The Collected Works of Hanserd Knollys

EARLY ENGLISH BAPTIST TEXTS

SERIES DESCRIPTION

The purpose of the series *Early English Baptist Texts* is to provide scholars, students, and church leaders with a contemporary, multivolume, scholarly edition of primary sources representative of English Baptists of the seventeenth century. While the series is intended to provide a valuable source to church leaders, it is also intended to make a long lasting contribution to scholarship in the areas of Baptists studies, the English Reformation, and the history of Christianity in general. It is anticipated that the series will consist of several volumes of primary source materials, the larger part of it never before edited. The selected works were penned by seven different English Baptists leaders, namely: John Smyth (d. 1612), Thomas Helwys (1550?-1616?), John Murton (d. 1625), William Kiffin (b. 1616), Katherine Sutton (1630-1663), Hanserd Knollys (c. 1599-1691), and Thomas Grantham (1634-1692). The collection aims to be diverse and inclusive, broad enough to transcend narrow confessional interests.

PROJECTED TITLES

—*The Extant Writings of Thomas Helwys (1608-1612).* [Publsihed 2009]

—*Collected Works of John Smyth (d. 1612)*, including: *The Bright Morning Star: Or, The Resolution and Exposition of the 22 Psalm* (Cambridge, 1603); *A Pattern of True Prayer* (London, 1605); *The Differences of the Churches of the Separation* (Middelburg, 1608); *The Character of the Beast* (Middelburg, 1609); *Parallels, Censures and Observations* (Middelburg: 1609).

—*John Murton (d. 1625) and the General Baptists*, including: *Objections* (1615); *A Description of What God Had Predestined* (London, 1620); *A Most Humble Supplication* (1621).

—*Collected Works of Hanserd Knollys (1599-1691)*, including: *A Moderate Answer* (London, 1645); *Christ Exalted* (London, 1646); *An Exposition of the First Chapter of the Song of Solomon* (London, 1656); *The Parable of the Kingdom of Heaven Expounded* (London, 1674); *The Baptists Answer to Mr. Obed Wills* (London, 1675); *Mystical Babylon Unveiled* (London, 1679); *An Exposition of the 11th Chapter of Revelation* (London, 1679); *An Answer to a Brief Discourse Concerning Singing* (London, 1691); *The Life and Death of that Old Disciple of Jesus Christ* (London, 1692); *An Exposition of Revelation* (London, 1689).

—*Katherine Sutton: A Christian Woman's Experience (1663).*

—*Collected Works of William Kiffin (1616-1701)*, including: *Observation upon Hosea* (London, 1642); *Confession of Faith* (London, 1644); *A Brief Remonstrance* (1645); *Confession of Faith* (London, 1652); *About Imposition of Hands* (London, 1654); *Letter to the Lord Mayor of the City of London* (London, 1660); *The Humble Apology* (London, 1660); *A Serious Answer* (London, 1692).

—*Thomas Grantham: Christianismus Primitivus (1678).*

SERIES FOREWORD

The series *Early English Baptist Texts* is inspired by the idea that a return to the sources, in the spirit of the Renaissance's ideal of *ad fontes*, can only inject new dynamism to Baptist theology. Serious engagement with historical Baptist sources can move Baptist theological reflection in the direction of robust ecumenical engagement as well as self-confident contributions based on historical Baptist theological insights. In fact, what this series offers is the opportunity to discover *de novo* the historical complexity, the plurality of voices, and the significant diversity of views that informed early English Baptists. This discovery will allow us to think of Baptists in new ways, ways that will allow for a broadening of Baptist identity.

The series is modeled after very successful collections of primary sources that have become standard resources for scholars, pastors, and other students of Baptist history, intellectual history of the Reformation, and Christian thought in general. Among the collections in mind are *Ancient Christian Writers* (Newman Press), and *Library of Christian Classics* (Westminster Press). Perhaps more in proportion with the editors' intentions is the collection, *Classics of the Radical Reformation* (Herald Press). Richard Groves' editions of Thomas Helwys' *A Short Declaration of the Mystery of Iniquity* (1998) and Roger Williams' *The Bloudy Tenant of Persecution* (2001), both by Mercer University Press, also provide an outstanding model for the present series. However, the texts of the collection are not limited to topics of religious liberty. Instead, the texts are meant to provide readily available primary sources for the study of early English Baptist thought in its broader manifestations.

Early English Baptist Texts stands to fill an important void in contemporary Baptist scholarship. The great majority of texts authored by early seventeenth century English Baptists remain buried in obscurity, only accessible to the expert scholar in research libraries throughout England and the United States. While accessibility to these works has greatly improved thanks to scholarly services of the digital age such as Early English Books Online, their access is still limited to a reduced specialized readership. Access to these works is further limited due to the historical gap between a potential contemporary American audience and the historical context that provided the backdrop against which early English Baptists articulated their ideas and composed their writings. Finally, the works for which there are existing modern editions are few in number and these very editions are now rare and hard to find. *Early English Baptist Texts* will be the first collection of its kind in Baptist scholarship. Many of the texts that are included will be edited for the first time, adapted to modern English usage, and properly set in their historical context in light of the best contemporary scholarship available.

Works to be included in the series have been selected according to the following criteria. First, they are representative of the complexity and rich diversity of English Baptists' of the seventeenth century. The editors of the collection affirm the continuing validity of the traditional classification of early English Baptists into General and Particular Baptists. Hence, a conscious effort has been undertaken to include texts that are representative of these theological impulses of the movement.

Second, works have also been selected based on their potential to illuminate the social history of the movement. In this sense the collection will be more than just an "anthology of classics." Indeed, some of the volumes of the collection will be dedicated to longstanding and well established classics, such as the collected works of John Smyth. However, careful thought has been given to include works that have traditionally been considered marginal either for the content matter or due to the status or gender of the author. Finally, the editors have sought to include in the collection works that are representative of different literary genres. Accordingly, confessions, books of sermons, journals, and controversialist literature are included side by side with more formal theological treatises and biblical commentaries.

In closing, while the editors are aware of the natural appeal of the series to a primarily Baptist audience it has been their intention to produce a scholarly work attractive to a broader public. Accordingly, the editors have invited renowned scholars to write introductions and notes to each volume, as well as other reading aids. It is hoped that the quality of the work will also inspire new generations of scholars to explore the rich history of the Baptists.

The Collected Works of Hanserd Knollys

Pamphlets on Religion

EARLY ENGLISH BAPTIST TEXTS

Edited and Annotated by

William L. Pitts, Jr.
and
Rady Roldán-Figueroa

Mercer University Press | Macon, Georgia
2017

MUP/ H933

Published by Mercer University Press
1501 Mercer University Drive
Macon, Georgia 31207

9 8 7 6 5 4 3 2 1

Books published by Mercer University Press are printed on acid-free paper that meets the requirements of the American National Standard for Information Sciences—Permanence of Paper for Printed Library Materials.

ISBN 978-0-88146-610-2
Cataloging-in-Publication Data is available from the Library of Congress

William L. Pitts dedicates this volume to
Ruth, Bill, Katherine, James, Ping Ting, Will, Emma, Ellie, and Adrian

Rady Roldán-Figueroa dedicates this volume to
Kretcha, Benjamin, Gabriela, Mercedes, and Marilu

CONTENTS

PREFACE

The conception of this volume dates back to a seminar on "theologians of anabaptism" that Rady Roldán-Figueroa offered in 2006-07 at George W. Truett Theological Seminary, Baylor University. A chance conversation with Professor Doug Weaver led to the creation of a new series, Early English Baptist Texts to be published by Mercer University Press. This first volume of the Collected Works of Hanserd Knollys is the product of collaboration of Bill Pitts and Rady Roldán-Figueroa. Both Pitts and Roldán-Figueroa are indebted to numerous individuals whose valuable help was critical. Ms. Ashley Williamson, then student of International/Global Studies at Baylor University, was responsible for the initial transcription of the edited texts found in this volume. Mr. Bryan Maine (Baylor University) served as research assistant in the early preparation of the work and Ms. Gina Zurlo (Boston University) provided superb editorial assistance as the project neared its completion. Ms. Sarah Sampas (Boston University) prepared an early draft of the bibliography. Professor Ruth Pitts (McLennan Community College) read and commented on several drafts of the manuscript, as did Professor Doug Weaver. Mr. John Parker and Dr. Joseph Tipton also read the last version of this work. The editors are indebted to Professor Bill J. Leonard (Wake Forest University) for his constructive comments. Generous funding for this project was provided by Baylor University through the Institute for Faith and Learning and its Vocation and Faculty Formation Grant Program (2009) as well as by the University Research Committee (2008-09). Finally, Roldán-Figueroa was able to further the project during a sabbatical leave granted by Boston University School of Theology (2012).

INTRODUCTION

Hanserd Knollys' life spanned much of the seventeenth century. He became a Baptist during the era of the English Civil War and served as a Baptist minister and apologist until his death in 1691. Knollys has been important for the history of dissent because of his active role in defining the theological underpinnings of early Baptists. He was imprisoned regularly, forced to move on several occasions, and endured two extended periods of exile from England. The driving factor in all of these experiences was coercion by the state to enforce religious conformity. For reasons of conscience he dissented. He became an important example of the necessity of establishing religious toleration by law. This goal was achieved in England just two years before Knollys' death.

Knollys has long been recognized as an important early Baptist writer. In explaining their position on baptism, Baptists defended their practice by addressing the more fundamental questions of what constitutes the church and who qualifies as members. On the former point Knollys and other Baptists wrote of the "gathered church," and on the latter issue, admitted only those who "repented and believed." Only following a personal act of commitment was baptism deemed appropriate. They therefore famously took the path of rejecting infant baptism. Knollys also argued for congregational governance of churches: there should be no supervision from outside the local church. He articulated the Baptist ideas in his literary debates with contemporaries, and emerged a Baptist leader.

Knollys is also increasingly being recognized for his apocalyptic millennial writings. He wrote extensively on the subject. This dimension of his thought has been neglected by earlier Baptist interpreters, perhaps because millennial views have not traditionally been considered among Baptist core principles or beliefs. But in the approach to the year 2000 millennial studies gained widespread attention, and interest in the topic has been sustained.

Knollys' life work revolved around religion and education. Religiously he was influenced by three major strands of seventeenth-century Protestantism. His father was a Church of England minister, and Knollys followed in his footsteps. At Cambridge he was influenced by Puritan thinking which eventually led him to suspend his own official parish appointment according to Church of England guidelines, but to continue to preach nonetheless. He found renewed energy in his preaching when he embraced the Puritan notion of the covenant of grace. The third strand of religious influence touched Knollys in 1645 when he embraced the practice of believers' baptism, the hallmark of the emerging Baptist movement, as well as their views on Christian salvation, the constitution and governance of the church and the appropriate relationship of the state to the church. He held Baptist views throughout the remainder of his life. However, when other groups arose to address problems of political and economic inequality in society, Knollys had to determine how he would relate to them. In the end, although he was sympathetic to aspects of other reform movements, he remained a Baptist. Having held three different confessional positions, Knollys' personal experience reflects the enormous religious upheaval that occurred in England during the seventeenth century.

Knollys is important not only for his religious identity but also for his relationship to the broader cultural milieu. He was highly educated as well as being deeply devoted religiously. He mastered the classical and Biblical languages and wrote grammars for Hebrew, Greek and Latin. He made his living as an educator. Many of his religious views reflect notions common in seventeenth-century England. He accepted popular notions of divine healing through prayer and annointing with oil. He believed in visions and dreams as a source of God's personal revelation to him. He believed in the direct power of Satan to tempt and harm people. In many ways his worldview was traditional and pre-modern. At the same time Knollys displayed devotion to logic and rationality throughout his writings. He experienced many encounters with episodes of skepticism—about the truth and authority of scripture, about the existence of heaven, and about God's power to answer prayer. In these respects his worldview appears to be very modern. Many of his experiences will sound very familiar to modern minds.

The structure of this book falls into three major parts. Part I is an introduction to Hanserd Knollys' life and work. Part II reproduces several of Knollys' publications. They cover a variety of topics, and we have called this volume *Pamphlets on Religion.* Each of these texts is preceded by a separate brief introduction and supplemented with extensive notes that illuminate the intellectual history behind his ideas and sources. This section allows the reader to engage in a first-hand encounter with early Baptist practice and thought as articulated by one of its key leaders. The following pamphlets by Knollys' are included in this volume.

A moderate answer and *A declaration concerning the public dispute* were published in 1645 at the time when Knollys decided to become a Baptist. They defend Baptist views on key beliefs regarding church membership and church governance. *The Baptists answer to Mr. Obed. Wills* explores the controversial Baptist view of baptism. In *Mystical Babylon availed* Knollys attacks claims made by the Roman Catholic Church, especially the papacy. In his "Preface" to Katherine Sutton's *A Christian woman's experiences* Knollys commends the spiritual value of her writing, and in *An answer to a brief discourse concerning singing* he offers his support for congregational singing in Christian worship services.

This volume also includes Knollys' autobiography, *The life and death of that old disciple of Jesus Christ.* Knollys' account of his life is brief, but enormously valuable. It tells us much more than we know about the lives of most early Baptist ministers. The autobiography reveals something of Knollys' character and religious convictions as well as his own assessment of failure and success during his life. The *Legacy*, a charge to his church during his final days, displays his concerns for his local Baptist church. Knollys provided personal leadership to churches throughout his lifetime, but he left an enduring legacy through his prolific authorship. The complete selections in this volume represent the broad range of his interest in numerous topics significant for seventeenth-century English Christianity. They also reveal much about early Baptist life.

Part III provides a summary of the historiography of Hanserd Knollys. This essay allows the reader to observe how Knollys has been interpreted during the past three centuries. Constant themes persist, of course, but also a significant number of new perspectives for interpreting Knollys have emerged, especially in recent years.

ABOUT THIS EDITION

We have edited Knollys' texts in order to assist the modern reader. We have modernized spelling and grammar where necessary for clarity except in the footnotes where we have usually provided the titles as originally printed. We retain the use of minimal capitalization of seventeenth-century titles when referred to in the main text. Although writers in the seventeenth century capitalized many words, presumably for emphasis, they often did not capitalize key words in their titles. They also used commas and semicolons excessively and apostrophes inconsistently. We have tried to bring these items into modern practice. The author also often used sentence fragments. Where they are clear, we have occasionally left these standing; otherwise, we have tried to supply complete sentences. Some of the publications appear to have been made in haste and some were written by a group of co-authors. For example, both of these factors appear to have been at work in *A declaration concerning a public dispute*. Knollys used a variety of ways of citing scripture. We have modernized these references. He also referred to arguments of opponents by page numbers. We have kept the abbreviation "p." in the narrative text. However, according to modern usage we have deleted "p." in our own footnotes. We have left some common Latin terms in the text and in the footnotes, such as ergo, viz., Ibid. and id. When we have supplied an occasional word in the text, we have used brackets. Where needed in footnote references we have used abbreviations "v" and "r" (for "verso" and "recto"). For several words no longer in common usage we have provided definitions in brackets or in footnotes. Unless otherwise noted, English translations are by the editors.

ABBREVIATIONS

BDAG:	Walter Bauer, *A Greek-English Lexicon of the New Testament and other Early Christian Literature*, rev. ed. Frederick William Danker, 3rd rev. ed. Chicago: University of Chicago Press, 2000.
Beza (1598)	Theodore Beza, *Iesu Christi Domini Nostri Novum Testamentum, sive novum foedus, cuius graeco contextui respondent interpretationes duae: vna, vetus: altera, Theodori Bezae.* Geneva: Sumptibus Haered. Eust. Vignon, 1598.
Beza	Theodore Beza, *Jesu Christi Domini Nostri Novum Testamentum, sive novum foedus, cujus graeco contextui respondent interpretationes duae: una, vetus; altera, Theodori Bezae.* Cantabrigiae: Rogeri Danielis, 1642.
Conciliorum oecumenicorum decreta	Giuseppe Alberigo, et al. (eds.), *Conciliorum oecumenicorum decreta*. Bologna: Instituto per la Scienze Religiose, 1973.
GNT	Barbara Aland, et. al. (eds.), *The Greek New Testament*, 5th ed. Stuttgart: Deutsche Bibelgesellschaft, 2014.
KJV	*The Holy Bible, conteyning the Old Testament, and the New: Newly translated out of the originall tongues: and with the former translations diligently compared and revised by his Maiesties speciall commandment appointed to be read in churches.* London: Robert Barker, 1611.

NRSV	*New Revised Standard Version Bible*, Division of Christian Education of the National Council of the Churches of Christ in the United States of America (1989).
PG	Jacques Paul Migne, *Patrologiae cursus completus, seu bibliotheca universalis, integra, uniformis, commoda, oeconomica, omnium SS. Patrum, doctorum scriptorumque ecclesiasticorum. Series Graeca*, 161 vols. in 166. Paris: Migne, 1857-1866.
PL	Jacques Paul Migne, *Patrologiae cursus completus, sive biblioteca universalis, integra, uniformis, commoda, oeconomica, omnium SS. Patrum, doctorum scriptorumque ecclesiasticorum. Series Latina*, 221 volumes in 212. Paris: Migne, 1844-1891.

PART I

HANSERD KNOLLYS' LIFE AND WORK

HANSERD KNOLLYS' LIFE AND WORK

by
Bill Pitts and Rady Roldán-Figueroa

I. INTRODUCTION

Hanserd Knollys was a leading figure in seventeenth-century Baptist life.[1] Influenced by current Puritan and dissenting traditions in England, he converted from the Church of England to the Baptists in 1645 and remained in this minority religious tradition throughout the remainder of his life.[2] He suffered imprisonment and periods of exile for his beliefs. Knollys was one of the most learned of early Baptists and was a successful educator. He was an active leader of Particular Baptists from his baptism in 1645 until his death in 1691. He served as a lifelong pastor of a local church throughout most of his life, and he offered his counsel to young Baptist churches on several controversial issues. Knollys was an itinerant who extended Baptist influence beyond London, and he used his financial resources to support the poor. He was a prolific writer who defended Baptist views, and played an important role in defining them for the young movement. He was also a signatory to important early Baptist confessions of faith. Historian Murray Tolmie judged that already in 1645 Knollys was

---

[1] Knollys also appears as Knowles, Knowls, Knols and Knollis. Baptist historian Joseph Ivimey or his printer spelled the name Knollys in his text and Knollis in his index. See Joseph Ivimey, *A History of English Baptists*, 4 vols. (London: Burditt and Morris, 1811). In Vol. II compare pages 261 and 616 for different spellings of Knollys. Modern editions usually spell his name Hanserd Knollys, which is the practice observed in this volume. For a succinct and complete biographical profile see Kenneth G. C. Newport, "Knollys, Hanserd (1598–1691)," in *Oxford Dictionary of National Biography*, edited by H. C. G. Matthew and Brian Harrison (Oxford: Oxford University Press, 2004). Online ed., edited by Lawrence Goldman, January 2010. http://www.oxforddnb.com/view/ article/15756 (accessed August 8, 2014).

[2] On the persistence of religious dissent in seventeenth-century England see the three works of Richard L. Greaves: *Deliver Us from Evil: The Radical Underground in Britain, 1660-1663* (New York: Oxford University Press, 1986); *Enemies Under His Feet: Radicals and Nonconformists in Britain, 1664-1677* (Stanford: Stanford University Press, 1990); *Secrets of the Kingdom: British Radicals from the Popish Plot to the Revolution of 1688-1689* (Stanford: Stanford University Press, 1992).

"the most popular of the sectarian preachers in London."[3] Knollys thus brought stability and leadership to the Baptist movement for almost half a century, and his Baptist legacy is substantial.

The life and death of that old disciple of Jesus Christ is the first and most influential account of Knollys' life.[4] Following the death of his wife and a child and his own serious illness, Knollys wrote the story of his life to 1672; his friend and fellow Baptist leader, William Kiffin, later added a general introduction and comments on the final two decades of Knollys' life. The book is brief and selective. Nevertheless, the autobiography provides valuable insight into his piety and his many activities. Moreover, this account inevitably shaped the content and chronological arrangement of subsequent studies of Knollys.[5] In his autobiography Knollys recorded several influences that shaped his life, including his family, his education, and his occupations, but it is clear that religion formed the center of his identity. Like fellow seventeenth-century dissenters who searched scripture for marks of the true church, in his quest for the truth Knollys demonstrated an openness to new religious ideas. This attitude led him to consider a variety of interpretations of Christianity. In this process of exploration he became a Baptist by 1645. This decision brought closure to his quest for confessional identity—but throughout the remainder of his life he continued to explore and publish his views on religious subjects, particularly Baptist beliefs and practices and apocalyptic interpretation.

---

[3] Murray Tolmie, *The Triumph of the Saints: The Separate Churches of London, 1616-1649* (Cambridge: Cambridge University Press, 1977) 147.

[4] Hanserd Knollys, *The life and death of that old disciple of Jesus Christ and eminent minister of the Gospel Mr. Hanserd Knollys who dyed in the ninety third year of his age written with his own hand to the year 1672; and continued in general in an epistle by Mr. William Kiffin* (London: Printed for John Harris, 1692). Page references in this section are to the nineteenth century edition, *The Life and Death of that Old Disciple of Jesus Christ, and Eminent Minister of the Gospel, Mr. Hanserd Knollys, who died in the Ninety-third Year of his Age. Written with His Own Hand to the Year 1672, and Continued in General, in an Epistle by Mr. William Kiffin. To Which is Added his Last Legacy to the Church* (London: E. Huntington, 1812).

[5] This biographical sketch is no exception. It makes extensive use of Knollys' own reflections on his life. For an account of the major studies of Knollys, see Part III: "The Historiography of Hanserd Knollys: Changing Interpretations of a Seventeenth-Century Baptist Leader."

II. RELIGIOUS PIETY AND EDUCATION

Knollys' early family experiences nurtured him in religious belief and practice. His father, Richard Knollys, was a graduate of Cambridge and a minister of the Church of England. Richard was serving as vicar at Cawkwell, near Louth, in Lincolnshire, when Hanserd Knollys was born.[6] His family moved when his father was appointed to serve churches at nearby Scartho and Grimsby. The Knollys family enjoyed a relatively respectable social standing.[7]

From this early period of his life Knollys recorded several events. He remembered a near death experience: "about the sixth year of my age, I fell into a great pond…my father came, leaped in, and pulled me out."[8] Knollys recalled several other formative events of his early life which helped shape his religious outlook. He remembered that when he was about ten years old his father "sought to dissuade me from the love and use of strong drink and said that he would give me twenty pounds if I would drink water."[9] Knollys reported that he drank only water for eleven years. His father also warned him not to make a vow to God since he was too young to "understand how sacred a thing a vow is, and how it binds the soul, and that it would be a sin not to perform my vow."[10] The parents also warned their children against Sabbath breaking and disobedience to their parents.[11] Knollys recalled an incident in which he and his brother fought on the way to school. Overcome with guilt, he confessed that the fight was sinful. The brothers knelt in a

---

[6] Hanserd Knollys, *The Life and Death* (1812) 8. The date of Knollys' birth is usually recorded as 1598, making him 93 at his death in 1691. However, based on Muriel James' examination of the records, modern scholars have challenged this view. See Muriel James, *Religious Liberty on Trial* (Franklin: Providence House Publishers, 1997) 26–27. Bustin summarizes the issue in his Appendix I, "Hanserd Knollys' Date of Birth" and adopts 1609 as the birth year. See Dennis C. Bustin, *Paradox and Perseverance: Hanserd Knollys, Particular Baptist in Seventeenth-Century England,* Studies in Baptist History and Thought, Vol. 23 (Milton Keynes: Paternoster, 2006) 324–328. This later date is persuasive, especially since it places Knollys' entrance into Cambridge when he was nearer 20 than 30 years of age.

[7] Murial James has established links to social privilege through Knollys' wife, Anne Cheney. Her relatives were able to give a modest inheritance to various family members. See James, *Religious Liberty on Trial*, 59–61.

[8] Knollys, *The Life and Death* (1812) 8.

[9] Ibid., 9.

[10] Ibid.

[11] Ibid.

field, prayed, and wept together, and "found great assistance from God."[12] The children were apparently well schooled in religious guidelines, and Knollys was keenly aware of his religious failures. All of these recollections of early life suggest that Knollys was deeply shaped by religious concerns.

Knollys attended Grimsby free school and also enjoyed the advantage of a private tutor in the home. He enrolled in St. Catharine's College, Cambridge.[13] In his remembrance of university life Knollys reflected chiefly on his religious formation rather than his academic pursuits.[14] He recalled a sermon he heard at Cambridge from Hosea in which the minister stressed that "often committing [a sin] after conviction of conscience for it, did provoke God."[15] He confessed that he had often broken the Sabbath, disobeyed his parents, and told untruths.[16]

At Cambridge Knollys came under the influence of Puritans such as his tutor, Richard Sibbes.[17] The Puritans believed that the Church of England should be purified of practices for which they found no biblical support, such as the wearing of vestments, kneeling at communion, and use of the wedding ring. The Puritan influence was powerful both in England and in New England and did much to shape English-speaking Protestant Christians of the seventeenth century.[18] Puritanism was particularly well established at

[12] Ibid., 9–10.

[13] According to Cambridge University records he was admitted to St. Catharine's Hall in 1629. See J. Venn and J.A. Venn, eds., *Alumni Cantabrigiensis,* 4 vols. (Cambridge: Cambridge University Press, 1922–1927) 3:31. See also Anne Laurence, *Parliamentary Army Chaplains, 1642-1651*, Royal Historical Society Studies in History, vol. 59 (Woodbridge: The Boydell Press, 1990) 142–143.

[14] Knollys, *The Life and Death* (1812) 10. Conflicting evidence suggests the date of entry was either 1627 or 1629. Since he was ordained in 1629, 1627 seems the more probable date according to Dennis C. Bustin, *Paradox and Perseverance,* 35n44.

[15] Knollys, *The Life and Death* (1812) 10.

[16] Ibid.

[17] James Culross, *Hanserd Knollys: "A Minister and Witness of Jesus Christ," 1598-1691* (London: Alexander and Shepherd, 1895) 13. For Sibbes, see Mark S. Dever, *Richard Sibbes: Puritan and Calvinist in Late Elizabethan and Early Stuart England* (Macon: Mercer University Press, 2000).

[18] For recent perspectives on many aspects of Puritanism see, John Coffey and Paul Chang-Ha Lim, eds., *The Cambridge Companion to Puritanism* (Cambridge: Cambridge University Press, 2008).

Cambridge University, especially at colleges such as St. John's, Trinity and Christ's.[19]

Although Knollys eventually became a leading Baptist, his early outlook was shaped by Puritan influence, probably in his home and definitely at Cambridge.[20] Knollys' account of his personal conviction of sin demonstrates his Puritan ethos. At university he was still haunted by his failures: "I was more convinced of my sinful condition, and that I was a child of wrath, without Christ, and grace...which work of conviction remained strongly upon me above one year...[and] under which I was filled with great horror and fears of hell." [21] Also typical were his many efforts to find religious peace: "yet I prayed daily, heard all the godly ministers I could, read and searched the holy scriptures, read good books...kept several days of fasting and prayer alone...begged pardon and grace of God for Christ's sake; grew strict...in reformation of my own life, examining myself every night, confessing my sins." [22] Knollys here describes a common pattern of conversion among Puritans. This account reveals serious engagement in his quest for salvation during his time at university.

Puritanism would also shape Knollys' theology. Whereas the earliest Baptists—John Smyth and Thomas Helwys—adopted the General or Arminian position that Christ died for all, Knollys adopted a Calvinist or Particular Baptist position, holding that Christ died for the salvation of the elect.[23] The debate that developed between followers of Calvin and followers of Arminius is one of the great dividing lines in the history of Protestant theology, and it affected Baptists from their early history.

When he sought ordination, Knollys delivered numerous trial sermons to prove his ability as a preacher. The bishop of Peterborough approved of his preaching, ordained Knollys a deacon in the Church of England on 29 June 1629, and then ordained him as priest the following day.[24] Unable to

---

[19] Patrick Collinson, *The Elizabethan Puritan Movement* (Oxford: Clarendon Press, 1967) 128.

[20] Patrick Collinson demonstrated the pervasive influence of Puritans in the seventeenth-century Church of England. See Patrick Collinson, *The Religion of Protestants: The Church in English Society, 1559-1625* (Oxford: Oxford University Press, 1982).

[21] Knollys, *The Life and Death* (1812) 11.

[22] Ibid.

[23] See Alistair Mason, "Arminianism," and "Reformed Theology" in *The Oxford Companion to Christian Thought*, ed. Adrian Hastings, Alistair Mason and Hugh Pyper (Oxford: Oxford University Press, 2000) 41 and 603–604.

[24] Knollys, *The Life and Death* (1812) 11–12.

secure a ministerial living immediately following his training at Cambridge, Knollys taught for two years at the Gainsborough Grammar School. Here he also met a Brownist and engaged the person in conversation.[25] The Brownists took a decisive step: they advocated separation from the Church of England and called for immediate reform. The title of Robert Browne's 1582 book, *A treatise of reformation without tarrying for anie*, conveys the sense of urgency for reform.[26] Whereas Puritans advocated reform of the church from within, many dissenters thought this was a failed strategy and left the church to establish a true church. The eventual result of their separation was the formation of the Presbyterian, Independent (Congregationalist), Baptist, and Quaker denominations—all successful products of the religious ferment in late Tudor, Stuart and Cromwellian England.

In 1631 Knollys was appointed vicar of Humberstone, a town near Scartho and Grimsby. His routine duties centered on regular preaching, always twice and sometimes as many as four times on Sunday.[27] During the week he devoted his mornings to study and his afternoons to visitation. In his autobiography Knollys records several experiences of what he considered to be divine healing. The first of these occurred when he was a young minister at Humberstone. Once again his focus is on religious experience. He wrote:

> A very religious widow, who falling sick sent for me, and charged me that I would not depart her house in the day-time until she ended or mended, lest Satan should tempt her above her strength. The doctor of physic had given her over; some godly ministers, friends, and relatives did take leave of her as a dying woman. She received nothing for several days but a little julep [and lay] speechless two or three days, her family mourning over her, and expecting her death every hour.[28]

---

[25] Ibid., 18.

[26] Robert Browne (c. 1550–1633) *A booke which sheweth the life and manners of all true Christians and howe vnlike they are vnto Turkes and Papistes, and heathen folke. Also the pointes and partes of all diuinitie, that is of the reuealed will and worde of God are declared by their seuerall definitions and diuisions in order as followeth. Also there goeth a treatise before of reformation without tarying for anie, and of the wickednesse of those preachers, which will not refourme them selues and their charge, because they will tarie till the magistrate commanude and compell them* (Middelburgh: Richarde Painter [i.e. Richard Schilders], 1582).

[27] Knollys, *The Life and Death* (1812) 12.

[28] Ibid., 11–12.

Knollys attended to the woman and spent some of this time preparing her funeral service. He recorded that at this point "the devil set upon me with a violent suggestion that the Scriptures are not the word of God."[29] Knollys reported that he had often suffered this temptation. On this occasion, "now the tempter assaulted me with this argument: whatever you ask in the name of Christ, God will do it, but that scripture was not [true]; and if I would put it [that scripture] now upon trial I should find it not to be true for if I would ask the woman's life in the name of Christ, God will not grant it."[30] Knollys decided to take up the challenge that was warring within his mind. He affirmed the truth of the promise of scripture and appealed to God to vindicate him. He recalled that he said:

> I will...go and pray for her, and believe that God will hear my prayers through the intercession of Jesus Christ, and restore her life and health.... I went into the parlour where she lay speechless.... I kneeled down by her bedside and prayed above a half hour, using my voice, and then she began to stir, toss and struggle.... I was assisted by the Holy Spirit to pray and believe.... I kneeled down again and prayed fervently and within half an hour, she said, 'The Lord hath healed me; I am restored to health.... O sir,' said she. 'God hath heard your prayers, and hath made me whole. Blessed be his holy name.[31]

Knollys wrote that the Lord had healed "for his own glory and to silence Satan."[32] In this passage Knollys clearly affirmed the intervention of God not only in the recovery of the woman's physical health but also in his overcoming temptation to doubt and in convincing him once and for all of the truth of scripture. He records that at a later time he himself was healed of illness by intercessory prayer.[33] Knollys does not indicate whether or not

---

[29] Ibid., 13.

[30] Ibid.

[31] Ibid., 14–15.

[32] Ibid., 16.

[33] Ibid., 43, 48. A contemporary General Baptist, Henry Denne, also reported miraculous cures. See Michael Watts, *The Dissenters,* 2 vols. (Oxford: Clarendon Press, 1978, 1995) 1:205. Watts cites Thomas Edwards, *The first and second part of Gangraena, or, A catalogue and discovery of many of the errors, heresies, blasphemies and pernicious practices of the sectaries of this time, vented and acted in England in these four last years also a particular narration of divers stories, remarkable passages, letters: an extract of many letters, all concerning the present sects: together with some observations upon and corollaries from all the fore-named premisses. Second part of Gangraena. Fresh and further discovery of the errors, heresies, blas-*

he adopted the practice of prayer for divine healing as a regular part of his ministry. But he records these two instances of healing in some detail and also mentions other cases of healing, especially during the plague.[34] Knollys' extended account of the healings reveals much about his piety—the importance of scripture in his life; his belief in the reality of Satan; the power and threat of temptation; the presence of skepticism in his own thinking; and his conviction that the power of God defeated sin and temptation as well as disease.[35] His account of the healing of the woman seems to have been as much about his own spiritual struggle over the truth of scripture as it was about her divine healing. These accounts provide a useful lens into beliefs regarding the relationship of prayer to healing and struggles to believe in the worldview of seventeenth-century England.

On May 22, 1632, Knollys married Anne Cheney of Wyberton. They lived together for thirty-seven years and had seven sons and three daughters. Knollys praised Anne as "a holy, discreet woman and a meet help for me in the ways of her household, and also in the way of holiness; who was my companion in all my sufferings, travels, and hardships, that I endured for the gospel."[36] She died April 30, 1671.

III. DISSENTING MINISTER

Knollys not only adopted Puritan views, he also acted on them early in his own ministry. He was troubled by three issues in particular: he opposed the Church of England practices of the minister wearing a surplice, the use of the sign of the cross in baptism, and the admission of "wicked persons" to the Lord's Supper.[37] He could not find scriptural justification for any of these practices. He therefore resigned his position as minister. Knollys reported to John Williams, bishop of Lincolnshire, that he could not conform to these practices any longer; however, he announced that he would

---

phemies, and dangerous proceedings of the sectaries of this time (London: T.R. and E.M. for Ralph Smith, 1646) 3.

[34] Knollys, *The Life and Death* (1812) 43.

[35] Knollys records the dramatic healing forty years later, but it remained vivid in his mind. This episode is generally ignored in modern accounts. However, the nineteenth-century Baptist minister Jackson Goadby quotes the episode at length and describes it as "the prayer of faith without the anointing with oil." See Joseph Jackson Goadby, *Bye-Paths in Baptist History* (London: Elliott Stock, 1871) 294–296.

[36] Knollys, *The Life and Death* (1812) 16.

[37] Ibid., 17.

continue to preach. Williams, anti-Laudian and well known for his tolerance of Puritans, supported Knollys' desire to continue to preach. Knollys' action suggests that he continued to reflect on the nature of true Christianity. He was not content passively to accept the status quo. Instead, his conscience compelled him to act against the norm—in short, to dissent from Anglican practice.

Knollys recalled that during his two or three years of preaching without an established parish appointment, no one had been converted under his preaching. He therefore resolved "not to preach any more until I had a clear call and conviction from Christ to preach the gospel."[38] He wrote that although he had been formally ordained by the bishop, he "had not received any seal from Christ of my ministry."[39] Knollys placed his ministry on hold and wondered if Christ had indeed called him. He struggled to establish his identity as a minister and "prayed with loud cries and tears that Christ would count me worthy and put me into the ministry."[40] The resolution of Knollys' ministerial crisis came through discussions with the Puritan minister, John Wheelwright, who told him his error was that he had tried to build his faith on a covenant of works. Knollys acknowledged that he had indeed "sought righteousness as it were by the works of the law, and got my peace by performing duties."[41] But Wheelwright counseled him to embrace the idea of a covenant of free grace. Knollys accepted this guidance and shifted his theological perspective and ministerial practice. During the next three or four years he preached in Lincolnshire and reported that "very many sinners were converted."[42] Positive results now confirmed Knollys in his ministerial work. Wheelwright had helped Knollys renew his life in ministry.

In 1636, Knollys was arrested for his preaching on a warrant from the Court of High Commission and taken to the house of the man who had arrested him. He persuaded his captor to let him go. This was a difficult time for English dissenters, and many made their way abroad to America or to the Netherlands, especially during the decade of the 1630s.[43] Knollys became part of this migration.

---

[38] Ibid.

[39] Ibid.

[40] Ibid., 18.

[41] Ibid., 20.

[42] Ibid., 26.

[43] James Culross' study views Knollys from the perspective of persecution of dissenters by authorities. See James Culross, *Hanserd Knollys* (1895) 13.

IV. AMERICAN SOJOURN

The arrest prompted Knollys' rapid departure from Lincolnshire. He took his family to London and arranged passage to Boston, Massachusetts. This self-imposed exile was not a planned stage in Knollys' life. Instead it was the result of religious persecution in England. The ocean passage was long and arduous, and personally very costly: during the voyage his young son died.[44] He spent about three and one-half years in America.[45] He seems to have arrived in the summer of 1638. He records that he had little money and no means of support; the family lived in a house loaned by a friend and Knollys immediately began doing manual labor with his hoe.[46]

In New England Wheelwright, along with his follower Anne Hutchinson, denounced the preaching of the covenant of works; instead, they adamantly taught the covenant of grace—that salvation comes only from the grace of God. They were labelled Antinomians because they stressed that keeping the law had nothing to do with salvation.[47] The authorities banished Wheelwright from Massachusetts in 1637 and Hutchison in 1638. The Antinomian problem was very much on the minds of ministers, and the clergy of Boston reported to the magistrates that Knollys was also alleged to be an Antinomian.[48] John Winthrop later confirmed that the authorities banished Knollys because he held Mrs. Hutchinson's Antinomian opinions.[49] The clergy granted him only limited time to remain in Boston before he had to move again.

Knollys recorded few details of his stay in Boston.[50] Circumstances of his move from Boston are also obscure. Knollys wrote only that two

---

[44] Knollys, *The Life and Death* (1812) 26–27.

[45] Ibid., 27.

[46] Ibid.

[47] For orientation to Antinomianism, consult David D. Hall, ed. *The Antinomian Controversy, 1636–1638: A Documentary History*, 2nd ed. (Durham: Duke University Press, 1990).

[48] Knollys, *The Life and Death* (1812) 27.

[49] John Winthrop, *Winthrop's Journal: History of New England 1630-1649*, ed. James K. Hosmer, 2 vols. (New York: Charles Scribners, 1908) 1:295.

[50] Histories of New Hampshire and Winthrop's *Journal* provide information for this phase of Knollys' life. Knollys' autobiography devotes only one page to his American experience.

strangers came from Piscataqua and invited him to come there to preach. Piscataqua was located far to the north of Boston very near the later site of Dover, New Hampshire: "Known as Dover from 1637, the 'plantation of Cocheco' had been set up in 1631."[51] Knollys established the first Congregational Church in Dover in 1638. Wheelwright, Knollys' old mentor in England, had been banished from Boston in 1637, and organized the church at Exeter, near Dover, in 1639.[52] Knollys may have maintained contact with Wheelwright during his stay in Dover.

Knollys created a serious problem for himself by writing home to England that he had met with nothing but oppression in America. He criticized the governing of the magistrates, the pervasive religious oppression, and the failure by the clergy and the people to observe religious practices.[53] The contents of the letter were made known in New England, and readers resented his censorious attitude. Knollys feared the consequences of his indiscretion and wrote a letter of abject apology to the Massachusetts authorities.[54] Another major problem arose for him when Thomas Larkham, a minister from Northam, England, moved to Dover in 1640; he was wealthy, able, and popular. Historian of Puritan Atlantic crossings Susan Hardman Moore notes that many small towns, unlike larger settlements, could not afford two ministers.[55] When the settlers chose Larkham to replace Knollys as their pastor, Knollys criticized Larkham for not observing church discipline, for using the sign of the cross in baptism and for following the Church of England rite for burial.[56] Disagreement between the two ministers led to open division and the formation of two churches. Tensions mounted, and the magistrates intervened to restore

---

[51] Susan Hardman Moore, *Pilgrims: New World Settlers and the Call of Home* (New Haven: Yale University Press, 2007) 61. The Piscataqua River is formed by the convergence of the Cocheco and Salmon Falls River near Dover.

[52] Albert Dunning, *Congregationalists in America: A Popular History of their Origin, Belief, Politics, Growth and Work* (New York: J.A. Hill, 1894) 158.

[53] Winthrop, *Journal,* 1:309–328.

[54] Hanserd Knollys, "Hanserd Knollys to Robert Simon, February 19, 1640," in *Suffolk Deeds,* vol. 1 (Boston: Rockwell and Churchill, City Printers, 1880) 18–20.

[55] Moore, *Pilgrims,* 61.

[56] Winthrop, *Journal,* 2:27, cited by George B. Spalding in "A Discourse Delivered in the First Church of Dover, May 18, 1873, on the Two Hundred and Fiftieth Anniversary of the Settlement of Dover, New Hampshire" (Dover: Freewill Baptist Printing Establishment, 1873) 13–14.

order.[57] Winthrop also reported that Knollys faced charges of sexual misconduct during his stay in Piscataqua, a report contested by modern authorities.[58] Dunning summarizes Knollys' time in Dover as "a short and stormy pastorate."[59] Knollys next moved to Long Island where once again a protest was filed against him. Having faced poverty, charges of Antinomianism and immorality, having struggled with a fellow minister, forced to apologize to Massachusetts's authorities with whom he did not agree, and forced to move twice in less than four years, Knollys was doubtless relieved to be called home to assist his aging father.[60] He arrived back in England with his wife and child on December 24, 1641.[61]

V. BECOMING BAPTIST

Knollys had not experienced success in America, and when he arrived in England, he once again faced economic hardship. His first task was to find a means to support himself and his family. He wrote, "I had rather work for my bread than be maintained by the charity of good Christians."[62] He

---

57 Bustin, *Paradox and Perseverance*, 63.

58 Winthrop declared Knollys a "weak minister." Winthrop, *Journal,* 1:295. However, Winthrop's editor, James Kendall Hosmer, rejects that notion and takes just the opposite view. Modern scholarship tends to discredit Winthrop's report, suggesting that he wanted to undermine anyone who did not support the majority belief system of Boston and was willing to believe and report the worst circulating rumor regarding opponents. See Bustin, *Paradox and Perseverance*, 69n202. This charge apparently did not seem credible to Winthrop's early readers. Daniel Neal stated that Knollys was "universally esteemed and beloved by all his brethren in England." Daniel Neal, *The History of New England Containing an Impartial Account of the Civil and Ecclesiastical Affairs of the Country to the Year of Our Lord, 1700*, 2 vols. (London: Printed for J. Clark, R. Ford, and R. Cruttenden, 1720) 197; Dunning, *Congregationalists in America*, 158–159. Cotton Mather, American Puritan historian and pastor, spoke kindly of Knollys in his *Magnalia Christi Americana.* See Charles Knowles Bolton, *The Founders: Portraits of Persons Born Abroad, Who Came to the Colonies in North America Before 1701* (Boston: The Boston Athenaeum, 1919) 2:410. In *The life and death* Knollys makes no reference to sexual immorality. Knollys' conscience moved him to confession often in life; yet he makes no reference to moral failure in America. On the other hand, he does seem to have wanted to forget (or at least not record) his American wilderness experience and other episodes of failure during his life.

59 Dunning, *Congregationalists in America,* 159.

60 Moore, *Pilgrims,* 190.

61 Knollys, *The Life and Death* (1812) 28; Moore, *Pilgrims,* 34, 190.

62 Knollys, *Life and Death* (1812) 30.

therefore returned to teaching school, first at Great Tower Hill and later at St. Mary-Axe free school. He was very successful in this venture. Within one year he had attracted above one hundred forty students and sixteen boarders.[63] Although English society suffered religious contentions and political upheaval during the seventeenth century, educational institutions seem to have flourished, and Knollys was well prepared by his Cambridge education for a lifetime of teaching. However, when the English Civil War broke out in 1642, the restless Knollys determined to serve as a chaplain in the Parliamentary Army where his major task was to preach to the soldiers.[64] But he soon abandoned this work since he "perceived the Commanders sought their own things more than the cause of God and his people, breaking their vows and solemn engagements."[65] He returned to London where he was arrested for preaching without license, but the authorities soon released him.[66] After his release from prison Knollys engaged in a preaching tour in Suffolk where he was again accused of disturbance and was "stoned out of the pulpit" for his efforts. He was arrested and acquitted.[67] This brief comment provides an important insight into the early dissenters' practice of itinerant preaching. Nonconformists promoted growth by many pragmatic methods of communication, including itinerant preaching, holding disputations, and publishing tracts and confessions of faith. Their strategies were also aided by favorable social conditions including relative freedom to preach and establish churches during the era of the Civil War and Cromwellian rule (1642-1660). All of these factors allowed several dissenting groups to grow strong enough to survive despite repressive legislation and punishment during the years ahead.[68]

---

[63] Ibid; also see Anon., "Dissenters' Schools, 1660–1820," *Transactions of the Baptist Historical Society* 4.4 (1914): 220–227; W. T. Whitley, "A Retrospect: The Contribution of Nonconformity to Education to the Victorian Era," *Transactions of the Baptist Historical Society* 4.4 (1914): 1–16.

[64] Anne Laurence, *Parliamentary Army Chaplains: 1642-1651* (Woodbridge: Boydell, 1990). Lawrence's book discusses the role of the chaplains and also provides a biographical directory of those who served the Parliamentary Army. Knollys' biography appears on pp. 142–143.

[65] Knollys, *The Life and Death* (1812) 30.

[66] Ibid., 32.

[67] Ibid., 32–33.

[68] Susan Doran and Christopher Durston, *Princes, Pastors and People: The Church and Religion in England, 1500-1700*, 2nd ed. (London: Routledge, 2003) 134.

Knollys became a Baptist in the mid-1640s. By 1644 he had joined the congregation of Independents in London founded by Henry Jacob in 1616, an influential congregation for separatists, including Baptists. That same year Knollys told the current minister, Henry Jessey, that he and his wife were not prepared to have their infant son baptized. At the church there were discussions for at least two months about the mode and especially the timing of baptism. Jessey had originally favored infant baptism, but now changed his views and Knollys baptized him in June, 1645.[69] Alexander Gordon judged that Jessey was Knollys' "most important convert."[70] From this time the composition of the Jessey church seems to have been predominantly people convinced of believer's baptism, but some pedobaptists remained as members.[71] It was a "mixed congregation."

Knollys does not give the exact date marking his acceptance of the Baptist position, but it seems to have occurred in late 1644 or 1645. He resisted infant baptism for his son in 1644 and baptized Jessey in 1645. In 1645 he gathered a Baptist church in London, one of the early Particular Baptist congregations.[72] The church met next door to the Church of Great St. Helen's, Bishopgate. Knollys was evicted in 1646, reportedly for praying for John Lilburne, the Leveller leader. The church moved several times, settling at length at Boston Wharf, Thames Street.

Seven small Calvinist Baptist churches produced the London Confession in 1644. The reason for writing the confession was to set forth their beliefs and dispel rumors that they were Anabaptists. Opponents frequently charged early Baptists with holding Anabaptist views.[73] Because of the radical social implications associated with the Anabaptists, this was a serious charge. The Baptists responded: the opening of the 1644 Confession of Faith reads, "A Brief Confession or Declaration of Faith set forth by

---

[69] Barrington R. White, *Hanserd Knollys and Radical Dissent in the 17th Century* (London: Dr. Williams's Trust, 1977) 7–8.

[70] Alexander Gordon, "Hanserd Knollys," *Dictionary of National Biography, 1885-1900*, vol. 31. Tolmie agreed with this assessment (Tolmie, *Triumph of the Saints,* 59); Newport, "Knollys, Hanserd (1598–1691)."

[71] White, *Hanserd Knollys,* 8.

[72] Knollys, *The Life and Death* (1812), 34.

[73] Baptists attracted numerous formidable opponents. Daniel Featley, Ephraim Pagitt, Robert Baille and Thomas Edwards all charged them with Anabaptist views. See Barry H. Howson, *Erroneous and Schismatical Opinions: The Question of Orthodoxy Regarding the Theology of Hanserd Knollys (ca. 1599-1691)* Studies in the History of Christian Thought, no. 98 (Leiden: Brill, 2001) 203.

many of us, who are (falsely) called Ana-baptists."[74] They shared with Anabaptists the radical theological views of believer's baptism, democratic ecclesiology, and separation of church and state. However, the Confession showed that the Baptists were not social revolutionaries.[75] Knollys had cast his lot with the Baptists and he signed the revised 1646 version of the London Confession. Confessions of faith provided effective vehicles for identity and growth, and Knollys would also be the first signatory on the Second London Confession, yet another major Baptist confession produced near the end of his life in 1688.[76]

Knollys served as pastor of his small Baptist church in London for the remainder of his life. He wrote that he had been with the members since he gathered the church in 1645.[77] However, he conceded that he was "absent from them sometimes upon just occasions and with their leave, or forced from them by violent persecution."[78] In fact he was gone for extended periods of time. Presumably he had their continuing support despite his absence for his preaching tours, and also when he was imprisoned or living in exile. Knollys also had the assistance of co-pastors such as John Perry.[79] His pastoral work included preaching and visiting the sick. He says that the church enjoyed fellowship, breaking of bread, and prayer without serious division within the church, although a few members "have forsaken the assembling of themselves as the manner of some is."[80] He leaves the impression of a close and stable relationship between the pastor and his small Baptist congregation.

In 1646 Knollys published the sermons he had delivered on an itinerant preaching tour of Suffolk in 1645. Together these three early Baptist

---

[74] *London Confession* (1644) in William Lumpkin, *Baptist Confessions of Faith*, rev. ed. (Philadelphia: Judson Press, 1969) 144–171, here 145.

[75] Baptist apologists argued for the legitimacy of their new theology and also argued against the stigma brought on by false charges. For example, they assured officials that they had no desire to subvert the state and the law by denying authority of the magistrates or refusing to take oaths.

[76] For the text of the *Second London Confession* (1688) see Lumpkin, *Baptist Confessions of Faith*, 235–295.

[77] Knollys, *The Life and Death* (1812), 34.

[78] Ibid.

[79] Bustin, *Paradox and Perseverance*, 136n94, citing W.T. Whitley, "London Churches in 1682," *The Baptist Quarterly* 1 (1922–1923): 82, 86.

[80] Knollys, *The Life and Death* (1812), 35.

sermons reveal key features in his approach to preaching.[81] The first sermon, "Christ Exalted," celebrated ways Christ is present for others: Christ is king, priest, prophet, preserver, finisher of faith, light, bread of life, mediator, and so forth.[82] Moreover, the new heart produces virtues and moral habits.[83] The second sermon is entitled "A Lost Sinner Sought and Saved by Christ." This sermon is based on Luke 15:10: "For the Son of Man is come to seek and to save that which was lost." Knollys retells the story of Zaccheus,[84] and his message is that Christ seeks and saves sinners.[85] The third sermon is "God's People are a Holy People" based on the phrase "that we should be holy" (Ephesians 1:4). He affirms that this doctrine needs no proof, noting that other passages such as I Thessalonians 4:3 also confirm it: "This is the will of God, your sanctification."[86] Knollys spells out three reasons why God will have his people to be holy and five ways holiness is useful in the Christian life.[87] This set of sermons offers a summary of three messages Knollys wanted to convey: Christ exalted, the sinner saved by Christ, and the living of the Christian life. He reveals his Protestant orientation, particularly by his heavy reliance on scripture. Much of the sermon content is simply a restatement of Biblical metaphors for Christ or scripture quotation, collected without reference to original context. He refers to the Beza text he is using and also to the translation by Jerome. In all of the sermons Knollys follows common Puritan practice. He enumerates his points: e.g., "first," "second," "third," thereby making the sermon easier for listeners to follow. In the sermons he includes doctrinal discussions and also offers several practical applications of the sermons to Christian life and experience.

Although Knollys formed his own congregation and early emerged as a Baptist leader in the capital city, he nevertheless had to continue to rely on teaching to support his family. He wrote that his "chiefest means of livelihood hath been by teaching school, wherein God was pleased to make me serviceable in my generation; to communicate liberally to the poor of the

[81] The 1646 edition is Hanserd Knollys, *Christ Exalted; A Lost Sinner Sought and Saved by Christ; God's People Are a Holy People. Being a Sum of diverse Sermons Preached in Suffolk* (London: Iane Coe, 1646).

[82] Knollys, *Christ Exalted,* 2–7.

[83] Ibid., 10–11.

[84] Knollys, *A Lost Sinner,* 15.

[85] Ibid., 25.

[86] Knollys, *A Holy People,* 30.

[87] Ibid., 31–38.

church, and to strangers that stood in need."[88] He wrote that he received from the church "according to their ability, most of the members of the church being poor."[89] He thought that support of ministers by their congregation was appropriate and biblical. But since his church was small and poor, he continued to support himself and his family by teaching. For Knollys preaching was absolutely imperative. In "Christ Exalted" he wrote: "Now the ordinary means which God hath in his infinite wisdom appointed to convert sinners, and also to build them up in Christ, is the Word preached."[90] Yet preaching alone would not support Knollys and his family. He was bi-vocational.

VI. BAPTIST APOLOGIST, 1645–1650

The year 1645 appears to be the pivotal point in the development of Knollys' religious identity. First, he baptized another religious leader who accepted the argument of believer's baptism. Second, he also published tracts defending key Baptist positions. Third, Knollys had suffered on several occasions for his views and had advocated religious freedom. Knollys' religious quest had led him to adopt and defend Baptists positions, and he clearly confirmed his Baptist identity by forming a Baptist church in London in 1645 and by signing the revised *London Confession* of 1646. In defending his views, Knollys became an apologist for Baptists.

Dissenters, including Baptists, were prolific authors. Knollys authored or co-authored several important tracts, stating and defending Baptist positions. In 1645-1646, Knollys defended three historic Baptist principles that remain Baptist markers to the present day: congregational governance, believer's baptism, and religious freedom. An early tract by Knollys centered on church organization and governance. John Bastwick and Knollys were friends for a while; in fact, Bastwick had assisted Knollys' family financially when they returned from America. But the two men disagreed on the structure and authority of the church. Bastwick, a Presbyterian, had written

[88] Knollys, *The Life and Death* (1812), 34. During the Interregnum he held government employment under Oliver Cromwell as Examiner at the Customs and Excise until March 29, 1653, and Clerk of the Check until March 23, 1655. See Newport, "Knollys, Hanserd (1598–1691)." Otherwise, he supported himself primarily as an educator.

[89] Knollys, *The Life and Death* (1812), 34. The Baptist churches of this era were small according to Ivimey, *History of the Baptists*, 1:231.

[90] Knollys, *Christ Exalted*, 12.

Independency, not God's ordinance (1645), an argument attacking congregational governance of churches. On this point the Brownists or Independents and the Baptists agreed against the Presbyterians. They both argued that the authority of a church is a local congregation of believers who make all decisions of the church. Seventeenth century English non-conformists objected not only to the papal authority of the Roman Catholic Church but also to the Church of England's practice of investing the authority of the church in bishops. Presbyterians also rejected episcopal authority but nevertheless retained a hierarchical structure that extended beyond the local congregation. Typical Presbyterian churches were governed by a group of elected local elders gathered in a consistory or session, and groups of churches gathered under a presbytery. Presbyteries, in turn, came together in synods, and delegates from synods formed a general assembly. Hence, in Presbyterian polity the presbytery played an important role in the governance of local churches, but Baptists refused to accept what they perceived as an encroachment on the biblical prerogative of believers in a local church.

Knollys wrote *A moderate answer to Dr. Bastwick's book* (1645) to refute Bastwick's Presbyterian position on church governance. Knollys made two central arguments: one addressed the structure of the church and the other focused on church membership. He began with a review of Bastwick's unique argument which held that there were many congregations of believers in Jerusalem, that together they all comprised one church, that the apostles and elders governed by a common council called a Presbytery and that this form of church government "is to be a pattern for all...congregations...in any...vicinity to unite into one church, and for the officers of those congregations to govern that church jointly in a college or presbytery."[91] Knollys challenged this view, arguing that there is neither historical nor Biblical evidence sufficient to sustain Bastwick's claim for a Presbyterian hierarchy of authority in the New Testament.[92] As a counter argument Knollys cited New Testament references to several individual

[91] Hanserd Knollys, *A Moderate Answer Unto Dr. Bastwicks* [*sic*] *Book, Called, Independency not God's Ordinance. Wherein, is declared the manner how some churches in this city were gathered, and upon what tearmes their Members were admitted; That so both the Dr. and the Reader may judge, how near some Beleevers who walk together in the Fellowship of the Gospell, do come in their practice to these Apostolicall rules which are propounded by the Dr. as God's method in gathering Churches and admitting Members* (London: Printed by Iane Coe, 1645).

[92] Ibid., 7–9.

churches and individual church leaders. He argued that there is no New Testament evidence for multiple congregations under one authority. Knollys also addressed the related question of church membership. Whereas Bastwick had focused on the authority of the minister, Knollys responded that "the conditions of terms which [Christians] were to propound unto all nations and people" for admittance to church membership were faith, repentance and baptism.[93] The Baptists appealed to Mark 16:15-16 to support their position. Knollys' tract defends Baptist teachings regarding both qualification for membership and congregational authority of the church. These were two essential principles articulated by Baptists from the beginning. Knollys' brief pamphlet offers an exposition and defense of these core Baptist ideas.

In addition to publishing tracts and confessions of faith, Baptists engaged in public debates as a forum for presenting and defending their views and recruiting followers.[94] We have a vivid record of a proposed debate between Presbyterians and Baptists in 1645. *A declaration concerning the publike dispute* has unusual historical interest in that it provides full background for a public debate on baptism, including the reason for the debate, proposed procedures, arrangements, and arguments for the event. The debate was scheduled for December 1645. The Baptists—Benjamin Coxe, Hanserd Knollys, and William Kiffin—were to defend their views against Edmund Calamy, James Cranford and other Presbyterians. The occasion for the debate was the interest of a merchant of the city who wanted this issue debated since his wife was "great with child."[95] A private disputation took place at his house, but there was no resolution of the issue. Since seating space was limited in the home, the organizers proposed that it be moved to a public place. The London mayor approved the plan to hold the debate in the Parish Church of Aldermanbury, on 3 December 1645, 9:00 A.M.–3:00 P.M. This was Calamy's church, located east of St. Paul's Cathedral. Terms of the debate were set (no hissing or talking, and so forth). But the mayor cancelled the debate the day before it was to take place, citing

---

[93] Ibid., 18.

[94] A. S. Langley, "17th Century Baptist Disputations," *Transactions of the Baptist Historical Society* 6 (1918–1919): 216–243.

[95] Benjamin Coxe, Hanserd Knollys, and William Kiffin, *A declaration concerning the publike dispute which should have been in the publike meeting-house of Alderman-Bury, the 3rd of this instant moneth of December; Concerning infants-baptisme. Together, with some of the arguments which should then have been propounded and urged by some of those that are falsly called Anabaptists, which should then have disputed* (London: no printer, 1645) 1.

as his reason fear of public disturbance.[96] The Baptists denied that they would resort to violence, but their arguments did not prevail, and the debate did not take place. The authors therefore decided to publish the main points of the argument they would have made in public debate had they had opportunity to do so. Knollys shared authorship of this treatise with Benjamin Coxe and William Kiffin.

The *Declaration* is a deeply significant document for both Baptist history and Baptist theology: it offers insight into the way Baptists extended their influence by public debate and it articulates the central notion of Baptist identity. The authors wrote that "we were going to maintain…that no infants ought to be baptized."[97] Indeed "only believers…ought to be baptized."[98] They supported their argument with appeal to John's baptism, which they argued was for those who repented and believed. The Baptists noted that to those who said to John that they were children of Abraham and therefore included in the covenant (a favorite Presbyterian argument), John had replied that they must bring forth fruit showing repentance. In addition to John's practice, they cited Acts 2:38 to emphasize the requirement for repentance before baptism.[99] The Baptists also argued that infants are incapable of expressing their faith, another condition for baptism.[100] Further, the Baptists argued that "rantizing" (baptism by sprinkling) was an "invention of man."[101] Their position was that infants are unable to undergo any of the preconditions for baptism set forth in the New Testament. Because of the sequence of the command to make disciples and then baptize them, Matthew 28:19-20 was a favorite passage of the Baptists. Of course this summary of a proposed debate offers only one side of the argument. Nevertheless, the *Declaration* sets forth the central Baptist

---

[96] Coxe, Knollys, and Kiffin, *A Declaration*, 3. Kiffin collaborated with Knollys on many projects, including publications of tracts and confessions of faith, preaching tours, and protests against persecutions. He supplemented and published Knollys' *The Life and Death*.

[97] Coxe, Knollys, and Kiffin, *A Declaration,* 6.

[98] Ibid.

[99] Ibid., 7.

[100] Coxe, Knollys, and Kiffin, *A Declaration,* 10.

[101] Ibid., 9. Baptists accused their opponents of "rantizing" in this text, which means to baptize by sprinkling. According to the *Oxford English Dictionary*, the term was first used in the seventeenth century. See "† rantize, v.," *Oxford English Dictionary Online* (Oxford: Oxford University Press, 2014) http://www.oed.com/view/Entry/158114? redirectedFrom=rantizing (accessed December 5, 2014).

position with clarity and force. The Baptist definition of the true church rested on its fundamental assertion of the necessity of personal individual commitment to Christ by each person. Only these believers could be counted true Christians and members of a true church. Baptists defined themselves in dialogue with other religious positions through both oral and written debates.

Religious persecution was a problem Knollys faced throughout more than fifty years of his life. In his later autobiographical narrative, Knollys documented his experience of persecution for his beliefs. Knollys suffered imprisonment several times in England, and fled England twice to escape threat of imprisonment. Knollys experienced rejection, persecution, and financial hardship in America and on the Continent. He would continue to suffer intermittent religious persecution, including incarceration near the end of his long life.[102] Knollys became an important example that Baptists would cite as evidence of the need for religious liberty, another key tenet of Baptist writing in the seventeenth century.

In fact, along with other dissenters, Knollys became an apologist for toleration of dissenters, although he retained typically strong anti-Roman Catholic views. In the earliest stages of Cromwell's leadership dissenting groups enjoyed *de facto* religious toleration. By 1645 the Presbyterians had gained significant power, and it appeared that they would seek privileged religious status in England, including denial of religious freedom to all others.[103] On this occasion Knollys wrote to John Dutton of Norwich,

---

[102] Stephen Wright notes that in 1646 Knollys "contributed a foreward to Thomas Collier's *Exhaltation*, which advocated toleration." At the same time, Knollys' "willingness to get involved in rowdy scenes stemmed from Knollys' desire to contest for the truth...even at the risk of disturbance and imprisonment." See Stephen Wright, *The Early English Baptists, 1603-1649* (Woodbridge: The Boydell Press, 2006) 159.

[103] The terms religious toleration and religious liberty/religious freedom are important in Baptist history, and they are usually distinguished. Religious toleration describes a church privileged by law, conceding limited rights to minority or outside groups. Under full religious liberty/religious freedom the state allows full and equal religious opportunity for all of its citizens. Early English Baptist Thomas Helwys articulated a plea for religious liberty in *A Short Declaration of the Mystery of Iniquity* (1612) where he famously affirmed, "For we freely profess that our lord the king...has no authority as a king but in earthly causes.... For man's religion...is between God and themselves.... Neither may the king be judge between God and man. Let them be heretics, Turks, Jews, or whatsoever, it appertains not to the earthly power to punish them in the least measure. See Thomas Helwys, *A Short Declaration of the Mystery of Iniquity*, ed. Richard Groves (Macon, GA: Mercer University Press, 1998) 53. Knollys also affirms the language of

protesting loss of religious toleration.[104] In 1646 the Independent John Saltmarsh published *The smoke in the temple,* which was a plea for toleration of all religions.[105] Knollys replied to Saltmarsh in *The shining of a flaming fire in Zion.*[106] He debated Saltmarsh on baptism, but he agreed with Saltmarsh's call for more unity and toleration, and he agreed that church membership should be voluntary, not compulsory. In 1647 and 1652 Knollys and Richard Wollaston twice petitioned Parliament for abolition of tithes.[107] In 1651, he was among a group of Baptist and Congregationalist leaders who signed *A declaration of divers elders and brethren of congregational*

---

conscience and protests religious taxation. This sentiment provides the foundation for Baptist affirmations of religious liberty, most influentially enshrined in the United States Constitution's Bill of Rights, where the state takes a neutral position on religions practiced in its realm. Knollys suffered repeated persecution for his beliefs—exile, arrest, and imprisonment—and he repeated appeals for relief. English religious dissenters finally achieved religious toleration in 1689. Thus in the seventeenth century English Baptists envisioned and articulated religious liberty, but they lived only under limited toleration. Religious liberty would come later. Hence we have usually used the term "religious toleration" in discussing Knollys.

[104] Thomas Crosby, *The history of the English Baptists: From the Reformation to the Beginning of the Reign of King George I* (London: no printer, 1738) 1:230–232; Ivimey, *History of the Baptists,* 1:189. The letter is reproduced in Crosby as well as in Benjamin Brook, *The Lives of the Puritans: A Biographical Account of those Divines who Distinguished Themselves in the Cause of Religious Liberty, from the Reformation under Queen Elizabeth, to the Act of Uniformity of 1662* (London: Printed for James Black, 1813) 3:495.

[105] John Saltmarsh, *The smoke in the temple. Wherein is a designe for peace and reconciliation of believers of the several opinions of these times about ordinances, to a forbearance of each other in love, and meeknesse, and humility. With the opening of each opinion, and upon what Scriptures each is grounded. With the several exceptions which may be made against each opinion from the Scriptures. With one argument for liberty of conscience, from the national covenant. With another argument to prove the Gospel, or New Testament of Jesus Chirst the very Word of God; tendered to all the beleevers, to show them how little we have attained, and that there is a more glorious fulnesse to be revealed. With a discovery of the antichristian way of peace, etc. for opinions. With a full answer to Master Ley, one of the assembly of divines, against my late new Quere. With some spiritual principles drawn forth of the controversie* (London: Ruth Raworth, 1646).

[106] Hanserd Knollys, *The shining of a flaming-fire in Zion. Or, A clear answer unto 13. exceptions, against the grounds of new baptism; (so called) in Mr. Saltmarsh his book; intituled, The smoke in the temple, p. 15, &c. Which exceptions, were tendered by him to all believers, to shew them, how little they have attained; and that there is a more glorious fulnesse to be revealed. Also, a postscript; wherein (to the like end) some queries are propounded unto believers* (London: Iane Coe, 1646).

[107] White, *Hanserd Knollys,* 14; Anon., "Jottings by John Lewis of Margate, 1742," *Transactions of the Baptist Historical Society,* 4.4 (1914): 206.

societies, who sought religious toleration and fair treatment for non-conformists.[108]

The growth of sectarian views alarmed the Presbyterians, who wrote critical responses to other dissenters. In 1645 Daniel Featley, Anglican apologist who had Presbyterian sentiments, attacked the Baptists and their recently published *Confession* (1644) in *Katabaptistai kataptüstoi, The dippers dipt, or, The anabaptists duck'd and plung'd over head and eares.*[109] In 1646, the Presbyterian Thomas Edwards published the first part of his extensive *The first and second part of Gangraena, or, A catalogue and discovery of many of the errors, heresies, blasphemies and pernicious practices of the sectaries of this time*, one of the most famous attacks on sectarianism of the century.[110] Edwards included Knollys by name, writing that he had done "a great deal of mischief."[111]

Baptists formed their identity over against rival confessional positions, but also by debating internal differences. No point was more significant than

---

[108] White, *Hanserd Knollys*, 27n44; Anon., *A declaration of divers elders and brethren of congregationall societies, in and about the city of London. Decrying and disclaiming two bookes; one called a cry; and the other book called A model of a new representative. Wherein their judgements touching the qualifications of electors, and eligible persons, are tendered to consideration, in way of vindication of themselves from unjust aspersions* (London: M. Simmons for L. Chapman, 1651) 8.

[109] Daniel Featley, *Katabaptistai kataptüstoi, The dippers dipt, or, The anabaptists duck'd and plung'd over head and eares, at a disputation in Southwark: together with a large and full discourse of their 1. Original. 2. Severall sorts. 3. Peculiar errours. 4. High attempts against the state. 5. Capitall punishments, with an application to these times* (London: Printed for Nicholas Bourne and Richard Royston, 1645).

[110] Thomas Edwards, *The first and second part of Gangraena, or, A catalogue and discovery of many of the errors, heresies, blasphemies and pernicious practices of the sectaries of this time, vented and acted in England in these four last years also a particular narration of divers stories, remarkable passages, letters: an extract of many letters, all concerning the present sects: together with some observations upon and corollaries from all the fore-named premisses. Second part of Gangraena. Second part of Gangraena. Fresh and further discovery of the errors, heresies, blasphemies, and dangerous proceedings of the sectaries of this time. Fresh and further discovery of the errors, heresies, blasphemies, and dangerous proceedings of the sectaries of this time* (London: T.R. and E.M. for Ralph Smith, 1646); Watts, *The Dissenters*, 1:111. Ann Hughes has noted how *Gangraena* shaped contemporary perceptions of dissenting groups. See Ann Hughes, *Gangraena and the Struggle for the English Revolution* (Oxford: Oxford University Press, 2004).

[111] Thomas Edwards, *The first and second part of Gangraena... The third edition, corrected and much enlarged* (London: T. R. and E. M. for Ralph Smith, 1646) 1:39-40; Watts, *The Dissenters*, 1:113.

the debate over divine and human roles in salvation. In 1646 Knollys defended Particular Baptist ideas against the General Baptists Henry Denne and Thomas Lamb.[112] He wrote the preface to *Mysteries unveiled,* a tract in which Calvinist Robert Garner attacked Denne and Lamb.[113] Knollys rejected the idea of the universality of the death of Christ for all persons.[114] The Baptist debate over redemption appeared early and remained a key source of division among them. Knollys also made clear his Calvinist position by signing the 1646 London Confession, thus positioning himself as a leader in the Particular Baptist camp.[115]

In 1648 Knollys published *The rudiments of Hebrew grammar in English.*[116] His goal for this volume was to provide guidance in English rather than Latin for people who wanted to read the Old Testament in Hebrew. He was reputed to be a student of the Orientalist, Christian Ravis (1613-1677).[117] On January 17, 1649 Kiffin and Knollys were granted official permission to preach in Suffolk.[118] The two ministers journeyed to Ipswich on a preaching mission. That same year John Miles was sent to Wales to preach and plant churches, and Knollys later also went to Wales as

---

[112] McBeth places the emergence of Particular Baptists at 1638 or earlier. See H. Leon McBeth, *The Baptist Heritage* (Nashville: Broadman Press, 1987) 44.

[113] See Knollys' preface, "To the Churches of God in London and elsewhere in all places with the Bishops and Deacons," in Robert Garner, *Mysteries unvailed wherein the doctrine of redemption by Jesus Christ, flowing from the glorious grace and everlasting love of God, the very fountain of life and salvation unto lost sinners, is handled: the most usuall Scriptures explained and reasons answered, which are urged for the universality of the death of Christ for all persons: vvherein the unsoundness of this opinion, together with divers other conclusions as depending upon it, are discovered and the truth unvailed* (London: no printer, 1646).

[114] White, *Hanserd Knollys,* 14.

[115] *The London Confession* (1644). Lumpkin emphasizes changes in the 1646 edition and refers to Knollys as a "notable signer." See Lumpkin, *Baptist Confessions of Faith,* 144-152 and 171. Barry Howson evaluated the question of Knollys' Calvinism at length. See Howson, *Erroneous and Schismatical Opinions*, 157, 192–193. Knollys would reaffirm his Particular Baptist position by signing the 1688 *Second London Confession.* See Howson, *Erroneous and Schismatical Opinions*, 151; White, *Hanserd Knollys,* 9.

[116] Hanserd Knollys, *The rudiments of the Hebrew grammar in English. Published for the benefit of some friends, who being ignorant of the Latine, are desirous to understand the Bible in the originall tongue* (London: Moses Bell, 1648).

[117] Newport, "Knollys, Hanserd (1598–1691)"; also see Knollys' "The Epistle to the Reader," in his *Hebrew Grammar*, where he makes reference to Ravis and his lexical works. Knollys, *The rudiments of the Hebrew grammar*, no pagination.

[118] Wright, *Early English Baptists,* 215.

an evangelist.[119] By mid-century Baptist ministers were extending the Baptist movement into England and Wales through itinerant preaching.

VII. CIVIL WAR AND COMMONWEALTH: THE FLOURISHING OF ENGLISH DISSENT, 1642-1660

Religion and politics were closely intertwined in English culture throughout the sixteenth and seventeenth centuries. The Church of England replaced Catholicism by law. Many Protestants remained dissatisfied. Some of them separated from the established church, and by 1646 had created four denominations that enjoyed long-lived success to the present day—Presbyterians, Independents (or Congregationalists), Baptists and Quakers (or Friends). King Charles I promoted conformity to the Church of England, and he appointed William Laud as Archbishop of Canterbury in 1633.[120] Laud pursued a vigorous program of enforcing Anglican worship and practice. Many dissenters did not conform, prompting them to seek refuge in The Netherlands or in the American colonies. Many others who remained in England and resisted government policy suffered fines and imprisonment. Charles also sought to exercise political authority without restraint, claiming divine authority to rule. King and Parliament were increasingly estranged and assertive of their respective rights. The result was the civil war that began in 1642 and ended with the beheading of the King in Whitehall in January, 1649, and government without monarchy until 1660. Oliver Cromwell, the dominant military and political figure of the era, favored religious toleration. Thus the new denominations had several years to establish themselves. Not only did the Presbyterians, Independents, Baptists and Quakers grow, more radical dissent flourished creating many new sectarian groups such as the Levellers, Ranters, Diggers, Muggletonians, Seekers and Fifth Monarchy Men. These movements combined radical theological views with radical demands for dramatic political, economic and social changes in English society.[121] These groups

[119] White, *Hanserd Knollys,* 15; Wright, *Early English Baptists*, 244.

[120] On the religious policy of Charles I and Laud see Peter Marshall, "Charles I's Reformation 1625-42," in *Reformation England, 1480-1642*, 2nd ed. (London: Bloomsbury Academic Press, 2012) 215–242.

[121] Christopher Hill wrote a classic study of these groups. See Christopher Hill, *The World Turned Upside Down: Radical Ideas During the English Revolution* (New York: Penguin, 1975).

were small: their membership reached only seven per cent of the population at most.[122] However, they created alarm since they were often perceived as dangerous subversives. Their influence declined sharply after the Restoration of 1660.

With the growth of many new forms of Christianity the religious landscape was thus increasingly fluid at mid-century. Baptists faced the problem of drawing boundaries in this pluralistic religious ethos. Thus they were prompted to articulate their basic views by publishing numerous tracts and the *London Confession of Faith* (1644, 1646). But some people, including Knollys, also heard and considered sympathetically the claims of the new groups who argued for political and economic equality, for the imminent end of the present age, and also for the relationship between these two ideas.

Although Knollys was drawn to elements of the teaching of some of these new groups, he ultimately rejected their full agendas.[123] Levellers advocated broad extension of suffrage and abolition of the monarchy. John Lilburne, leader of the Levellers, called for dissolution of the current Parliament and its re-establishment on democratic lines.[124] He was also a strong advocate for religious toleration for separatist groups. According to Thomas Edwards, Knollys made the following public prayer at his church in Great St. Helen's on 10 August 1645, upon Lilburne's commitment to prison by the Commons: "Lord, bring thy servant Lilburne out of prison, and honor him, Lord, for he hath honored thee."[125] Leveller influence was strong in the Army and in the House of Commons in 1646 and 1647, but support declined rapidly for fear that Leveller influence would lead to anarchy.[126] By 1649, while Knollys was serving in Whalley's regiment in Essex, most of the regiment "published a declaration against Leveller

[122] Doran and Durston, *Princes, Pastors and People,* 131.

[123] This dimension of his life has received extended attention in Knollys' historiography.

[124] "Levellers." In *The Oxford Dictionary of the Christian Church*, edited by Cross, F. L., and E. A. Livingstone, 3rd rev. ed. (Oxford: Oxford University Press, 2005) http://www.oxfordreference.com/view/10.1093/acref/9780192802903.001.0001/acref-9780192802903-e-4055 (accessed December 5, 2014).

[125] Edwards, *The first and second part of Gangraena* (1st ed.) 1:35; Bustin, *Paradox and Perseverance*, 122; Andrew Sharp, "Lilburne, John (1615?–1657)," in *Oxford Dictionary of National Biography*, edited by H. C. G. Matthew and Brian Harrison (Oxford: Oxford University Press, 2004). Online ed., edited Lawrence Goldman, October 2006. http://www.oxforddnb.com/view/article/16654 (accessed August 13, 2014).

[126] Bustin, *Paradox and Perseverance*, 122–123.

principles on which Knollys' name appears."[127] Since the authorities suspected him, Knollys sought to distance himself from these more radical sectarians.[128] Anti-Leveller declarations were published in 1647 and 1651, the latter signed by sixteen leaders, including William Kiffin, Hanserd Knollys and Richard Wollaston.[129] Bustin argues that although the Baptists appreciated Lilburne's defense of religious toleration, they distanced themselves from the Levellers because they "wished to be perceived by the government as good citizens" and had no wish to alter civil government.[130] Influential during the Civil War, by 1660 the Levellers had almost completely disappeared.[131]

In 1652 Knollys, Richard Wollaston and others petitioned the Rump Parliament, asking for abolition of tithes. Knollys signed a petition, and yet another followed. The dissenting churches relied on voluntary contributions by members and they appealed for fair treatment for all. During this period Knollys also wrote *An exposition of the first chapter of the Song of Solomon.*[132] In this study he dwells on a favorite dissenter theme—the contrast between the true church and the false church. His Baptist views are once again transparent: church members must be believers, and together they form a gathered church. During this stage of his life, Knollys' identity as a Baptist leader was firmly settled.

---

[127] Lawrence, *Parliamentary Army Chaplains*, 143.

[128] This was an important issue for Knollys. Pope Duncan and Barry Howson give particular attention to Knollys' relationship to other sectarian groups. See Pope Duncan, *Hanserd Knollys: A Seventeenth Century Baptist* (Nashville: Broadman Press, 1965) and Howson, *Erroneous and Schismatical Opinions*. Because eschatology was a major preoccupation of Knollys, his relationship to the Fifth Monarchy movement (organized c. 1651) would be particularly controversial in 1660–1661. By 1649 he had already dealt with charges of being an Anabaptist and a Leveller.

[129] Bustin, *Paradox and Perseverance*, 124.

[130] Ibid., 126–127.

[131] "Levellers," *Oxford Dictionary of the Christian Church* (3rd rev. ed.).

[132] Hanserd Knollys, *An exposition of the first chapter of the Song of Solomon. Wherein the text is analysed, the allegories are explained, and the hidden mysteries are unveiled, according to the proportion of faith. With spiritual meditations upon every verse* (London: W. Godbid, 1656).

VIII. KNOLLYS DURING RESTORATION AND REVOLUTION, 1660-1691

Knollys' autobiographical *Life and death* is highly informative for his early years, but it offers very little information about the last two decades of his life. Other records indicate the major contours of his activities. Along with other dissenters, Knollys experienced alternating persecution and toleration under the Restoration until legal toleration was more firmly established in 1689. He lived through the experience of imprisonment and the struggle for toleration in church-state relations. Fear of revival of Catholic rule and a popish plot provided a key social dynamic of the period. Knollys turned his attention to extensive apocalyptic studies of scripture, with heavy emphasis on the role of persecution by the state and the papacy in his interpretations. During this era Knollys suffered personal losses, including serious illness, financial setbacks, and the death of close family members. Finally, there are numerous additional examples of his continuing leadership of the Particular Baptists during the last three decades of his life. Most of his publications, in fact, appeared after 1660.

When it became clear that Charles II would be called to England to restore the monarchy, he issued from Breda in the Netherlands a declaration of religious toleration (1660).[133] This document lifted hopes of dissenters. However, Parliament's legislation undercut this promise. Not only was there general sentiment to restore the monarchy, there was also widespread support in Parliament to restore the authority of the Church of England after an interval of two decades which permitted growth of dissenters. In May of 1660 riots broke out against dissenters in London, apparently wrecking the church of William Kiffin. The Baptists presented two "Anabaptist Petitions" to the House of Lords in 1660 and 1661.[134] The first petition bears only one signature—that of Hanserd Knollys.[135] Larry Kreitzer judged that at the beginning of the Restoration "the relative degree of religious freedom enjoyed by Baptists and other sectarian groups during

[133] The text of the *Declaration of Breda* is available in Henry Gee and William Hardy, *Documents Illustrative of English Church History* (London: Macmillan and Co., 1896) 585–588.

[134] See Larry J. Kreitzer, "The Anabaptist Petitions of 1660 and 1661: William Kiffin and the Particular Baptists," *Exploring Baptist Origins,* ed. Anthony R. Cross and Nicholas J. Ward (Oxford: Regents Park College, 2010) 81–99.

[135] Kreitzer, "The Anabaptist Petitions of 1660 and 1661," 81.

the Protectorate was in danger of being lost altogether," and that Knollys appealed to the King's promise in the Declaration of Breda and presented the petition with the hope that "promises made for religious freedom and toleration continue to be extended to Baptists."[136] The second petition reiterated the Baptist plea for toleration.[137]

During the 1650s and early 1660s Knollys was attracted to the Fifth Monarchy Men, a new religious group with radical millennial proposals. Duncan observed that many Baptists were caught up in this movement.[138] These included notable leaders such as Major General Thomas Harrison, the evangelist Vavasor Powell, and numerous ministers.[139] The Fifth Monarchy idea derived from the Old Testament book of Daniel which describes the passing of four successive kingdoms followed by the rule of God's representative, the Messiah. Led by Thomas Venner, this group wanted to see the rule of God in England. The more radical members advocated violent intervention in order to hasten the return and rule of Christ in the new millennium. In January 1661 the radical Fifth Monarchy Men staged the Venner Uprising, challenging the King's right to rule. Venner was captured and executed January 19, 1661. The revolt was put down, and the Fifth Monarchy movement was discredited. Knollys was arrested, along with some four hundred others suspected of sympathizing with Venner.[140] Imprisoned for eighteen weeks, he was released by the general Act of Pardon issued in conjunction with the new king's coronation. The Venner uprising created alarm and more suspicion of dissenting sectarian groups.

Barrie White noted that Knollys was nowhere near the heart of the Fifth Monarchy Movement, but there is evidence of his sympathies. In 1654 he visited Anna Trapnell, the Fifth Monarchy prophetess, and fourteen members of Knollys' church signed *A declaration of several of the churches of Christ,* a Fifth Monarchy manifesto.[141] Moreover, he had Baptist minister

[136] Ibid., 86–87.

[137] Ibid., 87–91.

[138] Duncan, *Hanserd Knollys*, 46.

[139] This movement is treated by Bernard Capp, *The Fifth Monarchy of Men: A Study in Seventeenth-century English Millenarianism* (London: Faber, 1972) and Duncan, *Hanserd Knollys*, 46–50.

[140] White, *Hanserd Knollys*, 18–19.

[141] Anon., *A declaration of several of the churches of Christ, and godly people in and about the citie of London; concerning the kingly interest of Christ, and the present suffrings of his cause and saints in England* (London: no printer, 1654).

friends who were drawn to the movement—especially Henry Jessey and John Simpson.[142] The historian of dissent Geoffrey Nuttall helpfully distinguished four gradations of engagement with The Fifth Monarchy movement: those who accepted the view intellectually, those who were emotionally excited by hope for divine justice in the millennium, those who adopted it as a political policy, and finally, those who were engaged in outright plots to overthrow the government.[143] Bustin judged that Knollys shared some of their apocalyptic ideas but was at best only a mild sympathizer.[144] The response of the government to all dissenting groups over the next few years was to pass a series of laws meant to curtail their growth and influence. Collectively called the Clarendon Code, these laws, when enforced, made life difficult for anyone who did not worship according to the established norms of the Church of England.

After he was released from prison Knollys took his wife and two children to Holland and then on to Germany. He took sufficient funds to live there for about three years. Meanwhile his house and property in London were seized—a loss of about seven hundred sixty pounds sterling. He initiated legal efforts to reclaim his property, but was ultimately unsuccessful. While in Germany, Knollys turned his attention to writing grammars for learning Hebrew, Greek and Latin. He published these books in England in 1664. Knollys was an educator. He tutored upper class children for university, but he also taught the children of tradesmen, and he worked with students preparing for ministry. In this way he was not only assuring a good income when he taught; he was also establishing respectability and acceptance of Baptists.[145] While abroad Knollys also addressed questions about Baptist practices. Prior to his return to England Knollys wrote a formal preface to Katherine Sutton's *A Christian woman's experiences of the glorious working of God's free grace,* commending readers to heed this woman's spiritual teachings.[146] Knollys also wrote a preface endorsing Benjamin Keach's *Instructions for children: On the child's and youth's*

---

[142] White, *Hanserd Knollys*, 17.

[143] Geoffrey F. Nuttall, "Abingdon Revisited, 1656–1675," *Baptist Quarterly* 36 (April 1995): 96–103, here 101.

[144] Bustin, *Paradox and Perseverance,* 169.

[145] Ibid., 177.

[146] Hanserd Knollys, "Courteous Reader," in Katherine Sutton, *A Christian woman's experiences of the glorious working of God's free grace* (Rotterdam: Henry Goddaeus, 1663).

delight.[147] Keach was fined and imprisoned for publishing the book without authorization—yet another example of religious persecution during the early years of the Restoration.

When he returned to England, Knollys resumed teaching. He eventually achieved good financial standing, indicated by the pension he created for his son, also a Baptist pastor. London experienced disasters in the mid 1660s—first the plague in 1665 and then the fire of 1666. Knollys thought of these disasters in terms of the judgment of God. It is not surprising that he published *Apocalyptical mysteries*, an eschatological study, during the following year.[148] Knollys suffered intermittent persecution and difficulties throughout his life. But his experiences of loss in 1671 were overwhelming. He personally suffered life-threatening illness. He called on two friends, Kiffin and Powell, to pray for his healing.[149] Death visited the household. He lost two grandsons, two sons, and also Anne, his wife of thirty-seven years.[150] Knollys fell ill again but recovered and lived another nineteen years. He wrote his *Life and death* the following year, doubtless now keenly aware of his own mortality.[151] The illnesses and deaths also led to much spiritual soul-searching—"the trial of my faith"—as Knollys expressed it.[152] Knollys fell into some financial difficulties and accepted

[147] Hanserd Knollys, "To the Courteous Reader," in Benjamin Keach, *Instructions for children: or, The child's & youth's delight, teaching an easie way to spell & read true English. Containing the father's godly advice; directing parents in a right and spiritual manner to educate their children. With a Christian catechism, wherein all the chief principles of true Christianity are clearly opened. Together with many other things both pleasant and useful for the education of children* (London: Printed for Thomas Knowles at the corner of Tower-Street, and John How without Bishopsgate, 1683). In the preface, Knollys notes, "This little book, called, *Instructions for Children*, I have read, [who] have taught scholars above 40 years in London." The reference to his pedagogical activity is consistent with what we know about his transition from Independent to Baptist minister. In fact, as pointed out earlier in this essay he became a Baptist around 1645, nearly forty years before he penned this preface for Benjamin Keach. The original work is found in Jesus College Fellows' Library, University of Oxford.

[148] Hanserd Knollys, *Apocalyptical mysteries, touching the two witnesses, the seven vials, and the two kingdoms, to wit, of Christ, and of Antichrist, expounded. Wherein is contained some things necessary for the saints in this present generation to know* (London: no printer, 1667).

[149] Knollys, *The Life and Death* (1812) 48.

[150] Ibid., 46, 48–49.

[151] Ibid., 50.

[152] Ibid., 45.

assistance from funds established for "decayed" ministers.[153] His church seemed never to be able to support him fully. The congregation was poor and had limited resources.[154]

Charles II's 1672 Declaration of Indulgence provided some respite from persecution for dissenters during the decade 1672-1682.[155] During the 1670s Knollys engaged in several debates. One of these involved a spirited exchange between Baptist Henry Danvers and pedo-baptist Obediah Wills; Knollys, Kiffin and others intervened on behalf of Danvers.[156] Another debate arose among Baptists in Bristol over whether, in their quest to establish the true church, it was permitted for believers and nonbelievers to pray together. The London pastors assured them that both should be praying and that prayer together was to be encouraged.[157] The London Particular Baptist ministers also produced in 1677 a major new *Confession of Faith* based on the *Savoy Confession*. Duncan observed that "they wanted to ally with other Protestants" so they used the Presbyterian *Westminster Confession of Faith* (1646), and the Congregational *Savoy Declaration* (1658), and added Baptist emphases.[158]

In his later years, Knollys gave special attention to the question of the return and reign of Christ. He was deeply immersed in interpreting millennial expectations. In 1674 Knollys published *The parable of the Kingdom of Heaven expounded* based on the story of the five wise and five foolish virgins (Matthew 25:1-13).[159] In this study he explored the time, the nature and the Christian's preparation for the coming kingdom. Knollys published additional millennial studies in the 1670s and 1680s; it was the

---

[153] Crosby remarked that Knollys frequently had to move from place to place because of persecution, which explains why sometimes he was worth hundreds of pounds and other times he was penniless. See Crosby, *The History of English Baptists*, 1:338.

[154] Knollys, *The Life and Death* (1812) 34.

[155] White observed that "following the Declaration of Indulgence in 1672…it seems likely (if the records of regular and frequent meetings of the Petty France [Baptist] congregation accurately reflect the general situation in London) that the Baptists of the capital were not much troubled by active persecution during the period 1672-1682." White, *Hanserd Knollys*, 20.

[156] Hanserd Knollys, et.al., *The Baptists answer to Mr. Obed. Wills, his appeal against Mr. H. Danvers* (London: no printer, 1675).

[157] Ivimey, *A History of English Baptists*, 1:417–420.

[158] Duncan, *Hanserd Knollys*, 18.

[159] Hanserd Knollys, *The parable of the Kingdom of heaven expounded, or, An exposition of the first thirteen verses of the twenty fifth chapter of Matthew* (London: no printer, 1674).

chief theme of his theological writing. Fear of rule by Catholics pervaded much of this era, reaching a feverish level in the Popish Plot of 1678. Related to this issue Knollys published three more apocalyptic works, *An exposition of the 11th Chapter of Revelation* (1679), *Mystical Babylon availed* (1679) and *The world that now is and the world that is to come* (1681).[160]

The wide range of topics he addressed and the frequency of the appearance of his name in tracts and prefaces suggests Knollys' growing stature among Baptists. Knollys endorsed with fellow ministers an appeal for toleration of Baptists in Boston, Massachusetts.[161] Dissenters faced changing political fortunes in the early 1680s. In his political policy Charles II favored the Tories who supported the Church of England against the Whigs who favored dissenters' rights.[162] Undeterred by the risk, Knollys continued preaching. At an advanced age in 1684 he was arrested and spent six months in Newgate prison.[163]

The Catholic King James II succeeded Charles II in 1685, creating more anxiety for both leaders of the Church of England and for dissenters. In order to aid fellow Catholics he issued another declaration of indulgence for all. Dissenters also benefitted from this policy but they did not support the King.[164] When a male heir was born to James II, it was apparent that he would be reared in the Catholic faith. Protestants led the "Glorious Revolution" which removed James and established William and Mary as

---

[160] Hanserd Knollys, *An exposition of the 11th Chapter of Revelation wherein all those things therein revealed, which must shortly come to pass, are explained* (London: no printer, 1679); idem., *Mystical Babylon availed wherein is proved, I. That Rome-papal is mystical-Babylon, II. That the pope of Rome is the beast, III. That the Church of Rome is the great whore, IV. That the Roman-priests are the false prophet: also A call to the people of God to come out of Babylon* (London: no printer, 1679); idem, *The world that now is; and the world that is to come: or The first and second coming of Jesus Christ Wherein several prophecies not yet fulfilled are expounded* (London: Thomas Snowden, 1681).

[161] John Russell, *A brief narrative of some considerable passages concerning the first gathering and further progress of a church of Christ, in gospel order, in Boston, in New England, commonly (though falsly) called by the name of Anabaptists; for clearing their innocency from the scandalous things laid to their charge* (Boston: Printed by J. D., 1680). Six leading Baptist ministers, including Knollys, signed the foreword. See White, *Hanserd Knollys*, 29n79.

[162] Robert Bucholz and Newton Key, *Early Modern England, 1485-1714: A Narrative History*, 2nd ed. (Oxford: Wiley-Blackwell, 2009) 296–300.

[163] William Kiffin, "Epistle to the Reader," in Knollys, *The Life and Death* (1812), 5, and Ivimey, *History of the Baptists*, 1:411.

[164] Doran and Durston, *Princes, Pastors and People*, 135.

rulers in 1688. The Baptists issued yet another *Confession of Faith* in 1688, based on the 1677 *Confession*. The authority on Baptist confessions, William Lumpkin, judged that this confession "became one of the most important of all Baptist confessions."[165] The first signature to this confession is Hanserd Knollys's. In 1688, in the midst of upheavals, Knollys published his last apocalyptic essay, *An exposition of the whole Book of Revelation.*[166] Although historians have concluded the perceived threat from international Catholicism was greatly exaggerated, it was a perception that conditioned Protestant behavior.[167] The following year Parliament passed the Act of Toleration of 1689, granting the right to worship to all Trinitarian Christians except Roman Catholics. The long era of religious persecution for English Baptists and other dissenters came to an official close. It was a landmark decision. The religious dissenters were not large in numbers, but they had made a powerful and permanent impact on English society.[168] Despite his advanced age, Knollys continued to offer support and guidance to the Baptist movement. When the Baptists took up the debate over whether they should provide financial support of ministers, Knollys argued in favor of providing support.[169] He also joined his colleague Benjamin

---

[165] Lumpkin, *Baptist Confessions of Faith*, 239.

[166] Hanserd Knollys, *An exposition of the whole book of the Revelation wherein the visions and prophecies of Christ are opened and expounded: shewing the great conquests of our lord Jesus Christ for his church over all his and her adversaries pagan, arian, and papal* (London: William Marshall, 1689).

[167] Doran and Durston, *Princes, Pastors and People*, 79.

[168] Ibid.

[169] Anon., *The gospel minister's maintenance vindicated. Wherein, a regular ministry in the churches, is first asserted, and the objections against a Gospel maintenance for ministers, answered. Also, the dignity, necessity, difficulty, use and excellency of the ministry of Christ is opened. Likewise, the nature and vveghtiness of that sacred vvork and office clearly evinc'd. Recommended to the baptized congregations, by several elders in and about the City of London* (London: John Harris, 1689). The authorship of *The gospel minister's maintenance vindicated* has traditionally been attributed to Benjamin Keach (1640–1704). See discussion in Thomas Crosby, *The History of the English Baptists, from the Reformation to the Beginning of the Reign of King George I: Containing their History from the End of the Reign of King William III to the Reign of King George I, including some Part of his Reign* (London: Printed for the Author, 1740) vol. 4, pp. 292–298 and A. J. Klaiber, "The Gospel Minister's Maintenance Vindicated," *Baptist Quarterly* 2(5) (1925): 224–231. However, Bustin believes that the work was co-authored by Knollys with other London Particular Baptist ministers from London. See Bustin, *Paradox and Perseverance*, 269–275.

Keach in endorsing congregational singing in Baptist worship services.[170] These debates were not over what Baptists would later call their principles, but they did provide guidelines for future Baptist practices. The Baptists addressed many practical issues as they shaped their identity, and Knollys contributed to many of these discussions.

Following the Act of Toleration, Baptist leaders established yet another way of promoting the Baptist cause. They summoned Baptist churches to a general meeting to secure ministers for the future, improve zeal, promote worship and urge establishment of a central fund.[171] Over one hundred churches were represented, suggesting that Particular Baptists were beginning to demonstrate characteristics of a denomination.[172] Knollys was also present at the general assembly of Baptists in both 1690 and 1691. These broadly representative Baptist meetings were a fitting conclusion to a life rich in service to Baptists. Pope Duncan judged that "Knollys…in his latter years was perhaps the most influential Baptist in England.[173] Knollys died September 19, 1691 and was buried with other distinguished dissenters in Bunhill Fields.

---

[170] Hanserd Knollys, *An answer to a brief discourse concerning singing in the publick worship of God in the Gospel-church, by I. M. [Isaac Marlow] 1690* (London: Printed for the author H. K. [Hanserd Knollys], 1691).

[171] White, *Hanserd Knollys*, 22.

[172] Ibid., 22, 24. On the number of churches, White cites Ivimey, *History of the Baptists*, 1:480. The characterization of Particular Baptist as a "settled denomination" is White's observation.

[173] Duncan, *Hanserd Knollys*, 33.

PART II

PAMPHLETS ON RELIGION

A MODERATE ANSWER

(London, 1645)

INTRODUCTION

In *A moderate answer*, Knollys issued one of the earliest Baptist defenses of Congregationalism. His tract was prompted by the criticism of the Presbyterian controversialist John Bastwick (1595?-1654). At the time he published *Independency not God's ordinance* (London, 1645), Bastwick enjoyed considerable popularity among Presbyterians. In this tract, Knollys displayed for the first time his aptitude as an apologist for Congregationalism while drawing on his extensive philological abilities. Consequently, *A moderate answer* captures the major fault lines between Congregationalists and Presbyterians.

At the heart of the debate was the question of the "right" church polity, i.e. how the churches ought to be governed and organized along biblical lines. Knollys articulated an argument for Congregationalism that was solely based on exegetical proofs. Of particular relevance was his detailed exegesis of Acts 2:46 and 2:47, passages which he argued demonstrate that the early church followed the Congregational model that he and other Independents intended to restore. Of similar significance was the interpretation of passages such as Acts 14:23 and Titus 1:5, which Bastwick used to argue that the early church was "aristocratically and presbyterianly governed." In response, Knollys not only endeavored to refute his interpretation but also offered a more democratic, if not egalitarian, view of the early church based on Acts 15:28. The tract reflects the enormous influence that Theodore Beza (1519-1605) had on early Baptists. In fact, Knollys based his exegetical arguments on Beza's *Novum Testamentum* (Geneva, 1598).

A MODERATE ANSWER[1]

(London, 1645)

A Moderate Answer to Dr. Bastwick's[2] Book, called *Independence not God's Ordinance.*[3]

---

[1] Hanserd Knollys, *A Moderate Answer Unto Dr. Bastwicks* [*sic*] *Book, Called, Independency not God's Ordinance. Wherein, is declared the manner how some churches in this city were gathered, and upon what tearmes their Members were admitted; That so both the Dr. and the Reader may judge, how near some Beleevers who walk together in the Fellowship of the Gospell, do come in their practice to these Apostolicall rules which are propounded by the Dr. as God's method in gathering Churches and admitting Members* (London: Printed by Iane Coe, 1645).

[2] John Bastwick (1595?–1654) Puritan controversialist, studied medicine at Leiden and Padua. In 1624, he published *Elenchus religionis papisticae*, in which he attacked Roman Catholicism. The *Elenchus* went through a number of editions; the edition of 1634 landed him in trouble with the Court of High Commission leading to his arrest and imprisonment in 1635. He continued writing from prison and in 1637 was found guilty of seditious libel along with William Prynne (1600–1669) and Henry Burton (c. 1578–1647/48). He was condemned to life imprisonment. The sentence was carried out on June 30, 1637. He was, however, released in 1640 He eventually embraced the cause of Presbyterianism and in 1645 published his *Independency not God's Ordinance* (London, 1645). He fell out of favor with a number of leaders and died in relative obscurity in 1654. See Frances Condick, "Bastwick, John (1595?–1654)," in *Oxford Dictionary of National Biography*, edited by H. C. G. Matthew and Brian Harrison (Oxford: Oxford University Press, 2004). Online ed., edited by Lawrence Goldman, January 2008. http://www.oxforddnb. com/view/article/1659 (accessed December 5, 2014); T. B. Howell, ed., "Proceedings in the Star-Chamber against Dr. John Bastwick, Mr. Henry Burton, and William Prynn, esq. for several libels," in *A Complete Collection of State Trials and Proceedings for High Treason and other Crimes and Misdemeanors from the Earliest Period to the Year 1783, in 21 Volumes.* 21 vols. (London: T.C. Hansard for Longman, Hurst, Rees, Orme, and Brown, 1816) 3:711–770.

[3] John Bastwick, *Independency not Gods ordinance: or A treatise concerning church-government, occasioned by the distractions of these times. Wherein is evidently proved, that the Presbyterian government dependent is Gods ordinance, and not the Presbyterian government independent. To which is annexed a postscript, discovering the uncharitable dealing of the independents towards their Christian brethren, and the fraud and jugglings of many of their pastors and ministers, to the misleading of the poor people, not only to their own detriment, but the hurt of church and state; with the danger of all novelties in religion* (London: Printed by John Macock, for Michael Spark junior, 1645).

Passing by many things less considerable, because I intend brevity, in the seventh page of the Doctor's book, "There is a twofold question between them called Presbyterians and their brethren who are termed Independents; the first is, concerning the government of the church, that is to say, whether it be presbyterian dependent, or presbyterian independent? The second question is, concerning the gathering of churches."[4]

Touching the former question concerning the government of the church, the Doctor acknowledges in the same seventh page, that the brethren on both sides agree, "that the government of the church is a presbyterian government, both acknowledging a presbytery."[5] But whether it be dependent, or independent is the main thing in the question, which the Doctor does determine, and says in the title page of his book he has evidently proved: "that the presbyterian government dependent is God's ordinance, and not the presbyterian government independent."[6]

I intend not to strive with the Doctor about words, and therefore touching the two terms, to wit, dependent, and independent I shall only say this at present: that if by independent the Doctor indeed means—as it does appear so to my understanding by many passages in his book he does intend—a presbyterian government, which has not dependence upon any in matters merely ecclesiastical but upon the Lord Jesus Christ, who is the head of the church, and if by dependent he also intends—as in many other passages in his book seemed to me to be his meaning—a presbyterian government, which has a dependence upon a supreme judicature of a common council of presbyters, and who must in matters ecclesiastical be subject unto the decrees, sentences, constitutions, and commandments of a common council, college or consistory of classical, provincial, or synodical presbyters, then I do conceive the Doctor has not proved, nor will he ever be able to prove, that the presbyterian government dependent is God's ordinance. And I hope to make the contrary plainly appear both from clear texts of scripture, and the Doctor's own books. And seeing that the Doctor has in the sixth page of his book desired all his Christian brethren in the

---

[4] Bastwick's text reads: "There is a twofold question between us, they call the Presbyterians, and our Brethren they tearme Independents. The first is concerning the government of the church, *viz.* whether it be Presbyterian Dependent, or Presbyterian Independent. The second question is, concerning the gathering of churches; but that in its due place." Bastwick, *Independence not God's Ordinance*, 7.

[5] Ibid., 7.

[6] Ibid.

deciding of this question to take the word of God into their hands, and with the noble Bereans[7] to sit down and examine, whatsoever shall be said on either side according to the Scriptures, I willingly make the same request, as most desirous, that this short answer may abide the like trial, and be weighed in the other balance of the sanctuary against the Doctor's book.

Now that all things may be handled in good order, and in a methodical way, the Doctor has reduced the whole disputation concerning this first question into four propositions: "The first, that there were many congregations and several assemblies of believers in the church of Jerusalem, in the which they enjoyed all acts of worship, and all the ordinances amongst themselves, and did partake of all acts of church fellowship, especially of preaching, and in the administration of the sacraments, and prayer, and that before the persecution we read of (Acts 8:2). The second, that all these congregations and several assemblies made but one church. The third, that the apostles and elders governed, ordered, and ruled this church jointly, and by a common council and presbytery. The fourth, that this church of Jerusalem, and the government of the same is to be a pattern for all several congregations and assemblies in any city or vicinity to unite into one church, and for the officers of those congregations to govern that church jointly in a college or presbytery." These are his four propositions.

But before he comes to the proof of these particulars he says it will not be amiss in general to take notice, "That all the churches we read of in the New Testament were aristocratically and presbyterianly governed, and were all dependent upon their several presbyters," and produced diverse places of Scripture to prove the same.[8] And two sheets are spent wholly in proving thereof from the twelfth page to the twenty-ninth! All which—should it be granted—only proves: First, that in every city or church there was a

---

[7] "Bereans" is a reference to Jewish converts to Christianity in the historical city of Beroea, modern day Véroia in Greek Macedonia. According to Acts 17:11: "they welcomed the message very eagerly and examined the scriptures every day to see whether these things were so."

[8] "But before I come to the proof of these particulars, it will not be amiss in general to take notice that all the churches we read of in the New Testament, were aristocratically and presbyterially governed, and were all dependent upon their several presbyteries, and that the ordering and managing of that government lay only upon the presbytery and was their peculiar who had the power of the keys." Bastwick, *Independence not God's Ordinance*, 12.

presbytery: χειροτονήσαντες δὲ αὐτοῖς πρεσβυτέρους κατ' ἐκκλησίαν;[9] *cumque per suffragia statuissent illis per singulas Ecclesias seniores* (Acts 14:23).[10] That is, "when they had ordained them elders in every church by the suffrage or stretching forth of hands."[11] Also, Titus 1:5, καὶ καταστήσῃς κατὰ πόλιν πρεσβυτέρους, *O constituas oppidatim seniores.*[12] That is, "And thou mayest ordaine elders towne by towne, or city by city, or village by village."[13] Secondly, that as there were apostles and elders in the church of Jerusalem (Acts 15:2, 4), so there were elders in the church of Ephesus (Acts 20:17, 28), and in the church of Corinth, and in the church of Galatia, and in Philippi, etc. Thirdly, that these several churches were dependent upon their several presbyters, and were to obey them who had the rule over them (Hebrews 13:7, 17, 24). Or who were their guides, Πείθεσθε τοῖς ἡγουμένοις ὑμῶν, *Obedite ducibus vestris*[14] [Hebrews 13:17]. That is, "obey

---

[9] The frequent Greek NT quotations that appear throughout the pamphlet were drawn from Theodore Beza's *Novuum Testamentum.* Beza provided the *textus receptus* of the New Testament, the Latin translation of the Vulgate, and his own Latin rendering. He also provided his own extensive commentary with frequent references to Erasmus and his own codex of the first four books of the NT, the famous *Codex Bezae.* Here we have consulted the 1598 edition and a reprint that appeared in Cambridge in 1642. Cf., Theodore Beza, *Iesu Christi Domini Nostri Novum Testamentum, sive novum foedus, cuius graeco contextui respondent interpretationes duae: vna, vetus: altera, Theodori Bezae* ([Geneva]: Sumptibus Haered. Eust. Vignon, 1598); *Jesu Christi Domini Nostri Novum Testamentum, sive novum foedus, cujus graeco contextui respondent interpretationes duae: una, vetus; altera, Theodori Bezae* (Cantabrigiae: Rogeri Danielis, 1642). Unless otherwise noted, all page references are to the 1642 reprint.

[10] Here and in other places, Knollys provides an alternative Latin rendering that does not conform to either the Vulgate or Beza's translation. In this particular case, as well as in the subsequent quotation of Titus 1:5, Knollys uses "seniores" instead of "presbyteros," a move clearly intended to undermine the Presbyterians in their claims. Cf., Beza, "Nova," "Cúmque ipsi per suffragia creassent per singulas ecclesias presbyteros"; "Vetus," "Et cùm constituissent illis per singulas ecclesias presbyteros," 339.

[11] Knollys draws most English Bible quotations from the Authorized Version. Cf., "And when they had ordained them elders in every church, and had prayed with fasting, they commended them to the Lord, on whom they believed." Acts 14:23 (KJV).

[12] Cf., Beza, "Nova," "& constituas oppidatim presbyteros"; "Vetus," "& constituas per civitates presbyteros," 647.

[13] Cf., "For this cause left I thee in Crete, that thou shouldest set in order the things that are wanting, and ordaine elders in every citie, as I had appointed thee." Titus 1:5 (KJV).

[14] Cf., Beza, "Nova," "Parete ductoribus vestris"; "Vetus," "Obedite praepositus vestris," 691.

your guides."[15] Fourthly, that this presbyterian church government, God has appointed as his ordinance to be continued to the end of the world, the which, whosoever resisted, resisted the ordinance of God.

But it does not prove that this presbyterian church government is dependent upon a supreme judicature of a common counsel of presbyters, or that they must submit, and subject them themselves and their churches unto the decrees, sentences, constitutions, and commandments of a common council, college, and court of classical, or synodal presbyters, which the Doctor should have proved. For such a presbyterian government he intends, as may appear by the Doctor's own words in pages seventeen and eighteen: "As for the presbyterian government, in the sense that I understand it, there is nothing more clear to me in all the Scripture. Yea the very word and name of presbytery signified, a magistracy, or aristocracy, or signory, or court. And as the word is taken in the civil polity and government, so in the ecclesiastical, by a presbytery we understand," says the Doctor, "a religious, grave, solid, learned, and wise council of divines, ministers, etc., without whose joint and mutual accord, or agreement and common consent nothing ought to be done or transacted of public concernment."[16] And to make this good, to wit, that the presbyters of particular congregations, or assemblies of believers, and their churches ought to be subject to a common council or

[15] Cf., "Obey them that have the rule over you, and submit yourselves: for they watch for your souls, as they that must give account, that they may do it with joy, and not with grief: for that is unprofitable for you." Hebrews 13:17 (KJV).

[16] Knollys frequently provides partial and incomplete quotations of Bastwick's original statements. Here the editors of the present work are providing Bastwick's original statements as needed. Cf., "As for the presbyterian government, in the sense that I understand it, there is nothing more clear to me in all the holy Scripture. Yea the very word and name of presbytery signified a magistracy, or aristocracy, or signory, or court. That is, a company, or senate, or counsel of grave, wise, and understanding men, invested with authority and power of ruling, ordering, and commanding, and in whose hands the government is put. And as the word is taken in the civil polity and government, so in the ecclesiastical, by a presbytery we understand a religious, grave, solid, learned, and wise council of divines and ministers, or men of inveterate experience, and such as know how to rule and govern those that are under their command, with wisdom and moderation, and according to the word of God. And the which men likewise are invested with authority and power, for to exercise a jurisdiction over others, and are hereunto called by such as are able to judge and discern of the sufficiency of their gifts and abilities for this work, which the ordinary and common people cannot." Bastwick, *Independence not God's Ordinance*, 17–18.

court of presbyters, the Doctor urged that Scripture, the Third Epistle of John, the ninth, tenth, and eleventh verses, as an invincible argument.

You shall find it thus expounded by the Doctor: "And therefore when Diotrephes assumed to himself, and his particular congregation a power and authority to rule according to his will and pleasure, without the consent of the presbytery, and opposed John the Presbyter, he sharply reproves his proceedings, and signifies to the church that when he came he would remember his words, and teach him how to prate against the presbytery with malicious words, which is an evil thing in him, says St. John. It was evil in him to assume unto himself, and his particular congregation, that power that belonged unto the college or council of presbyters, and was to be moderated and exercised only by the conjoint, and common consent of the presbytery. For God has appointed that the church should be governed by a presbytery, and Diotrephes would have his congregation independent, and have an absolute jurisdiction within itself, which says St. John is an evil thing."[17]

Now let the reader judge, whether the Doctor be not much mistaken in his commentary-exposition and application of this place of Scripture. And let me give you to understand [w]hat St. John says in verse nine: "I wrote unto the church." Or as Beza[18] upon that verse, Ἔγραψά τῇ ἐκκλησίᾳ, *Scripsi nonnihil Ecclesiae* [3 John 9].[19] That is, "I have written something to

[17] "And therefore when Diotrephes assumed unto himself and his particular congregation a power and authority to rule according to his will and pleasure, without the consent of the presbytery, and opposed John the Presbyter, he sharply reproves his proceedings and signifies to the church (*Epist. 3*) that when he came he would remember his words, and teach him how to prate against the presbytery with malicious words: 'For he (saith S. John) contenteth not himself onely to prate maliciously against us, but he will not receive the brethren, nor suffer others, but casteth them out of the church; which is an evil thing in him,' saith Saint John. 'But for you,' saith he, speaking to the church, 'follow not that which is evil but that which is good.' It was evil in him to assume unto himself alone, and his particular congregation, that power that belonged unto the college or council of presbyters, and was to be moderated and exercised only by the conjoint and common consent of the presbytery. For God had appointed that his church should be governed by a presbytery, and Diotrophes would have his congregation independent, and have an absolute jurisdiction within itself, 'which,' saith Saint John, 'is an evil thing'." Bastwick, *Independence not God's Ordinance*, 15–16.

[18] Theodore Beza (1519–1605) the note is indicative of Knollys' use of Beza's New Testament.

[19] Cf., Beza, "Nova," "Scripsi Ecclesiae"; "Vetus," "Scripsissem forsitan Ecclesiae," 739; cf. "Ἔγραψά τι τῇ ἐκκλησίᾳ," GNT, 798.

the church."[20] But seeing no mention is made of any particular congregation, how can the Doctor so confidently affirm that it was his particular congregation? Now the reader may see plainly that the Doctor can expound those brethren and their elders or presbyters, which the Scripture calls a church, to be a particular congregation. And what it was which St. John had written to the church is not in this epistle, nor any other Scripture, declared, except it was to receive those brethren, which he says in verse eight ought to be received, and in verse ten whom Diotrephes would not receive. How then does the Doctor say, "That Diotrephes assumed that power to himself, which belonged unto the college and council of presbyters without whose joint and mutual agreement and common consent nothing ought to be done or transacted of public concernment"? Is the receiving of brethren or casting out of brethren a power which belongs to a college of presbyters, and neither the one nor the other may be transacted by the elders and brethren of a particular congregation unless the court or common council of presbyters conjointly consent unto it? Let it be also considered that Diotrephes opposed the brethren and forbade them that would have received those who St. John says in verse eight we ought to receive, yea and cast them ought in verse ten: καὶ τοὺς βουλομένους κωλύει καὶ ἐκ τῆς ἐκκλησίας ἐκβάλλει, *volentes (admittere) prohibet, & de Ecclesia deiicit* [3 John 10].[21] That is, "and forbiddeth them, that would, or are willing to admit them and casted [cast] them out of the church"; to wit, excommunicated them.[22] Does it hereby appear that Diotrephes would have his congregation independent, and have an absolute jurisdiction within itself? No, but Diotrephes would lord it over the church, and have the pre-eminence above his brethren, whether fellow elders or fellow saints [as in] verse nine: ἀλλ' ὁ φιλοπρωτεύων αὐτῶν Διοτρέφης, *sed amans primatum gerere in eos Diotrephes* [3 John 9].[23] That is,

---

[20] Cf., "I wrote unto the Church, but Diotrephes, who loveth to have the preeminence among them, receiveth us not." 3 John 9 (KJV).

[21] Cf. Beza, "Nova," "& volentes admittere prohibet & ex Ecclesia eiicit"; "Vetus," "[et] eos qui suscipiunt, prohibet, [et] de Ecclesia deiicit," 739.

[22] Cf., "Wherefore, if I come, I will remember his deeds which he doeth, prating against us with malicious words: and not content therewith, neither doth he himself receive the brethren, and forbiddeth them that would, and casteth them out of the church." 3 John 10 (KJV).

[23] Cf. Beza, "Nova," "sed qui primatum inter eos ambit Diotrephes, non admittit nos."; "Vetus," "sed is qui amat primatum gerere in eis Diotrephes, non recipit nos," 739.

"but Diotrephes loving the primacy amongst them."[24] He would be the primate and metropolitan of the church, and have the pre-eminence of all the presbyters in it, and brethren of it. The Doctor could have urged this Scripture against the domineering prelates. And why should he marvel that his brethren should now urge it against the court of presbyters?

It is confessed Diotrephes did that which was evil in usurping authority over the church and those brethren whom he cast out of the church. But that he was the first that opposed the presbyterian government, or that he did affront a court and common council of presbyters is more than I know, or the Doctor can prove. For had Diotrephes done so, why was he not convented[25] before them, surely the apostle and elder St. John would rather have written to the college of presbyters—if there were any such—than to the church, or in writing to the church, would rather have sent him a summons to appear at some consistory before the court and common council of presbyters, than to warn them to take heed of his evil, that they did not follow it. And doubtless St. John would have written thus, "Diotrephes loves to be a primate among you, wherefore when the presbytery, that is to say, the magistracy or signory of grave, solid, learned, religious, and wise divines and ministers come to keep order, and met [meet] together in a court and common council, I will remember his deeds, and inform, or complain to the court and common council of presbyters, that he prates against us—the presbyters—with malicious words."

But the apostle St. John did not know any court or common council of presbyters, neither classical, nor synodical, to appeal unto. Nor can the Doctor make good those appeals he mentioned on page ten to be according to the Scripture of truth; to wit, that "every particular man, as well as any assembly or congregation, may have their appeal to the presbytery of their precinct, hundred, or division under whose jurisdictions they were; and if they find themselves wronged there, then they have appeals to some other higher presbytery or council of divines for relief and justice."[26] I only ask the

---

[24] Cf., "I wrote unto the church: but Diotrephes, who loveth to have the preeminence among them, receiveth us not." 3 John 9 (KJV).

[25] *Oxford English Dictionary Online,* s.v. "convent," "to cause (persons) to come or appear; to call to a meeting or interview, to summon." The earliest recorded use of the term dates to 1540. See *Oxford English Dictionary Online* (Oxford: Oxford University Press, 2014) s.v. "† convent, v.," http://www.oed.com/view/Entry/40702?rskey= QwD-lut&result=2&isAdvanced=false (accessed December 05, 2014).

[26] Knollys seems to paraphrase the original. Cf., "[T]o the which every particular man, as well as any assembly or congregation, may have their appeal for the redress of any

Doctor how he can prove these appeals by Scripture, and if he could, whether that higher presbytery or council of divines, especially if they may say "the Holy Ghost and we" [cf., Acts 15:28], be not as independent as these brethren and their churches, against whom the Doctor has written. And if so, then such a high presbytery or council of divines is not God's ordinance, by the Doctor's own confession and affirmation. Therefore the Apostle writes to the church or particular congregation whereof Diotrephes was a member and an elder, whom he knew had power to judge him as well as the church or particular congregation of Corinth had power to judge them that were members therein (1 Corinthians 5:12–13). And therefore might as warrantably admonish Diotrephes, as the church of Colossae might Archippus (Colossians 4:17): "And if nothing of public concernment ought to be done or transacted without the joint and mutual accord or agreement, and common consent of the presbytery."[27] John the Presbyter would not have transgressed so far as to take upon himself this authority over Diotrephes to tell the church of his faults, and to say he would remember him and sharply reprove him, and teach him to prate against the presbytery with malicious words, which belonged to the court and common council of presbyters. But I shall have a just occasion to say more touching this matter in the answer unto the third question, and therefore passing by the objection with its answer mentioned on page 19 to 29 unto its due place.

I shall desire seriously to consider the Doctor's proof of his first proposition which he labored first by producing such scriptures as he conceived made for the manifestation of the truth, and from thence framed and formed his arguments. His scriptures are these, viz. Matthew 3:1, 2, 5, 6; Mark 6:20, 23; Matthew 14:5, and; Luke 20:4, 6. And diverse other Scriptures, which you have at large set down in the Doctor's book with his

---

abuses or enormities, and if they find themselves wronged there, then they have appeals to some other higher presbytery or council of divines for relief and justice." Bastwick, *Independence not God's Ordinance*, 10.

[27] Knollys is here quoting Bastwick. Cf., "Here Timothy and all ministers in him are to the end of the world bound to maintain that government unblamable that was appointed by the apostles, and that was the presbyterian government, and the ruling of all churches by joint consent and a common council or college of presbyters, so that nothing ought to be done or transacted of public concernment without their joint and mutual accord or agreement and common consent of the presbytery." Bastwick, *Independence not God's Ordinance*, 15. Knollys' point is that 3 John assumes a context in which there is no "college of presbyters" governing over the local church and that the latter had authority over Diotrephes.

arguments framed from thence on pages 29 to 82, where this first proposition ended. The sum of all, which I shall give the reader to understand as briefly as I can, to wit: "Where there was an infinite multitude of believers, or a very city of believers, so that they kept a tyrannical king in awe, and all the magistrates and elders in whose hands was all the power and authority, even a world of believers with many rulers and men of great place and office, with such an increase of multitudes of believers, 8,000 new converts besides women and children, yea many 10,000 of believers, and where there were almost a hundred preachers and ministers besides the twelve apostles, and all these continually taken up in prayer and preaching, there must of necessity be many congregations and assemblies. But in the church of Jerusalem there was an infinite multitude of believers and a very city of believers—which kept Herod himself, the tyrant in awe, and all the magistrates and elders—even a world of believers, with many rulers and men of great place and office, with an increase of multitudes of believers, and 8,000 new converts besides women and children, yea and many 10,000 after all the persecutions, and almost a hundred preachers and ministers beside the twelve apostles, and all these were continually taken up in prayer and preaching. Ergo, they must of necessity be dispersed into many congregations and several assemblies."[28]

I do deny the minor proposition of this argument. Neither has the Doctor proved that there was an infinite number of believers, nor a very city of believers in the church of Jerusalem. The scriptures quoted by the Doctor speak of no such thing; those places in Matthew, Mark and Luke, tell us of very many who were baptized by John, and by Christ's disciples, but do not

---

[28] Knollys provides a somewhat modified version of the original passage taken from Bastwick's *Independence not God's Ordinance*, 35: "Where there was such an infinite company and multitude of Christians and believers, as kept a tyrannical king in awe, and all the magistrates and elders in whose hands was all the power and authority; and struck such a fear and terror into them all, that they durst not exercise their cruelty and tyranny over them, though they were their inveterate enemies, and desired it: there of necessity the number of believers must be so great, as they could not all meet together in one place or room, or in one congregation, for the enjoying and partaking in all the acts of worship, but if they would be edified, must be distributed into diverse congregations and assemblies. But in Jerusalem there were such an infinite company and multitude of Christians and believers, as kept Herod himself, the tyrant, in awe and all the magistrates and elders, in whose hands was all the power and authority; and struck such a fear and terror into them, that they durst not exercise their cruelty and tyranny over them though they were their inveterate enemies, and desired it."

declare how many of these baptized persons were of the church in Jerusalem, and the Scripture witnessed, [i.e.] Acts 9:31, that there were churches throughout all Judea, as well as in Jerusalem, and for ought I know, or the Doctor either, many of those baptized persons might be in these churches, yea the most of them, and but a few, it may be no more but those 120 mentioned in Acts 1:13–15, to whom were added about 3,000 souls who continued in the apostles' doctrine, and fellowship, and in breaking of bread and in prayers (Acts 2:41–46). And as for the world of believers mentioned in another argument drawn from John 12:19, "behold the world is gone after him."[29] That Scripture does not say they believed in him, much less that there was a world of believers in the church in Jerusalem. Neither is there mention in any Scripture quoted by the Doctor of 8,000 new converts besides women and children. Neither does that Scripture produced, [i.e.] Acts 4:4, prove any such thing. For the reader may consider that the number of them there mentioned are but 5,000. And albeit the Doctor makes them up 8,000, those 5,000 men were added to the church and joined to the former believers (page 57).

Yet there is a twofold mistake in the Doctors' addition. To wit, first, that some of the 3,000 (maybe) were women, and how then can the Doctor say there were 8,000 new converts besides women. Secondly, these 5,000 are only called men and not converts, not believers. For howbeit many of them hearing the word believed, yet it is not said the 5,000 men believed. And the truth is the text well considered only holds forth that the number of men was made up five thousand: καὶ ἐγενήθη ο ἀριθμὸς τῶν ἀνδρῶν ωσει χιλιάδες πέντε, *factus est numerus virorum, quasi millia quinque*[30] [Acts 4:4]. And the number of men was made about five thousand, not 8,000. And as for the many 10,000s mentioned in Acts 21:20, μυριάδες comes of μυριάς,[31] *infinitus*[32] and though the word μυριάδες does sometimes signify *numerum decem millium*, yet not always, but for some great number which cannot suddenly be told as Luke 12:1. And Beza, both according to the old and new version of the Greek into Latin, reads it *millia*, [i.e.] 1,000, not *decem millia*,

---

[29] Cf., "The Pharisees therefore said among themselves, Perceive ye how ye prevail nothing? Behold, the world is gone after him." John 12:19 (KJV).

[30] Cf., Beza, "Nova," "& factus est numerus virorum quasi quinquies mille"; "Vetus," "& factus est numerus virorum quasi quinque millia," 306.

[31] "μυριάς," "a group/collective of 10,000," "a very large number, not precisely defined," BDAG, 661.

[32] Cf., Beza, "Nova," "millia"; "Vetus," "millia," 359.

[i.e.] 10,000s and so we have it in our English Bibles translated thousands.[33] And the following verse 22 will make it probable that there were not many 10,000s, for there we thus read: "The multitude must needs come together" [Acts 21:22]. So that I say it's probable that they were not so many 1,000s but they could, yea must assemble together. Neither can the Doctor make good from those Scriptures he produced on page 62, to wit, Acts 1:21, 22, 6:2–4, and 8:1, that there were almost a hundred preachers and ministers besides the twelve apostles in the church of Jerusalem. The twelve are named indeed in Acts 6:2–4, but not 100 besides, nor any one preacher but them twelve. And as for the other two places, [i.e.] Acts 1:21–22 and Acts 8:1, there is not any word concerning preachers or ministers, only some directions touching the choice of Matthias, who was one of the twelve mentioned in Acts 6:2. And although they who were scattered preached the Word (Acts 8:4), yet the Scripture does not declare that they were preachers or ministers of the church in Jerusalem.

But the Doctor has one argument, which is more to the purpose than all the others, which I desire the reader seriously to consider. On page 64 he thus further argues: "That which the Holy Scriptures in express words and in diverse places has declared unto us, that every Christian is bound to believe. But the Scripture in express words and in diverse places has declared unto us that there were diverse assemblies and congregations of believers in the church of Jerusalem, and that the apostles and all the believers in Jerusalem did continue daily with one accord in the temple, and that they broke bread from house to house, and that daily in the temple, and in every house, they ceased not to teach and preach Jesus Christ. Ergo, there were diverse congregations and several assemblies of believers in the church of Jerusalem where they did duly partake in all the ordinances and enjoyed all acts of worship."[34]

Now I do desire the reader to consider how the Doctor proves his minor, which he says is manifest from Acts 2:46, 5:12, 42 and 3:11–12, and many more places that might be produced (pages 64–66). In all which discourse, the Doctor gives you nothing, but his own suppositions and conclusions for the proof of his minor proposition which is his manner of discourse throughout his book. This argument I answer first by denying the assumption, or minor proposition, and the reason of my denying all is because the Scriptures produced by the Doctor do not in express words

[33] Cf., Beza, 359.

[34] Bastwick, *Independence not God's Ordinance*, 64.

declare that there were diverse assemblies and congregations of believers in the church of Jerusalem. The Scriptures quoted do in express words declare the contrary to what the Doctor would prove. For in Acts 2:44, 46 [it says], "all that believed were together,"[35] and "they continued daily with one accord in the temple."[36] And in Acts 3:11–12 it is expressly said that, "all the people ran together to them, in the porch, which is called Solomon's" [Acts 3:11].[37] [In] Acts 5:12, "and they were all with one accord in Solomon's Porch."[38] So that these Scriptures produced by the Doctor to prove that there were diverse assemblies and congregations of believers in the church of Jerusalem, who met together in several places at one and the same time, to wit, upon the first day of the week, where they did partake daily in all ordinances, does expressly prove the contrary, [namely], that the apostles and all the believers in the church of Jerusalem met together with one accord, in one place, to wit, the temple and in Solomon's Porch, and broke bread from house to house, κατ' οἶκον, domatim, not κατ' οἶκος, *per singulas domos*[39] [Acts 2:46],

---

[35] "And all that believed were together, and had all things common." Acts 2:44 (KJV).

[36] "And they, continuing daily with one accord in the temple, and breaking bread from house to house, did eat their meat with gladness and singleness of heart." Acts 2:46 (KJV).

[37] "And as the lame man which was healed held Peter and John, all the people ran together unto them in the porch that is called Solomon's, greatly wondering." Acts 3:11 (KJV).

[38] "And by the hands of the apostles were many signs and wonders wrought among the people; and they were all with one accord in Solomon's porch." Acts 5:12 (KJV).

[39] Knollys employs a grammatical argument to bolster his contention that there was only one church in Jerusalem. He maintains that in Greek, Acts 2:46 reads κατ' οἶκον and not κατ' οἶκος. Since the noun οἶκος appears in the original in its accusative singular form οἶκον, it is clear that it is the object of the preposition. Hence, according to Knollys the phrase κλῶντές τε κατ' οἶκον ἄρτον should be rendered "broke bread from house to house." He asserts that in the New Testament text the noun does not appear in its nominative singular form οἶκος. In that case the noun would have been the subject of the verb and hence it would have been adequate to construe each house as performing the action of breaking bread, hence *per singulas domos*. However, that is not the case. Knollys here also reveals his reliance on Beza. In his commentary on Acts 2:46, Beza took issue with Erasmus' use of *per singulas domos* and rejected it "on account of its ambiguity": "Erasmi verò interpretatio *per singulas domos*, videtur quidem idem esse atque Domatim, sed tamen repudianda es propter ambiguitatem." Beza, 303–4; Cf., Beza, "Nova," "Et quotidie perdurantes concorditer in templo, ac frangentes domatim panem,"; "Vetus," "Quotidie quoque perdurantes unanimiter in templo, et frangentes circa domos panem," 303.

and thus they did καθ' ἡμέραν, *quotidie*[40] [Acts 2:47], day by day, and they continued steadfastly in the apostles' doctrine, and fellowship, and in breaking of bread, and in prayers, and all that believed were together (Acts. 2:42, 44, 46). Yea, the Doctor himself says in his minor proposition, the latter part of it: "That the apostles and all the believers in Jerusalem did continue daily with one accord in the temple, and that they broke bread from house to house."[41] And this shall suffice for refutation of what the Doctor has written touching the first proposition.

The second now follows on page 81, namely, that all the congregations and several assemblies made but one church. And to this the Doctor says the brethren themselves acknowledge that all believers in Jerusalem were all members of that church, and they accord further that it was but one church. And it is manifest out of the Holy Scripture, Acts 2:45–46, to which I also consent. But the brethren have not acknowledged, neither has the Doctor by Scripture proved, that in this one church of Jerusalem there were [diverse] congregations and several assemblies of believers, and therein I must manifest my difference from the Doctor's opinion, promising him that whensoever he shall soundly prove it by express words of Scripture (which he has undertaken) I will acknowledge it.

The third proposition, which the Doctor comes next to prove is, "that the apostles and elders, or presbyters governed, and ordered, and ruled this church jointly and by a common council and presbytery,"[42] which the Doctor says is evident by these places following: Acts 11:27 to the end. The words of this Scripture which the Doctor makes use of to prove his assertions are these, verse 30: "And sent it to the elders by the hands of Barnabas, and Saul."[43] "Here in these last words," says the Doctor, "we see that the presbyters and none but the presbyters in all churches were the men of Government."[44] It is not denied by the brethren that the presbyters in all

---

[40] Cf. Beza, "Nova," "quotidie"; "Vetus," "quotidie," 303.

[41] Bastwick, *Independence not God's Ordinance*, 64.

[42] "I now come to prove my third assertion, viz. That the apostles and presbyters governed, ordered, and ruled this church, consisting of many congregations and assemblies by a common council and presbytery." Bastwick, *Independence not God's Ordinance*, 82.

[43] "Which also they did, and sent it to the elders by the hands of Barnabas and Saul." Acts 11:30 (KJV)

[44] "Here in these last words we see that the presbyters, and none but the presbyters, received the alms for it is said, 'they sent it to the presbyters by the hands of Barnabas and Saul' [Acts 11:30], which sufficiently proves that the presbyters in all churches were the

churches were the men in the government of the churches in which they are elders. But this I conceive, by the Doctor's favor, does not prove it, to wit: because the alms were sent to the elders [cf., Acts 11:30]. Much less does that Scripture prove that the apostles and presbyters governed and ruled the church in Jerusalem by a common council and presbytery, which is the assertion that the Doctor undertakes to prove: "But in the 15th chapter verses 2, 4, 6, 22, and in chapter 16:4, and in Acts 21:17–18, the presbyters of Jerusalem by name," says the Doctor on page 83, "are expressed."[45] Out of which places of Scripture before the Doctor frames his arguments, he pleases to make a digression from page 88 to 90. Wherein he highly extols the presbyters, making them equal with the apostles in all the acts of church government. As appears by the Doctor's own words: "I do verily believe," says the Doctor, "that the presbyters did act as authoritatively as the apostles" and "that the presbyters might as well conclude, 'it seemed good to the Holy Ghost and to us', as well as the apostles."[46] And not only the presbyters, who sat in council with the apostles, and other presbyters who were ordained elders by the apostles, [but also] the assembly now of divines, or any other, may "congregate and meet together in some one place," for the "deciding of controversies, and differences of opinions in religion," "to state the questions, and to debate them from Scripture, or warrantable authority and evidence of reason deduced from thence, and may determine the question by "joint consent," or by the "most voices," and may say "it seemed good to the Holy Ghost, and us."[47] And that Presbyters "have their authority

---

men in government, as who had the ordering and authority of appointing unto the deacons, how they should distribute those moneys, that they might be best improved and disposed of, which is an act of government, as all men (that know what belongs unto government) will acknowledge." Bastwick, *Independence not God's Ordinance*, 82.

[45] Bastwick, *Independence not God's Ordinance*, 83.

[46] "I do verily believe that the presbyters sitting at any time in council with any one or more of the apostles, did act as authoritatively as the apostles themselves [and] I am ever able to prove it and make it good against any man that the presbyters might as well conclude, 'it seemed good to the Holy Ghost and to us,' as well as the apostles, and may say, 'we have written and concluded,' as well as the apostles." Bastwick goes on to compare the presbyters to Parliament. Bastwick, *Independence not God's Ordinance*, 88.

[47] "In this action also, and their so doing, the apostles and presbyters left an example and precedent to all the presbyters of all succeeding ages, what they should do upon the like occasions for the deciding of controversies and differences of opinions in religion. Viz., To congregate and meet together in some one place, to state the questions, and to debate them from Scripture, and to follow the written Word, as their rule in all things, and whatsoever they do, to do it by joint consent, and the common council of them all, or

as well grounded in the word of God, as Kings and States have theirs."[48] And the Doctor does more especially extol the presbyters of this kingdom in these our days, telling what they have deserved from the church, parliament, and kingdom more than any of their predecessors.

Having ended his digression, he gives you his argument on page 90. To wit: "They that in the holy Scripture are called presbyters, and acted and ordered things in a joint body, and common council with the presbyters, and exercised that ordinary power committed to them in the 18 of Matthew, they acted as presbyters. But the apostles in governing the church of Jerusalem, consisting of many congregations and assemblies, acted and ordered things in a joint body and common council with the presbytery of that church, as presbyters. Ergo, the church of Jerusalem was presbyterianly governed, and by a common council of presbyters. The major and minor of this syllogism being proved," says the Doctor, "the conclusion will necessarily ensue."[49] I know not that the brethren ever denied that the church of Jerusalem was presbyterianly governed, and although the Doctor be pleased to make that his conclusion, yet—under Reformation be it spoken—that conclusion does not follow upon the premises. For if the Doctor pleases to review his argument he shall find, first, that the subject of his major proposition is left out both in his minor, and in his conclusion. The first part of the Doctor's minor should have been this, to wit: "But the apostles in the holy Scripture are called presbyters, and whoever denied this..." Also the first part of the Doctor's conclusion should have been this, from these two premises, to wit: "Ergo, the apostles acted as presbyters," which conclusion is not the thing in question. Secondly, that from the

---

by the most voices, but in all this their proceedings they must ever cleave to the rule of the Word of God, or warrantable authority and evidence of reason deduced from thence, as then the apostles and presbyters did. Yea, the very name of the presbyters in Jerusalem signified the judges, councilors, magistrates, and rulers of the church who had the keys committed unto them as well as the apostles." Bastwick, *Independence not God's Ordinance*, 87–88.

[48] "And they are not to be looked on and stirred as the fage ends of the clergy, as many black mouthers and profane lips speak of them; for the presbyters, they have their authority as well grounded in the word of God as kings and states have theirs, and therefore as they are employed in a more supreme orb, and in matters of eternal concernment, so they should be venerated as men watching over our souls, and all contumelious speeches against them deserve severe punishment and ought not to be tolerated." Bastwick, *Independence not God's Ordinance*, 89.

[49] Bastwick, *Independence not God's Ordinance*, 90.

second part of the Doctor's two propositions, to wit: "they that acted and ordered things in a joint body and common council, which the presbyters, acted as presbyters; but the apostles in governing the church of Jerusalem acted and ordered things in a joint body, and common council with the presbytery (or presbyters either) of that church. Ergo, the apostles acted as presbyters." This should have been the Doctor's conclusion.

Now the truth is, though the apostles were called presbyters in the Scripture, yet it follows not that they acted as presbyters, but as apostles (Acts 15). And they cannot therein be a pattern and precedent for presbyters. First, because the apostles had the care, and charge of and over all churches (2 Corinthians 11:28). But the presbyters had the care and oversight of some one church only, as Ephesus (Acts 20:28) or Philippi (Philippians 1:1). And this the Doctor often inserts in his book, that all the churches we read of in the New Testament, though they were presbyterially governed, were dependent upon their several presbyters (p. 12). And secondly, because this would make the presbyters independents indeed—for so the apostles were in the government of all the churches— the presbyters of Jerusalem, of Ephesus, and of all the churches were dependent upon the apostles, and the apostles only depended on Christ, by whose Holy Spirit they were all always guided in the government of their churches, and therefore they said, "it seemed good to the Holy Ghost and us (Acts 15:28)." And though the Doctor says the presbyters might say so as well as the apostles because the elders or presbyters are mentioned there, the Doctor might have also considered that the brethren, even the whole church, the multitude—how many soever the Doctor can make of them—were present as well as the presbyters (Acts 15: 4, 12, 22, 23, 25, 27, 28). And so have made the brethren, the multitude, even the whole church independent also. And the Doctor might as well have affirmed that the brethren, even the whole church, might say, "it seemed good to the Holy Ghost and to us" [Acts 15:28].[50]

To the fourth proposition, "That the church of Jerusalem and the government of the same, is to be a pattern for all congregations and assemblies in any city or vicinity to unite into one church, and for the officers and presbyters of those congregations to govern that church jointly

---

[50] At this point the distinctively congregational, and therefore egalitarian, character of the ecclesiology of London Baptists is clearly defined in contrast to the aristocratic view of the church articulated by the Presbyterians. Acts 15:28 is the Scriptural linchpin of the Baptist egalitarian view of the church that Knollys is defending.

in a college or presbytery" (p. 97).[51] And for the proof of this fourth proposition the Doctor says: "That all men acknowledge that the mother church must give an example of government to all the daughter churches."[52] "Neither do the brethren deny," says the Doctor, "but the government of the church of Jerusalem must be the pattern of government to all churches."[53] But the Doctor knows that the brethren deny that the church of Jerusalem consisted of diverse congregations and several assemblies under a common council, consistory, college, or court of presbyters. And this they have not granted, neither has the Doctor proved. And this may be sufficient to be said in answer to the four propositions touching the first question.

And now I come to the second question, which is concerning the manner of gathering of churches and admitting of members and officers (p. 98). Which question the Doctor thus states: "Whether ministers of the Gospel may, out of already gathered assemblies of believers, select and choose the most principle of them into a church fellowship peculiar unto themselves, and admit of none into their society, but such as shall enter in by a private covenant and are allowed by the consent and approbation of all the congregation?"[54] And this question the Doctor branches into six queries (pp. 98–99). Wherein the judicious reader may perceive the Doctor, through misinformation I conceive, has mistaken the stating of the questions, which he partly acknowledges on page 100. "But now I shall set down," says the Doctor, "God's method and the apostles practice in gathering of churches, and the manner they used in making members in every church, and compare it with the method our brethren the Independents use, etc."[55] And to this purpose the Doctor begins with Christ's commission [found in] Matthew 28:19–20, and Mark 15:15–16, and Acts 26:15, 16, 17, 18, and 20.

Out of these several Scriptures the Doctor observes these three things (pp. 101 and 102). To wit, first, "That they should teach no other things but what Christ commanded them, and appeared to them in, and for which they

---

[51] Bastwick, *Independence not God's Ordinance*, 97.

[52] Ibid.

[53] Ibid.

[54] Bastwick refers to "congregated," and not "gathered," assemblies: "Whether ministers of the Gospel may out of already congregated assemblies of believers, select and choose the most principle of them, into a church fellowship peculiar unto themselves and admit of none into their society, but such as shall enter in by a private covenant and are allowed by the consent and approbation of all the congregation." Bastwick, *Independence not God's Ordinance*, 98.

[55] Bastwick, *Independence not God's Ordinance*, 100.

had his word and warrant."[56] Secondly, the condition which "they were to propound unto all nations and people upon which they were admitted into the church, was faith, repentance, and baptism."[57] And thirdly, "that this commission was delivered only to the apostles and ministers of the Gospel, that they should admit whosoever believed, and were baptized; and they that believed not would not be baptized, were not to be admitted."[58] These are the Doctor's own words on page 102 and page 103. The Doctor for proof quotes the third chapter of Matthew, and Luke 3:7. And the sum of John's

---

[56] "Out of these several places, from the commission of Christ given to his blessed apostles and to all ministers and preachers of the Gospel to the end of the world, here observe these things. First, that their bounds and limits were set them, how far they should go in their teaching all nations, and beyond which they might not pass, and they were these; that they should teach no other things but what Christ commanded them and appeared to them in, and for the which they had his word and warrant, and so long as they should do this, he promised them and all that should succeed them in the ministry to the end of the world to be with them." Bastwick, *Independence not God's Ordinance*, 101.

[57] "We also further observe the condition in the executing of this their commission, they were to propound unto all nations and people upon which they were to be admitted in to the church, and that was faith and repentance, and they were to receive all such as believe and were baptized, and that upon the profession of their faith and repentance, without any further testimony of others, unless they had been formerly known to be open enemies and persecutors of the church, and then they were justly to be suspected, till they had given public evidence by witness to the apostles and ministers of their true conversion, as it happened to Paul, who for a time the disciples feared (Acts 9:26–27) till they had better information and proof that he now preached the faith that he had once persecuted and had suffered for it, which is the only precedent we have in all the Acts of the Apostles of any that were refused to be admitted into the communion and fellowship of the apostles, as I remember—for he was a minister before—but all the others that came in were admitted upon their own offer, if they tendered themselves and embraced the Gospel [and] were baptized, and that without any reluctance or scruple." Bastwick, *Independence not God's Ordinance*, 101–102.

[58] "The third thing we may observe is that this commission was delivered only to the apostles and ministers of the Gospel and that it was their place only, who had the keys delivered unto them to open and shut the doors of the church, to admit such as they thought for their faith, knowledge and repentance were sufficiently qualified and fitted to be made members, and to refuse such as they conceived not fit to be received into the fellowship of the church, either for their ignorance or other sins and offenses, and to cast such out of the church, as through their malversation declared themselves to be no believers: for the commission was only delivered unto the apostles and ministers, that they should admit whosoever believed and were baptized, and they that believed not and would not be baptized, were not to be admitted." Bastwick, *Independence not God's Ordinance*, 102.

preaching says the Doctor is mentioned in verse three: "it was the baptism of repentance for the remission of sins" [Luke 3:3].[59] Also he there cites Luke 7:29: "that all the people that heard him, and the publicans justified God, being baptized with the baptism of John. But the Pharisees and the lawyers rejected the council of God against themselves, being not baptized of him" [Luke 7:29–30] (pp. 103-104).[60] "But now to go on," says the Doctor on page 104, "after the resurrection and ascension of Christ, etc.,"[61] where he quotes Acts 2:37–38 [*sic*]:[62] "Then they that gladly received the word were baptized, and the same day were added unto them about three thousand souls."[63]

Hence the Doctor observes that the apostles "propounded no other condition or terms for their making all and every one of them members of the church, but repentance and baptism, the which, when the people had accepted of," says the Doctor, "they were forthwith admitted," etc. (p. 104).[64] For another proof the Doctor produces Acts 10:44, 47, 48; where the Doctor affirms on page 106 that these brethren who came with Peter did not intermeddle in that business, to wit, of their admittance by baptism into

[59] "And he came into all the country about Jordan, preaching the baptism of repentance for the remission of sins." Luke 3:3 (KJV); "And for the sum of his preaching, it is said verse the third, that it was the baptism of repentance for the remission of sins." Bastwick, *Independence not God's Ordinance*, 103.

[60] "And all the people that heard him, and the publicans, justified God, being baptized with the baptism of John. But the Pharisees and lawyers rejected the counsel of God against themselves, being not baptized of him." Luke 7:29–30 (KJV).

[61] Bastwick, *Independence not God's Ordinance*, 104.

[62] "Now when they heard this, they were pricked in their heart, and said unto Peter and to the rest of the apostles, Men and brethren, what shall we do? Then Peter said unto them, Repent, and be baptized every one of you in the name of Jesus Christ for the remission of sins, and ye shall receive the gift of the Holy Ghost." Acts 2:37–38 (KJV). Bastwick does quote Acts 2:37–38 and Acts 2:41, but Knollys provides only the second quotation.

[63] Acts 2:41 (KJV).

[64] "Here we may observe these two things. The first, that the apostles by themselves alone without the multitude or church admitted the people into the society [and] company of believers. Secondly, that in the execution of their commission they did nothing but according to their warrant and according to their injunction that was given unto them by Christ, they propounded no other condition or terms for their making all and every one of them members of the church, but baptism and repentance, the which when the people had accepted of, they were forwith admitted, and that upon their own word and testimony, without any more ado, or further inquiry." Bastwick, *Independence not God's Ordinance*, 104.

the Church.[65] Now I conceive the reason why those brethren did not intermeddle to hinder their admittance to that ordinance of Jesus Christ—to wit, baptism in water—and so to an entrance into the church was not because they had not such liberty, but because the brethren had no just objections, or hindrance to declare to Peter.

That the brethren had a liberty to have declared anything which might justly have hindered the administration of that ordinance of baptism unto them, does appear by the question which the apostle expounded in verse 47: "Can any man forbid water that these should not be baptized?"[66] And the Doctor himself acknowledges on page 102 that the brethren or disciples of the church of Jerusalem, who "must be a pattern," says the Doctor, "of all churches," had this liberty to except against some sorts of persons, and hinder their admittance into the church, though baptized according to Christ's commission, and [by] preachers chosen and sent by Christ himself. And that in case such persons have been formerly known to be open enemies and persecutors of the church, then they are "justly to be suspected," says the Doctor on page 102, "until they have given public evidence by witness to the ministers of their true conversion," and there he produces a plain instance to prove this on page 102 (Acts 9:26, 27, 28): "And when Saul was come to Jerusalem (ἐπείραζεν κολλᾶσθαι, *tentabat iungi*[67]), he assayed to join himself to the disciples, but they were all afraid of him, and believed not that he was a disciple, etc." [Acts 9:26].

Now this liberty have all the disciples in the like case, because Jerusalem the mother church is the pattern of all other the daughter churches, as the Doctor confesses, yea affirms in page 197 and says, "all men acknowledge, that the mother church must give an example of government to all the daughter churches."[68] And this is also by the Doctor acknowledged in page 102 to be a part of the power of the keys, "to open and shut the doors of the church; that is, to admit such as are for their faith, knowledge, and repentance sufficiently qualified, and fitted to be made members and to

[65] "Neither did those that came with Peter intermeddle in that business or require a covenant at their hand, or a public confession of faith." Bastwick, *Independence not God's Ordinance*, 106.

[66] "Can any man forbid water, that these should not be baptized, which have received the Holy Ghost as well as we?" Acts 10:47 (KJV).

[67] Cf. Beza, "Nova," "Cùm verò Saulus advenisset Hierosolymam, tentabat se propiùs ad jungere discipulis."; "Vetus," "Cùm autem venisset in Jerusalem, tentabat se jungere discipulis.," 323.

[68] Bastwick, *Independence not God's Ordinance*, 97

refuse such as are not fit to be received into the fellowship of the church, either for their ignorance or other sins and offences," etc.[69] Now then when it does evidently appear, that the disciples or brethren—not to say sisters though they are disciples also—of the church in Jerusalem—in her most flourishing condition—had this liberty to declare their fears, and the ground thereof against Paul, who was at that time a believer, a baptized person, and a preacher, or minister of the Gospel, so that although he came and assayed to be joined to the disciples and be admitted a member among them that he might have fellowship with them in the worship and ordinances of the Gospel, yet was thereby hindered from admittance until Barnabas witnessed his condition and conversation to the apostle, and then he was with them coming in and going out at Jerusalem. How can the Doctor make good that, "the presbyters alone without the consent of brethren may admit members, and cast out members, and that the brethren or the congregation has nothing to do to hinder any such thing" (pp. 102, 106)?[70]

For further proof hereof the Doctor urges Acts 8:35 to 40. The example of the Eunuch to whom Philip being sent preached Jesus and baptism in his name, and it is related that when they came to a certain water the Eunuch said unto him: "See, here is water; what doth hinder me to be baptized? And Philip said, If thou believest with all thine heart, thou mayest (ἔξεστιν, *licet*).[71] And he answered and said, I believe that Jesus Christ is the Son of God.[72] And he commanded the chariot to stand still: and they went down both into the water, both Philip and the eunuch, and he baptized him" [Acts 8:36–38]. "Here we see," says the Doctor, "that Philip admits him into the number of believers, and makes him a member of the church."[73] But the

[69] Bastwick, *Independence not God's Ordinance*, 102.

[70] "This commission I affirm, was only given to the apostles and ministers, and it was and is that office that peculiarly belonged unto them." Bastwick, *Independence not God's Ordinance*, 102; "The congregation has nothing to do to hinder any such, nay, they may not, it is more than belongs unto them; neither did those that came with Peter intermeddle in that business or require a covenant at their hand, or a public confession of faith." Bastwick, *Independence not God's Ordinance*, 106.

[71] Knollys' annotation. Cf., Beza, "Nova," "Dixit verò Philippus, Si credis ex toto corde, licet."; "Vetus," "Dicit autem Philippus, Si credis ex toto corde, licet," 321.

[72] Verse 37, "And Philip said…is the Son of God," appears in ancient authorities but is not part of the majority text of UBS 5th ed., see GNT, 426.

[73] "Here we see that Philip and not the church was sent unto the Eunuch and that Philip by his own authority, and upon the Eunuch his own testimony, without any reference unto the Church or without consulting with the congregation admits him into the number of believers, and makes him a member of church and here was neither a public

Doctor says, this was "without consulting with the congregation, by his own authority, and upon the Eunuch his own testimony" (p. 106).[74]

I answer that Philip had a special command from God for what he did herein, and so had Ananias (Acts 9:15) touching Saul, which is the next instance which the Doctor brings on this same page 106. And albeit the Doctor affirms that Ananias did not say to Saul, "I will consult with the church to see whether they will admit thee to be a member, for thou hast greatly wasted the church, and made havoc of the saints, and therefore I will have their approbation, and consent, and thou shall give in evidences of thy true conversion, etc., and so be received and admitted."[75]

"But without all this ado," says the Doctor on page 107, "he baptized Paul and admitted him into the number of believers, and made him a member of the church."[76] Yet if the reader looks back into page 102 of his book, the Doctor there makes an exception from the power which he a little before had affirmed the presbyters have to admit members, by virtue of Christ his commission, upon the profession of their faith and repentance, and receiving baptism, without any further testimony. "Unless," says the Doctor, "they had been formerly known to be open enemies, and persecutors of the church, and then they were justly to be suspected, till they had given public evidence by witness of their true conversion."[77] And gives an instance in Paul, "who for a time the disciples feared (Acts 9:26–27) till they had better information, and proof, that he now preached the faith, that he had once persecuted, and had suffered for it."[78]

---

confession required of him by any of the church, or any covenant exacted by the people." Bastwick, *Independence not God's Ordinance*, 106.

[74] Ibid.

[75] "And so when Saul in the 9 of the Acts was fallen down out of astonishment, and afterwards was converted as the story there fully declared the whole manner of it, the Lord sent one Ananias a disciple and minister unto him, he did not send the church unto him, neither did Ananias when he came to Saul, say unto him, I will consult with the church to see whether they will admit thee to be a member for thou hast greatly wasted the church, and made havoc of the saints, and therefore I will have their approbation and consent, and I will have thee first walk with the church sometime, that they may behold thy conversation, and then thou shalt make a confession of thy faith publicly before the congregation, and give in thy evidences of the truth of thy conversion and enter in a private and solemn covenant, and so be received and admitted." Bastwick, *Independence not God's Ordinance*, 106–107.

[76] Ibid., 107.

[77] Ibid., 102.

[78] Ibid.

To rehearse all the Scriptures alleged to prove this method of God and practice of the apostles were needless. But passing by such as are not so plain and clear for the proof thereof, and also omitting, what the Doctor has said touching the brethren in comparing their practice with the apostles, [is not possible]. Because the Doctor is mistaken in stating the question, and also in his queries, as before I mentioned in the page fourteen of this my answer, and the reader may see on pages 98, 99, and 100 of the Doctor's book. I shall give the reader the result of all that the Doctor has written from page 100 to the end of his book. Touching God's method, and the apostles' practice in gathering of churches and admitting members…that Christ having given a commission to his apostles to teach all nations, and baptize them (Matthew 28:19–20, Mark 16:15–16) the apostles practiced accordingly (Acts 2:37–38, Acts 10:44–48), and so did Philip (Acts 8:35–38), and Ananias (Acts 9:10, 19). Secondly, that the condition or terms, which they were to propound unto all nations and people upon which they were to be admitted into the church, were faith, repentance, and baptism (Mark 16:15–16). For the commission was delivered to the apostles, that they should admit whosoever believed and would be baptized, and they that believed not, and would not be baptized, were not to be admitted (pp. 102, 104). "The apostles," says the Doctor, "propounded no other condition or terms for making all, and every one, members of the church but repentance, and baptism" (Acts 2:37–38).[79] Thirdly, that the apostles and all succeeding ministers of the Gospel should admit whosoever believed, and were baptized, to be members of the church, and teach them to observe no other things but what Christ commanded them, and for which they had his Word and warrant (pp. 101–102) (Matthew 28:19–20). And this, says the Doctor, the apostles did practice, without requiring them to "take a private covenant, or enter into the church by way of a particular covenant" (Acts 2:37–38).[80]

This being the sum and result of that method and practice, which the Doctor conceives should be done in gathering churches and admitting members, which the Scriptures will warrant and Christ Jesus approve of as his Father's will, I shall now take liberty to declare what I know by my own experience to be the practice of some churches of God in this city. That so both the Doctor and the reader may judge how near the saints who walk together in the fellowship of the Gospel do come in their practice to these apostolical rules and practice[s] propounded by the Doctor as God's method

[79] Ibid., 104.
[80] Ibid., 105.

in gathering churches, and admitting members. I say that I know by my own experience—having walked with them—that they were thus gathered. That is, some godly and learned men of approved gifts and abilities for the ministry, being driven out of the countries where they lived by the persecution of the prelates came to sojourn in this great city, and preached the Word of God both publicly, and from house to house, and daily in the temples and in every house they ceased not to teach and preach Jesus Christ. And some of them have dwelt in their own hired houses, and received all that came in unto them, preaching the Kingdom of God, and teaching those things which concern the Lord Jesus Christ. And when many sinners were converted by their preaching of the Gospel, some of them that believed consorted with them and of professors a great many, and of the chief women not a few. And the condition which those preachers both publicly and privately propounded to the people, unto whom they preached, upon which they were to be admitted into the church [were] faith, repentance, and baptism, and none other. And whosoever—poor as well as rich, bond as well as free, servants as well as masters—did make a profession of their faith in Christ Jesus, and would be baptized with water into the name of the Father, Son, and Holy Spirit, were admitted members of the church. But such as did not believe, and would not be baptized, they would not admit into church communion.[81] This has been the practice of some churches of God in this city, without urging or making any particular covenant with members upon admittance, which I desire may be examined by the Scriptures cited in the margin, and then compared with the Doctor's three conclusions from the same Scriptures, whereby it may appear to the judicious reader, how near the churches some of them come to the practice of the apostles' rule, and practice of the primitive churches, both in gathering and admitting members. And my humble request to the Doctor is, that he will use all means, that the method of God, and practice of the apostles in gathering of churches, and admitting members may be conscionably practiced by his brethren of both sides according to the revealed Word and Will of the Father.

Finis.

[81] Knollys emphasizes congregational authority over the admission of new members into the congregation.

A DECLARATION CONCERNING THE PUBLIC DISPUTE

(London, 1645)

INTRODUCTION

In 1645, Hanserd Knollys participated in a major debate between Baptists and Presbyterians on the question of believer's baptism, or credobaptism. The debate was prompted by the inquiries of a London merchant who was formerly torn by the differences between paedobaptists and credobaptists, but had made his mind in favor of the latter. As a result, a public disputation was arranged with the initial consent of the Lord Mayor of London, Sir Thomas Adams. The Presbyterian standard-bearers included Edmund Calamy and James Cranford, while Benjamin Coxe, William Kiffin, and Hanserd Knollys would defend the Baptist position. However, the disputation, which was initially programmed for 3 December 1645, never took place. The Lord Mayor cancelled it fearing that it would degenerate into open confrontation. The Baptists were accused of plotting a violent attack against the Presbyterians and fears of "Anabaptist" anarchy were conjured against them.

In response the Baptist leaders Coxe, Kiffin, and Knollys composed and published the present tract, *A declaration concerning the public dispute*. It was not the first time that Baptists endeavored to articulate their views on credobaptism. In 1641, Edward Barber published his defense of believer's baptism, *A small treatise of baptisme, or, dipping* (London, 1641). Moreover, the *London Confession* of 1644—the first public confessional statement by English Baptists—defined immersion as the proper "way and manner of the dispensing of this ordinance," namely, baptism.[1] Yet, the *Declaration* was the finest attempt by early Baptists to justify and explain their observance of the distinctively Christian initiation rite. Among its merits one can point to its

---

[1] *The Confession of faith of those churches which are commonly (though falsly) called Anabaptists presented to the view of all that feare God, to examines by the touchstone of the Word of truth, as likewise for the taking off those aspersions which are frequently both in pulpit and print, (although unjustly) cast upon them* (London: Matthew Simmons, 1644) C2*r*.

systematic presentation and logical argumentation. The arguments presented in the *Declaration* flow in an unbroken chain of syllogistic theses that demonstrate the theological reasonableness of credobaptism. Furthermore, the authors were keenly interested in showing that credobaptism was the practice observed by the early church. Hence, they provided biblical proofs to buttress their position. In the process, they displayed the scholarly rigor of their position by citing such ancient sources as Nonnus of Panopolis (c. 400) as well as more contemporary scholars like the Dutch humanist Gerardus Joannes Vossius (1577–1649).

A DECLARATION CONCERNING THE PUBLIC DISPUTE[1]

By Benjamin Coxe, Hanserd Knollys, and William Kiffin
(London, 1645)

A merchant of this city, taking knowledge of different doctrines and administrations of baptism publicly held forth both in preaching and practice, some doubts did arise in his mind, which of the said doctrines and administrations was according to the will of God; who being desirous to try all things, and hold fast that which is good, searched the Scriptures daily, and upon examination found the doctrine and administration of baptism touching believers who make profession of faith, and manifest the fruits of repentance, to be more agreeable to the Scriptures, than the doctrine and administration of baptism touching the infants of believers, so far forth as he could discern. Yet because he would not lean to his own understanding, he earnestly desired, and at length—after much pains and entreaties—obtained a conference and private disputation between us and Mr. Calamy,[2] and some

---

[1] Hanserd Knollys, et al., *A declaration concerning the publike dispute which should have been in the publike meeting-house of Alderman-Bury, the 3rd of this instant moneth of December; Concerning infants-baptisme. Together, with some of the arguments which should then have been propounded and urged by some of those that are falsly called Anabaptists, which should then have disputed. By Benjamin Coxe, Hanserd Knollys, and William Kiffen, etc.* (London: no printer, 1645). [At bottom of title page: "For the weapons of our warfare are not carnal, but mighty through God to the pulling down of strong holds [*sic*]" (2 Corinthians 10:3–5)]. For Kiffin, see the Introduction to this volume. Knollys and fellow pastor Benjamin Coxe were trained at Cambridge and according to Bustin "were two of very few Particular Baptists who had any advanced education and theological training." See Dennis C. Bustin, *Paradox and Perseverance: Hanserd Knollys, Particular Baptist Pioneer in Seventeenth-Century England* (Milton Keynes: Paternoster, 2006) 100–101.

[2] Edmund Calamy (1600–1666) attended Pembroke College, Cambridge, from 1616 to 1620 and obtained an MA in 1623. In 1639, he was elected "perpetual curate" of St. Mary Aldermanbury, London. At the time St. Mary was a wealthy parish with influential members. See Sharon Achinstein, "Calamy, Edmund (1600–1666)," in *Oxford Dictionary of National Biography*, edited by H. C. G. Matthew and Brian Harrison (Oxford: Oxford University Press, 2004). Online ed., edited by Lawrence Goldman, October 2007. http://www.oxforddnb.com/view/ article/4355 (accessed November 21, 2014); Richard L. Greaves, *Saints and Rebels: Seven Nonconformists in Stuart*

of his brethren at the merchant's own house unto which were admitted divers [many] of his friends and some strangers, that he might hear both parties face to face maintain their own doctrine and practice about baptism, for his own and his wife's satisfaction—being great with child. At the end of which private dispute, the merchant and divers others present not having received satisfaction touching the lawfulness of baptizing the infants of believers, there was appointed another day for dispute at Mr. Mascall's[3] house, and Mr. Calamy undertook to prove that some of the infants of believers ought to be baptized. But the multitude of people that came thither hindered that dispute, for we could not get in to dispute for the crowd of the people; whereupon we all agreed to crave leave of the civil magistrate to have liberty to dispute in some public place.

And it is not unknown to many in this city that a public dispute touching the lawfulness of paedobaptism, between us and Mr. Calamy, Mr. Cranford,[4] with some others, was agreed upon. And having first obtained

---

England (Macon: Mercer University Press, 1985). In 1645, Calamy was involved in a pamphleteering war with the Independent Henry Burton (1578–1647/8) who was a catechist at Aldermanbury until the year before when Calamy had him locked out of the church. See Edmund Calamy, *The door of truth opened: or, A brief and true narrative of the occasion how Mr. Henry Burton came to shut himself out of the church-doors of Aldermanbury: published in answer to a paper, called, Truth shut out of doors: for the vindication of the minister and people of Aldermanbury, who are in this paper most wrongfully and unjustly charged; and also for the undeceiving of the underwriters, and of all those that are misinformed about this businesse. In the name, and with the consent of the whole church of Aldermanburie* (London: Printed for Christopher Meredith at the Crane in Pauls-Church-Yard, 1645).

[3] John Mascall was a Presbyterian merchant later associated with the East India Company. See Gary Stuart De Krey, *London and the Restoration, 1659–1683* (Cambridge: Cambridge University Press, 2005) 81, 82, 99, 412.

[4] James Cranford (1602/3–1657) was a Presbyterian divine who attended Balliol College, Oxford, graduating with a BA in 1621 and an MA in 1624. In 1641, he was appointed lecturer at St. Christopher-le-Stocks, London, becoming its rector in 1643. See E. C. Vernon, "Cranford, James (1602/3–1657)," in *Oxford Dictionary of National Biography*, edited by H. C. G. Matthew and Brian Harrison (Oxford: Oxford University Press, 2004). Online ed., edited by Lawrence Goldman, January 2008. http://www.oxforddnb.com/view/article/6610 (accessed November 21, 2014). He published controversial works against Independents, Baptists, and other sectarians. See James Cranford, *Haereseo-machia: or, The mischiefe which heresies doe, and the means to prevent it. Delivered in a sermon in Pauls, before the Right Honourable, the Lord Maior, and the aldermen of the famous citie of London, February the first, M. DC. XLV. And now printed, for the satisfaction of the hearers, and others. / By James Cranford, pastour of Christopher Le Stocks, London* (London: Printed by James Young for Charles Green, 1646).

leave of the Lord Mayor,[5] by the request of three common council men—whom we jointly entreated to move his Lordship in all our names—we privately consulted together at Mr. Calamy's house how we might manage that public dispute, to the glory of God, and the satisfaction of the people. And we mutually agreed to hold that public disputation in the parish church—as men call it—of Aldermanbury, upon the third day of this instant December, from nine a clock in the morning, until three a clock in the afternoon.[6] There should have been six in each party, whereof two were to be appointed moderators. One of the moderators was to begin with prayer, and the other to conclude with prayer after the dispute was ended. Also both parties chose Mr. Hade to be our notary, whom we all desired, that—prayer being ended—before we begun the dispute, he would read this following agreement in the ears of all the people there present.

THE AGREEMENT

It is agreed on both sides that this disputation shall continue for six hours. They that begin to dispute, shall dispute for two hours, and then the contrary party for two hours more, and then the first party shall dispute again the fifth hour, and the other party the sixth hour, with this proviso, that if any desire liberty to exceed the time allotted, the same liberty shall be granted to the other side, not exceeding half an hour.

It is likewise agreed, that at the end of each dispute the moderator of that party that disputes shall faithfully and conscientiously give the result both of the arguments and the answers.

It is likewise agreed, that the disputation shall be logical, and each side shall endeavor to make his answers as short as he can possibly.

---

[5] The mayor was Sir Thomas Adams (1586–1668) a Presbyterian politician of pro-royalist inclination in 1645–46. See Keith Lindley, "Adams, Sir Thomas, first baronet (*bap.* 1586, *d.* 1668)," in *Oxford Dictionary of National Biography*, edited by H. C. G. Matthew and Brian Harrison (Oxford: Oxford University Press, 2004). Online ed., edited by Lawrence Goldman, January 2008. http://www.oxforddnb.com/view/article/132 (accessed November 21, 2014); John Stoughton, *History of Religion in England from the Opening of the Long Parliament to 1850: Church of the Commonwealth*, 4th ed. (London: Hodder and Stoughton, 1901) 2:225.

[6] Based on this and other documents we can conclude that the exact date for the projected dispute was December 3, 1645.

It is also much desired by both parties that there be no disturbance offered by any one whatsoever, either by hissing, or humming, or laughing, or talking.

It is likewise professed, that both sides are willing to declare, and will as occasion shall serve, declare ingenuously what they hold, according as they shall be desired in the disputation about the subject matter of the dispute.

And lastly, both parties do seriously and solemnly profess that they come hither with a resolution to give or receive light, according as God shall offer it, and not to dispute for victory, but truth.

The question to be disputed this day is:

Whether the infants of believing parents ought to be baptized or no?

Mr. Calamy is to prove, that all or some infants of believing parents ought to be baptized.

And the other parties are to prove, that no infants ought to be baptized.

But the evening before the day agreed upon for that public dispute, some of us passing over the exchange, saw an order published by the Lord Mayor to this effect:

That his Lordship thought fit upon serious consideration, for prevention on the inconveniences that might happen thereby, to forbid the same meeting and disputation, upon that day or at any other time, in a public way, before his Lordship shall receive the pleasures of the Honorable Houses of Parliament touching the same, which with all convenience, his Lordship will endeavor to know, lest otherwise there might be hazard of the disturbance of the public peace.[7]

---

[7] As stated by the proclamation in full: "Whereas, at the entreaty of Mr. Calamy and other ministers, as it was represented unto me by certain citizens, I did lately give an allowance to them to meet and dispute with certain Anabaptists; and whence, I understand you, in pursuance of that allowance, there is a public dispute intended on Wednesday next, December 3rd, in the church of Aldermanbury, and there is likely to be an extraordinary concourse of people from all parts of the city, and from other places; and

Whereupon we—who are falsely called Anabaptists—being as ready to obey our civil magistrates, as to profess our subjection to his authority in all lawful commands—whatever is preached or printed of us by any to the contrary, and whosoever have or shall accuse us, either to the magistrates, or to the common people, that we will not obey authority, are false accusers of the brethren, and we hope that both the magistrates, and the people have found them liars and will find them so to be still so often as just occasion shall be offered to manifest our willing and loyal subjection to the magistrate's civil authority—we were constrained in obedience to his Lordship's lawful power, to forbear that intended and earnestly desired disputation, and wait until Mr. Calamy and his brethren obtain leave from authority to have liberty of a public dispute with us and our brethren, which we hope the Lord Mayor will with all convenience endeavor, according to his Lordship's promise and engagement. Hoping also that when they have said what they can by way of argument for their doctrine and practice, touching the baptizing of the infants of believers, we shall obtain the like equal liberty, both from the civil magistrates and themselves, as publicly to say what we can from the Scripture of truth for our doctrine and practice, touching the baptizing of believers that they who shall hear our public disputations, may try all things, and hold fast that which is good. But, lest some reports of us or our brethren which have been given out—by whom we know not, nay, we care not—with respect to ourselves—for we have learned to pass through good and evil reports, through the strength of Christ—yet lest we say those reports coming to the ear of authority should hinder them from granting this so much desired liberty or public dispute, we are forced to make this short apology. We will only at this time make mention of two reports, amongst others, which we conceive are pertinent to the matter. To wit, first, it was reported as if we intended to manage that dispute with our swords, clubs, and staves. Secondly, that if Mr. Calamy escaped with his life it would be well.

---

that in these times of distraction there may be hazard of the disturbance of the public peace, I have therefore thought fit, upon serious consideration, for prevention of the inconveniences that may happen thereby, to forbid the same meeting upon Wednesday next, or at any other time, in a public way before I shall receive the pleasure of the honourable House of Parliament touching the same, which, with all conveniency, I shall endeavour to know." Stoughton, *History of Religion,* 2:225n†.

And here we think meet [suitable], first to declare how we came to get some hint of these two base and scandalous reports. We could not but take notice of the reason expressed by the Lord Mayor, why his Lordship thought fit to prohibit our public dispute—after he had granted that favor—to wit, the hazard of the disturbance of the public peace, and for the prevention of the inconvenience that may happen thereby. Whereupon we went to Mr. Calamy and asked him if he knew what occasioned the Lord Mayor to fear the disturbance of the peace by such a disputation, especially seeing we had his Lordship's leave, and had agreed to manage it in so peaceable a manner. Mr. Calamy told us, that it was reported at the Lord Mayor's table by somebody—he knew not whom—that an Anabaptist—but he knew not who—said that he would bring his sword with him to the dispute, or he would not come without his sword, or words to that purpose. And Mr. Calamy also told us that a woman told him that some—nobody knows who—should say that if the public dispute [were] held, Mr. Calamy would scarce escape with his life. And other strange reports are whispered touching that dispute, as if we were the cause of the Lord Mayor's forbidding of it; when as we were, and still are most desirous to have liberty to dispute publicly with Mr. Calamy and his brethren.

Now, as concerning those two reports before mentioned, we do abhor the thoughts of such a thing as to manage our dispute with any other sword than the sword of the Spirit, which is the Word of God. For the weapons of our warfare are not carnal, but mighty through God, to the pulling down of strongholds. And our agreement may give a sufficient testimony of the contrary, especially in these words, "It is much desired by both parties, that there be no disturbance offered by any one whatsoever," etc.

And truly, we cannot but marvel, that either the magistrates, or inhabitants of this city—who have had so much experience of the peaceable conversation of us, and our brethren, called Anabaptists—should at any time hear such reports of us, without a just reproof to those that do bring them. Yea, let any rational man judge, whether we, who think it an unreasonable thing that we should be beaten with club-law instead of arguments, should go about to do that to others, which we would not have them do to us. And as for that other report concerning Mr. Calamy, it appeared to us that Mr. Calamy neither feared, nor apprehended any such danger. For he professed himself to be very willing and desirous that the dispute should have [been] held, and told us he was much grieved that it was put off, and that he went to the Lord Mayor and desired his Lordship not to forbid it, but could not prevail with his Honor. Only the Lord Mayor promised Mr. Calamy to endeavor to know the pleasure of the honorable Houses of Parliament about it. And Mr. Calamy told us, that Mr. Recorder would take a fit opportunity to move the honorable House of Commons concerning it, that so the Lord Mayor might know the pleasure of both the honorable Houses of Parliament. And for as much as these reports, with divers others, are dispersed both in the city and also in the Army, we are constrained to publish to the view of the world, some of the arguments which we intended to have propounded to Mr. Calamy and his brethren at that public dispute, which were all the swords and clubs, or weapons, with which we intended to pull down that stronghold of infant baptism. That part of the question which we were to maintain against Mr. Calamy and his brethren was, "That no infants ought to be baptized."

NO INFANTS OUGHT TO BE BAPTIZED

Argument I

If only believers themselves ought to be baptized, then none of their infants; but only believers themselves ought to be baptized; ergo, none of their infants, etc.

That believers only ought to be baptized, we thus prove. Such persons as we read in the Scripture of truth—John, Christ's disciples, and apostles—administered baptism unto, such only ought we to administer baptism unto. But we read in the Scripture of truth, that John, Christ's disciples, and apostles, administered baptism to such of the Jews only as repented, and to such of the gentiles only as believed. *Ergo,* such only ought we to administer baptism unto, who do believe and repent. That John administered baptism to such only as repented, appears both by his doctrine and practice. His doctrine you may read [in] Matthew 3:1–2, and Acts 19:4–5. And John's practice was suitable to his doctrine, [see] Matthew 3:5–6 and Luke 3:3, 12–18. And when some came to John's baptism, who thought that they might have been baptized because they were the children of Abraham, John said unto them, "Bring forth [therefore] fruit meet for repentance; and think not to say within yourselves, We have Abraham to our Father (Matthew 3:8–9)."[8] Giving them thereby to understand that they must not have this Gospel

[8] Unless otherwise indicated, readers can assume that the London Baptist ministers obtained their biblical references from the Authorized Version. We have revised the quotations and indicated with square brackets ([]) any editorial additions. Occasionally we

ordinance of baptism administered unto them—though they were the children of Abraham—until they did actually repent (Acts 2:38), as if he had said, "What though you be the fleshly seed of your believing father Abraham, must you therefore be baptized before you repent? Think not so." Hereupon the Pharisees rejected the counsel of God against themselves, not being baptized of him (Luke 7:29–30). For they are not all Israel which are of Israel; neither because they are the seed of Abraham are they all children. That is, they which are the children of the flesh, these are not the children of God, but the children of the promise are counted for the seed (Romans 9:6–8 and Galatians 3:26–29).

That Christ's disciples and apostles did administer baptism unto such only as believed and repented also appears by their doctrine and practice. Their doctrine you may read [in] Acts 2:38, Acts 8:35–37, [and] Acts 16:30–33. Also their practice was according to their doctrine both in Judea (Acts 2:41), and in Samaria (Acts 8:12); also in Caesarea (Acts 10:44–48), and in Macedonia (Acts 16:32–34), and in Achaia (Acts 18:8), and in Asia the less (Acts 19:1–5), and wheresoever there is mention made in the Scripture of their administration of baptism, it was according to their doctrine of baptism, and both their doctrine and practice was according to the commission and institution of Christ: "Make disciples of all nations, baptizing them" (Matthew 28:19), to wit, who are made disciples by preaching.[9] John 4:1–2, so expounds (μαθηταὶ αὐτοῦ), "Disciple ye" [*sic*] (μαθητὰς ποιεὶ καὶ βαπτίζει), "he made and baptized disciples."[10] Also Mark 16:15–16 declares what our Savior intended by the word "disciples"; to wit, "believers." He that believeth the Gospel preached unto him, and is

provide the rendering of the Authorized Version and/or the New Revised Standard Version for comparative purposes.

[9] "Go therefore and make disciples of all nations, baptizing them in the name of the Father and of the Son and of the Holy Spirit." Matthew 28:19 (NRSV).

[10] "When therefore the Lord knew how the Pharisees had heard that Jesus made and baptized more disciples than John, (though Jesus himself baptized not, but his disciples)." John 4:1–2 (KJV). In other writings, notably in his *A Moderate Answer* (1645) Hanserd Knollys made extensive use of the Greek text of Theodore Beza's *Novum Testamentum*, perhaps in its Cambridge edition of 1642. See Theodore Beza, *Jesu Christi Domini Nostri Novum Testamentum, sive Novum Foedus, cujus graeco contextui respondent interpretationes duae: una, vetus; altera, Theodori Bezae* (Cantabrigiae: Rogeri Danielis, 1642).

baptized, shall be saved.[11] Thus the unprejudiced reader may plainly perceive that the harmony of Scriptures does witness that believers themselves, and not their infants, ought to be baptized according to the doctrine and practice of John the Baptist, [the] disciples and apostles of Christ, also according to the institution of baptism by our blessed Savior.

Argument II

Every administration of baptism that differs essentially from the doctrine of baptism taught by Christ, his disciples and apostles, is unlawful. But your administration of infant baptism differs essentially from the doctrine of baptism, etc. Ergo, your administration of infant-baptism is unlawful.

That your administration of infant-baptism differs essentially from the doctrine of baptism taught by Christ, his disciples, and apostles we thus prove. Whatsoever administration of baptism differs from the doctrine of baptism, in respect of the subject matter, or form, differs essentially; but your administration of infant-baptism differs from the doctrine of baptism in respect of the subject matter and in regard of your form; *Ergo*, it differs essentially. The subject matter of baptism, according to the doctrine of Christ, Matthew 28:19 compared with John 4:1–2, are such men and women as are made disciples, [that is, made] believers by preaching (Mark 16:15–16). The subject matter of your baptism are the infants of your parishioners, whom you dream are born Christians, and are children of believers, because their parents are members of Aldermanbury Church, or some other parish church. The subject matter of baptism according to the doctrine of the disciples and apostles of Christ, Acts 2:38 compared with Acts 8:12, 35–37 and Acts 19:4–5, are such men and women as actually repent and believe. And all the ministers of England have with one consent acknowledged this truth. Witness against them that passage in their church catechism where they used to ask their communicants, "What is required of persons to be baptized?", and taught them this answer; to wit, "Repentance, whereby they forsake sin"—that is, actual repentance—"and faith, whereby they steadfastly believe the promises of God"—which is faith that comes by hearing the word.[12] And then they ask them another question, wherein they

[11] "And he said unto them, Go ye into all the world, and preach the gospel to every creature. He that believeth and is baptized shall be saved; but he that believeth not shall be damned." Mark 16:15–16 (KJV).

[12] Here the authors cite the *Westminster Shorter Catechism*: "*Maister.* What is

all confess that infants cannot perform that which is required, and query, "Why then are infants baptized?" To which they taught them an answer, whereof both themselves and their people are ashamed.[13] And now they have invented another, whereof they will in time be more ashamed; to wit, the infants of believers are Christians, and federally holy before they be baptized, and therefore to be baptized.[14] And these are the subject matter of your baptism; to wit, infants born in sin and children of wrath, who neither do actually believe nor repent, whom you say must be baptized, though there be no warrant in the word of God for such an administration.

---

required of persons to be baptized? *Scholler.* Repentance, whereby, they forsake sin; and faith, whereby, they steadfastly believe the promises of God, made to them in that sacrament." *The A. B. C. with the catechisme that is to say, an instruction to be taught and learned of every childe before he be brought to be confirmed by the* bishop (London: Printed for the Company of Stationers, 1605) B*v*; Compare to the Westminster Shorter Catechism published in 1646: "Q. To whom is baptism to be administered? A. Baptism is not to be administered to any that are out of the visible church, till they profess their faith in Christ, & obedience to him, but the infants of such as are members of the visible church are to be baptized." *The grounds and principles of religion, contained in a shorter catechism (according to the advice of the Assembly of Divines, sitting at Westminster) to be used througout the kingdom of England and dominion of Wales* (no printer, 1646) 25.

[13] "*Maister.* Why then are infants baptized, when by reason of their tender age they cannot perform them? *Scholler.* Yes: they do perform them by their sureties, who promise and vow them both in their names: which when they come to age, themselves are bound to perform." *The A. B. C. with the catechisme*, B2.

[14] The reference is to the *Westminster Directory* of 1645: "That children by baptism are solemnly received into the bosom of the visible church, distinguished from the world, and them that are without, and united with believers; and that all who are baptized in the name of Christ, do renounce, and by their baptism are bound to fight against the devil, the world and the flesh: That they are Christians, and federally holy before baptism, and therefore are they baptized: That the inward grace and virtue of baptism is not tied to that very moment of time wherein it is administered, and that the fruit and power thereof reaches to the whole course of our life; and that outward baptism is not so necessary, that through the want thereof the infant is in danger of damnation, or the parents guilty, if they do not contemn or neglect the ordinance of Christ when and where it may be had." *A Directory for the publicke vvorship of God throughout the three kingdoms of Scotland, England, and Ireland with an act of the Generall Assembly of the Kirk of Scotland for establishing and observing this present directory: together with an act of the Parliament of the kingdom of Scotland approving and establishing the same: an act of the committee of estates concerning the printing thereof: and an act of the commission of the Generall Assembly for the printing and for the present practice of it throughout the said kingdom of Scotland* (Edinburgh: Printed by Evan Tyler, 1645) 35.

The form or manner of baptism, according to the doctrine of Christ, his disciples, and apostles is such a dipping or washing of the person baptized in or with water, as holds forth their communion with Christ in his death, burial, and resurrection, as appears by these Scriptures: Matthew 28:19, Acts 8:38, Hebrews 10:22, Romans 6:3–4, Colossians 2:12, [and] 1 Corinthians 15:29. But your babe-baptism is administered after the invention of men, by sprinkling their faces with water, not dipping or washing their bodies in water; which we affirm is to rantize[15] and not to baptize. The Greek word (βαπτίζω) signifies to dip or to wash, but never to sprinkle. [So in] 2 Kings 5:14: καὶ ἐβαπτίσατο ἐν τῷ ιορδάνῃ ἐπτάκι; Et immersit se in Iordane septies; "and he dipped himself seven times in Jordane." So the Septuagint. *Nonnus paraphrasis* in John (page 8, line 12): καὶ σὺ τί βαπτίζεις; πόθεν ὕδατι φῶτα καθαίρεις. Et tu cur immergas, unde aqua hominem mundificas [And why do you dip, whence you clean man with water?].[16] Also Vossius in his Dispute, Thes. I, Hist. Theolog [*Theses*

[15] *Oxford English Dictionary Online*, s.v. "rantize," "to sprinkle; spec. to baptize by sprinkling, as opposed to immersion." The earliest recorded use of the term dates to 1645. See *Oxford English Dictionary Online* (Oxford: Oxford University Press, 2014) s.v. "† rantize,v.," http://www.oed.com/view/Entry/158114?redirectedFrom=rantize (accessed November 21, 2014).

[16] The reference is to the Egyptian poet Nonnus of Panopolis (c. 400). His *Metabole kata Ioannen*, a paraphrase of the Gospel of John, appeared first in print in Venice in 1501; see Frederic Adolphus Ebert, *A General Bibliographical Dictionary* (Oxford: The University Press, 1837) 3:1187. The quotation, "καὶ σὺ τί βαπτίζεις; πόθεν ὕδατι φῶτα καθαίρεις" was taken from Nonnus' paraphrase of John 1:25. See Nonnus Panopolitanus, *Conversio Evangelii secundum Ioannem, Graecis versibus conscripta* (Cologne: Apud Maternum Cholinum, 1570) 7; id., *Translatio vel Paraphrasis S. Evangelii secundum Ioannem... cum versione Latina* (Basel: Ex officina Chalcographica Petri Perna, 1571) 3*v*–4*r*; id., *Paraphrasis sancti Evangelii secundum Joannem*, PG 43:753. The Latin translation offered here by the London Baptists, "Et tu cur immergas, unde aqua hominem mundificas," comes close to the Latin rendering of the Dutch humanist Daniel Heinsius (1580–1655) whose translation of 1627 was used for PG 43. There the phrase is rendered as follows: "Et tu cur baptizas? Unde aqua hominem mundificas." See Daniel Heinsius, *Aristarchus sacer, sive ad Nonni in Iohannem metaphrasin exercitationes* (Lugduni Batavorum: ex officina Bonaventurae et Abrahami Elzevier, 1627) 6–7; id., *Paraphrasis sancti Evangelii secundum Joannem*, PG 43:749–942. Another similar Latin translation appears in the 1528 edition of Panopolitanus' *Metabole kata Ioannen*: "Et tu cur nam aquae Iordanis hoies immergis? [Et] unde hominum sordes aqua eluis?" Id., *In Evangelium S. Ioannis Paraphrasis Graeca* (Hagenau, 1528) Bii*v*.

theologicae et historicae]: "Κυρίως βαπτίζειν, notat mergere," and there he said, "it is more than ἐπιπολάζειν, and less than δύνειν."[17]

And in our reasons why baptism ought to be thus administered by dipping or washing the body in water are these, to wit:

1. Because it was administered in much water (John 3:23).

2. Because it must represent a death, burial, and resurrection (Romans 6:3–4, I Corinthians 15:29, Colossians 2:12).

3. Because the parties baptized are to go into the water (Matthew 3:13, 16 and Acts 8:38–39).

Thus the judicious reader—if not prejudiced—may plainly perceive that your administration of infant baptism differs essentially from the doctrine of baptism which was taught by Christ, his disciples, and apostles: *ergo,* unlawful. And your own mouths and doctrine to your communicants have borne witness against yourselves in that you have taught your people that truth which the Scriptures bear witness of; namely, that actual repentance and faith is required in persons to be baptized. And you and all your brethren have with one mouth confessed that infants cannot perform that which is required. And yet you go about to invent a reason why they should be baptized, contrary to Scripture and your own confession, Christ's doctrine and your own.

---

[17] The reference is to the Dutch Humanist, Gerardus Joannes Vossius (1577–1649) and his "Disputatio theologica prima de baptismo," in *Theses theologicae et historicae de variis doctrinae Christianae capitibus; quas, aliquot abhinc annis, disputandas proposuit in Academia Leidensi* ([Oxford]: Excudebat Guilielmus Turner, impensis Guilielmi Webb, [1628]). In the "Disputatio theologica prima de baptismo," Vossius made the following observations about βαπτίζειν (to dip, or to plunge): "Κυρίως βαπτίζειν notat mergere, quomodo in Glofs. vett. ab H. Stephano primùm editis explicatur. Ut plus omnino sit, quam ἐῶιπολάζειν, quod est leviter innatare: minùs autem, quàm δύνειν, quod est pessum ire: sive ad sui exitium fundum petere." Vossius, "Disputatio Theologica Prima de Baptismo," in *Theses theologicae et historicae*, 343. In essence, Vossius argued that βαπτίζειν means to "submerge," a more definitive action than ἐπιπολάζειν, that is, "to float," or as he put it, "to float smoothly"; yet, "less than δύνειν," "to cause to sink," or in his words, "to sink to the bottom." For a study of Vossius see, C. S. M. Rademaker, *Life and Work of Gerardus Joannes Vossius (1577–1649)* (Assen: Van Gorcum, 1981).

Argument III

That religious worship for which there is no command or example in the Scripture of truth is will-worship, and unlawful.[18] *But your infant baptism is a religious worship for which there is no command, nor any example written in the Scripture of truth: ergo, your infant baptism is will-worship, and unlawful.*[19]

Here Mr. Calamy and his brethren are put hard to it, and know not how to give a satisfying answer to either of the propositions of this syllogism. Some of his brethren being persuaded in their hearts that the major is a truth, dare not deny it, but would answer to the minor. Mr. Calamy not knowing how to avoid the truth of the minor would answer to the major.[20] And when the light of truth that is in both the major and the minor did so shine forth, that Mr. Calamy and his brethren could not deny either proposition, yet they did distinguish upon both propositions, and would grant neither, although true, and they thus distinguish. Mr. Porter said, "though there be no express command nor example written in the Scripture to baptize infants, yet there is an implicit command"—which distinction was in our dispute thus taken away. If there be any command at all to baptize infants, it is written either in the Old or New Testament. But there is no command at all to baptize infants, neither express nor implied, written in the Old or New Testament. *Ergo*, and we say further, that seeing secret things belongs to God, and things that are revealed belong to us and to our children, let the indifferent reader judge how such an unwritten tradition as infant baptism is—which is nowhere revealed either in the Old or New Testament—can belong to us and our children. But Mr. Calamy, not liking his brother's distinction and answer to our minor proposition, he gave us this answer to our major, which in his own words we will set down: "I would deny their major, for, if a thing by just consequence, by necessary consequence, whatever it be, proved out of the Scripture by necessary consequence, though there be no command, nor no example, yet it is Scripture, as much as if there was command or example." Although we grant

[18] In the King James Version, Colossians 2:23 condemns "will worship." The New American Standard version translates the text as "self-made religion."

[19] Marginal annotation: "The reader may here take notice that these distinctions were given us by Mr. Calamy and Mr. Porter at our private dispute at Mr. Priggs."

[20] This paragraph mentions the syllogism, which is a three-part logical train of reasoning that states a major and a minor premise and a conclusion. Use of syllogisms is common in seventeenth-century apologetic literature.

that the necessary consequences which the apostles and prophets—who were inspired by the Holy Spirit of God—did deduct from the Scriptures of the Old Testament, and left recorded in the New Testament, are Scripture and written for our instruction. Yet we do deny that the consequences which Mr. Calamy or his brethren—being men subject to like infirmity as ourselves and may err—do deduct from Scriptures—not by divine inspiration, but by natural or artificial logic—which Mr. Calamy called, necessary consequences, are Scripture. And the reason of our denying of such necessary consequences to be Scripture is because they are nowhere written in the Scripture of truth, but bring in that popish tenet of non-written verity, and so ushers in all popish innovations as prelacy, common prayer book, ceremonies, etc., and therefore is unsound, absurd, and sinful. Which we make good by this syllogism: Every tenet that brought in prelacy, common prayer book, and all popish ceremonies, hath proved to be unsound, absurd, and sinful, and is not now once to be named—without an odium—by any of the teachers of God's people. But this, to wit; that necessary consequences—as Mr. Calamy calls them—are Scripture, is one of those tenets that brought in prelacy, etc., *ergo*.

This was the tenet by which the parish ministers subjected their people to prelacy, and bound their consciences by their necessary consequences. They used thus to argue from Romans 13:1–2: "Every soul ought to be subject to the higher powers; but the archbishop and lord bishops are higher powers, *Ergo,* every soul ought to be subject to the archbishop and lord bishops."[21] By this tenet also they brought the people to worship God by the *Book of Common Prayer* and proved it lawful by their necessary consequences. They used thus to argue from Matthew 6:9: "If a set form of prayer be lawful, then the common prayer book is lawful, but a set form of prayer is lawful. *Ergo,* it follows by necessary consequence, that the common prayer book is lawful." And by this tenet they brought their people to submit to all their popish ceremonies, namely surplice, cross in baptism, and bowing at the name of Jesus, etc.

They used thus to argue from I Corinthians 14:40, "All things in the church ought to be done decently and in order." But it is very decent to wear a surplice, cape and hood, to sign the infant with the cross in baptism, and

[21] "Let every person be subject to the governing authorities; for there is no authority except from God, and those authorities that exist have been instituted by God. Therefore whoever resists authority resists what God has appointed, and those who resist will incur judgment." Romans 13:1–2 (NRSV).

to bow at the naming of Jesus, and to kneel at the receiving of the sacrament. Also, the uniformity of pews in the church, and the setting of the table altar-wise and railing it in is both very decent and orderly; *ergo,* all these ceremonies ought to be in the church.

Thus any who will not shut their eyes against the light may clearly see that men's necessary consequences have ushered in all popish innovations. Thereby the parish ministers have subjected their parishioners' consciences unto their own traditions, and have greatly endangered the damnation of many of their parishioners' souls thereby, while they have taught as doctrine the commandments of men. And we dare not but tell the people that if they will believe Mr. Calamy and his brethren, that their necessary consequences are Scripture, and whatsoever they can prove by their necessary consequences from the Scripture binds their consciences, and they ought to obey and practice whatsoever they so teach though there be no command nor example in the Scripture for the same. They will still be brought into as great an observance of the traditions of men, under the classical presbytery, as ever they were under lordly episcopacy. And we dare affirm and maintain—if we may have liberty of public dispute with them by the leave of authority—that the presbyters have nothing else [to] persuade the people to subject their consciences unto their synodical and classical authority, their newly devised parish/church-worship, their rantizing of the babes of their parish believers, and all the rest of their old and new traditions, but such necessary consequences. For we dare say the presbyters—whenever we shall dispute with them—will be forced to confess that there is no command nor example written in the Scripture of truth for all these things. But yet, it is likely they will say that they can prove all these by necessary consequences from the Scripture, and these necessary consequences are Scripture, and bind the consciences of their parishioners to observe them. The time was, when Mr. Calamy and his brethren did think that this was a good argument against the cross in baptism because there was no command nor example for it in the Scripture, and it was an adding to the Word to bring in such a thing, and men could not make it an action of faith, because they have no warrant for it in the Word of God, and therefore it was sin. This was a good argument against the bishops. Whatsoever is not of faith, is sin. Whatsoever we have no command, or example for, written in the Scripture of truth, we have no faith for. *Ergo,* was it a sin to sign a child in the forehead with a cross in the bishops' time? Because there is no word of God for it; and is it not a sin now [among] the presbyters, to sprinkle a little water upon a child's forehead or face, and say, "I baptize thee in the name, etc.," seeing they confess there is no Word of God for it, but their own necessary consequences?

Argument IV

That which does deny Christ to come in the flesh, ought not to be done. But the baptizing of infants does deny Christ to come in the flesh. Therefore, ought it not to be done.

We know that no man can deny the major, which is so clearly confirmed (1 John 4:3) with divers other places. We will prove the minor, that baptizing of infants does deny Christ to have come in the flesh. That which does take from Christ that which the Holy Spirit gives to Christ, considered come in the flesh; that denies Christ come in the flesh. But the baptizing of infants does take from Christ that which the Holy Spirit gives to Christ, considered come in the flesh; therefore it denies Christ come in the flesh.

And for the proof of this, we shall declare to you what we mean by that which the Holy Spirit gives to Christ considered come in the flesh. The Holy Spirit gives to Christ a pre-eminence above all others that were before him in his prophetical and kingly office [Marginal Annotation: Colossians 1:18, Philippians 2:9]. In his prophetical office: that neither Moses nor the prophets were to be compared with him, but far inferior to him and his office [Marginal Annotations: John 6:[32], Matthew 11:9, Luke 24:19]. So inferior, that he was not to be expounded by them; but in giving out his mind, considered come in the flesh, he was to expound and unfold them. But now men in their going about to plead for the baptizing of infants do exceedingly undervalue Christ's prophetical office in this, that they make the Old Testament expound the New, whereas the New should expound the Old. Christ should, and does expound Moses [Marginal Annotation: Matthew 5:21–28]. But there is no warrant for us to bring Christ under the exposition of Moses, and men do undervalue the Lord Christ in making Moses speak that which Christ speaks not, or bringing Moses to Christ, as a greater light to unfold the lesser. They do—we say—exceedingly undervalue Christ and that thus the light unfolding, or the wisdom unfolding, must be greater than the matter unfolded. Therefore, he that goes about to make Moses' mouth to speak out Christ's mind in things that concern Christ as come in the flesh, sets up Moses above Christ, and denies Christ to become in the flesh.

Secondly, they exceedingly take from Christ's kingly office. Whereas, the Holy Spirit sets up Christ [as] king in his church, and a lawgiver as equal to, [and] so transcending all others that were before him [Marginal Annotations: Isaiah 9:6–7, Revelation 15:3]. But men in the baptizing of infants do undervalue the kingly office of Christ in giving laws to his people. That's clear in these two things.

First in this, that they say it is a duty to baptize infants, and answer the mind of Christ, and yet cannot show a command from Christ. Whereas the Apostle said, "Christ was as faithful in his house as Moses." And you know the faithfulness of Moses did consist in this: that he gave laws and commands to the Israelites to declare their duty, and laid nothing upon them as a duty, but what they had a command for. And seeing he gave them laws for everything they were to observe, and if Christ was as faithful in his house as he, we will leave this to the judgment of the wise whether or not that this does not undervalue the kingly office of Christ, to say, that baptizing of infants is a duty that they owe to Christ. And yet [they] can show no command for it from Christ. [Marginal Annotation: Hebrews 3:2–3]

Secondly, they undervalue the kingly office of Christ in giving laws to his church in this: that they go about to perform—as they say—a duty to Christ, but can show no command for it from Christ, but must use their own art and reason to make Christ's law strong enough to hold it out to be a duty. And whether the joining of man's art, policy, and reason to the laws of Christ does not exceedingly undervalue Christ, as though his laws were not perfect enough for his people, we leave the wise to judge. And in so doing, they do exceedingly take—as before we said from the prophetical, so here in the kingly office of Christ—that honor and preeminence from him, which the Holy Spirit gives to him considered as come in the flesh. Therefore, so to do, denies Christ as come in the flesh.

Argument V

That which is no part of righteousness, ought not to be observed. But the baptizing of infants is no part of righteousness. And therefore it ought not to be observed.

The major proposition none can deny. I will prove the minor, and that thus: whatsoever is considered as a part of righteousness was seen either in the person or practice of Jesus Christ.[22] But neither in the person nor practice of Jesus Christ is the baptizing of infants seen or held forth. Therefore, it is no part of righteousness. And that whatsoever is a part of righteousness was seen in the person or practice of Jesus Christ, is clear from this scripture, Matthew 3:15: "And Jesus said, 'suffer it be so: for thus it to becometh us to fulfil all righteousness'." If all righteousness, then there was no righteousness but was considered either in the person or practice of Christ. And that the baptizing of infants is not held out in the person or practice of Christ, we leave the wise to judge. He himself was not baptized when he was an infant, though he might have pleaded the same privilege as they do, who say they are children of believers. Had it been a part of righteousness Christ would, nay, Christ should have done it.

Objection Answered:

If you object, and say, "There was none to baptize him before," we answer, had it been a part of righteousness, God in a providence would have provided one before, as well as then, for he was to fulfill all righteousness. And for his practice—though he baptized not, but his disciples, John 4:2—yet, in all their baptizing where Christ was, you never hear that ever they baptized any infant, or gave any command for it. Therefore, it is no part of righteousness, and ought not to be done.

Argument VI

Those only ought to be baptized who are accounted the seed of Abraham, either after the flesh, or according to the faith. But none of the infants of believing gentiles are accounted the seed of Abraham, either after the flesh, or according to the faith, ergo, they ought not to be baptized.

The major proposition, Mr. Calamy and his brethren will not deny because it is their own doctrine, and one of their principles, whereby they would prove that the infants of believers ought to be baptized. We do but borrow their own weapon to give their infant baptism its deadly wound. The assumption, to wit, that none of the infants of believing gentiles are

---

[22] The first person singular pronoun, "I," that opens this sentence points to two possible scenarios that may explain the question of authorship. The first possibility is that the entire *Declaration* was the work of one of the three Baptist ministers whose name appeared in the title page, i.e. Coxe, Knollys, and Kiffin. The other possibility is that each one of them was responsible for one or more of the nine arguments, which were later incorporated into the final document.

accounted the seed of Abraham, either after the flesh, or according to the faith, we thus prove.

First, because the Jews or Israelites only, and not any of the gentiles, are counted the seed of Abraham after the flesh: to wit, by natural generation or offspring. So then none of the infants of believing gentiles are accounted for the fleshly seed of Abraham. Secondly, because believers only themselves, and not the infants, are accounted the spiritual seed of Abraham, or his seed according to the faith, Galatians 3:29: "If you be Christ's, then you are Abraham's seed, and heirs according to the promise." And Abraham is called the father of them that believe (Romans 4:12). But it is nowhere said in Scripture, that Abraham is the father of all their children too. Nay, the contrary is witnessed by the Apostle Paul: "They which are the children of the flesh, these are not the children of God: but the children of the promise are counted for the seed" (Romans 9:8–9).

We conceive that this Scripture does expound Genesis 17. God made an everlasting covenant of grace with Abraham and his seed. Now the Scriptures declare that Abraham had two kinds of seed: the one born after the flesh, the other born after the Spirit (Galatians 4:29). The question is, who are counted for Abraham's seed according to the covenant of grace? We answer, not Ishmael, nor any one born after the flesh, but Isaac and every one born after the spirit. And the Apostle delivers this as the mind of God: Neither because they are the seed of Abraham, are they all children; but in Isaac shall thy seed be called: "That is," said the Apostle, "they which are the children of the flesh, these are not the children of God: but the children of the promise are counted for the seed" (Romans 9:8). Also Paul further clears this truth, in the 4th chapter to the Galatians, verse 22 to the end: "For it is written, that Abraham had two sons, the one by a bondwoman, the other by a freewoman. But he who was of the bondwoman [to wit, Ishmael] was born after the flesh; but he of the freewoman [to wit, Isaac] was by promise; which things are an allegory: for these are the two covenants," etc. [Galatians 4:22–24]. The Apostle witnessed that there are two covenants, which God made with Abraham and his seed; to wit, a covenant of works with Abraham's fleshly seed, and a covenant of grace with Abraham's spiritual seed, which was set forth allegorically in Ishmael and Isaac. And here have Mr. Calamy and his brethren been mistaken in bringing an argument to prove infant baptism, drawn from Abraham's fleshly seed, affirming that there is but one covenant in that Scripture, and that is a covenant of grace. And so have concluded that all the fleshly seed of Abraham—and by their necessary consequences—all the fleshly seed of believing gentiles are the children of God, and are to be counted for the seed with whom God hath made an everlasting covenant of grace. Contrary to these Scriptures, [see] Romans 9:6–9 and Galatians 4:22–24 to the end.

Neither does that promise, i.e. Genesis 17:7, in the least concern the seed of the Gentiles but the Jews only, who were Abraham's seed after the flesh. Thus then we understand the Scripture: that the children of the flesh, to wit, those who are born after the flesh, or of the flesh, are flesh (John 3:6). That is, are sinful, being conceived in sin and shaped in iniquity (Psalm 51), and by natural generation are the children of wrath as well as others (Ephesians 2:3). They are not the children of God, until they be born again, or born of God (John 1:13 and John 3:3–6). But the children of the promise, that is, those who are in Christ, are counted for the seed (Galatians 3:29). And we brethren—to wit, who are believers—as Isaac was, are the children of the promise (Galatians 4:28).

But some may think that this will put the children of believers into as bad a condition as the children of the Turks, heathens, and any other wicked men, and this they are persuaded is an horrible thing, and a dangerous opinion. We put not the children of believers into as bad a condition as the children of Turks, etc. It was Adam's disobedience in eating the forbidden fruit that put all his posterity equally into a sinful and miserable condition (Romans 5:12, 19). And the doctrine, which Mr. Calamy and his brethren teach, agrees. They say—and it is truth—that all the infants of believers are shaped in iniquity and in sin their mothers conceive them. Yea, they are born in sin and are by nature children of wrath as well as others. And now let the reader judge, whether this their own doctrine does not put the children of believers into as bad a condition, as any Turk's, heathen's, or wicked men's children. Why then should they go about to persuade the people that our opinion, that the infants of believers should not be baptized, is by no means to be received because—they say—it puts their children into as bad a condition as the children of the Turks, heathens, etc. when as their own doctrine does the like. And some of their doctrines touching the infants of believers put them into a worse condition; to wit, into a condition of falling away from grace. For they affirm that the infants of believers are within the covenant of grace, and therefore are to be baptized. So Mr. Marshal's sermon about infant baptism (p. 8 & 37)[23] and Mr. Blake's (p.

[23] Stephen Marshall wrote: "My first argument is this, the infants of believing parents are a *foederati*, therefore they must be *signati*, they are within the covenant of

16).[24] Also, this their judgment appears by the *Directory*,[25] where parish ministers are directed at baptizing children to teach that the promises of the covenant of grace is made to believers and their infants. And that the

---

grace, belonging to Christ's body, kingdom, family, therefore are to partake of the seal of his covenant, or the distinguishing badge between them who are under the covenant of grace, and them who are not." Stephen Marshall, *A sermon of the baptizing of infants preached in the Abbey-Church at Westminster, at the morning lecture, appointed by the Honorable House of Commons* (London: Richard Cotes for Stephen Bowtell, 1644) 8; "And the same command which enjoyed [enjoined] Abraham to seal his children with the seal of the covenant, enjoys [enjoins] us as strongly to seal ours with the seal of the covenant, and that command of God which expressly bound Abraham to seal his with the sign of circumcision which was the sacrament then in force, *pro tempore*, does virtually bind us to seal ours with the sign of baptism, which is the sacrament now in force, and succeeds in the room of the other by his own appointment." Marshall, *A sermon*, 37. Stephen Marshall (1594?–1655) was an Anglican clergyman, at the time vicar at Finchingfield in Essex. He was a very popular Puritan preacher who served both the Short and Long Parliament in that capacity. Marshall became a strong supporter of Presbyterianism and was a close associate of Edmund Calamy. See Tom Webster, "Marshall, Stephen (1594/5?–1655)," in *Oxford Dictionary of National Biography*, edited by H. C. G. Matthew and Brian Harrison (Oxford: Oxford University Press, 2004). Online ed., edited by Lawrence Goldman, October 2009. http://www.oxforddnb.com/view/article/ 18148 (accessed November 21, 2014).

[24] Thomas Blake (1597?–1657) Church of England clergyman and controversialist, wrote several tracts against Baptists and in defense of paedobaptism. The following passage, although it does not match with the page number offered by the London Baptists, is the closest to the subject under consideration: "Any ground—I say—which may secure the conscience of not having sinned against the souls of our infants, if by our default they die without this seal of the covenant, and so loose the benefit thereof? Have not infants need of Christ, and the application of his blood for the washing their souls from sin? Is there any hope of salvation without Christ? Is there any other way revealed by which any may have part in Christ, but by his ordinances? Is there any other ordinance by which infants may be made partakers of Christ and the covenant of grace except baptism?" Thomas Blake, *A moderate answer to these two questions, 1. Whether ther* [*sic*] *be sufficient ground in Scripture to warrant the conscience of a Christian to present his infants to the sacrament of baptism. 2. Whether it be not sinful for a Christian to receive the sacrament in a mixt assembly. Prepared for the resolution of a friend, and now presented to the public view of all, for the satisfaction of them who desire to walk in the ancient and long approved way of truth and holiness* (London: Abel Roper, 1645) 17; for more on Blake see William Lamont, "Blake, Thomas (1596/7–1657)," in *Oxford Dictionary of National Biography*, edited by H. C. G. Matthew and Brian Harrison (Oxford: Oxford University Press, 2004). Online ed., edited by Lawrence Goldman, January 2008. http://www.oxforddnb.com/view/article/ 2583 (accessed November 21, 2014).

[25] *A Directory for the publicke vvorship of God* (1645) 35.

Scripture, which they continually produce, tends to prove this their opinion, to wit, Acts 2:39. And yet they are forced to confess that some of the children of believers prove very profane, and notoriously wicked, yea live so, and die so, and are damned. So then by their own doctrine and confession some of the infants of believers who are in the covenant of grace, may perish in their sins, and be damned. Does not this uphold that Arminian tenet of falling away from grace? And the popish doctrine that persons may be in the state of Peter today, and in the state of Judas tomorrow? We would have said more to this thing, but Mr. Tombes in his *Examen* of Mr. Marshal's sermon about infant baptism (p. 45, 46–54), has handled this point very soundly.[26] And we could earnestly desire every one who questions infant baptism to read over Mr. Tombes' book very seriously.

Argument VII

It is not lawful to apply or administer any ordinance of Christ otherwise than according to the rule of the Word. But to baptize any infants is to apply or administer an ordinance of Christ, otherwise than according to the rule of the word. Ergo, it is not lawful to baptize any infants.

The truth of the Proposition appears:

1. All will-worship is expressly condemned in the Scripture (Colossians 2:23). But every administration and application of an ordinance of Christ, other than according to the rule of the Word is manifestly will-worship.

2. It is such an adding to that which God hath commanded which is forbidden in Deuteronomy 12:32.

3. In this case we should revive as doctrine the commandments of men, and our fear towards God would be taught by the precepts of men, the evil whereof appears in Isaiah 29:13 and Matthew 15:9.

4. In doing this we shall never be able to answer the demand in Isaiah 1:12: "Who hath required this at your hands?"[27] But we shall be found doers

---

[26]John Tombes (1603?–1676) *An examen of the sermon of Mr. Stephen Marshal about infant baptisme in a letter sent to him* (London: R. W. for George Whitington, 1645). Tombes wrote extensively as a theologian of anti-paedobaptism. His major work was his three volumes of *Antipaedobaptism* (1652, 1654, 1657). His views were very influential among Baptists, and he himself founded Baptist churches and help trained Baptist clergy. However, he did not endorse separation, and accepted the established church.

[27] "When you come to appear before me, who asked this from your hand? Trample my courts no more." Isaiah 1:12 (NRSV).

of those things which God commanded not, neither came they into his heart; touching which, see Jeremiah 7:31.

5. If Christ has not given complete directions in his Word concerning the use of his ordinances, how then is he faithful to him that appointed him—not only as the high priest, but also as the apostle of our profession, and as the prophet whom God raised up like unto Moses— even as Moses was faithful in all God's house? See Deuteronomy 18:15 and Hebrews 3:1–2. And if he has given such complete directions, is it not then unlawful to apply or use his ordinances otherwise than according to his own directions?

6. If it be lawful to apply or use the ordinances of Christ, otherwise than according to the rule of the Word, or otherwise than may be warranted and justified by the Word, then both Jews and Turks, and other such, both young and old, may be admitted to the ordinances. But this they all acknowledge to be unlawful.

Now that the baptizing of infants is an applying or administering of baptism—which is an ordinance of Christ—otherwise than according to the rule of the Word, and otherwise than may be warranted and justified by the Word; and so now proved unlawful, we thus confirm.

1. There is in the Scripture no precept enjoining us, nor rule directing us, nor any example showing it lawful for us to baptize infants.

2. The only written commission to baptize—which is in Matthew 28:19—directed us to baptize disciples only, "Go ye and disciple all nations, baptizing them," that is, the disciples. For this is the only construction and interpretation that the Greek word can bear, and infants cannot be made disciples because they cannot learn.

3. Those only of the Jews might be baptized that did repent, as appears in Acts 2:38, and they only of the gentiles that did sincerely believe, as appears in Acts 8:37.[28]

4. In Acts 8:12 it is fully related who were baptized in Samaria, *viz.* not infants, but men and women, when they believed.

5. Then only is baptism administered according to the rule of the Word when a disciple is baptized into the name of the Father, and of the Son, etc. (Matthew 28:19); that is, into the profession of faith in the Father, Son, and Holy Spirit. So the Apostle reminds the Corinthians that they had not been baptized into the name of Paul (1 Corinthians 1:13); that is, into the profession of faith in Paul. This necessarily excludes infants, who can make

[28] Acts 8:37, "And Philip said…is the Son of God," appears in ancient authorities but is not part of the majority text of UBS 5th ed., see GNT, 426.

no such profession. The supply of this want of profession by the profession of those that have been called sureties,[29] does now appear to all wise men to be as ridiculous and absurd as paedo-rantism—now falsely called, infant baptism—will shortly appear to be to all the godly.

6. All those that are baptized according to the rule of the Word are looked upon as persons submitting themselves to the use of baptism by the direction of the Holy Spirit (1 Corinthians 12:13). This also manifestly excludes all infants.

Argument VIII

If Christ commanded not his Apostles to practice or teach the baptizing of infants, then infants ought not to be baptized. But Christ commanded not his Apostles to practice, etc. Ergo [...]

That Christ commanded not his Apostles to practice, or teach infants baptism is manifest because the Apostles, in obedience to Christ's word (Matthew 28:20) taught the faithful to observe all things that Christ commanded them. But no man can say that the Apostles taught the faithful to observe the baptizing of infants, unless with the papists he will fly to unwritten traditions falsely called apostolic.

Argument IX

If the doctrine maintaining infants baptism be no part of the revealed counsel of God, then infants ought not to be baptized. For things that are revealed belong to us and to our children. But it is no part of the revealed counsel of God, as appears by the Apostles not declaring it (see Acts 20:27). Ergo, infants ought not to be baptized.[30]

---

[29] *Oxford English Dictionary Online*, s.v. "surety," "a person who undertakes some specific responsibility on behalf of another who remains primarily liable; one who makes himself liable for the default or miscarriage of another." The earliest recorded use of the term in this sense dates to 1428. See *Oxford English Dictionary Online* (Oxford: Oxford University Press, 2014) s.v. "surety," http://www.oed.com/view/Entry/194881?rskey=GHT2iY&result=6&isAdvanced=false (accessed December 05, 2014).

[30] Coxe, Knollys, and Kiffin identified an Argument IX but offered no defense of their assertion. Nor do they provide a proper conclusion to the tract. It appears to be unfinished. This omission was probably due to the author's rush to publish the *Declaration.*

"PREFACE" TO A CHRISTIAN WOMAN'S EXPERIENCES OF THE GLORIOUS WORKINGS OF GOD'S FREE GRACE

(Rotterdam, 1663)

INTRODUCTION

Very little is known about Katherine Sutton (fl. 1630–1663), a governess by vocation whose zeal for a pure form of religion led her to move with her children to the Netherlands.[1] Her only published work was *A Christian Woman's Experience of the Glorious Working of God's Free Grace* (Rotterdam, 1663). Presumably the original work was much more extensive, a record of "thirty years" of spiritual experiences. However, she lost her original text in a shipwreck and eventually set down in writing the present work, a reconstruction from memory. Hanserd Knollys was in the Netherlands at the time of publication and was personally acquainted with the circumstances of the author. We do not know more about their connection. In the preface he wrote for Sutton's work, he called her a "holy matron," and indicated with admiration that she "was not only a governess, but, as it were, a prophetess in her family." His sincere reverence for her spiritual gifts and the faithfulness of her account was unequivocally articulated in his commendation of her writings and the example of her life. He asserted that her experiences were written in her heart, "not with ink but by his Holy Spirit."

The preface reveals much of Knollys' own theology. In fact, his endorsement of Sutton's little work can be better understood in light of his own views on the gifts of the Holy Spirit and, specifically, what he calls the gift of spiritual singing. His understanding of the notion of spiritual gift is based on an eschatological reading of Joel 2: 28–32, in particular verse 28.[2]

---

[1] Michael Davies, "Sutton, Katherine (*fl.* 1630–1663)," in *Oxford Dictionary of National Biography*, edited by H. C. G. Matthew and Brian Harrison (Oxford: Oxford University Press, 2004). Online ed., edited by Lawrence Goldman. http://www.oxforddnb.com/view/article/69336 (accessed November 22, 2014); Bill J. Leonard, *Baptist Ways: A History* (Valley Forge: Judson Press, 2003) 61; Ian Mallard, "The Hymns of Katherine Sutton," *Baptist Quarterly* 20, no. 1 (1963) 23–33.

[2] "Then afterwards I will pour out my spirit on all flesh; your sons and your daughters shall prophesy, your old men shall dream dreams, and your young men shall see visions." Joel 2:28 (NRSV).

Accordingly, he refers to her work as a "testimony and witness of the free grace and fresh anointing of the Lord's Spirit, whom he had promised to pour forth upon his servants and handmaids in the last days (Joel 2:28–32)." More importantly, he claims a special regard for her writings on account of the anointing of the Holy Spirit: "do not judge her, for she has received an unction from the holy one, and is taught of God." It is interesting to note that this special anointing of the Holy Spirit permitted her, in Knollys' estimate, to overcome conventions of the day that defined women's proper private and public functions. He points to:

> …her extraordinary teachings of God by his Holy Spirit and word, when she could not enjoy the ordinary means of his own appointments. This godly woman—after God had begun the good work of grace in her soul—would not loose any opportunity she could get either in public or private for her precious soul, but would often break through some difficulties and endure some hardships to enjoy such opportunities.

Nevertheless, of greater importance was his way of thinking about spiritual singing. Knollys refined his views on spiritual singing towards the end of his career, in his *An Answer to a Brief Discourse Concerning Singing in the Publick Worship of God in the Gospel Church* (London, 1691). In that work he specified that spiritual singing was vocal and not silent. In this way he sought to distance his views from the positions of Quakers and Seekers. In 1663, however, he was laying the foundations of his understanding of spiritual singing. In short, he saw spiritual singing as a gift of the Holy Spirit, analogous to prayer or supplication. He also maintained that spiritual singing could not be from a book such as a hymnal, or from memory. Instead, the Holy Spirit extemporaneously inspired spiritual singing. He argued that, "singing of psalms, hymns, and spiritual songs being an ordinance of God's worship, ought to be performed by a gift and the assistance of the Spirit, as well as prayer (1 Corinthians 14:12–15)." For these reasons this short piece may attract the attention of present day Baptists.

"PREFACE" TO A CHRISTIAN WOMAN'SEXPERIENCES OF THE GLORIOUS WORKINGS OF GOD'S FREE GRACE[1]

(Rotterdam, 1663)

Courteous Reader:
When our Lord and Savior Jesus Christ had fed many with a few loaves, he commanded his disciples to gather up the fragments, that nothing be lost (John 6:12). And when God was pleased to pour out of his Spirit upon some of his faithful servants in our generation, he had also some of his handmaids who gathered up the crumbs of that spiritual bread, which the Lord blessed and distributed among his disciples, of which number this holy matron was one. Now there are three arguments whereby it may appear that God would not have these fragments—which she had gathered into her basket—to be lost. First, because God made them—by his blessing—food to her soul in the gathering and receiving them into her own heart, and also to the souls of several young virgins in her family, unto whom the Lord made some of these crumbs the bread of eternal life. Secondly, because when she had lost the manuscript—wherein these and many other of her experiences were written—in a sea storm wherein she suffered a shipwreck, yet God, who preserved her life, did also preserve these experiences in her heart where it seemed they were written, not with ink but by his Holy Spirit. Thirdly, because she being pressed in spirit to communicate them more publicly, the Spirit of the Lord did bring them again into her remembrance, and she has been made willing to publish them as her testimony and witness of the free grace and fresh anointing of the Lord's Spirit, whom he had promised to pour forth upon his servants and handmaids in the last days (Joel 2:28–32).

Now for as much as this little book is presented to you Christian reader, as a basket full of fragments, be not offended with the brokenness of

---

[1] Hanserd Knollys, "Preface" in Katherine Sutton, *A Christian Woman's Experiences of the Glorious Workings of Gods Free Grace Published for the Edification of Others* (Rotterdam: Printed by Henry Goddaeus, Printer in the Newstreet, 1663); See Elizabeth Skerpan-Wheeler, ed., *Life Writings*, The Early Modern Englishwoman: Printed Writings, 1641–1700, Series 2, Part 1 (Aldershot: Ashgate, 2000).

any matter, which you may meet within the reading thereof. Considering, that God, who has made them a blessing to others, may bless them unto you. You may take notice of three things in this little book, which I judge worthy of every Christian's observation. To wit, first, her extraordinary teachings of God by his Holy Spirit and word, when she could not enjoy the ordinary means of his own appointments. This godly woman—after God had begun the good work of grace in her soul—would not lose any opportunity she could get either in public or private for her precious soul, but would often break through some difficulties and endure some hardships to enjoy such opportunities. She did this at that time when many professors slighted and neglected (O grievous sin!), yea, contemned[2] the ministry of the word. Now, observe that as she followed the Lord, and waited upon him in the use of the means of grace, when she could enjoy it, so the Lord was pleased—of the exceeding riches of his free grace—not only to do her soul good by his presence and power therein. But also—when she could not enjoy the outward means of grace—the Lord waited to be gracious unto her soul, and followed her with the inward teachings of his Holy Spirit, and word, as she has witnessed in many particulars in this her book.

And if thy experience, courteous reader, cannot seal unto the testimony that she gives of those spiritual teachings, yet do not stumble at them, do not judge her, for she has received an unction from the holy one, and is taught of God. In the reading of her book, thou will meet with some sudden and unexpected transition from one thing to another, and you may think it to be somewhat abruptly, yet censure not too rashly but rather consider that even this also may, yea, does hold some proportion unto the course of heaven and heavenly communications. The husbandman will not wonder to see showers and shinings, bright and dark clouds succeed each other, knowing that the rain that comes from heaven has its seasons and its measure too. Will the mariner marvel to see the seas swell and rage in a great storm, or admire the stillness and smoothness of the deep waters in a great calm? Or will any who lives upon the seacoast think the frequent ebbing and flowing of the tide a strange thing? Neither will any experienced Christian marvel at the sudden ebbing and flowing of joys and sorrows in the hearts of saints. The operations and administrations of the Spirit are various (1 Corinthians 12:4–7). Sometimes the Spirit is poured out upon the souls of believers, as floods upon the dry ground, and those spiritual showers and shinings do make a

[2] Contemn, now rarely used, means to despise or to scorn.

spring of grace in the wilderness of their hearts, whereof the Lord [was] spoken by his prophets (Isaiah 51:3, 44:3–4 and 32:15–17; Jeremiah 31:12). But at other times the glory of the saints' comforts, joys, and light is so clouded and eclipsed that they are under great desertions (Isaiah 54:7, 8, 11). Yea, and may for sometime walk in darkness and have no light (Isaiah 50:10).

Secondly, another thing I judge worthy [of] the reader's observation in this book, is this Christian woman's experience of the presence and power of God, accompanying her conscientious endeavors to do good unto the souls of others both in her own family especially, and also in some other families, where she sojourned sometime. I mention not this for her praise, who desires that God alone may have all the glory of whatsoever he has done for her or by her—she needs no epistles of commendation from men. But seeing her experiences are made so public, my heart's desire is that parents and governors of families would follow her example therein. Endeavoring, as she did, the conversion and sanctification of them whom God had committed to their charge by instructions, counsel, and reproof, which she administered with so much love, wisdom, zeal, and tender heartedness, that they proved by God's blessing an effectual means of the conversion of many, some of whom are yet living witnesses of the truth hereof, and also of many other [of] her experiences related in this her book. She was not only a governess, but, as it were, a prophetess in her family, for she prayed constantly with her children and maidens, she also read the holy Scriptures daily unto them, and so spoke from them, that many of them, who heard her in her family duties believed and turned to the Lord. She opened her mouth with wisdom and in her tongue was the law of kindness, [as] Solomon spoke of the virtuous woman (Proverbs 31:26–29). She did so catechize the young children and instruct the elder maidens that they all learned to know, and many of them, to do their duty to God and man.

Thirdly, there is yet one thing more that I would have thee, courteous reader, to ponder in thy heart. To wit, the gift of singing spiritual songs and hymns, which she presents thee with some instances of in her book, here and there occasionally touching, which administration I am willing for thy edification to say [the following]. First, that singing of psalms, hymns, and spiritual songs being an ordinance of God's worship, ought to be performed by a gift and the assistance of the Spirit, as well as prayer (1 Corinthians 14:12–15). What is it then? *I will pray with the Spirit*, etc. *I will sing with the Spirit*, etc. Now as to take a book and read a prayer out of it, or to say a prayer without the book, is not to pray in the Spirit; so to read a psalm in a book and sing it, or to sing the same psalm without the book is not to sing in the Spirit. If the singing of psalms be a part of God's worship—as doubtless it is—then it ought to be performed by assistance of the Spirit, for the true worshippers ought to worship God in spirit and truth (John 4:23–24). Second, that Christians ought to sing spiritual songs and hymns, as well as psalms, unto the Lord, and that with grace in their hearts (Colossians 3:16). For the melody that the Lord loves is in the heart rather than in the voice (Ephesians 5:19). Third, they who perform this part of God's worship, whether they speak unto themselves in private, or unto others more publicly, ought to have the word of Christ to dwell richly in them, yea, and to be filled with the Spirit as the Apostle testifies (Ephesians 5:17–20; Colossians 3:16). I have known other godly and gracious Christians besides this grave and holy matron, who have this gift of singing, and I myself have some experience of this kind of anointing of the Spirit of praise, which will, I hope, ere long be poured forth upon the sons and daughters of Zion. And then they will praise Jehovah, singing to the Lord a new song and his praise in the congregation of saints, as is prophesied (Psalms 149:1–2, 5; Isaiah 51:11; 52:1, 8, etc.).

The Holy Spirit can dictate the matter, yea, and words of praise and singing, as well as the matter and words of prayer. And why may not the Lord assist a poor gracious humble soul to sing in the spirit, as well as to pray in the spirit, seeing there [is] nothing too hard for God to do? It was by many, and is still by some, denied that there is any such thing as a spiritual gift of prayer, save only that which is acquired. And yet the gracious experience of many godly persons does testify that there is such a gift of the Spirit, called a spirit of supplication, which is powered forth upon the Lord's people. And although many, nay most godly Christians do not believe there is any such spiritual gift as singing as I have intimated, yet some few poor gracious humble souls have good experience that there is sometimes a measure of the Holy Spirit powered upon them, whereby they are so filled with the Spirit that they break forth into singing. Pray therefore that you may sing and praise the Lord when the redeemed of the Lord shall return and come with singing to Zion (Isaiah 51:11). And the children of Zion be joyful in their King (Psalm 149:1). Unto whom be glory and dominion forever, Amen. So prays he who waits for his kingdom and coming.

HANSERD KNOLLYS

THE BAPTISTS' ANSWER TO MR. OBED [OBADIAH] WILLS, HIS APPEAL AGAINST MR. H. DANVERS

(London, May 13, 1675)

INTRODUCTION

In 1675, Hanserd Knollys coauthored *The Baptists' Answer to Mr. Obed. [Obadiah] Wills, his Appeal against Mr. H. Danvers.*[1] The occasion of the pamphlet was a renewed anti-paedobaptism controversy of the mid-1670s. A central figure in the debate was Henry Danvers (c. 1619–1687/88), who in 1673 published his *Treatise of Baptism.*[2] Within the year, the Puritan divine Obadiah Wills published a pointed retort entitled *Infant-Baptisme Asserted* (1674).[3] The debate between Danvers and Wills continued the next

[1] Hanserd Knollys, et al., *The Baptists answer to Mr. Obed. Wills, his appeal against Mr. H. Danvers* (London: Printed for Francis Smith, 1675). Knollys' name appears first; the additional five signatories are William Kiffin (1616–1701), Daniel Dyke (1614–1688), John Gosnold (1626?–1678), Henry Forty (?), and Thomas Delaune (d. 1685). Their names can be found on the last page of the pamphlet.

[2] Henry Danvers, *A treatise of baptism wherein that of believers and that of infants is examined by the Scriptures, with the history of both out of antiquity: making it appear that infants baptism was not practiced for near 300 years after Christ ... and that the famous Waldensian and old British churches and Christians witnessed against it: with the examination of the stories about Thomas Munzer, and John a Leyden: as also, the history of Christianity amongst the ancient Britains and Waldenses: and, a brief answer to Mr. Bunyan about communion with persons unbaptized* (London: Printed for Francis Smith, 1673); On Danvers see Richard L. Greaves, *Saints and Rebels: Seven Nonconformists in Stuart England* (Macon: Mercer University Press, 1985); for a discussion of Danvers' *A Treatise of Baptism* see, James M. Renihan, "Henry Danvers' *A Treatise of Baptism*: A Study in Seventeenth-Century Baptist Historiography," *BRT/RBT* 7, no. 1–2 (Spring/Fall 1997): 27–47.

[3] Obed [Obadiah] Wills, *Infant-baptism asserted & vindicated by Scripture and antiquity in answer to a treatise of baptism lately published by Mr. Henry Danvers: together with a full detection of his misrepresentations of divers councils and authors both ancient and modern: with a just censur of his essay to palliate the horrid actings of the anabaptists in Germany: as also a perswasive to unity among all Christians, though of different judgments*

year, as Danvers published his *Innocency and Truth Vindicated* (1675) and Wills responded with *Vindiciae vindiciarum* (1675).[4] Annexed to this last work was Wills' *Appeal*, which provoked Knollys and other Baptist leaders to issue this rejoinder.[5] In the *Appeal*, Wills accused Danvers of "abusing" and

---

about baptism (London: Printed by Jonathan Robinson, 1674). The Puritan minister Obadiah Wills has seldom attracted the attention of modern scholars. Here is what Edmund Calamy in his *Account* of the ejected and silenced ministers had to say about him: "This Mr. Wills was M.A. of the University of Oxford, a good scholar, and particularly well skilled in the Hebrew tongue on which he bestowed much study. He was a pious man, and very serious and excellent in prayer, but was not to be persuaded to preach, though he was ordained, and had made some little trial. After he came from the university, he lived many years in a private family as chaplain, where he only read the Scripture, and prayed. Having thus spent his youth and middle age, when he came to be advanced in years, and was by Dr. Grew and others, much solicited to preach, he could not be prevailed with. He thought himself so unfit and unable to study and preach, that he seemed quite discouraged from attempting either. He blamed himself for rashness in yielding to be ordained, and ascribed it to the persuasions of others. After Dr. Grew's death he removed to an estate he had at Stratton in Northamptonshire, where he died a few years ago." Edmund Calamy, *A Continuation of the Account of the Ministers, Lecturers, Masters and Fellows of Colleges, and Schoolmasters, who were Ejected and Silenced after the Restoration in 1660, by or before the Act of Uniformity* (London: Printed for R. Ford, 1727) 2:853; it is from Edmund Calamy (1671–1732) that we gather Wills' full name, Obadiah Wills. See Calamy, *A Continuation*, 2:878.

[4] Henry Danvers, *Innocency and truth vindicated, or, A sober reply to Mr. Wills' answer to a late treatise of baptisme wherein the authorities and antiquities for believers and against infants baptism are defended... with a brief answer to Mr. Blinmans essay* ([London]: Printed for Francis Smith, 1675); Obed [Obadiah] Wills, *Vindiciae vindiciarum, or, A vindication of a late treatise, entituled, Infant-baptism asserted and vindicated by Scripture and antiquity in answer to Mr. Hen. D'Anvers his reply: to which is annexed, the Right Reverend Dr. Barlow (now Bishop-elect of Lincoln) his apologetical-letter: also An appeal to the Baptists (so called) against Mr. Danvers, for his strange forgeries, and misrepresentations of divers councils and authors, both antient and modern / by Obed Wills* (London: Printed for Jonathan Robinson, 1675).

[5] The *Appeal* is missing from the copy of *Vindiciae vindiciarum* located at Union Theological Seminary, which was used for the microfilm collection *Early English Books*, and subsequently for *Early English Books Online*. The *Appeal*, however, can be found in the copy of *Vindiciae vindiciarum* housed in Harvard University's Houghton Library. See Obed [Obadiah] Wills, *An Appeal to the Baptists against Henry D'Anvers, Esq.* (London: Printed for Jonathan Robinson at the Golden-Lion in St. Paul's Church-yard, 1675) [155]–197. The *Appeal* appears with a separate title page, with errors in pagination, as part of *Vindiciae vindiciarum* (London, 1675) bound-copy with Obed [Obadiah] Wills, *Infant-baptism asserted and vindicated* (London, 1674) call number Houghton C 1396.65.

"misquoting" his sources.[6] Wills organized the *Appeal* into eight charges, all of which, with the exception of the last two, accused Danvers of misrepresenting his sources.[7] Danvers' poor handling of documentary sources was widely noted and gave his opponents ample opportunity for criticism. In fact, in the *Answer*, Knollys and his colleagues acknowledged Danvers' oversights. However, they also undertook to demonstrate that their coreligionist was fundamentally correct in many of his assertions. The authors checked the original sources and repeatedly found Wills guilty of more distortions and omissions in his citations of texts than Danvers. *The Baptists answer* was evidently written in haste, and its poor stylistic qualities obscure the Baptists' engagement with numerous scholarly sources. Other apologists of paedobaptism took issue with Danvers, including Richard Baxter (1615–1691) and William Wall (1647–1728).[8] Wills continued the controversy, and the next year he published a retort against Knollys and his friends, *Censura censurae* (1676).[9] The notes of the present edition seek to bring to light some of the intellectual complexities of the debate.

[6] Wills, *Appeal*, 159.

[7] "Mr. Danvers leaving out part of what his authors say, to make the sentence move for his purpose [p. 160]; Adding to authors without the distinction of a different character [p. 164]; Making his authors affirm one thing, when they affirm the directly contrary, yea contradicting himself [p. 169]; Perverting the sense of his authors, by the falseness of his translations [p. 175]; Fathering upon authors that which indeed they say not, at least in the places by him quoted [p. 180]; Picking out of authors here and there and joyning them together, as if they were one entire sentence [p. 184]; Asserting notorious untruths [p. 184]; Strange doctrines [p. 192]." Wills, *Appeal*, 160–192.

[8] Richard Baxter, "A Confutation of the Strange Forgeries of Mr. H. Danvers, Against the Antiquity of Infant Baptism," in *More proofs of infants church-membership and consequently their right to baptism, or, A second defense of our infant rights and mercies in three parts* (London: Printed for N. Simmons and J. Robinson, 1675) [183]–339; Wall's *History of Infant-Baptism* was first published in 1705 and went through several editions, see William Wall, *The History of Infant-Baptism*, ed. Henry Cotton, 4 vols. (Oxford: The University Press, 1835) here 2:45.

[9] Obed [Obadiah] Wills, *Censura censurae, or, A just censure of the unjust sentence of the Baptists upon an appeal made against Mr. Henry D'Anvers by Obed Wills* (London: Printed for Jonath Robinson, 1676).

THE BAPTISTS' ANSWER TO MR. OBED [OBADIAH] WILLS, HIS APPEAL AGAINST MR. H. DANVERS

(London, May 13, 1675)

Sir,

We have seriously considered your *Appeal* against Mr. Danvers, and have also heard and carefully weighed the *Defense* he makes thereto; and in order to give an impartial judgment, as you call us to do, have desired some of our number diligently to examine the authors cited by you both—although it appears to us that Mr. Danvers has earnestly endeavored an accommodation in a more private and friendly manner between you and him in order to rectify mistakes on any hand, which—had it been accepted—might have saved this trouble. The method you have used in this *Appeal* is unusual and unlike the pattern you seem to take—an appeal in these cases being then only proper when the party appealed against appears to be so contumacious and stubborn as to reject and stand out against just conviction and admonition, which we find not to be justly chargeable upon Mr. Danvers, and whether it be not rather your own oversight we hope you will in time be sensible of—yet, we say we shall not insist upon that consideration. In order to give you and the world that satisfaction expected from us, some of us whose names are subscribed have examined the particulars you charge him with and find some mistakes and escapes[1] on Mr. Danvers' side, which he ingeniously acknowledges and we hope may be to your full satisfaction as it cannot—in justice—but be to ours, since, as you seem to hint, a public owning is what you expect.

Some of the particulars in your *Appeal* we find to be so trivial and insignificant that they deserve not to be mentioned, and deem his answers respectively sufficient to satisfy the reader. Other of your charges he traverses

---

[1] *Oxford English Dictionary Online*, s.v. "escape," "an inadvertence, blunder, mistake; esp. a clerical or printer's error. Obs." The earliest recorded use of the term in this sense dates to 1570. See *Oxford English Dictionary Online* (Oxford: Oxford University Press, 2014) s.v. "† escape, n.1," http://www.oed.com/view/Entry/64236?rskey=C05IvB& result=1 (accessed December 05, 2014).

and joins issue with you at the bar you have brought it to, and the most material of these we now remark to you so that what he acknowledges, and what's inconsiderable, and what's here further examined comprehends your whole *Appeal*.

And we must observe to you, that you lie obnoxious to the return you made to Mr. Danvers[2] when he charged you with leaving out part of the sentence of Naziansus, namely, *si aliquid periculi immineat*, calling it on page seven of your *Vindication* "a frivolous charge," excusing yourself after such a manner as you will not be satisfied with from others.[3] Therefore, if we say many of your charges are frivolous, your reason in your own behalf will justify us, you being judge.

I

And therefore, we desire you to consider whether the stopping your translation out of Calvin where you did, on page 162 [of the] *Appeal*, be not unfair and misleading to an English reader.

II

You charge Colonel Danvers [in the] *Appeal* (p. 166) to add the words, "for it cannot be, that the body should receive the sacrament of baptism till the soul has before received the truth of faith," and say they are not Jerome's words, but of Mr. Danvers' adding. But upon examination of that place (Mat. 28, tom. 9, edit. Paris. an. 1546) we find them to be Jerome's words verbatim, as Mr. Danvers cites them.[4] And we observe in your quotation of Mr. Danvers, in that place you add, "*Magdeburg Centuries* 4, c. 6, 418," as if

---

[2] The phrasing is obscure. Presumably the authors are saying that his response to Danvers is obnoxious.

[3] St. Gregory of Nazianzus (c. 330–c. 389) friend of Basil, Bishop of Caesarea, was a champion of Nicene orthodoxy against Arianism and a leading voice at the Council of Constantinople (381); Wills, *Vindiciae vindiciarum*, 7.

[4] Indeed, the particular statement in question belongs to Jerome: "Primum docent omnes gentes, deinde doctas intingunt aqua. *Non enim potest fieri ut corpus baptismi recipiat sacramentum, nisi ante anima fidei susceperit veritatem.* Baptizantur autem in nomine Patris, et Filii, et Spiritus sancti, ut quorum una est divinitas, una sit largitio: nomenque Trinitatis, unus Deus est." Italics added for emphasis: "it cannot be that the body receives the sacrament of baptism if the soul does not first receive the truth of faith." Hieronymus Stridonensis, *Commentariorum in Evangelium Matthaei ad Eusebium libri quatuor*, PL 26, col. 218 B-C; The reference is to Charlotte Guillard's (d. 1557) edition of Jerome's works, *D. Hieronymi Opera Omnia*, 9 vols. (Paris: [C. Guillard], 1533–1546). At the time she was married to the printer Claude Chevallon (d. 1537).

Mr. Danvers had particularly quoted the *Magdeburg Centuries* there, which indeed he does not; but only Jerome upon Matthew, which double injury we conceive deserves your double consideration in order to a candid acknowledgment.[5]

III

You charge him [on] page 169 with abusing Calvin, fathering Estius' words upon him, though he hath owned it a mistake in his *Reply*. But we observe also that he quotes "Estius, *Annot. Gen. 17, 7*" at the end, which you leave out, though you took all his words to that, and yet reprove him so often for the same, which seems neither ingenious nor fair.[6]

IV

You charge him with abusing Dr. Hammond (p. 107 [sic, p. 170]) in affirming that, "βαπτίσμος signifies an immersion, or washing the whole body, answering the Hebrew בִילָהטְ," whereas you say the Dr. "tells us [λούσεις][7] signifies the washing the whole body, and answers to טְבִילָה, etc."[8]

---

[5] The *Magdeburg Centuries*, the first major ecclesiastical history published by Protestants, appeared in print between 1559 and 1574, *Ecclesiastica Historia: Integram ecclesiae Christi ideam, quantum ad locum, propagationem, persecutionem, tranquillitatem, doctrinam, haereses, ceremonias… & statum imperii politicum attinet, secundum singulas centurias… ex… historicis, patribus, & aliis scriptoribus congesta; Per aliquot studiosos & pios uiros in urbe Magdeburgica* (Basel: Oporinus, 1559–1574).

[6] The reference is to Guilielmus Estius [i.e., Willem Hesselszoon van Est, 1542–1613], *Annotationes in praecipua ac difficiliora sacrae scripturae loca* (Douai: Typis viduae et heredum Petri Borremans, 1621) and subsequent editions among them, *Annotationes aureae in praecipua ac difficiliora Sacrae Scripturae loca* (Cologne: Johann Crith von Witwe, 1622). Hesselszoon van Hest was professor and later chancellor at the University of Douay. For more on Estius see the insightful discussion found in Wim François, "Augustine and the Golden Age of Biblical Scholarship in Louvain (1550–1650)," in *Shaping the Bible in the Reformation: Books, Scholars and their Readers in the Sixteenth Century*, ed. Bruce Gordon and Matthew McLean (Leiden: Brill, 2012) 235–290, here 262–271.

[7] Both Hammond (1653) and Wills (1675) provide the Greek term λόσεις, while Hammond (1845) provides the correct λούσεις, from λούω, "I bathe." See Henry Hammond, *A paraphrase, and annotations upon all the books of the New Testament briefly explaining all the difficult places thereof* (London: Printed by J. Flesher for Richard Royston, 1653); Hammond, *A Paraphrase and Annotations upon all the Books of the New Testament, Briefly Explaining all the Difficult Places Thereof* (Oxford: The University Press, 1845) 3:328; BDAG, 603.

[8] "Mr. Danvers tells us the Doctor saith, Baptismos signifies an immersion or washing of the whole body and answers to the Hebrew word טְבִילָה. Whereas indeed he

We have examined the Doctor's book, printed for R. Royston, anno 1653 and find Mr. Danvers quoted his words truly, and the mistake to be yours, which we hope will convince you of the untrue and unjust reproach you subjoin that he understands not English authors, etc.

V

You charge Mr. Danvers for affirming from Walden that the Wicklevians, in agreement to the doctrine of Pelagius and others, denied infant baptism.[9] He acknowledges it to be his mistake to allege that it was agreeable to Pelagius and others, said to be for infant baptism. But if Walden is to be believed, it appears that the Wicliffists [i.e. Wycliffites] judged ecclesiastical baptism unprofitable to little ones, in these words: "nostri Wiclivistae baptismum ecclesiasticum inutile judicant parvulis contra omnes predictos."[10] [That is,] against all the aforesaid, [to be sure] Pelagius, Vincentius, Victor and those that baptized children as born of believing parents. And we must remark to you that in your quotation on page 172 of

---

tells us that λόσεις [sic., λούσεις] signifies the washing of the whole body, and answers to טְבִילָה. And that Baptismos signifies the washing of a part, as the hands or feet. No wonder Mr. Danvers mistakes Latin authors so often, when he cannot rightly understand those that are in English." Wills, *An Appeal*, 170–171. It appears, nevertheless, that, as the London Baptists indicated, Danvers was correct in his reading of Hammond. See Hammond (1653): "The Hebrews had their βαπτισμὸς, or λόσεις [sic., λούσεις], and their νίψεις [νίπτω, "I wash"], the former, washing of the whole body, which they call טְבִילָה, the other [Hammond (1845) 3:328, "the other two"], of the hands or feet, which they call קדוש, sanctifying." Hammond, *A Paraphrase* (1653) 340.

[9] Wiclevian(s) or Wicliffites, from the Latin form *Witclevistas* as used by Thomas Netter in the fifteenth century, followers of John Wyclif (d. 1384); Walden, i.e., Thomas Netter of Walden (c. 1374–1430) theologian and Carmelite friar, opposed to John Wyclif (d. 1384) the Lollards, and Hussites. He wrote the *Doctrinale fidei ecclesiae* sometime between 1428 and 1430, a voluminous refutation of Wyclif's doctrines. The *Doctrinale fidei ecclesiae* appeared in print in the sixteenth century, first in Paris (1521–1523) and then in Venice (1571) see Thomas Netter, *Tomus primus doctrinalis fidei ecclesiae catholicae contra Witclevistas et Hussitas: eorum[que] sectatores* ([Paris]: Josse Badius, 1532). For more on Walden see Kevin J. Alban, *The Teaching and Impact of the Doctrinale of Thomas Netter of Walden (c. 1374–1430)* (Turnhout: Brepols, 2010); Anne Hudson, "Netter, Thomas (*c.*1370–1430)," in *Oxford Dictionary of National Biography*, edited by H. C. G. Matthew and Brian Harrison (Oxford: Oxford University Press, 2004). Online ed., edited by Lawrence Goldman, May 2008. http://www.oxforddnb.com/view/article/19907 (accessed December 5, 2014).

[10] "In contrast to all the aforesaid, our Wicliffites consider ecclesiastical baptism of little ones to be unprofitable."

the *Appeal*, you leave out "parvulis" the principal word there, and with what design or end we leave you to consider.

VI

You charge him on pages 179 and 180 for adding the words "it is our will, that all that affirm that young children receive everlasting life, albeit they be not by the sacrament of grace or baptism renewed" to the *Milevitan Decree*.[11] We have examined that 4th tom. in *Collect. Reg.*[12] and find the canon quoted by Mr. Danvers on page 559 of it, taken out of a very ancient copy, immediately following the words you cite, thus: "Item placuit, ut si quis dicit, ideo dixisse Dominum, 'In domo Patris mei mansiones multae sunt,' ut intelligatur, quia in regno caelorum erit aliquis medius aut ullus alicubi locus, ubi beati vivant parvuli qui sine baptismo ex hac vita migrarunt, sine quo in regnum caelorum, quod est vita aeterna, intrare non possunt, anathema sit, an. Christi 424."[13] Now for you to affirm that the said

[11] Two significant councils were held in the fifth century in the ancient city of Milevum in Numidia (the modern day city of Mila in Algeria). The first was convened in 402 and the second in 416, known in Latin documents as Concilium Milevitanum I and II, respectively.

[12] This source is uncertain.

[13] The statement in question, i.e. "it is our will, that all that affirm, that young children receive everlasting life, albeit they be not by the sacrament of grace or baptism renewed," bears some similarities to two conciliar canons of the churches in north Africa. The first one is the second canon of the second Milevitan Council (416): "Item placuit, ut quicumque parvulos recentes ab uteris matrum baptizandos negat, aut dicit, in remissionem quidem peccatorum eos baptizari, sed nihil ex Adam trahere originalis peccati, quod regenerationis lavacro expietur: unde fit consequens, ut in eis forma baptismatis, in remissionem peccatorum, non vere, sed false intelligatur, anathema sit" (English trans.): ["Likewise that whosoever denies that infants newly from their mother's womb should be baptized, or says that baptism is for remission of sins, but that they derive from Adam no original sin, which is removed by the laver of regeneration, whence the conclusion follows that in them the form of baptism for the remission of sins is to be understood as false and not true, let him be anathema"]. This canon was included among the canons of the Council of Carthage of 418, as the second canon, and among the canons of the Council of Carthage of 424, as canon 77. In addition, a similar wording can be found in the third canon of the Council of Carthage of 418, and in a different version of canon 77 of the Council of Carthage of 424. It reads as follows: "Item placuit, ut si quis dicit ideo dixisse Dominum: In domo Patris mei mansiones multae sunt, ut intelligatur, quia in regno coelorum erit aliquis medius aut ullus alicubi locus, ubi beate vivant parvuli, *qui sine baptismo ex hac vita migrarunt, sine quo in regnum caelorum, quod est vita aeterna, intrare non possunt, anathema sit* (emphasis added)" (English trans.): ["Likewise, if someone says that

clause was of Mr. Danvers' own adding, whereas, as he says, here is an express anathema against those that affirmed children might be saved without baptism, is an instance—to give the most favorable conjecture of it—that you have made but a lame search. So that it is very just for us to acquit Mr. Danvers of this charge.

We presume you know that the *Magdeburg* [writers] give an account when they speak of that Milevitan Synod of some that affirmed infants' salvation without baptism, as by the instances Mr. Danvers gives from them undeniably appears. And in opposition to them was that anathema enacted and every circumstance concurs to evidence it as genuine as the other canons, and therefore upon a review of the place we question not but you will be satisfied here is no forgery or prevarication in Mr. Danvers in this particular.

---

the Lord said, 'In my father's house there are many dwelling places,' [John 14:2] so that it would be understood that in the kingdom of heaven there will be some intermediate place or some other place, where little ones who departed this life without baptism live blessed, without which [i.e. baptism] in the kingdom of heaven, which is eternal life, to enter is not possible, let him be anathema"]. This last canon was for long wrongly attributed to one of the Milevitan councils. Knollys and his colleagues argued that Danvers was citing the third canon of the Council of Carthage of 418, and 77 of some version of the Council of Carthage of 424. However, the statement bears a closer resemblance to a fragment from a letter by Pope Innocent I (r. 402–417) "Inter ceteras Ecclesiae Romanae," of January 27, 417. In his response to the Milevitan Council of 416, he stated: "...parvulos aeternae vitae praemiis etiam sine baptismatis gratia posse donari, perfatuum est" (English trans.): ["[that] young children have eternal life as reward even without the grace of baptism, is a treachery"]. For the second canon of the Milevitan Council of 416 see *Concilium Milevitanum II*, in *Sacrorum conciliorum nova et amplissima collectio*, ed. Giovanni Domenico Mansi (Florence: Antonii Zatta Veneti, 1760) vol. 4, col. 327; for the second and third canon of the Council of Carthage of 418 see Heinrich Denzinger and Peter Hünermann, *El magisterio de la Iglesia. Enchiridion symbolorum definitionum et declarationum de rebus fidei et morum*, 38th ed. (Barcelona: Herder, 2000) 129–133, pa. 223 and 224; for both versions of canon 77 of the Council of Carthage of 424 see *Concilium Africanum*, in Mansi, *Sacrorum conciliorum*, vol. 4, col. 504; for Pope Innocent I's letter "Inter ceteras Ecclesiae Romanae," see Denzinger, *El magisterio de la Iglesia/Enchiridion*, 128, pa. 219; For the English translation of the second canon of the second Milevitan Council (416) or second canon of the Council of Carthage (418) see Joseph Cullen Ayer, *A Source Book for Ancient Church History, from the Apostolic Age to the Close of the Conciliar Period* (New York: Charles Scribner's Sons, 1922) 464; The English translations of the third canon of the Council of Carthage of 418, or 77 of some versions of the Council of Carthage of 424, as well as of the fragment from Pope Innocent I's "Inter ceteras Ecclesiae Romanae" have been provided by the editors.

VII

Under the head of his "fathering upon authors that which they say not," you charge him with abusing Basil (*Appeal*, p. 181) in fathering those words upon him: "must the faithful be sealed with Baptism? Faith must precede, and go before." Whereas you say "there is no such speech in what the *Magdeburg* repeat of" Basil's *Contra Eunomium*, which we conceive to be a very weak ground for your charge.[14] For must it follow that the words are not Basil's because you find it not in the *Magdeburg*? We have searched Basil, and found his words to be lib. 3, p. 84, *Contra Eunomium* to the sense he is cited by Mr. Danvers, viz. "Πιστεῦσαι γὰρ δει πρότερον, ἐῖτα τῷ Βαπτίσματι ἐπισφραγίσασθαι," i.e. "It is necessary first to believe, and afterwards to be signed with baptism."[15] So, that this is also your own error and oversight.

VIII

You charge him with a notorious untruth on page 185, for affirming from the *Magdeburg* that Gulielmus added the Virgin Mary to the form of baptism. We have examined the *Magdeburg Centuries,* 13 (p. 419, cap. 4, edit. Basil, anno 1574), and find the words, "Malè Gulielmus ad formam baptismi addidit Mariam: Baptizo te in nomine patris omnipotentis, & filii, & spiritus sancti, & beate Marie virginis," as cited by Mr. Danvers, and therefore for you to affirm the contrary is a gross mistake.[16]

And thus, Sir, we have given a true and impartial representation of the particulars as we find them, being, as we conceive, the principal matters under our cognizance, omitting the less material, and do recommend them

[14] Basil the Great (329–379) Bishop of Caesarea, wrote *Contra Eunomium* c. 360, see Stephen M. Hildebrand, "A Reconsideration of the Development of Basil's Trinitarian Theology: The Dating of Ep. 9 and 'Contra Eunomium'," *Vigiliae Christianae* 58, no. 4 (2004): 393–406.

[15] The statement in fact belongs to Basil, Bishop of Caesarea, and it appears in the third book of *Contra Eunobius*: "Πιστεῦσαι γὰρ δει πρότερον, ἐῖτα τῷ Βαπτίσματι ἐπισφραγίσασθαι" (English trans.): ["For one must first believe, then be stamped with baptism"]. See Basillii Magni, *Libri quibus impii Eunomii apologeticus evertitur* [i.e. *Adversus Eunomium L. III.v*], PG 29, col. 665. The edition used by the London Baptists remains uncertain.

[16] Here again, the London Baptists were accurate in their assertion: "Malè Gulielmus ad formam baptismi addit Mariam: Baptizo te in nomine patris omnipotentis, & filii, & spiritus sancti, & beate Mariae virginis, & huiusmodi, non impeditur baptismus." *Decimatertia centuria, Ecclesiasticae historiae...* (Basileae [Basel]: Ex Officina Oporiniana [Oporinus], 1574) col. 419.

to your Christian consideration, hoping that your serious review of them will discover them to be your errors. And as Mr. Danvers has publicly owned what of mistake he is convinced of in his *Answer* to your *Appeal*, so it is justly expected you will also, according to your promise in the "Preface" to your *Appeal*, do the same in these particulars. And since your charges do not appear to be true to the satisfaction of all impartial persons, but on the contrary great mistakes on your side, you will not, we hope, think it unjust if we acquit him, and reflect the blame of the charge upon yourself, as you desire, in case you be found in the error. The particulars Mr. Danvers owns in his said *Answer* to your *Appeal*, we bring not under our discussion or censure, concluding it to be enough that he acknowledges them.

And such petty charges as he sufficiently answers, and are indeed of little weight, save to enhance the number of your particulars, as also things controverted, and only collateral to the grand proposition in dispute—as are those things you call strange doctrines, etc.—we think do not so properly offer themselves to our considerations. And therefore we conclude we may be excused if we wave them.

And lastly, we propose, that if the return we give to your *Appeal* should be deemed insufficient by you, or short in any thing, which we are not conscious of, and that thereupon you take yourself concerned to appear any further in this controversy, you would be persuaded that things may be transacted in an amicable and friendly way, which we hope may tend to our mutual satisfaction in the clearing up of truth, and to cherish that love, that all that fear the Lord should bear each other, though differing in some things, which is our very earnest desire, and to promote which, we shall endeavor to contribute the utmost we can.

London, the 13th of the 5th month, 1675.
Hanserd Knollys
William Kiffin
Daniel Dyke
John Gosnold
Henry Forty
Thomas Delaune

MYSTICAL BABYLON AVAILED

(London, 1679)

INTRODUCTION

The years after Knollys' self-imposed exile in the Netherlands and Germany, and leading to his death on September 19, 1691, were less eventful for him in spite of the difficulties generally faced by Nonconformists under the Clarendon Code.[1] In fact, the greater part of Knollys' literary output was published in the decades following the Restoration. He became intensely engaged with biblical literature of an apocalyptical character, and his millenarianism was certainly a response to the new political realities faced by Baptists after 1660. Indeed, Knollys articulated his apocalyptic views in a series of works that appeared between 1667 and 1689. Among them were two treatises that he published in 1679, namely *An exposition of the 11th Chapter of Revelation wherein all those things therein revealed, which must shortly come to pass, are explained* (London, 1679) and *Mystical Babylon availed, wherein is proved, I. That Rome-papal is mystical-Babylon, II. That the pope of Rome is the beast, III. That the Church of Rome is the great whore, IV. That the Roman-priests are the false prophet; Also, a call to the people of God to come out of Babylon* (London, 1679).

He composed the 1679 pamphlets during a time of heightened national anti-Roman Catholic frenzy. On September 6, 1678, Titus Oates (1649–1705) broke out news of an alleged Catholic conspiracy to assassinate King Charles II. The conspiracy, which became known as the Popish Plot, involved replacing the King with his Roman Catholic brother, James, Duke of York.[2] On September 28, 1678, Oates stated his allegations before the Privy Council in the presence of the King. Then, on October 17 the magistrate Sir Edmund Godfrey was found dead. Matters were compounded

---

[1] Collective designation for the *Corporation Act* (1661), the *Act of Uniformity* (1662), the *Conventicle Act* (1664), and the *Five Mile Act* (1665).

[2] For more on the "Popish Plot" see J. P. Kenyon, *The Popish Plot* (London: Heinemann, 1972); Richard L. Greaves, *Secrets of the Kingdom: British Radicals from the Popish Plot to the Revolution of 1688-89* (Stanford: Stanford University Press, 1992).

by the false testimony of the silversmith Miles Prance, who claimed to have witnessed the assassination of Sir Godfrey by hired hands in the presence of a Catholic priest.[3] The idea of a Catholic conspiracy to kill the King and reintroduce "popery" made Knollys inquire about the nature and character of the Church of Rome. He addressed this question in *Mystical Babylon availed.*

Knollys' argument in *Mystical Babylon availed* is extremely convoluted. One of his central contentions is stated in his second proposition, namely "that the pope of Rome is the beast." He is referring to the mythical beast described in Revelation 17:1–11. According to John the Seer he witnessed a scarlet beast with seven heads and ten horns. Of major significance for Knollys' interpretation of the beast are verses eight and eleven. In verse eight the Seer describes the beast as one that "was, and is not, and is about to ascend from the bottomless pit and go to destruction." Then in verse eleven the Seer again refers to the beast as "the beast that was and is not, it is an eighth but it belongs to the seven, and it goes to destruction."

For Knollys the beast described by the Seer is the papacy. Accordingly, the Seer's description found in verse eight refers to the continuity between the Roman Empire and the papacy. In a particular sense the beast was in a way that it is no longer, and at the same time it still is. In Knollys' words, the Roman Empire "was formerly, and even in St John's time, what it is not, now in our time." For him this particular way of being is defined by political power: "The Roman kingdom was then a power ordained of God." That is the Roman Empire was a legitimate political entity. He adduces the death of Jesus as evidence of its duly ordained character: "unto which Roman power our blessed savior Jesus Christ being then in the form of a servant was obedient to death." The Roman Empire was at the time of Jesus and the Apostles "God's ordinance of magistracy," even in spite of its persecution of Christ and Christians.

He then introduces the way in which the beast is not what it was. Invoking Revelation 13:2—"And the dragon gave it his power and his throne and great authority"—Knollys asserts that the power of the Roman Empire was transferred to the papacy. However, the papacy is not God's ordinance of magistracy; nor is it "a power ordained by God." He argues that this transfer of power occurred as an outcome of the investiture conflict

[3] Miles Prance, *A true narrative and discovery of several very remarkable passages relating to the horrid popish plot as they fell within the knowledge of Mr. Miles Prance* (Dublin, reprinted: no printer, 1679) 8–9.

between Emperor Henry V (r. 1111–1125) and Pope Paschal II (r. 1099–1118). In Knollys own words: "The Pope would not consent to his coronation until the emperor did give over all right of election of popes, and of investitures of bishops by staff and ring. And thus the pope gained the power of temporal sovereignty, and so is of the seven." Of course the resolution of the conflict that he is describing was not reached under Pope Paschal II, but with the Concordat of Worms of 1122 between Henry V and Pope Calixtus II (1119–1124). It is for these reasons that Knollys concludes that the papacy is the usurper of power par excellence. Again, he asserts that the papacy is not God's ordinance of magistracy, nor is it a "lawful power ordained of God." Later, he concludes that the "beast (the pope of Rome) hath the Roman power, but not *jure divino*, he is not by God's approbation." It is crucial that modern readers understand the historical context in which this tract was produced and not to misappropriate its content in a time of greater ecumenical harmony.

MYSTICAL BABYLON AVAILED[1]

(London, 1679)

Epistle to the Reader

Ingenuous Reader,

It is an astonishment beyond the ordinary comprehensions of nature, reason, and religion that the papists—especially the priests and Jesuits of the Church of Rome—so odious in their bloody tenets, so prodigious in their hellish plots, such inexecrable incendiaries, and furious assassins for murdering of princes, should be suffered to increase, and indulged to multiply in a Protestant nation, as of late years they have done in this kingdom.[2] Assuredly, it could never have been so, but that the Lord in his just indignation against us for our God-provoking sins of atheism, idolatry, profaneness, adultery, and other heinous wickedness, intends and suffers us to ripen and be prepared for some dreadful judgment; which God may justly bring upon this land and nation by the hand of the papists, if we repent not of those abominations, and do not reform them.

It is more than manifest by woeful experience that the main end of the papists in all their plots and conspiracies is the utter destruction of the protestants—whom they call heretics—and the Protestant religion in England especially, and the reestablishment of the popish religion of the Church of Rome in this kingdom; which end the popish recusants[3] in

---

[1] Hanserd Knollys, *Mystical Babylon availed wherein is proved, I. That Rome-papal is mystical-Babylon, II. That the pope of Rome is the beast, III. That the Church of Rome is the great whore, IV. That the Roman-priests are the false prophet: also A call to the people of God to come out of Babylon* (London: no printer, 1679). At the bottom of page: "Isa. 57. 14. *Take up the stumbling-block out of the way of my People.* Rev. 18. 6. *Reward her even as she Rewarded you.*" The specimen found in the Henry E. Huntington Library is the source that was used for *Early English Books Online* and, therefore, the one used for this edition. However, due to the imperfections of the Huntington specimen, the present edition was checked against the one found at the Beinecke Library, Yale University, call no. Mhc8 1679 K76.

[2] Knollys is here referring to the Popish Plot (see the introduction to this tract). See Robert Bucholz and Newton Key, *Early Modern England, 1685–1714: A Narrative History*, 2nd ed. (Oxford: Wiley-Blackwell, 2009) 295.

[3] Recusants were Roman Catholics who "refused" (from the Latin *recuso*) to be present at the services of the Church of England or to comply with the religious regulations

England—in this bloody and traitorous design, that damnable and hellish plot contrived and carried on by them for assassinating and murdering the King, subverting the government, and for rooting out and destroying the Protestant religion, as the King and Parliament have voted and declared[4]—are still endeavoring to effect, and bring to pass. The concurrent fury of our grand and greatest enemies in the world durst not entertain a thought of invasion, did they not hope—when time serves—to find amongst us a side and faction of numerous and seditious papists to join with them. Were we rid of the papists and were idolatry, atheism, whoredom, and blasphemy put away as in policy, reason, and religion these ought to be, the royal person of the King would be safe from assassination, and the government secure from subversion. And the Protestants, and Protestant religion free from utter destruction by the blessed protection of almighty God. Conformity unto all oaths, tests, and outward formal satisfactions of state, concurring with[5] a full resolution to continue in the popish religion of the Church of Rome is far more pernicious to the state, than open and professed recusancy. Papists, that can do so, either by power of some popish dispensation—which rich and noble men may easily procure—or by some mental reservation—which many of this popish equivocating generation have learned of the Jesuits and Roman priests—or by some promises of the pope's pardon for so doing, that may easily be obtained. I say again, such conformable papists are more pernicious to the state, King and kingdom, than open and professed

---

of the established church. See Michael Questier, "Conformity, Catholicism and the Law," in *Conformity and Orthodoxy in the English Church, c. 1560-1660*, ed. Peter Lake and Michael Questier (Woodbridge: The Boydell Press, 2000) 237–261, here 239.

[4] See among others, *An impartial account of divers remarkable proceedings in the last sessions of Parliament relating to the horrid Popish Plot, etc. Viz. The manner of choosing their speaker. The speeches of divers worthy members, relating to that. The vote of the House at large in defence of the King, and the Protestant religion. The articles of impeachment against the five Lords in the Tower. The articles of impeachment against Thomas Earl of Danby, and his letter. The Earl of Danby's pardon in Latin and English, and his plea. The reasons and narrative of the proceedings betwixt the two Houses of Parliament, concerning the Lords in the Tower, etc. The proceedings of the House of Lords, concerning the Lords in the Tower, and the names of those Lords that entered their protest. A copy of the bill relating to the Duke of York. The Earl of Shaftsburies speech in the House of Lords. Mr. Powel's speech concerning the Earl of Danby. Mr. Palme's report about the temporary laws* (London: no printer, 1679).

[5] The section starting at this point and stretching to the end of the "Epistle to the Reader" is missing in the digitized version of the text found in *Early English Books Online*. For the present edition we have relied on the seventeenth-century specimen located at the Beinecke Library, Yale University.

recusants. I have said but little against the Church of Rome, and popish recusants in comparison of what might be said. The four propositions handled in this small treatise, and fully proved, may serve both to discover the falsehood of the romish religion, and also to confirm and strengthen those that stagger, and are weak in the truth. God in mercy grant that the eyes of the papists in England may be opened to discern the depths of Satan, and the damnable principles and practices of the Church of Rome; and that their hearts may be turned from darkness to light, from the power of Satan unto God, and from the popish unto the Protestant religion. And that the common Protestants of England may not have their understandings darkened, and their minds blinded by the fogs and mists of popish doctrines and books, to turn papists. And my heart's desire, and prayer for both papists and common Protestants, which are yet unconverted, is that they may by the sound preaching of the Gospel be convinced, converted, sanctified, and saved with an everlasting salvation. God save the King, bless the Parliament, and preserve this nation from all the plots of the papists, and from all the hellish designs of the pope, Jesuits, and priests, and other adherents to the Church of Rome. Amen, and Amen. So prayed,

Hanserd Knollys.

THE MYSTICAL BABYLON AVAILED

The method that I have chosen to unveil mystical Babylon is by proving these four propositions, viz: 1. That Rome-papal is mystical-Babylon; 2. That the pope of Rome is the beast; 3. That the Church of Rome is the great whore; 4. That the Roman priests are the false prophet.

Proposition I.
That Rome-Papal is Mystical-Babylon

Eastern Babylon of Nebuchadnezzar[6] in Chaldea was a famous city, called the "lady of kingdoms"[7] and the "glory of kingdoms"[8] under whose kings the

[6] Nabuchadrezzar II (c. 630–c. 561 BC; r. c. 605–c. 561 BC) second Babylonian king of this name, part of the Chaldean dynasty of Babylonia.

[7] Knollys provides a series of marginal notes that include biblical references. They are arranged in alphabetic order. Because he provides other comments and other forms of bibliographical citations, we are reproducing all of them as footnotes instead of providing

people of God were captivated and oppressed violently.[9] For which violence done to Zion, and other God-provoking sins, that great city and kingdom was destroyed by Cyrus king of Persia[10] whom God raised up to execute his righteous judgments upon them for their iniquities, long before Saint John's time.[11] Therefore mystery, Babylon the great—so named [in] Revelation 17:5—is some other great city, which does resemble old Babylon for idolatry (Jeremiah 5:47), persecution (Lamentations 5:1–5), violence (Jeremiah 51:25), oppression (Jeremiah 50:33; Isaiah 14:4), and pride (Isaiah 47:1–7). "And thou saidst, I shall be a lady forever… I am, and none else besides me" [Isaiah 47:7–8]. And so does mystical Babylon say in her heart, "I sit a queen" (Revelation 18:7). Also blood guiltiness, "The blood of thy servants have they shed like water round about Jerusalem" (Psalm 79:[3]). And so does mystical Babylon (Revelation 26:6 [*sic*, Revelation 16:6]): "For they have shed the blood of saints and prophets" (Revelation 18:24). As the city Jerusalem was spiritually "called Sodom and Egypt where our Lord was crucified."[12] So Rome pagan and papal is mystically called Babylon, where the saints have been and shall be killed,[13] "and in her was found the blood of prophets and of saints and of all that were slain upon the earth" [Revelation 18:24].

That which Jesus Christ revealed by his angel unto his servant John touching mystical Babylon in this prophecy of the Revelation, can agree to no other city but Rome only. For first, no other city in Saint John's time was built upon seven mountains, or hills, but Rome only (Revelation 17. 5–18): "And the seven heads are seven mountains on which the woman sitteth," called the great city, verse 18, whose name is "mystery Babylon the great," verse 5. So Propertius,[14] Virgil,[15] Ovid,[16] Cornel. a Lap.,[17] Bellarmine.[18] So

biblical references in the main text. Doing otherwise may result in confusion for the reader. At margin, note *a*: Isaiah 47:1–5.

[8] At margin, note *b*: Isaiah 13:19.

[9] At margin, note *c*: 2 Chronicles 36:14–20; Jeremiah 51:34–35.

[10] Cyrus II (c. 590/80–c. 529) the Great, was the founder of the Achaemenian Empire of Persia. He is mentioned in the Bible as a patron of the Jews (cf. Isaiah 44:28).

[11] At margin, note *d*: Isaiah 45:1–4, 47:1–9.

[12] At margin, note *e*: Revelation 11:8.

[13] At margin, note *f*: Revelation 6:9–11; Revelation 11:7, 16, 6 [*sic*]; Revelation 18:13–24.

[14] At margin, note *g*: "Propert[ius], *Eleg*[iae], 10 l. 3 [Liber tertius, elegia decem], septem urbs alta iugis, toti quae praesidet orbi" (English trans.): ["...city high on the seven hills that presides over the whole world..."]. Sextus Propertius (55/43–c. 16 BCE) was

an ancient Roman poet, author of the *Elegies*, in four books. The quote is actually from Book III, elegy eleven. See Sextus Propertius, *Elegies*, ed. and trans., G. P. Goold, Loeb Classical Library, 18 (Cambridge: Harvard University Press, 1990).

[15] At margin, note *h*: "Virgil, *Georg*[icon], 2. ω. Pulcherrima Roma, septemque una sibi muro circumdedit arces" (English trans.): ["...beautiful Rome, enclosed seven [hills] behind one city wall..."]. Publius Vergilius Maro (70–19 BCE) was a Roman poet and author of the *Aeneid*. The quote is from *Georgics*, II.534–535. See Virgil, *Georgics*, ed. Richard F. Thomas, 2 vols. (Cambridge: Cambridge University Press, 1988) 1:67.

[16] At margin, note [i]: "Ovid. I. de Tristibus l.3.Elog.7. Dumq; suis victrix septem de montibus orbem prospiciet domitum, martia Roma legar" (English trans.): ["...while belligerent Rome from the seven hills the conquered world beholds, I shall be read..."]. The Roman poet, Publius Ovidius Naso (43 BCE–17 CE) or Ovid, is especially remembered by his *Ars amatoria*. The quotation is from Ovid, *Tristibus*, III.vii.52. See Ovid, *Tristium libri v*, ed. S. G. Owen (Oxford: Oxford University Press, 1889) 112.

[17] At margin, note *k*: "Cornel[ius] à Lap[ide] in Apoc. 17.3, 9. In septem montibus patet denotari Romam" (English trans.): ["...in 'seven mounts' evidently denotes Rome..."]. The Jesuit, Cornelius a Lapide (1587–1637) was a prolific biblical scholar. See Dominique Bertrand, "The Society of Jesus and the Church Fathers in the Sixteenth and Seventeenth Century," in *The Reception of the Church Fathers in the West: From the Carolingians to the Maurists*, ed. Irena Dorota Backus, 2 vols. (Leiden and New York: Brill, 1997) 1:889–950, here 932. For the full context of the quotation see Cornelio Cornelli a Lapide, *Commentaria in Apocalypsin S. Ioannis Apostoli*, in *Commentaria in Sacram Scripturam*, ed. Sisto Riario Sforza, 10 vols. (Naples: I. Nagar, 1859) 10:977. Knollys' reliance on Cornelius a Lapide may be wider than this note may intimate. For instance, in his commentary on Revelation, Cornelius a Lapide already mentions the classic Roman poets Virgil and Ovid and provides the same citations that Knollys uses to adduce the identity of Rome with the seven hills of Revelation 17. However, Lapide clearly rejects the identification of the Roman Catholic Church with the beast of Revelation 17: "Obiiciunt haeretici: Roma est Babylon; ergo Romana Ecclesia cum suo Pontifice est Babylon. Resp. consequentiam esse absurdam, aeque ac fallacem. Aliud est enim Roma urbs, aliud Romana Ecclesia. Rursum aliud est Roma ethnica, aliud Roma Christiana. S. Ioannes loquitur de Roma ethnica, qualis erat sio tempore sub Domitiano persecutore, non autem de Roma Christiana, multo minus de Romana Ecclesia" (English trans.): ["The heretics object: Rome is Babylon; therefore the Roman Church with its pontifice is Babylon. Answer: The consequence is absurd, and equally a fallacy. One is Rome the city, another Christian Rome. Again, one is pagan Rome, another Christian Rome. S. John speaks of pagan Rome, just as was in his time under Domitian the persecutor, not however of Christian Rome, much less of the Roman Church"]. Lapide, *Commentaria in Apocalypsin*, 10:971

[18] At margin, note *l*: "Bellar[mino] de R. P. l.2 c.2 & l.3 c.12." Robert Bellarmine (1542–1621) was one of the most influential Jesuit theologians of the early decades of the seventeenth century. In 1599, Pope Clement VIII (r. 1592–1605) created him a cardinal of the Roman Catholic Church. He was eventually canonized in 1930, and declared a doctor of the Church in 1931. Knollys is here referring to Bellarmine's controversy *De*

do Viegas,[19] Suarez,[20] Ribera,[21] and divers others affirm, that by Babylon in the book of the Revelation Rome is figured forth. And the Remists in their *Testament* acknowledge that by Babylon is meant Rome (See their notes on 1 Peter 5:13 and upon the 17th and 18th chapters of the Revelation).[22]

---

summo pontifice, which constitutes part of a larger controversial body, namely *De controversiis Christianae fidei*. See Robert Bellarmine, *Tertia controversia generalis, De summo pontifice, quinque libris explicata*, in *De controversiis Christianae fidei adversus hujus temporis haereticos*, 4 vols. (Venice: Joannem Malachinum, 1721) 1:241–446. Also, see Robert Bellarmine, *Opera omnia, Editio prima neapolitana iuxta Venetam anni 1721*, 6 vols. (Naples: Josephum Giuliano, 1856–1862) 1:299–540. When necessary further references to the Venice edition of 1721 will be accompanied with a reference to the nineteenth century *Opera omnia*.

[19] Blasius Viegas (1554–99) was a Portuguese Jesuit author of a popular commentary on the book of Revelation, *Commentarii Exegetici in Apocalypsim Ioannis Apostoli* (Evora: E. de Lyra, 1601). For a brief overview of Viegas' commentary see Bernard McGinn, "Wrestling with the Millenium: Early Modern Catholic Exegesis of Apocalypse 20," in *Imagining the End: Visions of Apocalypse from the Ancient Middle East to Modern America*, ed. Abbas Amanat and Magnus Bernhardsson (London: I. B. Tauris, 2002) 148–167, here 164–65.

[20] Francisco Suárez (1548–1617) is widely recognized as the most prominent scholastic theologian of the Society of Jesus. Although Knollys is not explicit, he may have been referring to the fifth book of Suárez's *Defense of the Catholic and Apostolic Faith*, in which Suárez expounded on the figure of the antichrist. See Francisco Suárez, *Defensio fidei catholicae, et apostolicae adversus Anglicanae sectae errores, cum responsione ad apologiam pro iuramento fidelitatis, & praefationem monitoriam serenissimi Iacobi Angliae regis* (Coimbra: Didacum Gomez de Loureyro, 1613); Francisco Suárez, *Selections from Three Works of Francisco Suárez, S.J.: De legibus, ac deo legislatore, 1612; Defensio fidei catholicae, et apostolicae adversus anglicanae sectae errores, 1613; De triplici virtute theologica, fide, spe, et charitate, 1621* (Oxford: Calrendon Press, 1944).

[21] The Jesuit Francisco de Ribeira (1537–91) was originally from Portugal. He was the author of an influential commentary on the book of Revelation. See Francisco de Ribeira, *In sacram b. Iohannis apostoli & euangelistae apocalypsim commentarij ... ; his adiuncti sunt quinq[ue] libri de templo & de ijs quae ad templum pertine[n]t ad multorum locorun tam apocalypsis quam reliquorum librorum intelligentiam cum primis vtiles* (Salamanca: Pedro Lasso, 1591). For a brief overview of Ribeira's commentary see McGinn, "Wrestling with the Millenium," 148–167, here 163–64.

[22] By "remists," Knollys is denoting the editors of the Douai-Reims Bible. English Catholics, mostly Jesuits, published the English translation of the New Testament at Rheims in 1582 and the Old Testament in 1609–1610 at Douai. The translation was chiefly the work of Gregory Martin (1540–1582) who had completed the translation of the Old Testament before his untimely death. The project was carried out under the auspices of William Allen (1532–1594). The Douai-Reims Bible was supplemented with polemical notes against Protestantism. Here Knollys made reference to three annotations

found in the Douai-Rheims New Testament. The first one was the annotation to 1 Peter 5:13 ("The church saluteth you, that is in Babylon, coelect: and Marke my sonne"). In the note the editors sought to explain the use of "Babylon": "That is in Babylon,) The Protestants shew themselves here (as in al [*sic*] places where any controversie is, or that maketh against them) to be most unhonest and partial handlers of God's word. The ancient Fathers, namely S. Hierom in *Catalogo de Scriptoribus Ecclesiasticis, verbo Marcus*: Eusebius *li. 2. c.14, hist. oecumenius* upon this place, and many moe [*sic*] agree, that Rome is meant by the word Babylon, here also, as in the 16 and 17 of the Apocalypse; saying plainely, that S. Peter wrote this epistle at Rome, which is called Babylon for the resemblance it had to Babylon that great citie in Chaldea (where the Jewes were captives) for magnificence, monarchie, resort and confusion of al [*sic*] peoples and tongues, and for that it was before Christ and long after, the seat of al [*sic*] ethnike superstition & idolatry, & the slaughter-house of the apostles & other Christian men, the heathen emperours then keeping their cheefe residence there. See S. Leo *Ser. I in nat. Petri et Pauli*." *The New Testament of Iesus Christ faithfully translated into English, out of the authentical Latin, diligently conferred with the Greek, & other editions in diuers languages: with arguments of books and chapters: annotations, and other helps, for the better vnderstanding of the text, and specially for the discouerie of corruptions in diuers late translations: and for clearing controuersies in religion of these dayes* ([Douai]: John Cousturier, 1633) rendering of 1 Peter 5:13 on 613, and the annotation on [614]. Knollys also alluded to the note explaining Revelation 17:18 ("And the woman which thou sawest: is the great citie, which hath kingdom over the kings of the earth"): "The great citie,) If it be meant of any one citie, and not of the universal societie of the reprobate which is the citie of the divel [*sic*], as the church & the universal fellowship of the faithful is called the citie of God, it is most like to be old Rome, as some of the Greeks expound it, from the time of the first emperours, til Constantine's daies, who made an end of the persecution. For by the authoritie of the old Romane Empire, Christ was put to death first, & afterward the two cheefe apostles, & the popes their successours, & infinit Catholike men throughout the world by lesser kings which then were subject to Rome. Al [*sic*] which antichristian persecutions ceased, when Constantine reigned, & yealded up the citie to the pope, who holdeth not the kingdom or empire over the world, as the heathen did, but the fatherhood and spiritual rule of the church. Howbeit the more probable sense is the other, of the citie of the divel [*sic*], as the author of the homilies upon the Apocalypse in S. Augustin, declareth." *The New Testament of Iesus Christ* (1633) rendering of Revelation 17:18 on 679, and the annotation on 680. Finally, Knollys also made a general reference to Revelation 18. It appears that he had Revelation 18:21 in mind: "And one strong angel tooke up as it were a great milstone, and threw it into the sea, saying: With this violence shal [*sic*] Babylon that great citie be throwen, and shal now be found no more." *The New Testament of Iesus Christ* (1633) 682. The annotation to Revelation 18:21, however, contradicted Knollys' interpretation: "By this it seemeth cleere that the Apostle meaneth not any one citie, but the universal companie of the reprobate, which shal [*sic*] perish in the day of iudgement. The old prophets also naming the whole number of God's enemies mystically, Babylon, as Jerem[iah] c. 52." *The New Testament of Iesus Christ* (1633) 682.

Secondly, no other city in the world had seven kings, that is, seven several kinds of governors succeeding one another, but Rome only: "And there are seven kings, five are fallen, and one is, and the other is not yet come" (Revelation 17:10). The five kings, that were fallen, past and gone before John's time, are mentioned by Titus Livius (1.6): "What the Romans did—said Livy—under their kings, and after under their consuls, dictators, decemvirs, and consular tribunes, whither as to wars abroad, or suppressing troubles at home, I have set forth in five books."[23] "And this one is,"[24] *viz.*, the emperor, for the caesars were the sixth head of Rome, who reigned in St. John's time: "the other is not yet come," viz., the seventh head of Rome, or the seventh king, or kind of roman governor, to wit, the popes of Rome: "And he—that is, the pope—is of the seven, and goes into perdition" (Revelation 17:11). This seventh kind of government of the Roman kingdom by popes was not come in Saint John's time. So then it is manifest that Rome is the city, which had seven kings, heads, or kinds of governors that succeeded one another. Now let anyone show us another city that has had seven kings, or several kinds of governors—*Et erit mibi magnus Apollo*—and let him be pope.

Thirdly, no other city in Saint John's time did reign over the kings of the earth, but Rome only: "And the Woman which thou sawest— ἔστιν ἡ πόλις ἡ μεγάλη, is that city the great, verse five, "mystery," "Babylon the Great," viz. Rome[25]—which reigned over the kings of the earth" (Revelation 17:18). Yea, it is very evident by the testimony and confession of many popish writers, who for their learning and dignity in the Church of Rome were eminent, that Rome is that great city, which by the emperor's authority in Saint John's time, and by the pope's power since, has reigned and still reigns over the kings of the earth. Bellarmine said that Rome is to be understood by the great whore.[26] Cardinal Pole said, "Christ has set Peter's

[23] The great Roman historian, Titus Livius (59/64 BCE–17 CE) was the author of *The History of Rome*. Knollys provides first the chapter and then the book in which the quotation is actually found. In modern editions and translations the quote can be found in Livy, *History of Rome*, 6.1. For the Latin version of the passage in question see Livy, *Ab urbe condita*, ed. Christina Shuttleworth Kraus (Cambridge: Cambridge University Press, 1994) 33.

[24] At margin, note *m*: "Rev[elation] 17:10 [...] ὁ εἷς ἔστιν."

[25] Knollys inserts this parenthetical note right in the middle of the quotation.

[26] At margin, note *n*: "Bellarm[mino], lib. 3 De Pont. R. c. 13. Per meretricem intelligi Romam" ["By prostitute understand Rome"]. The passage in question can be found in Robert Bellarmine, *Tertia controversia generalis, De summo pontifice, quinque libris*

chair above all the thrones of emperors, and above all the tribunals of kings."[27] But Christ did not sit in any such chair of kingly state as the pope does,

---

explicata, in *De controversiis Christianae fidei adversus hujus temporis haereticos*, 4 vols. (Venice: Joannem Malachinum, 1721) 1:241–446, here 368. However, Knollys appears to be intentionally misquoting Bellarmine, who was actually refuting the notion that the Roman Catholic Church was the seat of the anti-Christ. Here is the passage in full: "Nunc ad argumenta adversariorum supra explicata respondeamus. Ad primum respondeo tripliciter. Primo, dici potest cum Augustino in Psalmo 26. Aretha, Haymone, Beda & Ruperto, in cap. 17. Apocal. per meretricem, quae sedet super montes septem, & habet regnum super reges terrae, non intelligi Romam, sed universam diaboli civitatem, quae in Scriptura vocatur saepè Babylon, & opponitur civitati Dei, idest, ecclesiae, quae dicitur Hierusalem. Per septem autem montes intelligi universitatem superborum, & praecipuè regum terrae etc. Secundò, dici potest, & meo judicio meliùs: per meretricem intelligi Romam, ut exponit Tertullianus lib. cont. Jud. & lib. 3 cont. Marcion. & Hieronymus epist. 17 ad Marcell. & quaest. 11 ad Algasiam: sed Romam ethnicam regnantem, idola colentem, & Christianos persequentem, non autem Romam Christianam, sic enim iidem auctores exponunt" (English trans.): ["Now, concerning the injurious arguments set forth above, we respond. To the first, I respond in three parts. First, we can say with Augustine in Psalm 26, Arethas, Haymone, Bede, and Rupert, by harlot in chapter 17 of the Apocalypse, which sits on top of seven hills, and has power over the kings of the earth, by no means understand Rome, but the entire city of the devil, which the Scripture frequently calls Babylon and juxtaposes to the city of God, that is, the church, which it calls Jerusalem. On the other hand, by the seven hills understand all the haughty, especially the kings of the earth, etc. Next, we can say, and it is my honest judgment that by harlot we can understand Rome, as put forth by Tertullian in his book *Against the Jews* [*Adversus Iudaeos*] and in the third book of *Against Marcion*, as well as Jerome in his seventeenth letter to Marcella [Letter XLVI] and question eleven to Algasia. But in truth, pagan ruled Rome, idol worshipping, and Christians persecuting, not, however, Christian Rome. Thus in fact explain the very same authors"]. Robert Bellarmine, *De controversiis Christianae fidei* (1721) 1:368; *Opera omnia* (1856) 1:447.

[27] At margin, note *o*: "Polus Cardinal. *De Concilio*, p. 91. Petri cathedram super omnia imperatorum solia, & omnia regum tribunalia constituit Christus." Reginald Pole (1500–1558) studied at Oxford and Padua. Pope Paul III created him cardinal of the Roman Catholic Church in 1536. He returned to England in 1554 and became archbishop of Canterbury in 1556 under Mary Tudor. His book *De concilio* appeared in print in 1562, together with the *Reformatio Angliae.* The statement quoted by Knollys can be found on page ninety-one of the Dillingen edition printed by Sebaldus Mayer. It forms part of Cardinal Pole's "answer" to Question Sixty-One (Quaestio LXI). As it can be seen here, Knollys slightly departs from the text which reads as follows: "...hanc illorum sedem, quae Petri cathedra appellatur, supra solium omnium imperatorum, et supra tribunalia omnium principum mundi in oculis omnium sublatam, quasi suo loco positam, collocaret" (English trans.): ["...this seat, which is called the seat of Peter, he has placed above all the thrones of emperors and above all the tribunals of the princes of the world, lifted in the eyes of all, just as if set in his place"]. Reginald Pole, *Libri duo d. Reginaldi*

nor did Saint Peter, nor any of Christ's apostles, no not Saint Paul, the chiefest of all the apostles, 2 Corinthians 11:5 and 12:11. Isodorus Musconius said that the pope of Rome is the universal judge. He is King of kings, and Lord of lords.[28] However, that testimony recorded is undeniable:

Poli laudatissimi Cardinalis, quos pietate, gravitate, doctrina, ac eloquentia summa refertos, et ante hac in Germania nunquam excusos moriens reliquit. Primus liber de Concilio agit... (Dillingen: Sebaldus Mayer, 1562) 91. See also the Roman as well as the Venetian editions of the same year, Pole, *De Concilio liber* (Rome: Paulum Manutium Aldi F., 1562) 34v; Id., *Reginaldi Poli Card. amplissimi liber, De Concilio...* (Venice: Jordani Zileti, 1562) 55; Curt F. Bühler, "Observations on the 1562 Editions of Cardinal Reginald Pole's *De Concilio* and *Reformatio Angliae*," *Studies in Bibliography* 26 (1973): 232–234.

[28] At margin, note *p*: "Isodorus Musconius, *De majestate ecclesiae milit.* l. 1, c. 7, p. 26. Venetiis, anno 1602. Pontifex Romanus est judex universalis, rex regum, & dominus dominantium" (English trans.): ["The Roman Pontiff is universal judge, king of kings, and lord of lords"]. "Abra. Bzovius, De Pont. Rom. Coloniae Agrip. 1619, says, Papa est Christianorum monarcha, mortalium supremus, judex coeli, arbiter orbis, cap. 1.3, 16, 32, 45" (English trans.): ["The pope is the monarch of Christianity, the greatest of men, universal judge, overseer of the world"]. "Celsus Mancinus, *De juribus principatuum Romae* 1596. lib. 3, cap. 1, 2, etc. said, Papa est totius orbis Dominus: Potestas papae temporalis est omnium aliarum potestatum eminentissima, allaeq; potestates omnes ab illo dependent" (English trans.): ["The pope is lord of the world: the temporal power of the pope is more eminent than all other power; all power derives from there"]. The first reference is to Isidoro Mosconio (d. 1621) a little-known Italian priest who, according to the title page of his work *De maiestate*, was vicar-general of the diocese of Bologna. Isidoro Mosconio, *De maiestate militantis ecclesiae. Libri duo. Quibus ecclesiae maiestatem ex religione Christiana prodire demonstrator. Atque de ipsius religionis statu* (Venice: Florauantem Pratum, 1602). The next reference is to the Polish Dominican, Abraham Bzowski (1567–1637) best remembered as continuator of the monumental work of Caesar Baronius (1538–1607) the *Annales ecclesiastici*. Abraham Bzowski, *Annalium ecclesiasticorum post C.B. tomus XIII-XX, rerum in orbe christiano ab A.D. 1198 usque ad A.D. 1565 gestarum narrationem complectens* (Cologne: Boetzerus, 1616–1640). The third reference is to Celso Mancini (c. 1542–1612) Bishop of Alessano, Italy. He was born in Ravenna and in the 1550s joined the Institute of Regular Canons of Saint Mary in Porto (Ravenna) commonly known as the Canons Regular of the Lateran, or Canons Regular of the Congregation of the Most Holy Savior of the Lateran (C.R.L., or *Congregatio Ssmi Salvatoris Lateranensis*). He was appointed bishop of Alessano in 1597. See *Edit 16. Censimento nazionale delle edizioni italiane del XVI secolo.* Istituto Centrale perl il Catologo Unico delle Biblioteche Italiane e per le Informazioni Bibliografiche, http://edit16.iccu.sbn.it/scripts/iccu_ext.dll?fn=11&res=8559 (accessed December 5, 2014); Eubel Conradus, *Hierarchia catholica medii et recentionis aevi sive summorum Pontifucum*, 8 vols. (Münster: Regensberger, 1923) 4:77. His work *De juribus principatum* has an important place in the development of modern Italian political theory. See Celso Mancini, *De iuribus principatum libri novem* (Rome: Gulielmi Facciotti, 1596).

"And it came to pass in those days, that there went out a decree from Caesar Augustus," the Roman emperor, "that all the world should be taxed" (Luke 2:1–3). From what has been confessed and testified by the papists themselves, it is plain and evident that Rome-papal is mystical Babylon.[29]

Proposition II.
That the Pope of Rome is the Beast

The great monarchs and monarchies of this world have been figured forth by beasts of prey. God showed his prophet Daniel the four great kingdoms of this world, *viz.* the Assyrio-Caldean, the Medi-Persian, the Grecian, and the Roman kingdoms by a vision of four ravenous and devouring beasts: "And behold a fourth beast"[30]—the Roman kings and kingdoms with seven heads, and ten horns, and upon the horns ten crowns, and upon his seventh head two horns, like a lamb, Revelation 13:1–11—"dreadful and terrible," etc., "exceedingly," and "diverse from all the other" three beasts (Daniel 7:3–8). And Jesus Christ showed his apostle John the same fourth beast: "and the beast that I saw, was like unto a leopard, and his feet were as the feet of a bear, and his mouth as the mouth of a lion, and the dragon[31] gave him his power, his throne, and great authority" (Revelation 13:2); "and he spoke as the dragon" (Revelation 13:11). The most full description of the Roman-papal beast is expressly written in the seventeenth chapter of the Revelation: "And the Angel said unto me," verse 7, "I will tell thee the mystery of the woman, and of the beast," etc. This beast the angel described unto St. John

[29] At margin, note *q*: "Viegas in Apoc. 17, com. I. S. 3. Inquit, nomine Babilonis urbem Romam significari in hoc Apocalypsis opere, ubi toties Babilon nominatur. vid. Orosium lib. 2, c. 3 Hist. Par. in Apoc. 14.8. ["It is said, in name only Babylon signifies the city of Rome in the book of Apocalypse, as often as Babylon is named..."]." The passage quoted can be found in page 832 of the Parisian edition of 1606. Blasius Viegas, *Commentarii exegetici in Apocalypsim Ioannis Apostoli* (Paris: Dionysium Binet, 1606) 832.

[30] At margin, note *a*: "Daniel 7:7" [English trans.: "a fourth beast, terrifying and dreadful," NRSV].

[31] At margin, note *b*: "That old serpent, the devil and Satan. For the devil and the pope are alike (as father and son) in many things. The devil contradicted God's word (Genesis 3:4); so does the pope (1 Timothy 4:3), forbidding to marry. This confesses Christ [i.e. Satan] (Mark 3:11) but denies his laws; so does the pope (Revelation 13:11–17). The devil would be worshipped as God (Matthew 4:6). The pope would be exalted above all that is called God, or that is worshipped (2 Thessalonians 2:4). The devil challenges to be the disposer of all kingdoms of the earth, Luke 4:5–7. So does the pope of Rome, vid. Bellarmine, lib. 5, cap. 8, *De Pont. Rom.*"

in three particulars, which can agree with no other persons, powers, emperors, kings, nor dominion in the world but the popes of Rome only. First, by his past, present, and future state, verse 8: "The beast, that was, and is not, and yet is." Secondly, by his twofold number, verse 11: "He is the eight, and is of the seven." Thirdly, by his rise and ruin, verses 8 and 11: "The beast shall ascend out of the bottomless pit, and go into perdition"; that lawless one, the son of perdition, "and goeth into perdition."

First, the beast is described by his past state: "The beast which thou saw, was, and is not" (Revelation 17:8). That is to say, the Roman state and kingdom was formerly, and even in St. John's time, what it is not, now in our time, in diverse respects, *viz.* 1. The Roman kingdom was then a power ordained of God (Romans 13:1–7), unto which Roman power our blessed savior Jesus Christ being then in the form of a servant "was obedient to death" (Philippians 2:7–8). So were Christ's disciples, and the primitive Christians, search those scriptures.[32] The Roman powers though pagan persecutors of Christ and Christians, was [*sic*] God's ordinance of magistracy, until the ten kings gave the beast—the pope of Rome—his power, his throne and great authority (Revelation 13:2). And then the angel told St. John: "He is not." *Viz.* The beast of the seventh and eighth head is not God's ordinance of magistracy; nor a power ordained of God. Here let it be seriously considered that the dragon, which gave the beast his power, throne, and great authority, was [*sic*] not the Roman pagan emperors, for they never gave their power and great authority unto the beast of the seventh and eighth head, *viz.* the pope of Rome. The Roman heathen, yea and Christian emperors stood in the pope's way, and did let and hinder his rise and reigning power, until they were removed out of his way, as was foretold by the Apostle Paul, 2 Thessalonians 2:3–10.[33] And thus it came to pass.

---

[32] At margin, note *c*: "Mark 12:17; Acts 25:10–11; 1 Peter 2:13–15; Titus 3:1. Not only Paul, but Peter, and Christ himself was subject to the Roman pagan emperors, kings, and governors. But the beast of the eighth head, the pope of Rome will be the supreme power over all kings and kingdoms."

[33] The following note appears in the margin and, presumably due to a typographical error, it lacks the corresponding marker, in this case letter "d." We are placing it at the end of this section as it deals with the then disputed power of the pope to depose monarchs. At margin, note [*d*]: "In bull *Coena Domini*. Sect 3, 4, 5 against Queen Elizabeth and all heretics, vid. *Remonstran. Hibernorum* per R. Caron, part 1, cap. 3, sect. 4, pag. 7." Knollys appears to be conflating two different papal bulls. In 1568, Pope Pius V (r. 1566–1572) promulgated the bull *De Coena Domini*, in which, like popes before him, he asserted the temporal powers of the papacy. A few years later he proclaimed the bull *Regnans in*

Constantine the Great leaving Rome, and making Constantinople the imperial seat, thereby (*sede vacante*) the then bishop of Rome got full possession of that city. And so the chief bishop of Rome continued his primacy from that time until, at last, the Western Empire determined [under] Augustulus [in the year] 475 or thereabouts.[34] And about the year 607 the then bishop of Rome, Boniface III, obtained from Phecas [or Phocas] the emperor of the east, that not the patriarch of Constantinople but the bishop of Rome be universal bishop.[35] But for all this rise and advance, the beast of the eighth head, the pope of Rome, is not of the seven; that is to say, he is not supreme as the Roman emperors were. For although the emperors assumed the title of *Pontifex Maximus*[36] and added it to the

---

excelsis of 25 February 1570, in which he specifically excommunicated Queen Elizabeth. The sections mentioned by Knollys, i.e., 3, 4, and 5, coincide with the sections of *Regnans in excelsis* in which the Pope claimed the power and authority to excommunicate the Queen. For a succinct discussion of *De Coena Domini* see William J. Bouwsma, *Venice and the Defense of Republican Liberty: Renaissance Values in the Age of the Counter Reformation* (Berkeley: University of California Press, 1968) 327–328. For the Latin text of *Regnans in excelsis* see Pio V, *Regnans in excelsis*, in *Bullarum diplomatum et privilegiorum sanctorum romanorum pontificum, taurinensis editio*, ed. Francisco Gaude, et al., 25 vols. (Turin: Seb. Franco and Henrico Dalmazzo, 1862) 7:810–811. The third reference is of special interest. Knollys is calling on the authority of the Franciscan Redmond Caron (c. 1605–1666) whose views on the supreme authority of the monarch in all temporal matters put him at odds with his superiors and Rome. See Redmond Caron, *Remonstrantia Hibernorum contra Lovanienses ultramontanasque censuras, de incommutabili regum imperio, subditorumque fidelitate, et obedientia indispensabili : ex S.S. Scripturis, patribus, theologis, etc. vindicata* (London: no printer, 1665).

[34] Romulus Augustulus (fl. 5th century) is popularly remembered as the last emperor of the West (r. 475–476).

[35] Pope Boniface III (r. February 19 to November 12, 607) went to Constantinople in 603 as papal legate of Pope Gregory I (r. 590–604). There he successfully secured a decree from the Byzantine Emperor Phocas (r. 602–610) recognizing the primacy of Rome.

[36] At margin, note *e*: "Dionys. Halicarnas. Ant. Rom. 12. And Godwin's Antiq. l. 2, sect. 2, cap. 15." Knollys is alluding to the first-century BCE Greek historian, Dionysius of Halicarnassus (fl. c. 20 BCE). He was the author of the multi-volume history of Rome, known in Latin as *Antiquitates Romanas*. For a bilingual edition (Greek-English) see Dionysius of Halicarnassus, *The Roman Antiquities*, 7 vols. (Cambridge: Harvard University Press, 1984–1993). Next is Thomas Godwin (1586/7–1642); he was the author of a primer in Roman history for school children, *Romanae historiae anthologia* (1614) which went through several editions. See Thomas Godwin, *Romanae historiae anthologia: an English exposition of the Romane antiquities, wherein many Romane and Eng-*

imperial crown, yet the imperial crown of the roman government and kingdom was not added to the pope of Rome, until Emperor Henry IV,[37] whom Gregory VII excommunicated and deposed, and made Rodulphus [or Rudolf] emperor in his stead,[38] and afterwards when Henry V came to Rome to be crowned by Pope Pascal II, the Pope would not consent to his coronation, until the Emperor did give over all right of election of popes, and of investitures of bishops by staff and ring. And thus the pope gained the power of temporal sovereignty, and so is of the seven.

Nor did all this episcopal, pontifical, and imperial dignity, power, and authority fill and satisfy the beastly pope of Rome, until he obtained supremacy above all general councils,[39] and so the pope became *pontifex*

---

lish offices are parallel'd, and divers obscure phrases explained (Oxford: Printed by Iohn Lichfield, and Iames Short, for Henry Cripps, 1620).

[37] Due to a typographical error the marker for the following note was omitted in the original: "Avent. Annal. Boyor. lib. 5 and pag. 447 and lib. 9." The citation is to the Bavarian historian John Aventine of Abensberg, or Johannes Aventinus (1477–1534). He was the author of the multivolume history of Bavaria, *Annales Boiorum*. Johannes Aventinus, *Annalium Boiorum libri septem: accessit rerum et verborum memorabilium index copiosus* (Ingolstadt: Alexandrum et Samuelem Weissenhornios, 1554). For a complete study of his life and work see Gerald Strauss, *Historian in an Age of Crisis: The Life and Work of Johannes Aventinus, 1477–1534* (Cambridge: Harvard University Press, 1963). Knollys must have associated Aventine's chronicle with the life of Emperor Henry IV, of Bavarian origin.

[38] At margin, note *f*: "Petra dedit Petro, Petrus diadema Rodulpho. Bellar. De Concil. Lib. 2, cap. 1.2, c. 17." A literal translation of the statement would be, "The rock bestowed on Peter, Peter 'crowned' Rudolf." Better yet, however, would be, "Peter [the Apostle] bestowed on the pope, the pope bestowed the crown on Rudolf." The statement is often attributed to Pope Gregory VII (r. 1073–1085) on the occasion of his recognition of Rudolf of Rheinfelden (d. 1080) as king instead of Henry IV. For a detailed discussion of the investiture controversy from the perspective of the life of Pope Gregory VII see H. E. J. Crowdrey, *Pope Gregory VII, 1073–1085* (Oxford: Oxford University Press, 1998). Knollys identifies the source of the quote as Bellarmine's *Liber secundus, De conciliorum auctoritate*. See the full text in Robert Bellarmine, *De controversiis Christianae fidei* (1721) 2:27–51; *Opera Omnia* (1857) 2:43–72.

[39] At margin, note *g*: "Bellamine boasteth saying, the last Lateran Council under Leo 10th expressly and professedly teacheth, that the pope is above all councils, *Bellar. De Concil.* 1.2, c. 17." Bellarmine's complete statement, for which Knollys is providing a short translation, is as follows: "Denique lateranense ultimum sub Leone X, sess. 11, diserte et ex professo docuit, pontificem esse supra omnia concilia, et reprobavit contrarium decretum, editum in concilio basileensi." Robert Bellarmine, *De controversiis Christianae fidei* (1721) 2:48; *Opera Omnia* (1857) 2:68. In fact, Pope Leo X in session eleven (1516) of Lateran Council V declared that the pope has "authority over all councils" ("...tanque

maximus, the chief high priest, who translated kings and emperors at his pleasure. Bellarmine said, the Roman Empire was by the authority of the pope, translated from the Grecians to the French, and from Charles the Great and the French unto the family of Otto and the Saxons, which is now the Roman papal empire of Germany with its seven electors.[40]

Secondly, the Roman beast also—that was—is described by his present state; negatively, "and is not," [and] affirmatively, "and yet is."[41] Herein lays another mystery: "and here is the mind, that hath wisdom," to know in what respect the Roman beast is not, and yet is. I will not be positive, nor dare I presume to make a determinate judgment and to give a resolution herein. But I humbly offer my opinion, and submit it to the mind that has wisdom, and let him that has understanding in this mystery, judge what I say. It is said "he is not," with respect to those five kings, or kinds of kingly government, *viz.* kings, consuls, dictators, decemvirs, and tribunes, which were fallen, that is, past and gone before St. John's time. For this beast, which rose out of the sea of the troubles and confusions in Rome, and in the Roman Empire, and out of the earth of the apostasies[42] which the Apostle foretold should be in the latter days, and which the angel was now revealing unto John[43] *viz.* Papal Rome, is not yet come (Revelation 17:10) that is, he

---

auctoritatem super omnia concilia habentem..."). *Sa. Lateranen concilium novissimum, sub Julio et Leone X celebratum* (Rome: I. Mazochius, 1521) clxxxv.

[40] At margin, note *h*: "Bellar de trans. Imp. Rom. in tribus libris, per Episcopi Rom. authoritatem." Knollys summarizes Bellarmine's argument found in Robert Bellarmine, *De translatione imperii romani a graecis ad francos, adversus Matthiam Flaccium Illyricum, libri tres* (Antwerp: Christophori Plantini, 1589).

[41] At margin, note *i*: "Revelation 17:8–9."

[42] At margin, note *k*: "1 Timothy 4:1 and 2 Thessalonians 2:3–5."

[43] At margin, note *l*: "Revelation 13:1 and ver. 11 and Revelation 17:3–8." The marginal note continues providing three lists of "ancient," "modern," and "papist" sources that underscore the point: "Ancients: Ireneaus, l. 5 *Adversus haeresis*, c. 28. Tertullian, *De resur*[*rectione mortuorum*] [or *De resurrectione carnis*], c. 25. Ander. Caesar. Episc. cap. 36, *in Apoc.* 13, v. 1, Beda *in Apoc.* 13, v. 1. Modern: Joan. Viguer. *Instit. Theol.* c. 21, sect. 3, v.4, Nich. Sander, l. 8 *de visib. Eccl. Monarch.* c. 1 in libro octavo, Nich. Zegar *in Apoc. 13.* Papists: Benedict Pererias, l. 14, *in Dan.*, R. Bellarminus, l. 3, *de R. P.*, c. 2. 8., Francis. Rib. *In Apoc.* 13, sect. 1, hiomne bestiam, Apoc. 13.1, ipsistimum esse antichristum [...]." Below we are providing the complete bibliographical description of editions of works cited by Knollys in note *l* that might have been available to him: Andreae Caesareae Cappadociae Episcopi (Bishop of Caesarea in Cappadocia, c. 500) *In D. Ioannis Apostoli et Evangelistae Apocalypsin* (Ingolstadt: Sartorius, 1584); Bede, *Operum Venerabilis Bedae presbyteri tomus secundu, in quo subsequentes continentur eiusdem commentarii in Euangelium Marci Lib. IIII; in Euangelium Lucae Lib VI; in Acta Apostolorum Lib. I; Expositio nominum*

was not in being when St. John wrote this book. And yet "he is," that is to say "one is," to wit the Emperor, who is the sixth king, then in being in St. John's time, and sometime after: "And there are seven kings, five are fallen, and one is, and the other is not yet come" (Revelation 17:10). Viz., to be the seventh head of the Roman Empire, and the supreme governor of the Roman monarchy. The Roman papal beast is not, that is to say, he is not God's ordinance of magistracy, nor a lawful power ordained of God, but he is an usurper of the Roman kingdom, and an instrument of the great dragon, that old serpent, called the devil and Satan, (Revelation 12:3–9), viz. the Roman pagan emperor, and also the dragon, "that old serpent, which is the devil, and Satan" (Revelation 20:2). Viz. he that "beguiled Eve through his subtlety" (2 Corinthians 11:3) gave the beast his power, and his throne and his supreme authority. So that beast, the pope of Rome, has the Roman power, but not *jure divino*, "he is not," by God's approbation. And yet "he is" the supreme Roman governor. Yea "he is" of the seven, to wit, the seventh king or kind of kingly government, as is before said. And "he" even he is the eighth (Revelation 17:11).[44]

---

locorum in Actis contentorum, siue eiusdem, siue alterius au[to]ris; In Epistolas Catholicas; In Apocalypsim B. Ioannis Apostoli ([Paris]: Josse Bade, 1521); Joannes Viguerius, *Institutiones ad christinianam theologiam, sacrarum literarum, universaliumque conciliorum authoritate, necnon doctorum ecclesiasticorum eruditione confirmatae, ... His annecti curavimus eiusd. Viguerij commentaria antea nunquam excussa, in D. Pauli epistolam ad Romanos* (Antwerp: Viduae et Haeredum Ioannis Stelsii, 1572); Nicholas Sander, *De visibilii monarchia ecclesiae: libri octo* (Louvain: Fouler, 1571); Tacitus Nicolaus Zeger, *Scholion in omnes Novi Testamenti libros quo loci difficiles aut etiam ambigui juxta originalem Scripturae phrasim... sunt explicati... pars prima [Scholion in locos difficileis... epistolarum apostolicarum... pars secunda, scholia in locos difficileis... libri Apocalypseos... pars tertia* (Cologne: Haeredes Arnoldi Birckmanni, 1553); Benedictus Pererius, *Commentarius in Danielem Libri XVI* (Antwerp: no printer, 1594); Robert Bellarmine, *De Papa Romano libri decem, scholasticè et theologic collati cum disputationibus Roberti Bellarmini* (Franeker: no printer, 1594); Francisco de Ribeira, *In sacram b. Iohannis apostoli & euangelistae apocalypsim commentarij ... ; his adiuncti sunt quinq[ue] libri de templo & de ijs quae ad templum pertine[n]t ad multorum locorun tam apocalypsis quam reliquorum librorum intelligentiam cum primis vtiles* (Salamanca: Pedro Lasso, 1591).

[44] At margin, note *m*: "Bestia se Papa Rom. is octavus est, et de septem illis est, quia nimirum Papa se antichristus (Cornu illud parvulum Dan. 7, 20) oriturus erat de medio cornuum quartae bestiae, quae Imperium adumbrabat Romanum, etc. J. W. lib. de ultimo Romae Exitio. p. 6." The lack of bibliographical facts, i.e. no author's name, no title, and no publisher, in addition to irregularities in Latin usage, makes it quite difficult to identify the source of this reference. The problem is compounded by the fact, which should by now be evident to the reader, that Knollys does not always quote directly and

Thirdly, the Roman beast is described by his future state: "And the other is not yet come" (Revelation 17:10), that is to say, the other king or kind of kingly government, *viz.* popes had not gotten the supreme power, neither political, nor ecclesiastical. But this beast, that was to come, that is, to succeed the emperors, was the popes [*sic*], and they are the eight and of the seven (Revelation 17:11). Which will be made appear in the second particular of the angel's description of the beast by his twofold number.

The second particular, or part of the angel's description of the Roman beast is by his twofold number, seven and eight. The pope of Rome is of the seven, or the seventh king, or kingly kind of government with respect of his imperial or magisterial power[45] over emperors and kings of the Roman kingdom; and "he is" the "eight" with respect of his hierarchical, or pontifical power[46] or principality, which was also there before, under former Roman governments. For as to matters of religion, the Romans had of old instituted

accurately from the source. However, the declaration "bestia se papa Romano" leaves no doubt that the source must be a work by a non-Roman Catholic author. In addition, the initials "J. W." suggest that the provenance must be traced to John Wycliffe (c. 1330–1384). It must also be noted that Knollys' argument, which he hammers throughout this track, namely that the papacy is an usurper of the temporal power ordained by God, is consistent with Wycliffe's views. For the last point see John Wycliffe, *Tractatus de ecclesia. Now First Edited from the Manuscripts with Critical and Historical Notes*, ed. Johann Loserth (London: Published for the Wycliffe Society by Trübner & Co., 1886).

[45] At margin, note *n*: "Bellar. contra. Barcl. c. 5, Non solium in spiritualibus quoque imperatore & rege maior est Papa, sed etiam in temporalibus" (English trans.): ["Not only is the pope spiritual emperor and king, but also temporal"]. See Robert Bellarmine, *Tractatus de potestate summi pontificis in rebus temporalibus, adversus Gulielmum Barclaium* (Cologne: Sumptibus Bernardi Gualtheri, 1610); *Opera omnia* (1859) vol. 4, part 2, 257–344.

[46] At margin, note *o*: "[Indecipherable], Quanto creatura Deo, tanto imperatoria maiestas est papae inferior. The pope is the seventh head in nature and kind: and an eighth also in degree and power. Hen. Bish. of Meath, of Antichrist, pag. 11." The source of the first quotation remains uncertain as the author and title are deemed indecipherable. As for the second quote, it can be found in Henry Jones (1605–1682) *A sermon of antichrist preached at Christ-Church, Dublin, Novemb. 12. 1676* (London: for Nathaniel Ponder, 1679) 11. Jones' sermon originally appeared in print in 1676, followed by a "revised" edition of 1679. The pagination, moreover, of the 1679 revised edition matches Knollys' description; that is, the quotation appears on page 11 of the 1679 edition.

by Numa Pompilius[47] their pontifices or under-priests and over them a chief priest called *pontifex maximus*, which lower priests were exempted from civil jurisdiction, and only ordered and governed by him, who was their *pontifex maximus*, he himself not being accountable to any.[48] And therefore the pope is said to be of the "seven" with respect of his imperial and pontifical power, unto which he has advanced himself in his dominion and titles above all principalities and powers on earth, no kings nor emperors being excepted or exempted.[49] And so in his exalted power of imperial and pontifical horns the pope of Rome became the beast of the eighth head (Revelation 17:11), who did rise out of the earth having two horns like a lamb (Revelation 13:11). Horns do signify power in the prophesies of the Holy Scripture of truth, as in Daniel 8:20–24.[50] So that the two horns of that beast, the pope of Rome,

---

[47] Numa Pompilius (fl. C. 700 BCE) reigned Rome between 715 to 673. He was credited with the founding of Roman religious institutions including the office of the *pontifex maximus*.

[48] At margin, note *p*: "Dionys. Halicarnass Ant. Rom. 12. Godwin's Antiq. lib. 2 Sect. 2, cap. 15." The first reference is to Dionysius of Halicarnassus' *Antiquitates Romanas*. See Dionysius of Halicarnassus, *The Roman Antiquities*, 7 vols. (Cambridge: Harvard University Press, 1984–1993). The subsequent reference is to Thomas Godwin, *Romanae historiae anthologia: an English exposition of the Romane antiquities, wherein many Romane and English offices are parallel'd, and divers obscure phrases explained* (Oxford: Printed by Iohn Lichfield, and Iames Short, for Henry Cripps, 1620). The segment that starts with, "For as to matters of religion," and ends in, "not being accountable to any," is a verbatim copy from Jones, *A sermon of antichrist preached at Christ-Church* (1679) page 9–10. Even the source citations, namely Halicarnassus and Godwin, are found in the original Jones' text.

[49] At margin, note *q*: "Triplex imperium habet Papa, in terra, in coelo, et (ubi Christus nullum habet) in purgatorio, in eujus signum tiara papalis triplici corona ornata est, Caeremon l. 1. Sect, 5, c. 9 et sect. 7, f. 78. Hab. 3:4 and Zech. 1:18–21" (English trans.): ["The pope's supreme power is threefold; on earth, in heaven, and, where no one but Christ has it, in purgatory, after which the triple-crown papal tiara is decorated"]. The source of this statement is untraceable due to lack of bibliographical information.

[50] At margin, note *r*: "Purgatorium est peculium Papa (English trans.), ["Purgatory is the peculiar possession of the pope"], said Angelus Parisiensis. Antoninus part 3, tit. 22, cap. 5, sect. 6 et 7. Bal. in vita Leonis 10, etc. Patres concil. Lateran. sess 10, in orat. Steph. Patracensis." The paternity of the dictum, "purgatorium est peculium Papa," is enigmatic. John Jewel (1522–1571) bishop of Salisbury, in his *The Defense of the Apologie of the Church of Englande* (1567) attributed the phrase to Angelus Parisiensis. Richard William Jelf, the nineteenth-century editor of Jewel's works identified Angelus Parisiensis with Johannes Angelus. Bietenholz and Deutscher, in turn, equate Johannes Angelus with the sixteenth-century humanist from Aragon, Jean Lange. Because Jewel referred to Angelus Parisiensis as "one of youre allowed doctoures," it is very unlikely that

he was referring to a humanist associated with the circle of Meaux and former student of Lefèvre d'Etaples. Instead, it is more probable that Jewel had Angelus Dobelin (c. 1350–c. 1420) in mind. An Augustinian hermit, Angelus Dobelin lectured at the University of Paris on the *Sentences* in 1374–1375. Furthermore, since the second and fourth references in the present note *r* are almost identical to those Jewel provided contiguous to the quote in question, we can infer that Knollys appropriated the quote from Jewel's *Defense* and not from the primary source. See John Jewel, *A defense of the Apologie of the Churche of Englande Conteininge an answeare to a certaine booke lately set foorthe by M. Hardinge, and entituled, A confutation of etc. Whereunto there is also newely added an answeare vnto an other like booke, written by the saide M. Hardinge, entituled, A detection of sundrie fowle errours etc. Printed at Louaine, Anno. 1568. and inserted into the foremer answeare, as occasion, and place required, as by special notes added to the margine it maie appeare* (London: Henry Wykes, 1571) under "The Apologie, cap. 6, division 14," 572. See John Jewel, *The Works of John Jewel*, ed. Richard William Jelf, 8 vols. (Oxford: Oxford University Press, 1848) 1:xxxv; Peter G. Bietenholz and Thomas Brian Deutscher, *Contemporaries of Erasmus: A Biographical Register of the Renaissance and Reformation*, vols. 1–3 (Toronto: University of Toronto Press, 2003) 57 and 289–90. For a succinct overview of Angelus de Dobelin see William J. Courtney, *Ockham and Ockhamism: Studies in the Dissemination and Impact of his Thought* (Leiden/Boston: Brill, 2008) 224–225; a very influential discussion in Damasus Trapp, "Angelus de Dobelin, Doctor Parisiensis, and His Lectura," *Augustinianum* 3 (1963): 389–413. The second reference is to Antonino Pierozzi, or Antonino de'Forciglioni (1389–1459) archbishop of Florence, who was canonized in 1523. He was the author of *Summa theologica moralis* (Venice, 1477) and *Summa confessionum* (Mondovi, 1472). Knollys was citing the *Summa theologica*. John Jewel also mentioned Antoninus after alluding to Angelus Parisiensis. Jewel attributed the following quotation to the Archbishop of Florence: "Potestas papae maior est omni alia potestate creata, aliquo modo extendens se ad coelestia, terrestria, et infernalia: ut de ea verificari possit, quod dictum est, omnia subiecisti sub pedibus eius: The pope's power is greater, then any other power, that God ever made: and after a sorte stretcheth it selfe unto thinges in heaven, thinges in earth, and thinges in helle: so that, of that power the woordes maie be verified, that are written by the prophet David, Thou haste made al thinges subiecte to his feete." Jewel, *A defense of the Apologie* (1571) 572. The quote is found in Antoninus de Florentia, *Summae sacra theologie, iuris pontificii, et caesarei, pars tertia* (Venice: Bernardum Iuntam et Socios, 1571) 394*v*. Knollys cited the same title and chapter as Jewel, but specified sections 6 and 7, which suggests that he had access to an edition of Antoninus' *Summa theologica*. The material that Knollys was alluding to is found in Antoninus de Florentia, *Summae sacra theologie* (1571) 396*r*–397*r*. The third bibliographical mention is as encryptic as several others in this document. We would like to point out the possibility that Knollys was writing about Paolo Giovio, *Pauli Iouii nouocomensis episcopi Nucerini, De vita Leonis Decimi Pont. Max. libri quatuor.: his ordine temporum accesserunt Adriani Sexti Pont. Max. et Pompeii Columnae Cardinalis vitae* (Florence: Laurenti Torrentini, Florence, 1599). Finally, Knollys made mention once more of Lateran Council V. The citation matches the one Jewel offered in the same page as the previous two others. See Jewel, *A defense of the Apologie* (1571) 572. Moreover, signify his twofold power political and ecclesiastical, or imperial and pontifical, twisted and united together in his seventh and eighth headship, for even "he is the eight, and is of the seven" (Revelation 17:11). This number of the "beast" *viz.* the seventh and eighth can agree with none of the Roman heads, but popes only.

The third particular, or part of the angel's description of the Roman papal beast of the seventh and eighth head is by his rise and ruin: "The beast shall ascend out of the bottomless pit, and go into perdition" (Revelation 17:8); "And goeth into perdition" (Revelation 17:11). I shall here show briefly, first his rise, then his ruin. Whereby it will more plainly appear, that the pope of Rome is the beast.

First, as to the rise of the beast of the seventh and eight head, *viz* the pope of Rome; we find in the Roman histories, that Constantine the Great changed the seat of the emperor from Rome to Constantinople, thereby leaving the City of Rome, as it were vacant. After his death the Roman Empire was divided, and the Roman eagle having two great wings spread herself into the Eastern and Western empires. At last about anno 475 the Western Empire quite expired in Augustulus [or Romulus Augustulus].[51]

Knollys specifically called attention to the discourse of Stefan, titular archbishop of Patras. Jewell also made a direct quotation of Stefan's discourse in his *Defense*: "Stephanus the bishop of Patraca, in your late Councel at Laterane in Rome, saithe thus, in Papa est omnis potestas supra omnes potestates, tam coeli, quam terrae: Al power is in the pope above al the powers, as wel of heaven, as of earthe." Jewel, *A defense of the Apologie* (1571) 562. For the discourse of Stefan Teglatije (d. 1514) bishop of Torcello and titular archbishop of Patras, see *Oratio R. P. D. Stephani Archiepi. Patracen et Episcopi Torcellan. Habita in Concilio Lateranen cora Leone X Pont. Max. in decima sessione dicti Concilii Quarta Maii. M.D. XV*, in *Sa. Lateranen concilium novissimum, sub Julio et Leone X celebratum* (Rome: I. Mazochius, 1521) cliiii*r*–clxi*v*, the statement in question is found in clix*r*. Also see Stefan's *Oratio* in *Tomus Quartus Conciliorum omnium, tum generalium, tum provincialium atque particularium* (Cologne: Gervinum Calenium et Haeredes Iohannis Quentelij, 1567) 654–662.

[51] At margin, note *s*: "Ambrose, Cyrill, Theophylact [Theophylactus Simocattes, d. c. 640?] upon 2 Thessalonians 2:6–7. When the Roman Empire shall be taken out of the way, then shall Antichrist come. Chrysostome in 2 Thessalonians 2:6-7 τουτ ἑστιν, saith he, ἡ ἀρχὴ ἡ Ῥωμαϊκὴ." The last statement in this marginal note, "When the Roman Empire shall be taken out of the way," is a literal translation from John Chrysostom's *Homily IV* on 2 Thessalonians 2:6–9: "Οὕτω δὴ καὶ ἐνταῦθά φησι Μόνον ὁ κατέχων ἄρτι ἕως ἐκ μέσου γένηται τουτ ἐστιν, ἡ ἀρχὴ ἡ Ῥωμαϊκὴ ὅταν ἀρθῇ ἐκ μέσου, τότε ἐκεῖνος ἥξει" (English trans.): ["So indeed he also says here. *Only he who now letteth will let, until he be taken out of the way;* that is, when the Roman Empire is taken out of the way, then he shall come"]. See John Chrysostom, *In Epistolam Secundam ad Thessalo-*

For the Empire having been invaded by the Goths and Vandals, and other barbarous nations, by whom also Rome itself was taken and possessed about fifty years, the pope or bishop of Rome himself being also expelled out the City of Rome and put to seek for a time another place of abode. About the year 607, Boniface III[52] then bishop of Rome obtained from Phocas then emperor of the east, that not the patriarch of Constantinople, but the bishop of Rome should be universal bishop. And now was the title of pope appropriated to the bishop of Rome, which was before communicated to other patriarchs and bishops also indifferently. After this Pope Gregory VII contended with the Emperor Henry IV, whom he excommunicated and deposed, and gave the imperial crown to Rodulphus, with this verse: "Petra dedit Petro, Petrus diadema Rodulpho."[53] The pope of Rome being now risen above all bishops, patriarchs and emperors, he advanced himself above all general councils, which rise was fully attained by Pope Leo X, as Bellarmine boasted. The pope of Rome having ascended thus high, he was ambitious to rise yet higher. That so he might appear to be that man of sin, and son of perdition, who opposed and exalted himself above every one called God, or divine power, so that he as God might sit in the temple of God, showing himself that he is God [2 Thessalonians 2:4].[54] And to that end the pope of Rome confirmed those erroneous doctrines, and positions of the Church of Rome, and caused them to be concluded and decreed for doctrines and articles of faith, in the general councils of Constance, Lateran, and of Trent. Christophorus Mercelius speaking to Pope Julius II in the

---

nicenses Commentarius, *Homilia IV*, in *S.P.N. Joannis Chrysostomi, Opera Omnia Quae Exstant*, PG 62, col. 485–492, here col. 486, lines 36–39; translation from Charles Marriott and E. B. Pusey, eds., *The Homilies of St. John Chrysostom, Archbishop of Constantinople, on the Epistles of S. Paul the Apostle to the Philippians, Colossians, and Thessalonians* (Oxford: James Parker and Co., 1879) 491–501, here 492.

52 At margin, note *t*: "Prideaux, Introduction of Histories, Interval 7, sect. pag. 89." See Mathias Prideaux, *An easy and compendious introduction for reading all sorts of histories: contrived, in a more facile way then heretofore hath been published* (Oxford: Leonard Lichfield, 1648).

53 At margin, note *u*: "Bellarm. de Concil. lib. 2, cap. 17." See earlier notes on Bellarmine.

54 At margin, lacking proper marker, note [*v*]: 2 Thessalonians 2:4 ὁ ἀντικείμενος καὶ ὑπεραιρόμενος ἐπὶ πάντα λεγόμενον θεὸν ἢ σέβασμα, etc., σέβασμα Numen ["numen," object of worship]." See 2 Thessalonians 2:4: "He opposes and exalts himself above every so-called god or object of worship" (NRSV).

Council of Lateran, said: "Thou art another God upon earth."[55] And in the gloss on the canon law he is called, "Our Lord God the Pope," by the pope's allowance, as also divine adoration.[56]

The pope of Rome, the beast of the seventh and eighth head, having ascended out of the deep abyss, or bottomless pit, and risen at last unto this height of impiety; he having overcome the saints of God (Revelation 13:7) and killed the two prophetical witnesses of Christ (Revelation 11:7) must go into perdition: "and goeth into Perdition" (Revelation 17:8, 11). Which implies his gradual ruin, step by step. As he did rise gradually to the height of his grandeur, so he must fall by degrees into perdition: "Whom the Lord shall consume with the spirit of his mouth, and shall destroy with the brightness of his coming" (2 Thessalonians 2:8). So that this beast, the pope of Rome, shall be first consumed, and afterwards destroyed, as is foretold (Daniel 7:11–13). Now to be consumed is to decay, to wax weak, and by some sickness or distempers to waste, pine, and wear away, and at last to dye: even so shall the "beast," that "man of sin," the "son of perdition," the

---

[55] At margin, note *w*: "Tu es alter Deus in terrra (English trans.), ["You are another God on earth"]. Extra Joh. 22. de verb. signif. cap. cum interp. & lib. cerem. 1, sect. 1, fol. 16, Eberhardus Epist. Salisburgensis impress. Lugd. Anno 1555. Edit. nov. Ant. Papae Greg. 13. Credere dominum Deum nostrum Papam non sic potuisse statuere, prout statuit, haereticum censeatur." The first quote is from Archbishop Cristoforo Marcello (d. 1527) of Corfu, Greece. It can be found in *Christophori Marcelli in quarta Lateranensis Concilii Sessione habita oratio*, in *Sa. Lateranen concilium novissimum, sub Julio et Leone X celebratum* (Rome: I. Mazochius, 1521) liii*r*–lvii*r*, here lvi*v*. The second part of the note relates to the statement attributed to the fourteenth-century canonist Zenzelinus de Cassanis (d. 1334) "Credere dominum Deum nostrum Papam... ["Believe the lord our God the pope..."]. In 1325, or thereabout, Zenzelinus glossed a selection of decrees of Pope John XXII (r. 1316–34). These, together with other decrees of the same pope, were collected in the late fifteenth century by Joannes Chappuis and Vitalis de Thebis and are collectively known as *Extravagantes Joannis XXII*. The collection was incorporated in the sixteenth century to the new *corpus juris* of Pope Gregory XIII (r. 1572–1585) which was made public in 1582. See Constant Van De Wiel, *History of Canon Law* (Louvain: Peeters Press and Eerdmans, 1991) 111. Knollys' annotation is not clear. Hence, the edition that he might have handled or the edition of the *Extravagantes Joannis XXII* that was handled by his actual source remains unknown. However, the statement can be seen in *Sexti libri materia cum capitulorum numero* ([Paris]: Johannis Petit, 1508) folio liii*v*.

[56] At margin, note *x*: "Those words, *All that is called God, and worshipped*, 2 Thessalonians 2:4, are not to be interpreted πολιτικός of kings, etc., nor εκκλησιαστικός of prelates and priests, but θεολογικός of objects of divine worship, so the Athenian σεβάσματα, Acts 17:23, were their idols and models of devotion, and divine worship. So Dan. 11:36, 37, 40."

pope of Rome. Who has been consuming many years by the spirit of Christ's mouth, *viz* the powerful and spiritual preaching of the Gospel of free grace: by the prophetical witnesses of Christ, his godly and faithful ministers. Bellarmine's confession is a full confirmation of the pope's consumption, his words in English are these: "The Roman see has by little and little decayed, etc."[57] And it has much more decayed, and been consumed since that time, by the preaching of the Gospel through the powerful operation of the Holy Spirit.[58]

The utter downfall and destruction of the Roman beast, the pope, is also prophesied: "Babylon is fallen, is fallen, that great city" (Revelation 14:8), which is Rome as has been fully proved. Also Revelation 18:2, 8, 10, 19, 21: "Therefore shall her plagues come in one day... and she shall be utterly burnt with fire, for strong is the Lord God, who judged her... Alas, alas, that great city Babylon (that is Rome papal), that mighty city, for in one hour is thy judgment come." And verse 19: "Alas, alas, that great city (Rome)... for in one hour she is made desolate." And Revelation 19:19–20: "And the beast (that is the pope of Rome), was taken, and with him the false prophet... these both were cast alive into the lake burning with brimstone." Then shall Rome papal be found no more at all (Revelation 18:21). And then shall the beast (who is the pope of Rome), "be tormented day and night, for ever and ever" (Revelation 20:10).

Proposition III.
That the Church of Rome is the Great Whore

The church of God under the law was resembled by the prophet[59] unto a comely and delicate woman. And the church of Christ under the Gospel

---

[57] At margin, note *x* [2]: "Bellarm. de Rom. Pontif. lib. 3, cap. 21, scrip. 1577." See Robert Bellarmine, *Tertia controversia generalis, De summo pontifice, quinque libris explicata*, in *De controversiis Christianae* (1721) 1:241–446; *Opera omnia* (1856) 1:299–540.

[58] At margin, note *y*: "Mr. Rich. Bernar's Key of Knowledge, part. 4, pag. 126, 127, 128, 129. Since 1558 (saith he) the pope hath nothing increased upon us, but we by God's power have prevailed against him. Have not the papists had ill success in all their attempts against us? And in spite of their policy, trecheries, and treasons,—we stand and they fall; and so must they now (saith he) continually, for by an oath of God it is confirmed unto us, chap. 10. 5, 6. 'That there should be time no longer.' Read pag. 127, 128 & 129." See Richard Bernard, *A key of knowledge for the opening of the secret mysteries of St Iohns mysticall Reuelation* (London: Felix Kyngston, 1617).

[59] At margin, note *a*: [Blank].

was revealed to the Apostle[60] by the similitude of a woman clothed with the sun, having a crown of twelve stars on her head. Such was the church at Jerusalem, and the churches in Judea, in the days of the apostles. And such was the church at Rome, whose faith was famous throughout the whole world[61] and such also were the churches in Asia, those golden candlesticks—whilst Jesus Christ walked in the midst of them—and their shining lights, like stars, the able ministers of the New Testament called angels, whom the Lord Jesus Christ held in his right-hand.[62] But when the Church of Rome departed from the faith, as was foretold by the Apostle[63] and apostatized both in doctrine and manners and fell away, as was also foretold by the same Apostle,[64] then she became a false church, whom Jesus Christ showed unto his servant John, in a vision and revelation, like a woman, that is a harlot, and the mother of harlots, and calls her the great whore[65] whose name is mystery, Babylon the great, etc. which is papal Rome, as has been clearly, and fully proved. And I shall now prove, and plainly demonstrate, this third proposition: that the Church of Rome is the great whore.

That church which is the "mother of harlots,"[66] by maintaining, commanding, and practicing spiritual adulteries, whoredoms, and fornications, is the great whore. But the Church of Rome is the "mother of harlots," which maintained, commanded and practiced spiritual adulteries, whoredoms, and fornications; therefore the Church of Rome is the great whore.

The spiritual adultery, whoredom, and fornication of Judah and Jerusalem, which God did so much complain of by his prophets was their idolatry, and image worship: "with their idols have they committed adultery" [Ezekiel 23:37]. So God complained of Nineveh, by his prophet: "Because of the whoredoms of the well-favoured harlot, the mistress of witchcraft, that selleth nations through her whoredoms, and families through her witchcrafts... I will shew the nations thy nakedness, and the kingdoms thy shame" (Nahum 3:4–5). And so did Christ show the spiritual adultery, and idolatry of papal Rome under the similitude of a woman whose name is

[60] At margin, note *b*: "Revelation 12:1"
[61] At margin, note *c*: "Romans 1:7–8"
[62] At margin, note *d*: "Revelation 1:20 and 2:1."
[63] At margin, note *e*: "1 Timothy 4:1, 2, 3."
[64] At margin, note *f*: "2 Thessalonians 2:1, 2, 3, 4...12."
[65] At margin, note *g*: "Revelation 17:1, 5."
[66] At margin, note *a*: [Blank].

"mystery," "Babylon the great," the "mother of harlots," and of "the abominations of the earth." God's great prohibition against this sinful abomination of spiritual whoredom, of making and worshipping images in the second commandment (Exodus 20:4–5). And the grievous judgments, which God denounced against, and inflicted upon the worshippers of idols, yea against them false prophets, and any other persons, that shall entice and persuade any to go after other gods, and serve them (Deuteronomy 13:1–15) showed us the sinfulness of this sin of idolatry and how greatly God is provoked unto jealousy by it (1 Corinthians 10:20–22 and Revelation 3:20–22 and Revelation 18:1–8). So that idolatry and false worship is spiritual whoredom.

Now let us examine the second proposition, to wit, whether the Church of Rome be guilty of this great sin of spiritual whoredom, adultery, and fornication—called idolatry—and be indeed the "mother of harlots"? The ancients do with one consent assert that idolatry is an attributing of divine honor unto the creature, which is only due unto God. And Thomas Aquinas[67] out of all the Fathers and ancient writers concludes so, "that is idolatry," said he, "when the honor, that is only due to God, is given to the creature." The Church of Rome does attribute that divine honor to the creature, which is only due to God, for she does attribute trust and confidence in their prayers to saints deceased, yea to their feigned saints, as plainly appears in the public service books, rosaries, breviaries, psalters, and catechisms of the Church of Rome.[68] The papists praying to Saint John, say,

---

[67] At margin, note *a*: "Aquin. In Epist. ad Ephes. c. 5, Lect. 3. Quando honor soli Deo debitus, exhibetur creaturae. Concil. Trident. Sess. 9." Thomas Aquinas (1225–1274) may have lectured on Paul's Epistle to the Ephesians while at Rome, between 1265 and 1268. See Jean-Pierre Torrell, *Saint Thomas Aquinas: The Person and His Work*, 2 vols. (Washington: Catholic University of America Press, 2005) 340. His lectures on the epistles of Paul are collected under the title *Commentaria in omnes epistolas divi Pauli Apostoli.* For a seventeenth-century edition see Thomas Aquinas, *Commentaria in omnes epistolas divi Pauli Apostoli* (Paris: Dionysium Moreau, 1636) quotation on page 434. For an English translation see Aquinas, *Commentary on Saint Paul's Epistle to the Ephesians*, trans. Matthew L. Lamb (Albany: Magi Books, 1966). For a critical edition of the Council of Trent see "Concilium Tridentinum," in *Conciliorum oecumenicorum decreta*, 657–799.

[68] At margin, note *b*: "Catechis. Roman. Osorius tom. 3, concion. p. 681. Bellarm. De Sanctor. Beat. lib. 1, cap. 10." In this note, Knollys is referring to three separate works. First, is the *Catechism of the Council of Trent.* It was first published under Pope Pius V (r. 1566–1572) see *Catechismus, Ex Decreto Concilii Tridentini: Ad Parochos, Pii Quinti Pont. Max. iussu editus* (Rome: Manutius, 1566). The second allusion is to the Jesuit priest Juan Osorio and his collection of sermons published in Antwerp in four vol-

"Hail, o holy Apostle of our Lord Jesus Christ, I entreat thee that thou wouldest deliver me, thy unworthy servant, from all adversity, and receive my soul at the hour of death, and wouldst bring me to life everlasting." To Saint George they pray thus, "He saved us from our sins, that we may rest with the blessed in heaven." To Saint Erasmus, "O Erasmus! Grant, that by thy merits and prayers we may overcome all the snares of our enemies, and be freed from eternal death."[69] To Francis the Friar they pray thus, "O Francis, singular crucified saint, be thou to us the way of life, make satisfaction for us always, show to Christ the marks of thy wounds."[70] This Friar Francis they make equal to Christ, as those blasphemous verses of two

---

umes between 1594 and 1597; see Juan Osorio, *Concionum* (Antwerp: Joannem Keerbergium, 1594–1597). The third reference is to Robert Bellarmine, *Liber primus: De beatitudine et canonizatione sanctorum. Quarta controversia generalis de ecclesia triumphante, tribus libris explicata*, in *De controversiis Christianae* (1721) 2:341–376; *Opera omnia* (1857) 2:411–462.

[69] At margin, note *c*: "Possevin. bibl. select. pag. 295. Boz. de sig. Eccles. tom. 2. pag. 200." The first citation refers to the Jesuit priest, Antonius Possevin (c. 1533–1611) from Mantua. See Antonius Possevin, *Bibliotheca selecta, qua agitur de ratione studiorum in Historia, in Disciplinis in Salute omnium procuranda* (Rome: Typogr. Apostolica Vaticana, 1593). The second part of the citation cannot be identified with certainty due to a lack of bibliographic information. It is possible, however, that Knollys may be referring once again to Abraham Bzowski, *Annalium ecclesiasticorum* (1616–1640).

[70] At margin, note *d*: "Exue Franciscum tunica laceroq; cuculo: qui Franciscus erat, jam tibi Christus erit. Francisci exuviis (si qua licet) indue Christum: jam Franciscus erit, qui modo Christus erat" (English trans.): ["Strip Francis, from his coat and cowl, all naked, and you shall see, he that even now Saint Francis was, to Christ will turned be: Again, put Francis' coat and cowl on Christ (and mark the liar) he that even now, was Jesus Christ, will Francis be"]. The quote is found in Possevin, *Bibliotheca selecta, pars secunda* (1593) 295. Possevin attributes the prayer to Horatius Tursellinus (see next note). English translation from John White, *The way to the true church wherein the principall motiues perswading according to Romanisme and questions touching the nature and authoritie of the church and scriptures, are familiarly disputed, and driuen to their issues, where, this day they sticke betweene the Papists and vs: contriued into an answer to a popish discourse concerning the rule of faith and the marks of the church. And published to admonish such as decline to papistrie of the weake and vncertaine grounds, whereupon they haue ventured their soules. Directed to all that seeke for resolution: and especially to his louing countrimen of Lancashire* (London: [R. Field], 1608) A*v*. It should be noted that White, who also includes a diatribe against Catholic prayers in his preface, provides the Latin form of the prayer and cites Possevin by page number.

shameless Jesuits Turselline and Bencius do plainly declare.[71] And to the image Veronica, they pray thus, "Hail, holy face, imprinted on a clout, purge us from all sin within and without, etc."[72] Thus also the papists by the commandments of men, *viz* popes, Jesuits, priests, yea and general councils, and the Church of Rome do worship images, pictures, crosses, crucifixes, and relics, which—they say—are to be worshipped after the same manner as images are.[73] It's written of Dunstan the Abbot of Glastenbury, that he blessed the right thumb of Editha the Abbesse of Wilton, which being found uncorrupted, after all her body was turned to dust and ashes in her grave, became a relic.[74] How many things about our Savior are turned into relics? *Viz.* the manger, his linen cloth, his cradle, his shirt, the table on which Christ eat [ate] his last supper, the cup wherein he gave his blood to

---

[71] The first is the Italian historian Horatius Tursellinus, or Orazio Torsellini (1545–1599) and the other is the rhetorician Franciscus Bencius, or Francesco Benci (1542–1594).

[72] At margin, note *e*: "Chemnit. exam. Concil. Trident. de Imagin." Knollys is referring to the work of the Lutheran theologian Martin Chemnitz (1522–1586) *Examen concilii tridentini* (1565–1573). See the multivolume edition, Martin Chemnitz, *Examen Decretorum Concilii Tridentini. In Quo Ex Sacrae Scripturae norma, collatis etiam orthodoxis uerae & puriorus Antiquitatis testimonijs ostenditur, qualia sint illa Decreta, & quo artificio sint composita* (Frankfurt: Sigismundi Feyerabend, 1566–1573). Chemnitz's discussion on images is found in the fourth and last part.

[73] At margin, note *f*: "Vasq. De adoratione, lib. 3, dis. 3, cap. 2. Reliquiae eodem modo atque, imagines sunt adorande" (English trans.): ["Relics are honored in the same way as images"]. "Conci. Trident. Decret. De Reliq. Sanct." The first citation is to the work of the Spanish Jesuit Gabriel Vázquez (1549/51–1604) *De cultu adorationis libri tres* (Alcalá de Henares: Juan Gracian, 1594). The section cited by Knollys is found in pp. 205*r*–206*r* of the 1594 edition. For the Council of Trent on relics see *Decretum de invocatione, veneratione et reliquiis sanctorum, et de sacris imaginibus*, in *Conciliorum oecumenicorum decreta*, 774–776.

[74] At margin, note *g*: "Guliel. Malmsbur, lib. 2 de Pontific. Vincent. li. 25, cap. 33." The Benedictine monk William of Malmesbury (b. c. 1090–d. c. 1142) was author of the medieval chronicle *De gestis pontificum Anglorum libri quinque*. Several editions of the work appeared in print in the sixteenth and seventeenth century as part of the larger collection *Rerum anglicarum scriptores post Bedam*, among them *Rerum Anglicarum scriptores post Bedam praecipui, ex vetustissimis codicibus manuscriptis nunc primum in lucem editi. Willielmi monachi Malmesburiensis de gestis regum Anglorum lib. V. Eiusdem Historiæ nouellæ lib. II. Eiusdem de gestis pontificum Angl. lib. IIII. Henrici Archidiaconi Huntindoniensis Historiarum lib. VIII. Rogeri Houedeni Annalium pars prior & posterior. Chronicorum Ethelwerdi lib. IIII. Ingulphi abbatis Croylandensis historiarum lib. I. Adiecta ad finem chronologia* (London: G. Bishop, R. Nuberie, & R. Barker, 1596). The second reference cannot be identified with precision due to lack of bibliographical information.

be drunk are relics to be seen at this day—as the papists and other pilgrims and travelers report in several places and churches in Rome, Spain, Ravenna, Pisa, at Andegavum [i.e. Angers, France], etc. The Church of Rome is guilty of gross idolatry and spiritual adultery in adoring and worshipping the host, for at the priest's elevation of the host—the papists breaden God—they all fall down upon their knees, and worship it with very great devotion, and whosoever refuses so to do is counted a heretic.[75] And yet some priests have poisoned the host, intending to add murder, yea willful and sacrilegious murder thereby to their gross idolatry, as the monk Bernhardine, who poisoned the host to the intent that he might poison the Emperor Henry of Luxembourg, as he also did at the instigation of Robert King of Sicily.[76] Baronius[77] tells us of a priest that either did, or would have poisoned Pope Victor II at the sacrament. And William Archbishop of York was poisoned at the mass by his own chaplains by that which they put into the chalice. What can be more heathenish and palpable idolatry than to worship the bread consecrated by a priest, which is maintained, commanded and practiced by the Church of Rome, by all her priests and papists?

---

[75] At margin, note *h*: "Bellarm. De Sacrament. Euchar. l. a. cap. 29. Coster. Enchir. de Euchar. Rubric. in Missal. Rom." Bellarmine's thoughts on the eucharist are gathered in the six books of *De sacramento eucharistiae.* See Robert Bellarmine, *Tertia controversia generalis, De sacramento eucharistiae, sex libris explicata, De controversiis Christianae fidei, Opera omnia* (1857) 3:235–576. The next reference is to the work by the Jesuit priest Franciscus Coster (1532–1619) *Enchiridion controversiarum praecipuarum nostri temporis de religione* (Cologne: Arnoldi Mylij, 1596) chapters eight, nine, and ten deal with the eucharist. Lastly, Knollys mentions the Roman Missal. In 1570, Pope Pius V (r. 1566–1572) instituted the *Missale Romanum* as the standard liturgy of the Roman Catholic Church.

[76] It was held by many chroniclers, although not all, that Emperor Henry VII (c. 1269/74–1313) was poisoned by the Dominican Bernard de Montepulciano. For an overview see Sophia Menache, *Clement* V (Cambridge: Cambridge University Press, 2003) 172. Robert Anjou (1278–1343) was the king of Naples from 1309 to 1343.

[77] At margin, note *l*: "Cuspinian. Nauclerus, Egnat. et Baron. Spondan. An. *Eccles. an.* 1055. Volateran. Hoveden. Math. Paris. etc." Knollys provides a long list of medieval and late-medieval chroniclers, as well as humanist historians, whose authority he is claiming in his polemic against Rome. These are (in order of appearance): Johannes Cuspinian (1473–1529); Johannes Nauclerus (c. 1425–1510); Johannes Baptista Egnatius (c. 1478–1553); Caesar Baronius (1538–1607); Henricus Spondanus (d. 1643); Raphaelus Maffeus Volateranus (1455?–1522?); Roger of Hoveden (d. c. 1201); Matthew Paris (d. 1259). Spondanus was one of the continuators of Baronius, see Henricus Spondanus, *L'abregé des annales ecclesiastiques de ... cardinal Baronius* (Paris: Jacques d'Allin, 1655).

Another branch of the spiritual whoredom and adultery of the great whore, the Church of Rome, is the adoration and worshipping the cross itself, on which Christ suffered, say they, also the image of the cross and the sign of the cross. Vázquez the Jesuit affirms that this is the doctrine of the Church of Rome, and so does Bellarmine, Thomas Aquinas and many other great doctors of the Church of Rome.[78] It is testified that a famous papist, and a professor of divinity, who dedicated his book to Pope Clement VIII said thus, "we worship the cross with the same worship wherewith we adore Christ himself," etc.[79]

Again, whereas we assert that the Church of Rome is the mother of harlots, for a full proof thereof let it be considered: First, that the Church of Rome owns herself to be the catholic and mother church of all those churches in Italy, Spain, France, Germany, etc., whether national or parochial, that receive, believe, and practice her damnable doctrines and idolatrous worship which are false churches and harlots ("with whom the kings of the earth have committed fornication, and the inhabitants of the earth have been made drunk with the wine of her fornication," [Revelation 17:2]) and therefore the Church of Rome—mystical Babylon as before proved—is called the mother of harlots and abominations of the earth (Revelation 17:2–5).

Secondly, that the Church of Rome has begotten, born, and nourished all those national and parochial churches before mentioned, which are called the cities of the nations (Revelation 16:19) which national churches are harlots as Nineveh was called (Nahum 3:4) because of the multitude of their

---

[78] At margin, note *m*: "Vasques, *de Adorat.* l. 3, cap. 2. Bellarm. *de Imagin. lib. 3. c. 27, 28, 29.* Aquin. *Sum. part. 3, art. 4.*" Gabriel Vázquez, *De cultu adorationis libri tres* (Alcalá de Henares: Juan Gracian, 1594). The full and correct reference to the section cited by Knollys is Vázquez, *De Adoratione*, lib. 3, dis. 2, cap. 2 found in pp. 196*v*–198*v* of the 1594 edition. In the following reference Knollys calls the reader's attention to the "third book" ("lib. 3") of the *Fourth general controversy*. Note, however, that in the Venice edition of 1721 and the subsequent *Opera omnia* the alluded controversy appears as the "second book." See Robert Bellarmine, *Liber secundus: De reliquis et imaginibus sanctorum. Quarta controversia generalis de ecclesia triumphante, tribus libris explicata*, in *De controversiis Christianae* (1721) 2:412–418; *Opera omnia* (1857) 2:504–511. Knollys reference to Aquinas is incomplete. The full reference to the Leonine Edition is: Aquinas, *Sum*, Part III, 25, Art. 4. See Thomas Aquinas, *Opera omnia, iussu impensaque Leonis XIII P. M.* (Rome: Ex Typographia Polyglotta S. C. De Propaganda Fide, 1903) 11:281–282.

[79] At margin, note *n*: "Chrys. à Visitat. de virb. Domini tom. 4. Lib. 6. c. 7." Source is not discernible. Also, it is not clear either which "famous papist" Knollys is referring to, or what is the connection to the reference to Chrysostom.

spiritual whoredom and abominable idolatries. Whereby it appears that the Church of Rome is the mother of harlots for she has infused her false doctrines, worships, and all her idolatries into those churches.

Thirdly, that the Church of Rome, as the mother of harlots, imposes her false doctrines, idolatrous worships and damnable practices upon those and other national churches, whom she called her daughters, owning her authority over them as being their mother. And, first, it does appear that the Church of Rome is the great whore, by her spiritual whoredom and fornications: "And the woman... had a golden cup in her hand full of abominations and filthiness of her fornication" (Revelation 17:4). All kinds of idolatry, image worship, and superstitions in the service of God is spiritual whoredom, and such are those images and idols, those crosses and crucifixes, those pictures, and painted forms, or representations of our savior Christ, of the Virgin Mary, and of saints deceased, whom the papists set up, fall down before, and worship.[80] The kings of the earth have committed fornication—

[80] For some reason the sequence of marginal notes is now broken, reverting to letter "f." At margin, note *f*: "Prid. *de Antichristo,* Lect. 11. Non in Babilona solum, sed in Sodomam Roma degeneravit, ut non πόρνων modo meretricum, sed (ut habet liber Complutensis et Regius) πόρνων, hoc est, catamitarum et ganimedum mater habeatur (English trans.): ["Rome has fallen below the level not only of Babylon, but of Sodom, even if not only as πόρνων, as in the way of prostitutes, but also (as in the Complutensian and Biblia Regia) πόρνων, that is, considered as the motherland of effeminates and those who are like Ganymede"]. Sic Heptades *de Antichristo,* pag. 99, 129–131, et Doun. Diatr. *de Antichristo,* l. 1, c. 7. Etiam M. Antonius de Dom. Archiep. Spalat. *de Rep. Eccles.* lib. 4., cap. 3, n. 26–29, ac Hieron. *Adver. Jovin.* lib. 2, etc. Marlor in Apoc. 18.24, et in Apoc. 13, p. 37, 64, 65." Note *f* makes reference to the following sources, in order of appearance: John Prideaux (1578–1650) "Lectio XI: De Antichristo," in *Viginti-duae lectiones de totidem religionis captibvs, praecipve hoc tempore controversis, prout publicè habebantur Oxoniae in vesperiis quibus accesserunt Tredecim orationes inavgvrales de totidem theologiae apicibus scitu non indignis, prout in promotione doctorum in comitiis habebantur: subnectuntur Sex conciones pro more habitae ad artium baccalaurios in die cinerum* (Oxford: Hen. Cripps, Hen. Curteyn, & Thom. Robinson, 1648) 161–179; George Sandys (1578–1644) *Sacrae heptades, or Seaven problems concerning Antichrist 1. of his place. 2. Of his state. 3. Of his names. 4. Of his rising. 5. Of his raigne. 6. Of his words and actions. 7. Of his times. Necessarie to be read and knowne of all men, who professe Christ Iesus, and hope to be saved by no other name* (Amsterdam: Successors of Giles Thorp, 1625) 99, 129–131; George Downame (d. 1634) *Papa Antichristus, siue Diatriba de Antichristo cuius duae partes: prior, kataskeue, quâ orthodoxa serenissimi Regis Iacobi, de Antichristo sententia demonstratur; posterior, anaskeue, quâ Leonardi Lessii sedecim demonstrationes, monitoriae Regis praefationi oppositae, refutantur. Auctore Reuerendo in Christo Patre, Georgio Dounamo Episcopo Derensi* (London: Ioan. Billium, 1620) I.vii; Marco Antonio De Dominis (1560–1624) *De repub-*

that is, spiritual whoredom and adultery—with her: "And the inhabitants of the earth have been made drunk with the wine of her fornication" (Revelation 17:12). By receiving those idolatrous doctrines and by practicing those imaginary superstitions, which the Church of Rome teaches and practices in the worship of God.[81] "In vain do they worship God," said Christ, "teaching for doctrines the commandments of men" [Matthew 15:9]. To be sure, those notoriously known doctrines and practices of the Church of Rome, the mother of harlots. Namely, their worshipping of images of Christ and of the Virgin Mary; their invocation, adoration, and prayers to dead saints and their irrational and senseless doctrine of transubstantiation, sacrifice, and adoration of the host, that is, their breaden God which, they say, is by consecration changed into the very body and blood of Christ, which the papists adore, kneel unto, and worship, as their God and savior.[82]

But besides the idolatry and superstition of this part of their will-worship, let it be considered by the judicious and rational papists and Protestants, first, how irrational that doctrine and practice of the Church of Rome is, to wit, of transubstantiation. Admit the sacrament of the Lord's Supper be administered in the Roman Catholic Church in 100 to 500

---

lica ecclesiastica libri X (London: Ex officina Nortoniana apud Ioan. Billium, MDCXVII. [1617]) 558–583; Agustin Marlorat, *A catholike exposition vpon the Reuelation of Sainct Iohn. Collected by M. Augustine Marlorate out of diuers notable writers, whose names ye shal find in the page following* (London: H. Binneman, 1574); Hieronymus Stridonensis, *Adversus Jovinianum libri duo*, see PL 23, col. 221–352. The Greek myth of Ganymede was originally used to explain the ancient Cretan practice of pederasty; see William A. Percy, *Pederasty and Pedagogy in Archaic Greece* (Urbana: University of Illinois Press, 1996).

[81] At margin, note *g*: "Matth. 15.7, 8, 9. & Rev. 13.4, 8. Idem, in Apoc. 18. Meretricem babylonicam, ecclesiam nempè romanam, scortationibus, ad immundiâ antichristi romani, sanguino lentorum scil. at que belluinorum pontificum, quorum plerique magi, venefici, athei, adulteri,—non apostolici, sed apotactici, & apostatici, quales ipse Genebrardus lib. 4. Chronol. fatetur—superstitionum, & cultuum novorum inventores" (English trans.): ["Prostitute of Babylon, the Church of Rome, whoredom, dirty because of the Roman antichrist, blood dawdler [*sic*], because of the bestial pontiffs, most of them enchanters, sorcerers, atheists, adulterers, by no means apostolic, but rebels and apostates, such as Genebrardus himself confesses, inventors of superstition and new worship"]. The source of this quote remains unclear. Perhaps these are Knollys' own words. It does appear, however, that he attributes it to the Benedictine Gilbert Génébrard (1535–1597) *Chronographiae libri quatuor* (Paris: M. Sonnium, 1580).

[82] At margin, note *h*: "Doun. *de Antichristo* lib. 1. cap. 7. Dementatos & mente captos esse not at Apostolus, Apoc. 18.23. & 19.2. & 17.2, 4. qui cum ista Meretrice scortantur, ejusque scortationibus & idololatriis imbuuntur & fascinantur." The reference is to Downame (d. 1634) *Papa Antichristus, siue Diatriba de Antichristo* (1620).

places, as indeed it is, at the same time, and the bread be by virtue of each priest's consecration changed into the real body of Christ, then Christ had 100 to 500 real bodies at one time, which is absurd and irrational. Secondly, how senseless their doctrine of transubstantiation is. The Church of Rome teaches, and the papists senselessly are to believe, that the bread after consecration is the very body of Christ. And yet they that eat that bread, see it is bread after the consecration, yea they taste and know it is bread still, while they are eating of it. Thus, they delude their senses by a fond and false belief. Thirdly, how damnable their doctrine and practice of this part of their false worship of God is, (viz. transubstantiation). The doctrine is damnable, for the Church of Rome teaches her children, the papists, to believe in, to fall down unto, and to worship a breaden-God, which their priests have made an idol, with solemn and sacred adoration. And the practice is also damnable, for the papists eating that bread with a firm belief, that it is not bread, but the body of Christ, do eat that bread and drink that cup unworthily, and so eat and drink their own damnation (1 Corinthians 11: 29).

Secondly, it appears, that the Church of Rome is the great whore because she is become the mother of harlots, the lupan[83] of stews and of all abominations (Revelation 17:1, 5).[84] The Church of Rome calls herself the

---

[83] The original work displays an asterisk by the word "lupan," but does not provide either a marginal note under the sign of an asterisk or an explanation. He seems to be playing on the Latin term "lupanar," or brothel. Since in a now archaic use the noun "stew" means "prostitute," the phrase could be rendered as a "brothel of prostitutes."

[84] At margin, note *k*: "Prid. *de mille annis Apoc.* Lect. 13. Roma est Sodoma spiritualiter, quia similis Sodomae: quâ re similis? foeditate Sodomiticarum libidinum in urbe magnâ horribiliter grassantium, unde & mater scortationum, Apoc. 17.5. vocata, etc. Vide iam magnam urbem Papatus; Quid est nisi scortationum spiritualium & corporalium foedissima officina? Petrarcha queritur Ep. 20. Romae stupra, raptus, incestus, adulteria, iam Pontificialis lasciviae ludi sunt, quod cecinit Mantuanus. I pudor in villas, si non patiantur easdem et villae vomicas, Roma est iam tota Lupanar. Roma, vale, vidi, satis est vidisse; revertar, cum leno, meretrix, scurra, cinaedus, ero. Sic, Marulus in Epitaph. Ita Janus Pannonius, etiam Johannes Sapidus." Knollys cites John Prideaux, "Lectio XIII: De mille annis apocalypticis," in *Viginti-duae lectiones de totidem religionis captibvs* (1648) 199–179. Prideaux's lecture, however, is based on Revelation 20:1–8, while Knollys mentions Revelation 17:5: "Roma est Sodoma spiritualiter, quia similis Sodomae: quâ re similis? foeditate Sodomiticarum libidinum in urbe magnâ horribiliter grassantium, unde & mater scortationum, Apoc. 17.5. vocata, etc. Vide iam magnam urbem Papatus; Quid est nisi scortationum spiritualium & corporalium foedissima officina?" (English trans.): ["Rome is spiritual Sodom, because it is like Sodom, how is it similar to Sodom? In that shameful sodomitic lust roams horribly in the city, the source and origin

catholic church, and she teaches her children—the papists—to believe, that she is the mother of all national churches, and whosoever do not acknowledge her to be the holy catholic church, and submit not to her canons, constitutions, doctrines, discipline and worship, are heretics. All the national churches of Germany, France, Spain, and Italy, etc., are her harlots, false churches and idolatrous worshippers of images, crosses, crucifixes, etc., as said before.

The Church at Rome was a true church in the apostles' time, whose faith was famous throughout the whole world (Romans 1:7–8). But afterwards that church departed from the faith, apostatized both in doctrine

---

of whoredom, as named in Revelation 17:5. Go and see the great papal city, who is not in spiritual whoredom and the loathsome vestment of the eucharistic office?"]. Knollys attributes the following Latin quotation to Francesco Petrarch (1304–1374): "Petrarcha queritur Ep. 20. Romae stupra, raptus, incestus, adulteria, iam Pontificialis lasciviae ludi sunt..." (English trans.): ["In Rome shame, pillage, lewdness, adultery are now pontificall pastime..."]. Yet, the statement is a paraphrase based on Letter XVIII of Petrarch's *Liber sine nomine*, or *Book without a Name*. Cf., Francesco Petrarca, *Sine nomine*, ed. Ugo Dotti (Roma: Editori Laterza, 1974) 208–210. Knollys also alludes to the Carmelite poet Baptista Spagnuoli Mantuanus (1448–1516) whose *Adolescentia* was widely used in primary education throughout Protestant England. See Lee Piepho, "Mantuan's Eclogues in the English Reformation," *Sixteenth Century Journal* 25, no. 3 (1994): 623–632; Cf., Mantuanus, *Baptistae Mantuani Carmelitae theologi Adolescentia, seu, Bucolica, breuibus Iodoci Badij commentarijs illustrata: his accesserunt Ioannis Murmeillij in singulas eclogas argumenta, cum annotatiunculis eiusdem in loca aliquot obscuriora: accessit, & index, non ille vetus, & indigestus, sed nouus omnino, ac locupletior multo, opera Barthol. Laurentis* (London: Ioannes Kyngstonus, 1569). Knollys lumps together several verses, the first of which he credits to Mantuanus, "...quod cecinit Mantuanus" (English trans.): ["as celebrated by Mantuanus"]. The first two verses, "I pudor in villas, si non patiantur easdem, et villae vomicas, urbs est iam tota Lupanar" (English trans.): ["Also, decency in the country, even if it does not suffer the same, villages are gatherings of pus, Rome is all a brothel"], are the closing lines of Mantuanus' poem, "De carnis privii mala consuetudine," in Mantuanus, *De sacris diebus Carmelitae opus aureum* (Madiolani: Caluum, 1540) 38. Knollys' version replaces "urbs" with "Rome." The second verse was widely ascribed to Erasmus of Rotterdam, although some credited it to Mantuanus. Knollys attributes it to a certain Marulus, whose exact identity remains uncertain: "Sic, Marulus in Epitaph, 'Roma, vale, vidi, satis est vidisse; revertar, cum leno, meretrix, scurra, cinaedus, ero' " (English trans.): ["So Marulus in the Epitaph, 'Farewell Rome! I have seen you, and to have seen you is enough. I shall come back when I am a pimp, a whore, a buffon, a sodomite' "]. See Erasmus of Rotterdam, *Collected Works of Erasmus: Notes to Poems,* Collected Works, vol. 86 (Toronto: University of Toronto Press, 1993) 728. The last two figures mentioned in the note are the Hungarian poet Janus Pannonius (1434–1472) and Johannes Sapidus (1490–1561).

and in discipline, yea and also in manners.[85] And so became a false church and a synagogue of Satan, and she is now become the great whore and mother of harlots: she has left her first husband Christ Jesus the Lord, and has taken another head and husband, the pope of Rome. She has departed from her first faith, which was grounded upon the doctrines of Jesus Christ and his apostles and now she does believe the doctrines of her holy father the pope. And she is fallen from her first purity in discipline and manners into all manner of licentiousness and abominable wickedness, and so is become the mother of harlots, and of all the abominations which are in all false churches that are her daughters, whereby the Church of Rome is plainly manifested to be the great whore.

Thirdly, it appears that the Church of Rome is the great whore by her barbarous and bloody persecutions and murders added to her whoredomes (Revelation 18:24): "For in her was found the blood of prophets, and of saints, and all that were slain upon the earth." "And I saw the women (the

---

[85] At margin, note *l*: "J. W. de ult. *Romae* exitio. pag. 62. ait, Joannes 13. omni flagitiorum generi, scil. stupris, adulteriis, incestis, [...] aliisque sceleribus ab ipsâ adolescentia incumbens, Stephanam Concubinam Patris sui, & duas sorores vitiavit. [...] Nicholaus quidam de Bibrach Erphordiensis non obscure innuit se à Martino 2. velut Ganymedem [...] ad turpiora quaedam expetitum" (English trans.): ["he says, John XIII did all genre of crimes, that is, fornication, adultery, incest ... among Stephen's other wicked deeds from his very youth he forced his way with his father's concubine and vitiated his two sisters ... Nikolaus von Bibra, from Erfurt, clearly refers to Martin II just as [sic. Marinus II] Ganymedem ... according to a cerain indecent desire"]. Knollys is quoting the anonymous seventeenth-century work, *Romae ruina finalis anno dom. 1666. Mundiq; finis sub quadragesimum quintum post annum. Sive, literae ad Anglos Romae versantes datae, quibus (vel ex pontificiorum, scriptis evicto, Babylonis in Apocalypsi nomine, Romam Pontificiam designari, Papamque Romanum ipsissimum esse Antichristum, scripturis praedictum) & bestiam derelinquere, & Babylone, urbe nempe Romanâ anno jam dicto, millesimo sc. sexcentesimo, sexagesimo sexto, excidio, & incendio delendâ atque funditus evertendâ confestim exire admonentur* (London: T.C. for Johannene Sherlaeum, 1655). The preface is signed by a J.W. The volume is attributed to James Windet, or Jacobus Windus (d. 1664) a physician trained at Leiden and poet. See Norman Moore, "Windet, James (d. 1664)," rev. Michael Bevan, in *Oxford Dictionary of National Biography*, edited by H. C. G. Matthew and Brian Harrison (Oxford: Oxford University Press, 2004). Online ed., edited by Lawrence Goldman. http://www.oxforddnb.com/view/article/29718 (accessed May 27, 2014); Alfred Hackman, *Catalogus librorum impressorum Bibliothecae Bodleianae*, vol. 3 (Oxford: University Press, 1843) 848. Knollys abridges the much longer passage found in *Romae ruina finalis*, 62. The reference to the Greek myth of Ganymede, can be found in Nicolaus de Bibera (fl. 13th cent.) *Occulti Erfordensis, Carmen satiricum. Eine quelle de XIII jahrhunderts,* ed. Theobald Fischer (Halle: Buchh. des Waisenhauses, 1870) 41.

great whore, and mother of harlots) drunken with the blood of the saints, and with the blood of the martyrs of Jesus" (Revelation 17:1, 5–6). Particularly of the Waldenses, Albigenses, and other.[86] Vergerius, who was well acquainted with the romish bloody Inquisition, tells us that 150,000 Protestants suffered death in less than 30 years. The King of France in his letters to the pope boasted that in the year 1572, in the massacre of Paris and elsewhere, 70,000 heretics were slain in few days, that is 70,000 Protestants were then and there murdered by the papists.[87] And can we forget, or omit to mention the late bloody butcheries of Protestants by the barbarous cruel Irish papists in 1641, when 100,000 were murdered? And if the bloody invasion of 1588 and the horrid gunpowder treason of November 5th, 1605, and the bloody traitorous design of popish recusants—as the King calls it[88]—"even that damnable and hellish plot"—as the Parliament voted it—"contrived and carried on by popish recusants for assassinating and murdering the King, and for subverting the government and rooting out and destroying the Protestant religion" had taken effect, many more Protestants in England had been—ere this day—murdered and massacred by the bloodthirsty papists.[89] And these barbarous, bloody, and damnable persecutions and practices of the papists are grounded on the very doctrine, religion, and faith of the Church of Rome, which is not to be found in any other party of the whole Christian world—so called—besides. Whereby it is evident, to those that have understanding, that the Church of Rome is the great bloody

---

[86] At margin, note *m*: "*Abregè Chronol.* etc. par le Sieur de Mezeray, Paris. 1567. Tom. 3, p. 1082, 1086 ad Annum 1572." See François Eudes Mezeray, *Abrégé chronologique, ou Extrait de l'histoire de France... divisé en trois tomes* (Paris: T. Jolly, 1568).

[87] At margin, note *n*: "Thuanus *Hist.* l. 53. ad annum 1572, p. 837. Edit. 1620. Fam. Strada *de bello Belgico.* l. 7, p. 373. Edit. Romae 1648." See Jacques-Auguste de Thou (1553–1617) *Jacobi Aug. Thuani Historiarum sui temporis*, 5 vols. in 8 (Paris: Ambrosium & Hieronymum Drouart, 1604–1608); Famiano Strada, S.J. (1572–1649) *De bello Belgico decas prima [- secunda]*, 2 vols. (Rome: Francisci Corbelletti, 1632–1647).

[88] At margin, note *o*: "In his Majesties Declaration for banishing all papists ten miles from London, Octob. 30. 1678." See *By the King. A proclamation commanding all persons being popish recusants, or so reputed, to depart from the cities of London and Westminster, and all other places within ten miles of the same* (London: Printed by John Bill, Christopher Barker, Thomas Newcomb, and Henry Hills ..., 1678).

[89] At margin, note *p*: "The votes of the Commons read to the Lords, and by them also approved at a conference, 1st. Nov. 1678." See "House of Lords Journal Volume 13: 1 November 1678," *Journal of the House of Lords*, volume 13: 1675–1681 (1767–1830) 331–334, in British History Online. http://www.british-history.ac.uk/report.aspx? compid=11591 (accessed May 28, 2014).

whore; that is, that purple and scarlet colored whore, the mother of harlots and abominations of the earth (Revelation 17:1, 4–5).

Proposition IV.
That the Roman Priests are the false Prophet

By the "roman priests," I mean and intend the pope, the cardinals, the Jesuits, and all those priests that do receive orders of priesthood from the Church of Rome, and acknowledge her to be the Catholic Church, believe her doctrines, obey her canons, and teach her damnable heresies. That the roman priests are the false prophet does plainly appear by the false doctrines of the Church of Rome, which they believe and teach. I call them the doctrines of the Church of Rome, which are approved by the public authority of that church by their established laws, their [papal] bulls, decretals, and constitutions, or the canons of their provincial, national, or general councils. All which are approved and confirmed in their Council of Trent.[90] And all their secular clergy, and all who have cure of souls, etc., are sworn to approve, to profess, and teach the same, and to anathematize, reject, and curse all contrary opinions and doctrines.[91] I shall at present instance in three known doctrines of the Church of Rome.

1. The doctrine of the pope's supremacy over all princes, kings, and emperors of the earth. This pernicious doctrine of the Church of Rome is

---

[90] At margin, note *a*: "Con. Trident. Sess. 25. de Reformatione, cap. 20. Praecepit. Sancta Synodus, Sacros Canones, & Concilia generalia omnia, nec non alias Apostolicas Sanctiones in favorem Ecclesiasticarum Personarum & Libertatis Ecclesiasticae; & contra eius Violatores editos, quae Omnia presenti Decreto innovat, exactè ab omnibus observari debere" (English trans.): ["It decrees, therefore, and enjoins, that the sacred canons, and all the general councils, as also all other apostolic sanctions, published in favor of ecclesiastical persons, of the liberty of the Church, and against the violators thereof —all which it also renews by this present decree—be exactly observed by all men"]. Knollys is citing, with very little variation, chapter 20 of the *Decretum de reformatione generali*, Twenty-fifth Session of the Council of Trent. For a critical edition see *Concilium Tridentinum*, in *Conciliorum oecumenicorum generaliumque decreta: editio critica*, ed. Klaus Ganzer, Giuseppe Alberigo, and Alberto Melloni, 2 vols. (Turnhout: Brepols Publishers, 2008–2010) 2:9–178, here 174. Translation from, *Canons and Decrees of the Council of Trent*, trans. Theodore Alois Buckley (London: George Routledge and Co., 1851) 251.

[91] At margin, note *b*: "Vide Bullam Pii 4. Super formâ Juramenti Professionis fidei, in calce Sess. 25. Concilii Trident. datam Romae. Id. Nov. 1564. de Reformatione, cap. 12." See Pope Pius IV, *Bulla super forma juramenti* (Rome: no publisher, 1564).

taught by the roman priests.[92] Blasius Bagnus, a prior general, tells us that the pope's empire is over all the world and that he is the only vicar of God, who has supreme power and rule over all kings and princes of the earth. Jacobus Simanca, a roman bishop, whose book is printed *cum publico privilegio*, and commended by the *censor librorum*, the learned Benito Arias Montanus, who said, that he had read it and that it contained nothing offensive to the catholic faith. "Heretics," said Simanca, "are actually deprived of all dominion and jurisdiction, and their subjects freed from their obedience, and this comprehends kings and other lords."[93] And Emanuel Sa, a famous Jesuit, affirms that "if a clergyman rebels against his king, it is no treason, because," said he, "clergymen are not the king's subjects."[94] These false prophets have taught and maintained this false doctrine.

2. The doctrine of justification by works which are, say they, meritorious and satisfactory. I need not spend time and waste paper in proving that the Church of Rome and all her clergy own and teach this doctrine.[95] Therefore, I will briefly prove that it is false doctrine, whereby it

---

[92] At margin, note *c*: "Blasius Bagnus *de S. Romanae Ecclesiae dignitatibus*, Tract. 7. pag. 83, 84, 85." See Bagnus Blasius, *Ad sanctiss. D. N. Urbanum Octavum Pontificem Optimum Maximum. De praecipuis S. R. E. dignitatibus. Tractatus sexdecim* (Bologna: Nicolai Tebaldini, 1625).

[93] At margin, note *d*: "Sic. *Simanca Enchir. Judicum* Tit. 67. §. 12. p. 349. Antwerp. Anno, 1573. &c." See Diego de Simancas (1583) *Enchiridion judicum violatae religionis* (Venice: Jordani Ziletti, 1573).

[94] At margin, note *e*: "Eman. Sa *Aphor. Confess. Verbo Clericus*, pag. 41. Col. 1599." See Manuel de Sá, S.J. (1530–1596) *Aphorismi confessariorum, ex variis doctorum sententiis collecti* (Cologne: Petri Amorfortii, 1599).

[95] At margin, note *f*: "Conc. Coloniens, pag. 140, 141. Becan. Ibid. Concil. Trident. Sess. 6. cap. 6. Bellarm. lib. 1. *de just.* cap. 13. & *de Purgat.* lib. 1. cap. 14. Rhem. *Annot.* 2 Tim. 4.8. & Heb. 6.10. Greg. de Valen. tom. 3. disp. 7. q. 2. de Indulgent. Bellarm. lib. 4. cap. 16. *de Justif.* & lib. 5. cap. 16, 17. Andradius *orthod. Explic. Concil. Trident.* lib. 6." Note *f* makes reference to the following sources, only those for which there is sufficient bibliographical information are presented in order of appearance: *Canones concilii provincialis Coloniensis. Sub Reverendiss. in Christo patre ac dño, D. Hermanno S. Colonieñ. ecclesiae archiepiscopo* (Cologne: no printer, 1536); Robert Bellarmine, *De justificatione impii libre quinque* (Heidelberg: Johannis Lancelloti, 1615); Id., *Tertia controversia generalis, de ecclesia quae est in purgatorio. Duobus libris explicata*, in *Disputationes Roberti Bellarmini Politiani, S. R. E. cardinalis, de Controversiis Christianae fidei, adversus huius temporis Haereticos; quatuor tomis comprehensae* (Paris: Tri-Adelphorum Bibliopolarum, 1608) vol. 3, col. 557–656; Gregorio de Valencia, S.J. (1549?–1603) *Commentariorum theologicorum tomi quatuor. In quibus omnes materiae quae continetur in Summa Divi Thomae explicantur*, 4 vols. (Ingolstadt: David Sartorius, 1591–1597); Diogo Paiva de Andrade

will appear, that the roman priests are false teachers, deceivers, and the false prophet. The apostle Paul gives it in holy writ as the conclusion of all Christ's apostles: "Therefore we conclude," said he, "that a man is justified by faith, without the deeds of the law" (Romans 3: 28). And, "Knowing that a man is not justified by the works of the law, but by the faith of Jesus Christ, for by the works of the law shall no flesh be justified" (Galatians 2:16). It may be objected, that the apostle James said expressly that "by works a man is justified, and not by faith only" (James 2:24). And instanced in Abraham: "Was not Abraham our father justified by works?" (James 2:21). I answer that a man's person is justified by faith before God, and works justified his faith before men. And this seems to be the mind of both those apostles. For St Paul said expressly, "If Abraham were justified by works, he hath whereof to glory, but not before God" (Romans 4:2). And St James speaks of showing our faith by our works before men: "I will show thee my faith by my works" (vers. 18). And so Peter Martyr and other of the ancients used to distinguish: "Faith," said he, "justifies our persons, and good works justify our faith."

3. The doctrine of the false worship of God, which consists of many particular parts—that the Church of Rome practiced and the roman priests teach—all which are asserted, confirmed, and established by the laws, canons, and general councils of the Church of Rome. And the romish clergy, by teaching for doctrines the commandments of men touching the worship of God and thereby deceiving and seducing them, are become the false prophet. [96] Like Thyatira's Jezabel, which called herself a prophetess

---

(1528–1575) *Orthodoxarvm Explicationvm Libri Decem: In quibus omnia ferè de religione capita, quae his temporibus ab haereticis in controuersiam vocantur, apertè & dilucidè explicantur: Praesertim contra Martini Kemnicij petulantem audaciam, qui Coloniensem Censuram, quam à uiris Societatis Iesu compositam esse ait, unà cum eiusdem Sanctiß. Societatis uitae ratione, temerè calumniandam suscepit; Cum neceßariis indicibus, rerum verborum, et explicatae scripturae sacrae* (Cologne: Cholinus, 1564).

[96] At margin, note *g*: "Joan. Bal. in vitâ Innocent. 3d. saith that Innocent 3d. commanded, that the words of the canon of the masse should be held equal to the words of the Gospel. Card. Cusanus entitleth his book, *De Authoritate Ecclesiae & Concilii supra & contra Scripturam*. Henricus Doctor magister suori palatii Roma ad Legatos Bohemicos sub Felice Papâ, pag 1447. saith, The pope may change the holy Gospel, and may give to the Gospel, according to the place and time, another sense. Michael, Medina, Gratian, Abb. Panorm. Felinus, and all the Roman priests assert and teach, the pope may dispence against jus divinum and against the New Testament." The source alluded to in the first part of the note remains uncertain. The second part, however, refers to the 15th century theologian and philosopher, Nicholas of Cusa (1401–1464). John Jewel in *A defense of the*

(Revelation 2:20), viz. the false prophets in that church who taught and seduced the people of God to commit fornication, so the roman priests do teach them [to] worship the beast and his image, to worship saints deceased, yea to worship idols, crosses, crucifixes, and images which the Church of Rome has set up and commanded to be adored and worshiped, especially their breaden God and sacrilegious host. Teaching the people and seducing them to believe that the self same body of our Lord Jesus Christ, who was once in the fullness of time—and but once made of a woman (Galatians 4:4)—by the power of God is every sacrament day made of a wafer by the power of a romish priest. By all which, and by several other false doctrines, it is plain and evident to those that have understanding in the holy Scriptures of truth that the roman priests are the false prophet[s], meant and intended by Christ (Revelation 13:14 and 16:13 and 19:20). As for their doctrines of purgatory, penances, pardons and many other false doctrines taught by the roman priests, I pass by as not worth mentioning.

Having thus far unveiled mystical Babylon, that is Rome-papal, I shall now proceed to call the people of God to come out of Babylon and to forsake papal Rome, to renounce the Church of Rome, as the great whore and mother of harlots, to deny the pope's imperial and pontifical supremacy as the beast with his two horns like a lamb and not to hear nor hearken unto the roman priest, that false prophet which teaches the false doctrines of the Church of Rome, and seduces the servants of God. And this call I give the people of God, especially in England, in the name of our Lord Jesus Christ.

Apologie of the Churche of England (1567) refers to the mid-sixteenth century Basel edition of Cusa's works. See D. Nicolai de Cusa, *Utriusque juris doctoris, in omniqúe philosophia incomparabilis viri opera* (Basel: Sebastian Henricpetri, 1565). In light of Knollys' reliance on one of the early editions of Jewel's *Defense* (1567, 1570 or 1571) it is possible that he was citing from the same edition as Jewel. The source for the third part of the reference (i.e. "Henricus Doctor magister suori ...") is also uncertain. Nonetheless, Knollys copied the quote from George Downame (d. 1634) *A treatise concerning Antichrist divided into two bookes, the former, proving that the pope is Antichrist, the latter, maintaining the same assertion, against all the obiections of Robert Bellarmine, Iesuit and cardinall of the Church of Rome* (London: ImPrinted for Cuthbert Burbie, 1603). The quoted statement appears in its integrity in Downame, *Treatise*, p. 77. Moreover, the accompanying marginal note in page 77 has "Felice Papa 1447" separated by a hyphen, giving the typographical impression—in the next line of the marginal note—that the reference is to "pag. 1447" ("Pa-*pa 1447*," emphasis added). The year is an allusion to the reign of Antipope Felix V (r. 1439–1449). Knollys, however, erroneously transcribed the year 1447 as "pag. 1447." See Knollys, *Mystical Babylon*, 24. The fourth part of marginal note *g* ("Michael, Medina, Gratian...") consists of Knollys' own words.

A Call to all the People of God to come out of Babylon

"And I heard another voice from heaven, saying, come out of her my people, that ye be not partakers of her sins, and that ye receive not of her plagues" (Revelation 18:4). This call is the call of God our savior unto all his people in mystical Babylon, papal Rome, to come out of her. "Come out of her my people": which call of Christ was given by an audible voice, "and I heard another voice from heaven saying," etc. And this call from heaven is urged and enforced upon the people of God by two cogent arguments or reasons, 1. "that ye be not partakers of her sins," 2. "that ye receive not of her plagues." Two things in this call need explanation: 1. What this voice was? 2. What it is to come out of her? To both these I shall speak briefly, and then proceed to speak more largely of this call.

First, this voice has heaven's authority: "it was from heaven." To wit, the voice of Christ in the ministry of the Gospel ordinarily and by the powerful efficacy of the Holy Spirit also. "For our Gospel came not unto you in word only, but also in power, and in the holy Spirit, and in much assurance" (1 Thessalonians 1:5). So had the voice of the angels of God by whom Christ then spoke unto his servant John (Revelation 14:6–13) "with a loud voice (ver. 7), which St John heard from heaven (ver. 13). And so have the voices of the faithful ministers of God by whom Christ also now speaks unto his people: "He that heareth you, heareth me" (Luke 10:16). That is, heaven's authority.

Secondly, to come out of HER is to seperate themselves from the Church of Rome, which is now become a false church, called "the great whore and mother of harlots." "Wherefore come out from among them, and be ye seperate, saith the Lord" (2 Corinthians 6: 14–18, ver. 17). The Lord Jesus Christ would have his people to be seperated under the Gospel from the unbelieving Jews, and their false worship, which Christ calleth vain worship (Matthew 15: 8–9). And St Paul did seperate the disciples from the Jewish synagogue of unbelievers (Acts 19: 8–9). And also from idolatrous gentiles that worship images, as the Church of Rome does, and from their idol-temples, churches, and chappels. For the gentile papists and Church of Rome, their pope, cardinals, Jesuits, and all the Roman priests do tread under foot the holy city Jerusalem (Revelation 11:2), viz. the church and people of God. "What agreement hath the temple of God with idols? For ye are the temple of the living God, as God hath said, I will dwell among them, and walk among them, and I will be their God and they shall be my people.

Wherefore come out from among them, and be ye seperated saith the Lord, and touch not the unclean thing (2 Corinthians 6:16–17; Levitticus 20:24–26 and 26:12). The papists' images, crosses, crucifixes, their consecrated wafers, holy waters, and saints pictures, the image of the Virgin Mary and of our Savior upon the cross, unto which images the popish priests and people fall down and worship, yea their *Ave Maria*, and prayers to saints deceased, all their holy bells, beads, prayer-books, and candles, etc. are an unclean thing, and ought to be seperated from, and not touched by the people of God, whom Christ calls upon "with a loud voice" to come out from among them.

These two particulars explain the argument which Christ urged to inforce this his call unto his people, "that ye be not partakers of her sins, and that ye receive not of her plagues." As if Christ had said, "I do by the voice of my faithful ministers call and command you my people to come out of mystical Babylon (papal Rome) and to separate your selves from the Church of Rome, which is fallen, is fallen from her apostolical purity in doctrine, worship, and discipline or ecclesiastical government and is become a harlot, a false church, the great whore, the mother of harlots, and abominations of the earth, the synagogue of Satan, the habitation of devils, the hold of every foul spirit, and a cage of every unclean and hateful bird." "But if you my people," as if Christ had said, "will not obey my voice, nor hear my call, if you will not come out from the Church of Rome and seperate your selves from the papists, and leave going to and worshipping in their popish temples, churches, chappels, and private cloysters, nunneries, priories, religious houses, meeting places, and holy roods of auricular confession, etc., then in the first place you will be partakers of their sins, that is, you will become guilty of their will-worship and spiritual fornication (Revelation 17:2) of their idolatries, adulteries, thefts, murders, etc. (Revelation 9: 20, 21) and of their impenitency added unto their iniquities. And in the next place you shall receive of her plagues, death and mourning and famine, etc. (Revelation 18:8). "And these shall drink of the wine of the wrath of God, which is poured out without mixture into the cup of his indignation (Revelation 14:9–12).

The motives and encouragements, I shall propound to the people of God to come out of mystical Babylon and to seperate from the Church of Rome are these. 1. You cannot come to Sion, until you come out of Babylon: "And the ransomed of the Lord shall return and come to Zion with songs and everlasting joy upon their heads" (Isaiah 35:10). 2. You cannot worship

God in spirit and truth, unless you first seperate your selves from false worship and worshipers: "Ye worship ye know not what [...] The true worshipers shall worship the Father in spirit and truth" (John 4:22–24). 3. You cannot enjoy communion with God, whilst you hold a communion with idols and image-worshipers: "What communion hath light with darkness? And what agreement hath the temple of God with idols? Wherefore come out from among them and be ye seperate, saith the Lord" (2 Corinthians 6:14–17).

Consider whilst you continue in Babylon—the Church of Rome—you are under the guidance of the pope and Roman priests, who are so far from being infallible guides, as they pretend, that they are erroneous, false, and blind leaders of the blind into perdition. The Roman priests are those false teachers, seducers, and deceivers that were foretold by the apostles of Christ (2 Peter 2:1–2 and 2 John 7 and 2 Timothy 3:13 and 1 Timothy 4:1 and 1 John 2:26). "These things have I written unto you concerning them that seduce you" [1 John 2:26]. Therefore "look to yourselves," said the Apostle (2 John 1:8). "Beloved," said he, "believe not every spirit, but try the spirit, whether they be of God, for many false prophets are gone out into the world."[97] You may do well to consider also what diversities and divisions in principles, opinions, and practices in religion there are at this time, in the world, especially among teachers, false teachers, who privately bring in damnable heresies: "And many follow their pernicious ways by reason of whom the way of truth is evil spoken of" (2 Peter 2:1–22). Now God has in great mercy unto the souls of his people out of the exceeding riches of his free grace and marvelous loving kindness towards them—that they might not be led away with the errors of the wicked—appointed them a threefold guide, which God hath plainly declared in the holy Scripture of truth to direct, lead and guide his people in the way of truth until they come to heaven: namely, 1. His Holy Spirit, 2. His written Word, and 3. His faithful ministers.

First, God has given his Holy Spirit unto his people (Galatians 4:6) to lead them (Romans 8:14) and guide them into all the truth (John 16:13) and to teach them all things (John 14:26 and 1 John 2:20, 27). And least his people should be deceived, deluded, or seduced by Satan's transforming himself into an angel of light, or by false apostles, deceitful workers—who are his ministers—transforming themselves into the ministers of Christ (2

[97] Marginal note *a*: "1 Epist. of Joh. 4.1, 2. etc." The reference is to 1 John 4:1–2.

Corinthians 11:13–15). God has secondly given his people a sure word—his written word to guide them (Psalm 43:3; 2 Peter 1:14). Unto which they do well if they take heed, "as unto a light, that shineth in a dark place" [2 Peter 1:19] etc., and thus God counseled and cautioned his people of old by his prophet: "To the law and to the testimony; if they speak not according to that word, it is because there is not light in them" (Isaiah 8:20). And the Apostle testifies that, "all scripture is given by inspiration of God, and is profitable for doctrine and for instruction in righteousness" (2 Timothy 3:15–17), etc. And thirdly, God has also given his people able ministers of the New Testament, not of the letter only, but of the spirit (2 Corinthians 3:5–6). "And he gave some apostles; and some, prophets; and some, evangelists; and some, pastors and teachers, for the work of the ministry" (Ephesians 4:11–13), etc. And God set them in his church (1 Corinthians 12:4, 28) to be "guides" unto his people, Hebrews 13:7, 17: "Remember your guides" (ver. 7). "Obey your guides" (ver. 17). "And submit your selves, for they watch for your souls, as they that must give account."[98] Will any godly wise man or woman judge in themselves that it is safe for them to forsake and refuse this threefold sure guide of the Spirit, word, and ministry of Christ, which God has ordained, and to give up the conduct of their souls unto the Church of Rome to be guided by her laws, canons, councels, popes, cardinals, Jesuites, and the rest of the Roman clergy, who are blind guides and anti-Christian ministers and so to hazard their own eternal salvation?[99] Which false teachers and their false and damnable errors, doctrines, and practices our blessed Saviour and his holy apostles have forewarned us of in the Scripture of truth.

A Call to the Kings of the Earth to hate the Whore, to make her Desolate, and to burn her with Fire.

My warrant to give this call to the kings of the earth is that prophecy: "And the ten horns, which thou sawest upon the beast, these shall hate the whore, and shall make her desolate, and naked, and shall eat her flesh, and shall burn her with fire" (Revelation 17:16). The ten horns are those ten

---

[98] Marginal note *b*: "Heb. 13, 7, 17. Μνημονεύετε τῶν ἡγουμένων ὑμῶν, Πείθεσθε τοῖς ἡγουμένοις, etc." Knollys provides the Greek openings of Hebrews 13:7 and 13:17, respectively.

[99] Marginal note without symbol: "Math. 24: 4, 5; 11: 23, 24; 25:21.; Act. 20: 29, 30; 1 Tim. 4: 1, 2, 3; 2 Tim. 4:3,4; 2 Pet. 2:1.2, 3; 1 Joh. 4:1, 2, 3."

kings, which had formerly agreed and given their kingdom, power, and strength unto the beast [...] until the words of God shall be fulfilled (Revelation 17:12, 13, 17). These ten horns are the European kings of Italy, Spain, Germany, France, England, etc., who have formerly submitted themselves and their kingdoms unto the beast—the popes of Rome—and to the Church of Rome, that great whore and mother of harlots. As was hereof prophesied and as all historians have testified. But it is the revealed will of God recorded in the Scripture of truth, that the ten horns shall hate the whore, etc. And upon this scripture-ground, I take this humble boldness to give this *CALL* unto the kings of the European world to hate the whore, etc. And the reasons, which I shall humbly propose to them are these, viz. 1. Because it is the revealed will of God that they should so do (in this very Scripture, Revelation 17:16), and "they shall do so." 2. Because the great whore—the Church of Rome—has given her golden cup, full of abomination and filthiness of her fornication into the hands of the kings of the earth, and caused them to drink, and they and the inhabitants of the earth have been made drunk with the wine of her fornication (Revelation 17:1–4). 3. Because she—the Church of Rome—has raigned over the kings of the earth (Revelation 17:18). Deposing emperors and kings; putting down one and setting up another, at the pope's pleasure—who is her head, lord, and law-giver—as has been proved (pag. 3, 10, 11 of this treatise)[100] and appears.[101] 4. Because she has shed the blood of the prophets, saints, and

[100] Reference is to the page numbers in the orignal pamphlet.

[101] Marginal note *a*: "Century 8. Pope Zachary deposed Childerick King of France. Gregory the 7th, deposed Henry the fourth, Cent. 11. Pope Sylvester the third Excommunicated Henry the fifth, Cent. 12. Pope Innocent the 4th, deposed the Emperour Frederick 2d. Century, 13. Pope Gregory the 2d, deposed the Emperour Leo Isaurus, because he was against Images. Baron Annal, ad annum 730. Num. 5. and ad annum 593 Num. 86. and Tom. 8. ad An. Christi, 593. Num. 86. Non modo deponi, sed etiam excommunicari, & in aeterno examine damnari Decrevit" (English trans.) ["He decreed that he will not only be taken down, but also be excommunicated, and determined to be condemned in eternity"]. Damnatio & Excommunicatio Hen. 8. by Pope Paul the 3d. & Elizabethae. by Pope Pius the 5th. The Title fixed to the Pope's Bulls." Knollys bases his succinct account of papal entanglement in European dynastic politics on Caesar Baronius (1538–1607) *Annales ecclesiastici a Christo nato ad annum 1198*, 12 vols. (Rome, 1588–1609). The quotation, "Non modo deponi... damnari decrevit," can be found in the modern edition of Baronius' work, Cesaris Baronii, *Annales ecclesiastici (546–599)* ed. Augustino Theiner (Paris: Ludovicus Guerin, 1867) 10:525. It constitutes the central part of a letter from Pope Gregory VII (r. 1073–1085) to Bishop Hermann of Metz, dated March 15, 1081. Pope Gregory VII was invoking the authority of his forerunner, Pope

martyrs of Jesus (Revelation 16:6–7 and 17:6 and 18:24). "Therefore reward her even as she rewarded you; and double to her double, according to her work" [Revelation 18:6]. And of all the nations in Europe, no kings, or kingdoms have more just cause to hate and to be avenged on mystery, Babylon the great, the mother of harlots, that great whore, the Church of Rome, and her head the pope, that beast, and the Roman priests, the false prophet, than this our nation, King, and kingdom. If his Royal Majestie, and his great council assembled in Parliament seriously consider all the papists former plots and conspiracies against the kings and kingdom of England. But most especially this late bloody traiterous design of popish Recusants, even this damnable and hellish plot contrived and still carrying on by them to assassinate the King, to subvert the government, and to root out the Protestant religion, and all the Protestants in England.[102]

All which I most humbly submit to the wisdom of the King's Majesty and his great council when assembled in Parliament, for whom I daily pray.

FINIS

Gregory the Great (r. 590–604) against monarchs who were defiant of papal authority. See Sidney Z. Ehler and John B. Morrall, ed. *Church and State Through the Centuries: A Collection of Historic Documents with Commentaries* (New York: Biblo and Tannen, 1967) 29–39, here 32. Knollys then makes reference to the excommunications of Henry VIII, on December 17, 1538, and Elizabeth I, on April 27, 1570.

[102] Marginal note *b*: "The Votes of the House of Commons approved by the Lords in a Conference, Novemb. 1. 1678." See "House of Lords Journal Volume 13: 1 November 1678," *Journal of the House of Lords*, volume 13: 1675–1681 (1767–1830) 331–334, in British History Online. http://www.british-history.ac.uk/report.aspx?compid=11591 (accessed May 28, 2014).

AN ANSWER TO A BRIEF DISCOURSE CONCERNING SINGING IN THE PUBLIC WORSHIP OF GOD IN THE GOSPEL CHURCH

(London, 1691)

INTRODUCTION

Hanserd Knollys' *An answer to a brief discourse concerning singing* (1691) represents his small but significant intervention in an acrimonious dispute that embroiled Particular Baptists in the last decade of the seventeenth century. Benjamin Keach introduced the practice of regular hymn singing in his congregation at Horsleydown in Southwark. According to Thomas Crosby, when Keach "was convinced that singing the praises of God was a holy ordinance of Jesus Christ, he labored earnestly, and with a great deal of prudence and caution, to convince his people thereof, and first obtained their consent to the practice of it at the conclusion of the sacrament of the Lord's Supper." The novelty seems to have been accepted by most in the congregation, although a few saw it as an unwelcomed departure. The congregation eventually adopted the practice of singing hymns every Lord's day.[1]

The Particular Baptist Isaac Marlow was the first to publicly reject regular hymn singing. In his *A brief discourse concerning singing in the public worship of God in the Gospel church*, Marlow set forth several arguments against the singing of "precomposed hymns."[2] For Marlow the problem of hymn singing was analogous to that of using prescribed forms of prayer in public worship. He thus summarized the fundamental question as he saw it: "...the question is, whether David's Psalms, or any human prescribed, or precomposed matter, may or ought not to be vocally sung by all the church

---

[1] Thomas Crosby, *The history of the English Baptists, from the Reformation to the Beginning of the Reign of King George I. [Vol. IV] Containing their History from the End of the Reign of King William III to the Reign of King George I, including some Part of His Reign* (London: Printed for the author and sold by John Robinson, 1740) 4:298–299.

[2] Isaac Marlow, *A brief discourse concerning singing in the public worship of God in the Gospel-church* (London: no printer, 1690).

together, as part of the public, constant and ordinary worship of God, instituted in his Gospel church."[3] He argued that both the Holy Scriptures and the witness of the "purest churches in our age" were firmly set "not only against the humane prescribed and precomposed forms of prayers, but of singing of David's Psalms, and other hymns or songs precomposed by man, as they are frequently used as part of the constant and ordinary worship of God instituted in his Gospel church."[4] He further argued that the "essence of singing" consists in "an inward spiritual exercise of the soul or mind of man."[5] He sustained that the singing of the "Psalms of David is nowhere instituted, ordained or practiced either by Christ or his Holy Apostles." Consequently, he resolved that there is "no warrant for the singing of them."[6] Finally, in the third section of his tract Marlow concluded, "if the essence of singing consists in an inward spiritual exercise of the soul or mind of man, and that both the matter and the melody of it proceds from the inward graces and operations of the Holy Spirit with the Word, then surely no human prescribed form of singing can be accepted of God."[7]

In his response to Marlow, Knollys defended the practice of regular hymn singing in public worship. He questioned the logic of Marlow's argumentation. According to Knollys, Marlow's premise was contrary to reason as singing always "consists in the voice as well as in the soul or mind of man." That is, the essence of singing according to Knollys cannot be conceived without it involving the voice. He rejected the identification of silent with spiritual singing as one that was based in a false dichotomy. Knollys warned that this line of argumentation was similar to that of the Quakers, which led them to reject the ordinances of the Lord's Supper and baptism.

Moreover, Knollys argued that Marlow's argument was also deficient in terms of its weak scriptural foundation. Of crucial importance was the rendering of Acts 16:25, specifically of the Greek term ὕμνουν ("singing praises"). As in other places, Knollys here relied on Theodore Beza's *Novuum Testamentum* (Geneva, 1598). However, the tract reveals other sources of Knollys thought as he made reference to the lexicographical work

[3] Marlow, *A brief discourse*, 7.

[4] Ibid., 4.

[5] Marlow, *A brief discourse*, [6], pagination is incorrect in original with pages [5] and [6] showing incorrect page numbers.

[6] Ibid., 15.

[7] Ibid.

of Cornelis Schrevel (1608–1664) and Joseph Hill (1625–1707) as well as the exegetical writings of John Owen (1616–1683).

AN ANSWER TO A BRIEF DISCOURSE CONCERNING SINGING[1]

(London, 1691)

Beloved Brother,

The Apostle James says: "Brethren, if any of you do err from the truth, and one convert him; Let him know, that he which converteth a sinner from the error of his way, shall save a soul from death, and shall hide a multitude of sins" (James 5:19–20). I have read your little book, which you gave me, concerning singing. And now after prayers to God, and serious consideration of what you have said therein, I return you this brief answer, which I do entreat you to consider. So I remain,

Your brother, in our Lord Jesus Christ,

H. K.

AN ANSWER TO A BRIEF DISCOURSE CONCERNING SINGING

The subject that you intended to treat of—expressed in the title page of your book—is, "Singing in the Public Worship of God in the Gospel Church"; that is, say you (in page 5, lines 1, 2, 3), the primitive and apostolic church. Your words are these: "That spiritual and vocal singing was used in the primitive and apostolic church of Christ is undeniable." You also confess in your first [argument] (fifth page, lines 28, 29, 30) that "vocal singing [in Colossians 3:16] is there to be understood, etc." And in your second (fifth page, lines 20, 21, 22), "Intelligible singing," say you, "for teaching and admonishing others, cannot be without the use of the organic instruments of the voice."

I beseech you, my beloved brother, to consider that singing in the public worship of God, in the Apostle's days, was not only used and

[1] Hanserd Knollys, *An answer to a brief discourse concerning singing in the publick worship of God in the Gospel-church, by I. M.* [Isaac Marlow] *1690* (London: Printed for the author H. K. [Hanserd Knollys], 1691).

practiced, as you have confessed again and again, but commanded by the Apostle Paul [in] Colossians 3:16, where the word "let" has the force of a commandment of God, as Ephesians 4:29, Philippians 1:27, Ephesians 5:33, James 5:13. Read the words, especially consider what you say concerning women, 1 Corinthians 14:34: "Let your women keep silence in the church." And 1 Timothy 2:11, "Let the women learn in silence with all subjection." Read your own words (page 21, lines 12, 13, 14, 15, 16, 17). You say in page 5, line 5: "But the question is, whether David's Psalms, or any human prescribed or pre-composed matter may, or ought not to be vocally sung by all the church together as part of the public, constant, and ordinary worship of God, instituted in his gospel church."

You had done fairly, to have put this your question in the title page of your book, but there is not one word of it there, except what you have confessed and granted, again and again, as I have already noted out of divers pages of your book. And so, I proceed to offer something to your serious consideration, about the essence or being of singing, which, you say, "consists in an inward spiritual exercise of the soul or mind of man, and this must be granted," say you (p. 5, lines 24, 25, 26).

No Brother! You must not take it for granted until your reasons or arguments be examined, which you bring to prove it. You affirm that, "the Scriptures do clearly witness, that the essence of prayer and praises, and of sin, do all consist in an inward exercise of the soul and spirit" (p. 6, lines 9, 10, 11, 12). And from thence you conclude that the essence or being of singing consists in the inward spiritual exercise of the soul or mind of man. If you consult with any logician, he can show you the weakness of your consequence in this argument.

Now, the essence or being of singing in the church of God, unto edifying, consists in the voice as well as in the soul or mind of man (p. 16, lines 16, 17). You say right, "We find in Scripture another kind of singing, 1 Chronicles 16:32–33 and Psalm 65:13, that is, the virtual, or metaphorical singing of the creatures" (p. 9, lines 9 and 10). But there is no other kind of singing in the public worship of God in the gospel church, unto edifying without the voice. You should have put the voice into the essence or being of this kind of singing. The natural kind of the singing of birds and of little children is not without voices and organic instruments of the voice. You have neither scripture nor sound reason for your opinion about singing without the voice, unto edifying in the church of Jesus Christ. You bring a Scripture to prove silent singing in the church (1 Corinthians 14:26–28). All

I need to say in answer to what you have said (p. 7–9) is to show you that you are mistaken in the mind of Christ and his Apostle in that Scripture. The Apostle mentioned divers gifts (ver. 26) a psalm, a doctrine, a tongue, a revelation, an interpretation. Then he exhorted them saying, "Let all things be done to edifying," and verse 27, "If any man speak in an unknown tongue, let it be by two, or, at most, by three, and that by course, and let one interpret; but if there be no interpreter, let him keep silence in the church." What is this to silent singing in the church, any more than if you had brought it to justify the silent meetings of them called Quakers? Then, in page 8, lines 20 and 21, you say, "What can be more plain, than that singing and other gifts of the Holy Spirit have their essences in our spirits, wherein we are capable of worshipping God acceptably without the verbal and vocal instruments of the body."

O my Brother! I know you are not one of them that approve the silent meetings, who supposing that they have a light within them, whereby they are capable to worship God acceptably without his gospel ordinances of Baptism, the Lord's Supper, and singing without verbal and vocal instruments in their silent meetings. In a word, this unsound opinion of yours will lead you, and others of the same mind, into some erroneous principles of them called Seekers, Quakers, and such as are for non-churches, if God does not prevent by his Holy Spirit and Grace, or restrain.

The next particular you treat of is David's Psalms (p. 9, to p. 15), where you labor to prove that David's Psalms ought not to be sung in the churches of Christ, in the days of the gospel. I have proved that the Apostle Paul commanded the saints and faithful brethren in Christ (Colossians 1:2) to sing psalms (Colossians 3:16); that is, David's Psalms. Read those Scriptures: "And David himself saith in the book of Psalms, the Lord said unto my Lord, sit thou on my right hand. And he said unto them, these are the words which I spoke unto you, while I was yet with you, that all things must be fulfilled which were written in the Law of Moses, and in the Prophets, and in the Psalms concerning me" (Luke 20:42 and 24:44); "For it is written in the book of Psalms, Let his habitation be desolate, and let no man dwell therein: and, his bishopric let another take. God hath fulfilled the same unto us their children, in that he hath raised up Jesus again; as it is also written in the second Psalm, 'Thou art my son, this day have I begotten thee'" (Acts 1:20 and 13:33). You cannot show where the word "psalms" is understood of any other, but only David's Psalms, called The Book of Psalms.

But you having no Scripture against singing of David's Psalms, do seem to reason and argue against singing of them, first because the church of Christ is now in a wilderness condition, and in a mourning sackcloth state (p. 12, lines 13–21). But the wilderness state of the church under the Gospel ("How beautiful upon the mountains are the feet of him that bringeth good tidings, that publisheth peace, that bringeth good tidings of good, that publisheth salvation, that saith unto Zion, thy God reigneth! Thy watchmen shall lift up the voice, with the voice together shall they sing, for they shall see eye to eye, when the Lord shall bring again Zion. Break forth into joy, sing together ye waste places of Jerusalem: for the Lord hath comforted his people, he hath redeemed Jerusalem," Isaiah 52:7–9) should not hinder the churches and servants of God to sing [from singing] psalms, hymns, and spiritual songs, making melody in their hearts to the Lord. Was not Christ and his disciples in a mourning condition, the same night our blessed Savior was betrayed? Yet, they sung a hymn (Matthew 26:30 and Mark 14:26). Was not the condition of Paul and Silas a wilderness condition? Acts 16:23–30: "And when they had laid many stripes upon them, they cast them into prison, charging the jailor to keep them safely: Who having received such a charge, thrust them into the inner prison, and made their feet fast in the stocks: And at midnight Paul and Silas prayed, and sang praises unto God: and the prisoners heard them. And suddenly there was a great earthquake, so that the foundations of the prison were shaken: and immediately all the doors were opened, and every ones bands were loosed. And the keeper of the prison awaking out of his sleep, and seeing the prison doors open, he drew out his sword, and would have killed himself, supposing that the prisoners had been fled: But Paul cried with a loud voice, saying, Do thy self no harm, for we are all here. Then he called for a light, and sprang in, and came trembling, and fell down before Paul and Silas; and brought them out, and said, sirs, What must I do to be saved?" Yet they sang praises to God and God wrought a notable miracle of confirmation, not only an Earthquake, that shaked the foundations of the prison, opened all the prison doors, and every one's bands were loosed, and the keeper of the prison was terribly affrighted and converted (ver. 34).

You say, "The word 'sung' is not in the Greek, but it is there read, 'and they having hymned'." "Which word," you say, "is taken by divers learned men to be of a general signification of all kinds of praises or thanksgivings, and not confined to songs only." Neither do I confine the signification thereof only to songs. Yet Beza translates ὑμνήσαντες, *quum hymnum cecinissent*, "When they had sung an hymn."[2] Screvilius and Hill, in their Greek lexicon translate, ὑμνέω *celebro, hymnum cano.*[3] And learned Dr. Owen, upon Hebrews 2:12 (ἐν μέσῳ ἐκκλησίας ὑμνήσω σε, which the learned translators do read, "In the midst of the church will I sing praises unto thee" [KJV]) hath these words in his exposition: "It is declared further, first, what Christ will moreover do; 'He will sing praises unto God. Secondly, where he will do it; 'in the midst of the congregation or church'."[4] So that it is manifested, say you, from the aforesaid premises, that praising

---

[2] Interestingly, Knollys uses ὑμνήσαντες [English trans.: "having sung a hymn"], a form of the verb ὑμνέω (English trans.): ["I sing a hymn"]. This is the form of the verb that appears in Matthew 26:30: "Καὶ ὑμνήσαντες ἐξῆλθον εἰς τὸ ὄρος τῶν Ἐλαιῶν" ("When they had sung the hymn, they went out to the Mount of Olives," NRSV). The discussion, however, is based on Acts 16:25, where the form of the verb is ὕμνουν [English trans.: "were singing hymns"]: "Κατὰ δὲ τὸ μεσονύκτιον Παῦλος καὶ Σιλᾶς προσευχόμενοι ὕμνουν τὸν Θεόν, ἐπηκροῶντο δὲ αὐτῶν οἱ δέσμιοι" (English trans.): ["About midnight Paul and Silas were praying and singing hymns to God, and the prisoners were listening to them," NRSV]. Of course, the whole point of contention is the proper translation of the masculine noun ὕμνος. In both cases, Beza translates the Greek term as the Latin "hymnos": "Et quum hymnum cecinissent, exierunt in montem Olearum" (Matthew 26:30); "Media autem nocte orantes Paulus et Silas hymnos canebant Deo" (Acts 16:25). Beza (1598) 127 and 527.

[3] See Cornelis Schrevel (1608–1664) and Joseph Hill (1625–1707) *Lexicon manuale, Graeco-Latinum & Latino-Graecum primò conncinatum, térque editum à Cornelio Schrevelio: vocabulorum octo quasi millibus locupletatum, plurimisque praeterea in locis auctum & adornatum, prout ex praefatione constat / studio atque operâ Josephi Hill; ad calcem adjecta sunt sententiae Graeco-Latinae, quibus omnia Gr. L. primitiva comprehenduntur; item tractatus duo, alter De resolutione verborum, De articulis alter; uterque perutilis & adhuc desideratus* (London: John Field, 1663) 654.

[4] "In the second part of this first testimony is declared further: (1) What Christ will moreover do; he will sing praises unto God, and (2) Where he will do it; in the midst of the congregation." John Owen (1616–1683) *An exposition of the two first chapters of the Epistle of Paul the Apostle unto the Hebrews* (London: Robert White, 1668) 256. This book, although under a separate title page and with new pagination, is found in the first volume of John Owen, *Exercitations on the Epistle to the Hebrews also concerning the Messiah wherein the promises concerning him to be a spiritual redeemer of mankind are explained and vindicated, his coming and accomplishment of his work according to the promises is proved and confirmed, the person, or who he is, is declared, the whole oeconomy of the mosaical law, rites, worship, and sacrifice is explained : and in all the doctrine of the person, office, and work of the Messiah is opened, the nature and demerit of the first sin is unfolded, the opinions and traditions of the antient and modern Jews are examined, their objections against the Lord Christ and the Gospel are answered, the time of the coming of the Messiah is stated, and the great fundamental truths of the Gospel vindicated : with an exposition and discourses on the two first chapters of the said epistle to the Hebrews*, 4 vols. (London: Robert White, 1668).

of God is not limited to songs of praise. I do not limit the signification of the word ὕμνος only to songs. Neither you, nor all the learned men and books in Sion College can prove that the word signifies the essence of singing—without the voice—in heart and mind only.[5] Especially, if a minister of the church who has received a spiritual gift to sing a hymn or a spiritual song (Colossians 3:16), does sing in the church (as 1 Corinthians 14:15–16 and 26: "What is it then? I will pray with the Spirit, and I will pray with the understanding also; I will sing with the Spirit, and I will sing with the understanding also. Else, when thou shalt bless with the Spirit, how shall he that occupieth the room of the unlearned, say Amen at thy giving of thanks, seeing he understandeth not what thou sayest?"; "How is it then, brethren? When ye come together, every one of you hath a Psalm, hath a doctrine, hath a tongue, hath a revelation, hath an interpretation. Let all things be done to edifying") may, and in my opinion ought to administer his gift. "As every man hath received the gift, even so minister the same one to another, as good stewards of the manifold grace of God. If any man speak, let him speak as the oracles of God; if any man minister, let him do it as the ability which God giveth; that God in all things may be glorified through Jesus Christ; to whom be praise and dominion for ever and ever. Amen" (1 Peter 4:10–11). Yet, this I confess, that those hymns and spiritual songs, which they sing in the Spirit and with understanding unto edifying, are not those Psalms of David, which the Apostle mentions (Colossians 3:16), as I have proved before. Neither will those ministers or members of the churches of saints that sing hymns or spiritual songs affirm or assert that they are David's Psalms, hymns and spiritual songs (Colossians 3:16), no, nor given them by the inspiration of the Holy Spirit, as the Book of Psalms was.

And in page 14, lines 10–12, you say, "Some of the Psalms were clear prophecies of the sufferings of Christ, which to sing now were to deny that Christ is come in the flesh." If this argument was good, it would also follow that to read those Psalms now was to deny that Christ is come in the flesh. And in page 15, lines 4–8, you say, "There is no instance [sic.] can be given in the New Testament that any of David's Psalms were ever sung by any persons, or churches, etc." And yet you say, affirm, and confess that vocal singing of psalms, hymns, and spiritual songs was practiced in those

---

[5] Established under a royal charter of King Charles I in 1630, Sion College was founded by Thomas White (c. 1550–1624) for the Anglican clergy of London. See Anon., *Sion College, Founded by Thomas White, D. D.* (London: P. White and Son, [1854]).

churches of Ephesus and Colossians (p. 5, lines 20–23 & p. 5, lines 1–4). And you say vocal singing was used in the primitive and apostolic church of Christ.

But women may not speak in the church, and therefore they may not sing (p. 21), for singing is teaching. Why do the churches of saints require women to declare the work of conversion in the church? Or, to bear witness of the disorderly walking of any brother or sister, if they may not speak in the Church? Women have the essence of singing—as well as men—both in their souls and with their voices; and are allowed to speak by all the churches of saints.

Many other things you have said, and many objections you have propounded and answered, in which I am not willing to show your weakness. But leave you and others of your persuasion therein to consider what I have said, and pray, that God will convince you of your error and make known unto you his revealed will in the holy Scripture of truth.

FINIS

THE LIFE AND DEATH OF THAT OLD DISCIPLE OF JESUS CHRIST

(London, 1692)

INTRODUCTION

In this autobiographical piece, Hanserd Knollys traces the trajectory of his life from early childhood to the distressing events of his adult years. The account can be described as a "spiritual autobiography" due to its emphasis on his experiences of God's redemptive work. Scholar Kathleen Lynch has used the category of "Protestant autobiography" as a "more inclusive framework" for the analysis of a variety of narrative forms that can be described as spiritual autobiography, confession testimony, and conversion narrative.[1] Knollys' *Life and death*, fits very nicely into this literary pattern. It also has certain epic proportions that commend it to the reader. After all, the first part of the work depicts Knollys as a radical Puritan who runs into difficulties with religious and political authority in England. It describes his self-impossed exile in New England as well as his tragic losses and impoverishment in Boston and Dover. The account is no less interesting as it relates Knollys' return to England and how he and his family coped during the English Civil War. The account's frequent references to tragic developments in Knollys' life, such as the loss of children, reminds us of the frailty of human existence during such a tortuous period as the seventeenth-century.

The account is also important as it sheds light on the intellectual and spiritual sources of Knollys' theology. From his overly pious upbringing, through his studies at the University of Cambridge, to his encounter with John Wheelwright (1592?-1679) it maps his religious journey before becoming a Baptist. In fact, it also highlights the influence of the Brownists

[1] Kathleen Lynch, *Protestant Autobiography in the Seventeenth-century Anglophone World* (Oxford and New York: Oxford University Press, 2012) 4 and 19.

in his drift to radical Puritanism.[2] Knollys' later years as a Baptist minister are well represented, although not with the detail of his early life. Particularly intriguing are the gaps in the narrative in regards to his association with Thomas Venner's 1661 rising. The work was published posthumously, with the intervention of William Kiffin who penned the preface. The extent of Kiffin's editorial intervention(s) on the published text remains an important question.

---

[2] On "radical Puritanism" see, David R. Como, "Radical Puritanism, c. 1558-1660," in *The Cambridge Companion to Puritanism*, ed. John Coffey and Paul C. H. Lim (Cambridge: Cambridge University Press, 2008) 241–258.

THE LIFE AND DEATH OF THAT OLD DISCIPLE OF JESUS CHRIST[1]

(London, 1692)

THE EPISTLE TO THE READER

It was the special charge God gave to his people of old, that the many signal providences and mercies that they had received from him should by them be recorded and left to their children's children, to the end that the memorial of his goodness might cause them to love and fear his name, and therefore they are required to bless the Lord from the fountain of Israel, from the very beginning of all his favors towards them. It is no small favor the servants of God are made partakers of, that his people of old have left so many testimonies of the gracious goodness and providences of God towards them, being a means to strengthen the faith of his people in a dependency upon him in all those variety of dispensations that do attend them in this world.

That whatever troubles they meet withal in this life they may know that God deals no otherwise with them than he had done to those that formerly have feared his name and may be comforted with the same comforts and supports which his servants formerly have received from God. The author of these ensuing experiences was that ancient and faithful servant of God, Mr. Hanserd Knollys, who departed this life in the ninety-third year of his age, having been employed in the works and service of Christ as a faithful

---

[1] Hanserd Knollys, *The life and death of that old disciple of Jesus Christ and eminent minister of the Gospel Mr. Hanserd Knollys who dyed in the ninety third year of his age written with his own hand to the year 1672; and continued in general in an epistle by Mr. William Kiffin* (London: Printed for John Harris, 1692). See also the now rare nineteenth century edition of the work, *The Life and Death of that Old Disciple of Jesus Christ, and Eminent Minister of the Gospel, Mr. Hanserd Knollys, who died in the Ninety-third Year of his Age. Written with His Own Hand to the Year 1672, and Continued in General, in an Epistle by Mr. William Kiffin. To Which is Added his Last Legacy to the Church* (London: E. Huntington, 1812). The 1812 edition was consulted for the present work. An excerpted version of *The life and death* can be found in B. Evans, "Incidents in the Life of Hanserd Knollys," *The Baptist Magazine* (February 1866): 92–100.

minister for above sixty years. In which time he labored without fainting under all the discouragements that attended him, being contented in all conditions, though never so poor in this world, under all persecutions and sufferings so he might therein serve his blessed Lord and savior. I have my self known him for above fifty-four years, and can witness to the truth of many things left by him under his own hand. It is great pity that the last twenty years of his life cannot be found amongst his writings, which to the knowledge of many were attended with the same sufferings as formerly, and with the same holy behaviors under them. He in that time was a prisoner in the New Prison for the truth's sake many months, where with great cheerfulness he remained, comforting and encouraging all that came to visit him with many blessed exhortations to cleave to the Lord. None were sent empty away, without some spiritual instructions, and many of his fellow prisoners were greatly strengthened and comforted by that heavenly counsel that dropped from his lips, spending much of his time there in prayer and study of the word of God, daily preaching to them the things that concern the kingdom of God.

He was chosen an elder to a congregation in London, with whom he labored for nearly fifty years, under many difficulties that did attend him. But neither the poverty of the church, nor the persecutions that attended him, were any temptation to him to neglect his duty towards them, but was willing to be poor with them in their poverty, and to suffer with them in their sufferings, being willing to labor for his own and his family's bread by keeping a school when they were not able to supply his wants, although he wanted not opportunities to have advanced himself in the world if he would have accepted of them. But like a faithful pastor he chose rather to be poor and suffer affliction, than to leave the duty and work he was called unto, in which he was employed until he arrived to the age of above ninety years. When he found weaknesses attend him, his love and affection to that poor church was such that he was daily exercising his thoughts to have an able minister for them in his room [i.e. "in his place"]. Declaring to several of his friends what great satisfaction it would be to him to see one settled amongst them, and that he would be willing to part with something of that little which he had—if there was need—for his maintenance of the church, towards the supply of him. And it pleased God to provide one for them, to their great satisfaction and rejoicing. So great was his natural affection and tender care for his daughter and grandchildren, who he knew were likely to come to some distress, that he did accordingly at that great age again undertake the teaching of a school that he might do to the uttermost of his ability to provide for them.

And having finished his work he fell asleep in the Lord, the 19th of September 1691. That these experiences may be of use to all those that read the same, is the desire and prayer of yours in the Lord, William Kiffin.

THE LIFE AND DEATH OF MR. HANSERD KNOLLYS

I, Hanserd Knollys, was born at Cawkwell near Louth in Lincolnshire, and was removed thence with my parents to Scartho, near Market Grimsby in the same county. About the sixth year of my age, I fell into a great pond and was preserved from being drowned by the water bearing up my coats till my father came, leaped in, and pulled me out.[2] About the tenth year of my age, I having construed the thirty-fifth chapter of Jeremiah in my Latin Bible to my father, he took occasion to dissuade me from the love and use of strong drink, and said he would give me 20*l* [20 English pounds] if I would drink water. But withal told me he would not have me do it to the prejudice of my health and charged me to make no vow to God so to do, for I did not understand how sacred a thing a vow is and how it did bind the soul, and it would be sin not to perform my vow; whereupon, I drunk water eleven years and never in all that time drank any wine, nor strong drink. About that time my father kept a tutor in his house to teach me and my brother, who was a godly and conscientious young man. He gave us good instructions for our souls, and convinced us of the sin of Sabbath breaking, and of disobedience to our parents. After my father had preferred our tutor to a place of greater profit we went a little while to Grimsby free school, till my father got another tutor for us into his house. One day going to the free school we fell out and fought, upon which I was much convinced that we had sinned against God, and against our father, who had often told us we were brethren, and ought not to fall out by the way. And I said, "Brother, we have sinned, come let us be friends, and pray God to pardon this, and other our sins." Whereupon we both kneeled down upon the plowed land, and I prayed, wept and made supplication to God as well as I could, and found so

---

[2] His father was Richard Knollys, rector of Scartho, Lincolnshire from 1613 to 1647. See the *Clergy of the Church of England Database*, http://www.theclergydatabase.org.uk/jsp/persons/CreatePersonFrames.jsp?PersonID=71066 (accessed on December 8, 2014).

great assistance from God at that time, that I never used any set form of prayer afterwards; which done, we both kissed each other, and went to school.

Afterwards I went to Cambridge, and there a godly minister preached on Hosea 4:17.[3] His doctrine was that the joining to sin by often committing it after conviction of conscience for it, did provoke God to give over many to the power of their corruptions, and let them alone to die in their sins. I was thereby convinced that it was my case, for I had oftentimes broken the Sabbath after conviction, and I had disobeyed my parents, and had often told untruths. The same Lord's Day at night another godly minister preached at five o'clock upon Ephesians 2:3 and thereby I was much more convinced of my sinful condition, and that I was a child of wrath, without Christ and grace, etc. Which work of conviction remained strongly upon me above one year, under which I was filled with great horror and fears of hell, sore buffetings and temptations of the devil, and made to possess the sins of my youth. But yet I prayed daily, heard all the godly ministers I could, read and searched the holy scriptures, read good books, got acquaintance with gracious Christians, then called Puritans, kept several days of fasting and prayer alone, wherein I did humble my soul for my sins, and begged pardon and grace of God for Christ's sake; grew strict in performing holy duties, and in reformation of my own life, examining myself every night, confessing my sins, and mourning for them, and had a great zeal for God, and an indignation against actual sins, both committed by myself and others.

June 29, 1629. I was ordained deacon, and the next day, June 30th, I was ordained presbyter by the Bishop of Peterborough, having preached above sixteen sermons before I would be ordained, by way of trial of my ability for that great work of the ministry.[4]

After my ordination, the Bishop of Lincoln gave me a small living at Humberston, where I preached twice every Lord's Day, and once every

[3] The original reads "Hosea the 5th. Chap. and 17. ver." The reference is obviously incorrect and we are assuming that the text Knollys is referring to is Hosea 4:17: "Ephraim is joined to idols—let him alone" (NRSV).

[4] The bishop of Peterborough at the time of Knollys' ordination in 1629 was Thomas Dove (1555–1630). His consecration as bishop of Peterborough took place on April 26, 1601. See Kenneth Fincham, "Dove, Thomas (1555–1630)," in *Oxford Dictionary of National Biography*, edited by H. C. G. Matthew and Brian Harrison (Oxford: Oxford University Press, 2004). Online ed., editd by Lawrence Goldman, January 2008. http://www.oxforddnb.com/view/article/7952 (accessed December 5, 2014).

holyday.[5] That which made me strict and laborious in preaching was partly the work of conviction upon my conscience, but more especially a providential acquaintance that I had gotten with a very godly old widow in Gainsborough—where I taught at the free school before I came to Humberston—who told me of one called a Brownist, who used to pray and expound scriptures in his family, whom I went sometimes to hear and with whom I had conference and very good counsel.[6]

Whilst I was at Humberston there lived a very religious widow, who falling sick sent for me and charged me that I would not depart her house on the day-time until she ended or mended, least Satan should tempt her above her strength. The doctor of physic had given her over, and some godly ministers, friends, and relations did take leave of her as a dying woman. She received nothing for several days, but a little julep,[7] which was put into her mouth with a spoon, and ran most of it out again, laying speechless two or three days, her family mourning over her and expecting her death every hour. I had brought some of my books to her house and was studying her funeral sermon, and when I had almost finished the same, the devil set upon me with a violent suggestion; that the scriptures are not the word of God. He had suggested this temptation to me divers times before, but prevailed

[5] Knollys is referring to John Williams (1582–1650) who became the bishop of Lincoln in 1621, succeeding to George Montaigne (1569–1628). In that same year King James I appointed him as lord keeper of the seal. See Brian Quintrell, "Williams, John (1582–1650)," in *Oxford Dictionary of National Biography*, edited by H. C. G. Matthew and Brian Harrison (Oxford: Oxford University Press, 2004). Online ed., edited by Lawrence Goldman, January 2008. http://www.oxforddnb.com/view/article/29515 (accessed December 5, 2014). Whitley places the beginning of Knollys' tenure at Humberstone in 1631. See W. T. Whitley, "Debate on Infant Baptism, 1643," *Transactions of the Baptist Historical Society* 1 (1908–1909): 237–45.

[6] "Brownists" were Separatist followers of Robert Browne (1550?–1633) the Congregationalist church leader. Separatists wanted to separate from the Church of England and form independent churches. Some Separatists resented the label, especially on account of Browne's return to the Church of England in 1585. See Barrington R. White, *The English Separatist Tradition from the Marian Martyrs to the Pilgrim Fathers* (London: Oxford University Press, 1971) 44–66. Burrage saw the period between 1585 and 1633 in Browne's life as one of "outward conformity." See Champlin Burrage, *The True Story of Robert Browne (1550?-1633) Father of Congregationalism* (Oxford: The University Press, 1906) 40ff.

[7] "Julep," a sweet drink, sometimes sweetened with sugar or other sweeteners. See "julep, n.," *Oxford English Dictionary Online* (Oxford: Oxford University Press, 2014). http://www.oed.com/view/Entry/101996?redirectedFrom=julep (accessed December 5, 2014).

not. Now the tempter assaulted me with this argument: whatever you ask in the name of Christ, God will do it, but that scripture was not true. And if I would put it now upon trial, I should find it not to be true, for if I would ask the woman's life in the name of Christ, God will not do it, and thereby I should know the Scriptures are not true, nor are they the word of God, for his word is true. To which I answered, "Satan, you are a liar, a deceiver, and a false accuser. The Holy Scriptures are the word of God, and the scriptures of truth, and seeing you have often tempted me in this kind, that I may forever silence you, you wicked and lying devil, I will trust in God, and act faith in the name of Christ in that very word of his truth which you have now suggested. I will leave my study and go and pray for her, and believe that God will hear my prayers through the intercession of Jesus Christ, and restore her life and health, that you may be found a liar." Whereupon, I went into the parlor where she lay speechless, without any visible motion or use of any senses and having locked the door—candles being in the room—I kneeled down by her bedside, and prayed above half an hour, using my voice, and then she began to stir, toss, and struggled so much, that I was constrained to stand up, and holding her in her bed, still prayed over her. Satan then gave me a great interruption and suggested to me she was dying, and these were the pangs of death upon her. I, notwithstanding this assault of the devil, was assisted by the Holy Spirit to pray and believe still, and in a short time she lay very quietly, and I kneeled down again and prayed fervently. Within half an hour, while I was yet praying, she said, "The Lord has healed me, I am restored to health." Then, I returned praises to God, and she did joined with me, lifting up her eyes and hands, still saying, "I am healed." Then I rose up from my knees and asked her how she did: "O Sir," said she, "God has heard your prayers, and has made me whole. Blessed be his Holy Name." Then I unlocked the door, and some of her kinsfolk and servants being at the door, came in and asked me if she were dead. To whom I answered, "No." Then they asked me how she did, and I bade them go to her and ask her. She had been speechless four days. I told them she could speak now; and as soon as they came to her bedside, she lift up herself and said, "I am well, the Lord has heard the prayer, and healed me, I am very weak and sore in my bones, but I am in health, I pray you give me something to eat." And as soon as they brought her some broth, she sat up and ate it, and took some of her julep, and from that time received strength, and the next day she did rise and walked with a staff. Which being heard of, many godly ministers and Christians came to visit her and to know the truth of what was told them touching her recovery. I told them it was not anything in me, but it was the Lord that had done it for his own glory and to silence Satan, who has never suffered to tempt me in that kind afterwards. God bruised Satan under my feet, and my Lord Jesus Christ made a conquest of him and gave me the victory, and helped me to give him the Glory of it.

The next year after this, I married a wife, with whom I lived 40 years; by whom I had issue, seven sons and three daughters; who was a holy, discreet woman, and a meet help for me in the ways of her household, and also in the way of holiness; who was my companion in all my sufferings, travels, and hardships that we endured for the gospel. She departed this life the 30th of April 1671, in full assurance of eternal life and salvation.

Presently after I was married I was convinced of some things about the worship of God—which I had conformed unto—to be sinful, to wit, the surplice, the cross in baptism, and admitting wicked persons to the Lord's Supper, whereupon I resigned my living to the bishop, who offered me a better living. I told him I could not conform any longer,[8] and would do nothing but preach, which he connived at for two or three years. Shortly after, I was convinced that my ordination received from the bishop was not right and though I had preached some years by virtue of that ordination, I had not received any seal from Christ of my ministry.[9] For though many had been reformed and moralized, yet I knew not that I had been instrumental to convert any souls to God.[10] And to that end, I renounced that ordination

[8] In other words, Knollys reflects upon his past as a "non-conformist."

[9] Several decades later, and on the other side of the Atlantic, the Baptist preacher and civic leader Isaac Backus referred to this "seal" as an "internal call" to preach the Gospel. See Isaac Backus, *A Discourse Showing the Nature and Necessity of an Internal Call to Preach the Everlasting Gospel* (Boston: Printed by Fowle in Ann-Street, near the town-dock, 1754). The tract can also be found in Isaac Backus, *Isaac Backus on Church, State, and Calvinism: Pamphlets, 1754-1789* (Cambridge: The Belknap Press of Harvard University Press, 1968) 65–128.

[10] Note the contrasting language that he uses in relation to Catherine Sutton, whom he calls an "instrument for the effectual calling of many," as well as his reference below to Mr. Wheelwright, "he had been instrumental to convert many." The idea that a preacher could serve as the instrument of God for the "effectual calling" of a sinner was common among Calvinist divines and found expression in article ten of the Westminster Confession, approved by Parliament in 1648: "All those whom God has predestinated unto life, and those only, he is pleased, in his appointed and accepted time, effectually to call, by his word and Spirit, out of that state of sin and death in which they are by nature, to grace and salvation by Jesus Christ; enlightening their minds spiritually and savingly to

and silenced my self, resolving not to preach any more, until I had a clear call and commission from Christ to preach the gospel. And to that end I gave myself to prayer day and night, for several weeks together and at last being at prayer in a wood at Woodenderby [i.e. Wood Enderby] in Lincolnshire, where I had preached before, and prayed with loud cries and tears that Christ would count me worthy and put me into the ministry, and show me how to glorify God in the ministry. And though I was much melted and enlarged in prayer at that time, yet I had no answer from the Lord. After prayer I walked and meditated under the wood side till sunset and then went homeward, resolved not to preach till the Lord made my call to that great work of preaching the gospel clear to me. And as I was going home, an answer of my prayers was given to me in these words, "Go to Mr. Wheelwright, and he shall tell you, and show you how to glorify God in the ministry."[11] But, I heard no voice, nor did I see any vision, only those words

understand the things of God, taking away their heart of stone, and giving unto them an heart of flesh; renewing their wills, and, by his almighty power determining them to that which is good, and effectually drawing them to Jesus Christ: yet so as they can come most freely, being made willing by his grace." The "effectual calling" was conceived as the work of the Holy Spirit and the ministry of the word fulfilled the function of an outward call: "Elect infants, dying in infancy, are regenerated and saved by Christ through the Spirit, who works when, and where, and how he pleases. So also are all other elect persons, who are incapable of being outwardly called by the ministry of the word." See John MacPherson, ed., *The Westminster Confession of Faith, with Introduction and Notes* (Edinburgh: T&T Clark, 1881) 82–87.

[11] John Wheelwright (1592?–1679) was educated at Sidney Sussex College, Cambridge. In 1636, he moved to Massachusetts with his second wife, Mary Hutchinson, and his five children. In Boston he played a crucial role together with John Cotton and Anne Hutchinson in the antinomian controversy that lasted from 1636 to 1638. He was banished from the Massachusetts Bay Colony in 1637, and moved north to Piscataqua. In 1639 he helped establish the town of Exeter. The incorporation of Exeter to the Bay Colony forced him to move to Wells, Maine. The General Court, however, revoked the ban against him in May 1644. He was pastor in Hampton for eight or nine years and returned to England in 1655. The prevailing religious climate after the Restoration compelled him to go to New England in 1662, where he served as minister in Salisbury, New Hampshire, until his death in 1679. Knolly's account makes clear that Wheelwright had already articulated his "covenant of grace" theology before 1636. Their encounter must have taken place between 1632 and that year, since it is evident that Wheelwright was no longer vicar of Bilsby. The present section of Knollys' autobiography underscores the paramount importance of Wheelwright in Knollys' spiritual life and career. See Joseph L. Chester, "Rev. John Wheelwright," *The New England Historical & Genealogical Register* 21, no. 4 (October 1867): 363–365; Charles H. Bell, *John Wheelwright: His Writings, Including his Fast-day Sermon, 1637 and his Mercurius Americanus, 1645; With a Paper upon*

were plainly and articulately spoken into my ears and understanding. At which I was astonished, and said, Lord let me not be deluded, nor deceived. Then was brought to my mind that passage of Cornelius sent to Peter, who should tell him what he should do.[12] Whereupon, I was fully persuaded it was an answer of my prayers from the Lord, and I was filled with such joy that I went on my way rejoicing, leaping and praising God.

The next morning going to seek out Mr. Wheelwright, who was a silenced minister, whom I had heard of by some Christians that he had been instrumental to convert many souls, but I knew him not, nor did I know where he was, but I was resolved to find him out. For I had heard that he was near Lincoln, about twenty-five miles from me, where he lived privately. And as I was getting up on horseback, one of my neighbors coming by asked me whither I was riding, to whom I said I did not certainly know, I was going to Mr. Wheelwright who was, as I heard, about Lincoln. "No," said he, "Mr. Wheelwright and his family came to dwell at a village which was but three miles from my house, for," said he, "I saw him come thither but three nights since, with his family and household goods in a coach and a wagon." Thither I rid presently, and found it so; and I told Mr. Wheelwright that yesternight I was praying as before, and was sent unto him by the Lord, etc. And after he had asked me many things about the work of God upon my soul, and I had told him, he said I could not glorify God neither in the ministry, nor in any other way or work for I was building my soul upon a covenant of works, and was a stranger to the covenant of grace.[13] At which I was startled, troubled, and somewhat amazed, but I told

---

the Genuineness of the Indian Deed of 1629 (Boston: Printed for the Prince Society, 1876); Charles H. Bell, *History of Exeter, New Hampshire* (Boston: Press of J. E. Farwell & Co., 1888) 5–21; Maurice W. Armstrong, "Religious Enthusiasm and Separatism in Colonial New England," *The Harvard Theological Review* 38, no. 2 (1945): 111–140; Sargent Bush, "'Revising what we have done amisse': John Cotton and John Wheelwright, 1640," *The William and Mary Quarterly* 45 no. 4 (1988): 733–750; Michael P. Winship, "Wheelwright, John (1592?–1679)," in *Oxford Dictionary of National Biography*, edited by H. C. G. Matthew and Brian Harrison (Oxford: Oxford University Press, 2004). Online ed., edited by Lawrence Goldman. http://www.oxforddnb.com/view/article/66155 (accessed December 5, 2014).

[12] See Acts 10:1–8.

[13] The encounter with Wheelwright operated an important transition in Knollys' spirituality. His early years at Cambridge were characterized by the rigid discipline typical of Puritanism. In spite of their commitment to the Protestant principle of justification by faith alone, the godly, or Puritans, were also deeply concerned with sanctification. A corollary of their belief was a robust piety such as what Knollys described earlier in this ac-

him I was assured God had sent me to him, and by his mouth I should be instructed how to glorify God in the ministry of the gospel and I did

---

count in relation to his Cambridge years: "I was thereby convinced that it was my case, for I had oftentimes broken the Sabbath after conviction, and I had disobeyed my parents, and had often told untruths. The same Lord's Day at night another godly minister preached at five o'clock upon Ephesians 2:3 and thereby I was much more convinced of my sinful condition, and that I was a child of wrath, without Christ and grace, etc. Which work of conviction remained strongly upon me above one year, under which I was filled with great horror and fears of hell, sore buffetings and temptations of the devil, and made to possess the sins of my youth. But yet I prayed daily, heard all the godly ministers I could, read and searched the holy scriptures, read good books, got acquaintance with gracious Christians, then called Puritans, kept several days of fasting and prayer alone, wherein I did humble my soul for my sins, and begged pardon and grace of God for Christ's sake; grew strict in performing holy duties, and in reformation of my own life, examining myself every night, confessing my sins, and mourning for them, and had a great zeal for God, and an indignation against actual sins, both committed by myself and others." Knollys found a way out of the crisis of spiritual confidence that was afflicting him since around 1631. Wheelwright convinced Knollys that he was living under a "covenant of works" and not under the "covenant of grace." Wheelwright summarized his understanding of the "covenant of grace" in the sermon he preached at Boston on January 19, 1636/37: "No, no, this is a covenant of works, for in the covenant of grace, nothing is revealed but Christ for our righteousness; and so for the knowledge of our justification by faith, nothing is revealed to the soul but only Christ and his righteousness freely given, it was the very grace of God that appeared, that same apparition whereby the soul comes to know that he is justified, the object of it is Christ freely given, when the loving kindness of Christ appeared not by the works of righteousness, they are laid aside, and the Lord reveals only to them the righteousness of himself given freely to the soul; if men have revealed to them some work of righteousness in themselves, as love to the brethren and the like, and hereupon they come to be assured they are in a good state, this is not the assurance of faith, for faith has Christ revealed for the object, therefore if the assurance of one's justification be by faith as a work, it is not Gospel." Wheelwright, *Fast-day Sermon,* in *John Wheelwight: His Writings*, 164–165. Wheelwright's sermon, which reflects the teaching that Knollys received from him while still in England, contributed to his banishment as an antinomian from the Bay Colony. Antinomianism was an important reaction against the rigorous piety of the godly. As David R. Como indicates: "Antinomians rejected this ferocious regime of moral oversight, claiming that the godly obsession with sanctification and holy duties compromised the Protestant message of the free grace and seduced the people of God back into works righteousness and legalism." Como, "Radical Puritanism, c. 1558–1660," 249–250; Perry Miller, "'Preparation for Salvation' in Seventeenth-Century New England," *Journal of the History of Ideas* 4 no. 3 (1943): 253–286. For an overview of the antinomian controversy in the wider context of New England Puritanism see Francis J. Bremer, "The Puritan Experiment in New England, 1630-1660," in *The Cambridge Companion to Puritanism*, ed. John Coffey and Paul C. H. Lim (Cambridge: Cambridge University Press, 2008) 127–142, here 133–137.

earnestly entreat and beseech him to apply himself to give me his counsel and directions touching that matter.

Then Mr. Wheelwright opened to me the nature of the covenant of free grace, which I confessed to him I was a stranger to in a great measure, having been only under legal convictions, and a spirit of bondage. And though I had some discoveries of my want of Christ, yet I had sought righteousness as it were by the works of the law, and got my peace by performing duties, and rested on them. Mr. Wheelwright desired me to consider what he had said to me, and to come to him two or three days after.

So I left him at that time, and went home exceedingly sorrowful about my soul's condition. But I gave my self to prayer, and begged of God to teach me the covenant of grace, and to that end I searched the scriptures, and I heard one Mr. How preach upon Galatians 2:20: "I live by the faith of the Son of God."[14] Whereby I saw that I had lived a life of works, and not of faith. Then I began to see a necessity of believing in Christ for pardon and salvation. And hearing the minister say that Christ was the author, root, and only foundation of saving faith, and that God did give the faith of evidence (Hebrews 11:1) in some new covenant promise (Galatians 3:14) and that those promises were given of God (2 Peter 1:4), I prayed that night, and

---

[14] Knollys was surely referring to, as Whitley indicated, Samuel How. See Whitley, "Debate on Infant Baptism," 237. Also known as the cobbler, Samuel How was perhaps best known in his time by his *The sufficiencie of the spirits teaching, without humane-learning: or A treatise, tending to proue humane-learning to be no help to the spirituall understanding of the Word of God. Written (if it may be) for the silencing of such false and scandalous reports, as have been rumored about concerning this matter; and also for the affording of true information to all such as desire to know the truth* ([Amsterdam]: [Cloppenburg Press], 1640). *The sufficiency* was based on 2 Peter 3:16: "There are some things in them hard to understand, which the ignorant and unstable twist to their own destruction, as they do the other scriptures" (NRSV). How rejected what he called human learning, or theological intellectualism, and argued that 2 Peter 3:16 referred to, "that sound knowledge, and sure information that every Christian has in Jesus Christ, whereby he is so deeply rooted, and so surely grafted into him by faith, as that he abides immovably settled in him… these are taught and instructed by the teachings of the Spirit of God." How, *The sufficiency*, B2v. Like Wheelwright, How emphasized an inner experience of the work of the Holy Spirit over the external means of grace. According to Perry Miller he was "one of the first sectarians to turn the enthusiasm of Puritanism against the orthodox divines." Perry Miller, *The New England Mind: The Seventeenth Century* (Cambridge: Harvard University Press, 1983) 508n2. It is highly significant that Brownists, Wheelwright, and How were so influential in this period of Knollys' life, between 1629 and 1636.

next morning, and in the night season, that God would give me such a promise. The next day I locked myself in the church, and in the chancel, or choir so called, I prayed very earnestly, mourning and bemoaning myself and my soul's condition, fearing, and with great brokenness of Spirit, and many tears expressed my fears, that God would leave me and forsake me, and then I should utterly perish for ever. And then that promise (Hebrews 13:5), "I will never leave thee, nor forsake thee," was given me, which promise stopped me a little in prayer, and I broke forth into this kind of expostulation with God, saying, "Lord, who am I? I am a vile sinful sinner, the chief of sinners, most unworthy of pardon and salvation! How, Lord? Never leave me, nor forsake me? O infinite mercy! Oh free grace! Who am I? I have been a graceless soul, a formal professor, a legal performer of holy duties, and have gone about to establish mine own righteousness, which I now see is but filthy rags," etc. Then God gave me those two promises, Isaiah 43:22–25 and Isaiah 54:9–10, and filled my soul with joy and peace in believing, so that I broke forth into praises and thanksgiving.

The next day, I went again to Mr. Wheelwright and told him what God had done for my poor soul, who said unto me now I was somewhat prepared to preach Jesus Christ and the gospel of free grace to others, having been taught it of God, and having heard and learned Jesus Christ myself. And he advised me to wait still upon God in prayer, and Christ would appear again to me by his Holy Spirit in his word, and show me and teach me how to preach. Then I went home again and continued in prayer. And one day begging earnestly of God in prayer, that if he had designed me to that great work of preaching the gospel, that then he would give me some testimony out of his holy word of his calling me thereunto. Whereupon these words were spoken by his Spirit to my heart (Acts 26:16): "I have appeared unto thee for this purpose, to make thee a minister and a witness both of these things which thou hast seen, and of those things in the which I will appear unto thee." Whence I believed that now I had received a call and commission from my Lord Jesus Christ to preach the gospel of his free grace and I blessed God, and expected a further appearance of Jesus Christ unto me. That night in my sleep Christ put into my mind that the next Lord's Day I should preach on that text, Romans 8:1. And he dictated to me in my sleep what doctrine I should preach from that text. The next day, I went and told all this to Mr. Wheelwright, who said, "Now my beloved brother, and fellow laborer in the gospel of the grace of God, Christ has given you authority, a call and a commission to preach. I pray you be humble and holy, and delay not to do your master's work," or words to that effect.[15] That night in my sleep the Lord taught me more, and the third night also. And I retained it all in my memory, and wrote it down, and searched the scriptures, which I received in my sleep for the confirmation of my doctrine.[16] And the next day being the Lord's Day, I preached that which I had received from the Lord, and God made it useful and powerful to conversion, as appeared to me afterwards. Thus I was night by night taught of God to preach the doctrine of free grace, according to the tenor of the new and everlasting covenant for three or four years together, whereby very many sinners were converted, and many believers were established in the faith. In which three or four years space I preached in three several places, at Anderby [Woodenderby], at Fulleby on the Hill, and at Wainfleet, where I was silenced; and from thence removed to London, and thence to New England, with my wife and one child.

About the Year 1636, I was persecuted, and prosecuted in the High Commission Court by virtue of a warrant wherewith I was apprehended in Boston and kept a prisoner in the man's house who served the warrant upon me. But God helped me to convince him, and he was so greatly terrified in his conscience, that he set open his doors and let me go away. But before I went [to Boston], I tarried so long in London, waiting for a passage, that when I went aboard I had but six brass farthings left, and no silver or gold, only my wife had 5*l* that I knew not of, which she gave me when we came there. By the way my little child died with convulsion fits, our beer and water stank, our biscuit was green, yellow, and blue, molded and rotten, and our cheese also. So that we suffered much hardship, being twelve weeks in our passage. But God was gracious to us, and lead us safe through those great deeps. And e're we went ashore, came one and enquired for me, and told me a friend that was gone from Boston to Rhode Island had left me his house to sojourn in, to which we went, and two families more with us, who went suddenly to their friends and other relations in the country. And I being poor was necessitated to work daily with my hoe, for the space of almost three weeks. The magistrates were told by the ministers that I was an

---

[15] Wheelwright's words amount to a formal approval of Knollys' experience, a clear indication of the latter's theological alignment with Wheelwright's "covenant of grace" theology.

[16] It is important to underscore that Hanserd Knollys believed in charismatic gifts throughout his career. Here it is easy to see how important was the idea that dreams could serve as a means of divine revelation.

antinomian, and desired they would not suffer me to abide in their patent [district].[17] But within the time limited by their law in that case, two strangers coming to Boston from Piscataqua, hearing of me by a mere accident, got me to go with them to that plantation, and to preach there, where I remained about four years.[18]

Being sent for back to England by my aged father, I returned with my wife and one child about three years old, and she was great with another child, and we came safely to London on the 24th of December 1641. In which year the massacre in Ireland broke forth, and the next year wars broke forth in England between King and Parliament. I was still poor and sojourned in a lodging till I had but sixpence left, and knew not how to provide for my wife and child. But having prayed to God, [I] encouraged my wife to trust in God and to remember former experiences, and especially that word of promise God had given us and would perform to us (Hebrews 13:5). Having paid for my lodging, I went out not knowing whither God's good hand of providence would lead me to receive something towards my present subsistence. And about seven or eight doors from my lodging a woman met me in the street, and told me she came to seek me, and her husband sent her to tell me that there was a lodging provided and prepared in his house by some Christian friends for me and my wife. I told her my present condition and went along with her to her house, and there she gave me twenty shillings, which Dr. Bastwick, a late sufferer had given her for me, and some linens for my wife, which I received and told her and her husband I would fetch my wife and child, and lodge there.[19] So I returned with great joy, and

---

[17] As noted earlier, in 1636 the antinomian controversy was well underway in the Massachusetts Bay Colony.

[18] Knollys was pastor of the First Church of Dover in New Hampshire from December 1638 to 1641. See Alonzo H. Quint, "The Memorial Address," in *The First Parish in Dover, New Hampshire: Two Hundred and Fiftieth Anniversary* (Dover: Printed for the Parish, 1884) 94.

[19] Among Knollys' benefactors was John Bastwick (1595?–1654) with whom he would later have an important debate over the question of independency. In 1645, Bastwick published his *Independency not Gods ordinance: or A treatise concerning church-government, occasioned by the distractions of these times. Wherein is evidently proved, that the Presbyterian government dependent is Gods ordinance, and not the Presbyterian government independent. To vvhich is annexed a postscript, discovering the uncharitable dealing of the independents towards their Christian brethren, and the fraud and jugglings of many of their pastors and ministers, to the misleading of the poor people, not only to their own detriment, but the hurt of church and state; with the danger of all novelties in religion* (London: Printed by John Macock, for Michael Spark junior, 1645). The same year Knollys replied with his *A*

my wife was very much affected with this mercy and divine providence, being so suitable and seasonable a supply unto us. And she said, "Oh dear husband, how sweet is it to live by faith, and trust God upon his bare word, let us rely upon him whilst we live, and trust him in all straits," with many such like expressions. And after we had returned praises to God we went to our new lodging, where we found all things necessary provided for us, and all charges paid for fifteen weeks. And my wife being bruised much on shipboard, had sore labor, and lay under great weakness above ten weeks, all which time two doctors, an apothecary and a chirurgeon [surgeon] did daily attend her, and administered unto her freely without any money.

At the end of sixteen weeks we had 7*l* that were given us by some Christian friends. I had spoken to some of those friends to get me some scholars, and I would get me a convenient place to teach school. For I had rather work for my bread, than be maintained by the charity of good Christians. One morning came a friend and told me a schoolmaster on Great Tower Hill died last night, and if I would come presently I might probably get some of his scholars. So I went and got three or four scholars that day, and there I had a great school, and continued till I was chosen master of Mary-Axe free school; whither I carried sixty scholars from Great Tower Hill. Within one year, I had above seven-score scholars, and sixteen boarders.[20] [The] free school and all the benefits thereof, I left to go into the Parliament's Army, and preached freely to the common soldiers until I did perceive the commanders sought their own things more than the cause of God and his people, breaking their vows and solemn engagements; whereupon, I left the army and came to London again. Shortly after, the Committee for Plundered Ministers sent their warrant to the then keeper in Ely House to apprehend me, and bring me in safe custody before them.[21]

---

moderate answer vnto Dr. Bastvvicks book; called Independency not Gods ordinance. Wherein is declared the manner how some churches in this city were gathered, and upon what tearmes their members were admitted; that so both the Dr. and the reader may judge, how near some beleevers who walk together in the fellowship of the gospell, do come in their practice to these apostolicall rules which are propounded by the Dr. as Gods method in gethering churches and admitting members (London: Printed by Iane Coe, 1645).

[20] Seven-score; that is, seven times twenty, or one hundred and forty.

[21] In 1642, the House of Commons created the Committee for Plundered Ministers, commissioned with the handling of parish minsters and their appointments. According to Green, it was responsible for the twin mission of "finding places for puritan clergy driven out by the Cavaliers, as well as ejecting unsuitable clergy." I. M. Green, "The Persecution of 'Scandalous' and 'Malignant' Parish Clergy during the English Civil

[The keeper] took me out of my house, carried me to Ely House, and there kept me prisoner several days without any bail. At last [he] carried me before the Committee, who asked me several questions, to which I gave them sober and direct answers. Among others, the chairman Mr. White asked me who gave me authority to preach.[22] I told him, the Lord Jesus Christ. Then he asked me if I were a minister. I answered I was made a priest by the prelate of Peterborough, but I had renounced that ordination, and I did here again renounce the same. They asked me by what authority I preached in Bow Church. I told them [that] after I had refused the desire of the then churchwardens three times, one day after another, their want of supply and earnestness prevailed with me, and I went thither. They opened the pulpit door and I went up and preached upon Isaiah 58 and gave them such an account of that sermon—thirty ministers of the Assembly of Divines, then so called, being present—that they could not gainsay, but bade me withdraw, and said nothing unto me, nor would my jailor take any charge of me. For the Committee had called for him, and did chide him, and threaten to turn

---

War," *The English Historical Review* 94 (1979): 507–531, here 515; Stephen K. Roberts, "The House of Commons, 1640-60," in *A Short History of Parliament*, ed. Clyve Jones (Woodbridge: Boydell Press, 2009) 121. The Committee oversaw the financial governance of the Church of England and had the specific task of enforcing conformity with the Solemn League and Covenant with the Scots of 1643. See W. A. Shaw, ed., "Introduction," in *Minutes of the Committee for the Relief of Plundered Ministers, and of the Trustees for the Maintenance of Ministers; Relating to Lancashire and Cheshire, 1643-1660, Part I, 1643-1654* (London and Redhill: Wyman and Sons, LTD, 1893) xvi–xvii.

[22] The reference is to John White (1590–1645) who was elected as Member of Parliament in 1640 for Southwark. He came from a family of wealthy merchants and studied law at the Middle Temple. White was a lay Puritan leader and his participation in the Long Parliament was characterized by his strong stance against Archbishop Laud, the episcopacy, and Arminianism. He chaired the Committee for Plundered Ministers. He was the author of *The first century of scandalous, malignant priests made and admitted into benefices by the prelates, in whose hands the ordination of ministers and government of the church hath been, or a narration of the causes for which the Parliament hath ordered the sequestration of the benefices of severall ministers complained of before them, for vitiousness of life, errors in doctrine, contrary to the articles of our religion, and for practising and pressing superstitious innovations against law, and for malignancy against the Parliament* (London: Printed by George Miller, 1643). See Green, "The Persecution," 515; Jacqueline Eales, "White, John (1590–1645)," in *Oxford Dictionary of National Biography*, edited by H. C. G. Matthew and Brian Harrison (Oxford: Oxford University Press, 2004). Online ed., edited by Lawrence Goldman. http://www.oxforddnb.com/view/article/29254 (accessed December 5, 2014).

him out of his place for keeping me prisoner so many days. So I went away without any blame, or paying of any fees.

Not long after I was brought before the Committee of Examinations,[23] being accused to them that I occasioned great disturbance to ministers and people in Suffolk, which I gave so good and satisfactory an account of to them, that upon their report thereof to the House of Commons they ordered that I might preach in any part of Suffolk when the minister of that place did not preach.[24] Which was all I got for 60*l*, which that trouble cost me to clear my innocence and the honor of the gospel. Which expense I put upon Christ's score for whose gospel and preaching Jesus Christ upon that text (Colossians 3:11), "But Christ is all and in all," I was stoned out of the pulpit and persecuted at a privy session, and fetched out of the country sixty miles up to London and was constrained to bring up four or five witnesses of good repute and credit to prove and vindicate myself from false accusations.

---

[23] On June 14, 1643, Parliament passed "An Ordinance for the Regulating of Printing." The Ordinance turned the Commons' Committee of Examinations into what Mendle has called a "virtual Star Chamber for the governance of the press." The Committee was authorized to search and seize "all unlicensed printing presses, and all presses any way employed in the printing of scandalous or unlicensed papers, pamphlets, books, or any copies of books [...]." It also authorized the apprehension of authors and printers. See C. H. Firth and Robert S. Rait, eds., *Acts and Ordinances of the Interregnum, 1642-1660*, vol. 1 (London: His Majesty's Stationary Office, 1911) 184–186; Michael Mendle, "Grub Street and Parliament at the Beginning of the English Revolution," in *Media and Revolution*, ed., Jeremy D. Popkin (Lexington: University Press of Kentucky, 1995) 31–47, here 40; William M'Callum Clyde, *The Struggle for the Freedom of the Press from Caxton to Cromwell* (New York: Burt Franklin, 1970, repr. 1934) 66.

[24] In 1645, Knollys published his first work, *Christ exalted: in a sermon begun to be preached at Debenham in Suffolk, upon the 14. day of Febr. last, upon Coloss. 3. 11. / By Hanserd Knollys. Who was stoned out of the pulpit (as he was preaching) by a company of rude fellowes, and poor women of that town; who were sent for, called together, and set on by a malignant high-constable, who lives in the same town. Also, another sermon, preached at Stradbrooke in Suffolk, the 13. day of Febr. last, concerning sanctification; upon Ephes. 1. 4.* (London: no printer, 1645). He published a second edition of the work the next year, 1646, with a new title making reference to the intervention of the Committee of Examinations and a new preface dedicating the work to the members of the Committee. See Knollys, "To the Honourable Committee of Examinations," in *Christ exalted: a lost sinner sought, and saved by Christ: Gods people are an holy people. Being the summe of divers sermons preached in Suffolk; / by Hanserd Knollys. Who for this doctrine had the meeting-house doores shut against him, and was stoned out of the pulpit (as he was preaching) by a rude multitude; who were gathered together, and set on by a malignant high-constable. Which hath been proved by divers witnesses of good reputation, before the Honourable Committee of Examination at London* (London: Printed by Iane Coe, 1646) Av.

Some time after that I was summoned before a committee in the Chamber—called the Queen's Court—at Westminster, whereof Mr. Leigh was chairman, for preaching without holy orders.[25] To which I answered, that I was in holy orders. Some of the committee told the chairman I had renounced my ordination by the Bishop in the Committee for Plundered Ministers. I confessed that I did so, but I was ordained since in a church of God according to the order of the gospel of Christ, the manner whereof I then declared to the committee before Mr. Nye, and other ministers there present.[26] But at last the committee, by their chairman, commanded me to preach no more. I told them I would preach the Gospel both publicly and from house to house, for it was more equal to obey Christ, who had commanded me, than them who forbid me. So I went away and ceased not to teach and preach Jesus Christ and him crucified.

I was then pastor to a church which I had gathered two or three years before, in the year 1645, with whom I have walked ever since, except that I

---

[25] Knollys is most likely referring to the Puritan writer and politician, Edward Leigh (1603–1671) who was sitting in Parliament from 1645 to 1648. See John Sutton, "Leigh, Edward (1603–1671)," in *Oxford Dictionary of National Biography*, edited by H. C. G. Matthew and Brian Harrison (Oxford: Oxford University Press, 2004). Online ed., edited by Lawrence Goldman, January 2008. http://www.oxforddnb.com/view/article/16378 (accessed December 5, 2014). On March 9, 1647, the House of Commons ordered the following: "That power be given to the committee where Colonel Leigh has the chair, appointed to receive information against such persons as preach, and are not in orders, to enjoin all such as come before them, who shall be proved guilty of preaching, contrary to the ordinance, not to preach until further order taken: which if they shall refuse to promise; or shall, notwithstanding they have so promised, go on in the same offence, and still preach; that in such cases they shall have power to commit them." House of Commons Journal Volume 5: 9 March 1647, *Journal of the House of Commons: volume 5: 1646-1648* (1802) in British History Online, http://www.british-history.ac.uk/report.aspx?compid=25040 (accessed December 5, 2014).

[26] The reference, in all likelihood, is to the Independent minister Phillip Nye (bap. 1595, d.1672) who was an influential member of the Westminster Assembly of Divines. He was keen on marking a hard line of demarcation between the Independents and the Separatists while asserting the right of Congregationalists to maintain their own independence from a national church. See Barbara Donagan, "Nye, Philip (bap. 1595, d. 1672)," in *Oxford Dictionary of National Biography*, edited by H. C. G. Matthew and Brian Harrison (Oxford: Oxford University Press, 2004). Online ed., edited by Lawrence Goldman, January 2008. http://www.oxforddnb.com/view/article/20417 (accessed December 5, 2014); Francis J. Bremer, "Nye, Philip (1595–1672)," *Puritans and Puritanism in Europe and America: A Comprehensive Encyclopedia*, 2 vols. (Santa Barbara: ABC-CLIO, 2006) 1:184–86.

was absent from the church sometimes upon just occasions, and with their leave, or forced from them by violent persecution. My chiefest means of livelihood had been by teaching school. Wherein God was pleased to make me serviceable in my generation to communicate liberally to the poor of the church and to strangers that stood in need, and plentifully to provide all things necessary and convenient for my wife and children, through God's blessing upon my honest labors. I received from the church always according to their ability, most of the members of the church being poor but I coveted no man's gold or silver; but chose rather to labor, knowing, "It is more blessed to give than to receive" [Acts 20:35]. And I did not wholly neglect my duty as a pastor, but preached two or three times in a week and visited the members of the church from house to house, especially when they were sick. During twenty-five years now past the church has continued in the apostles' doctrine, fellowship, and in breaking of bread and in prayer, without division and separation of any part thereof, or party therein. Though some few particular members being led away by some error in their judgment have forsaken the assembling of themselves with the church, as the manner of some is and was in the apostles' time.[27]

In the year 1660, upon Venner's rising, and others that with him made an insurrection in the city of London, myself and many other godly and peaceable persons were taken out of their own dwelling houses and brought to Wood Street Compter, and many to Newgate, and other prisons, though we were innocent and knew not of their design.[28] At which time I suffered imprisonment eighteen weeks, till we were delivered by an act of pardon

[27] See mention of this breakaway group in *Mr. Knollys' Last Legacy to the Church*, included in the present volume.

[28] Although Knollys started this section by mentioning the year 1660, he was in fact about to elaborate on events that happened in the course of the decade. On January 1661, the Fifth Monarchist leader, Thomas Venner (1608/9–1661) headed an uprising against the restored monarchy. Fifth Monarchists were millenarians who believed in a literal thousand-year reign of Christ on earth. Their views led them to oppose Oliver Cromwell under the Protectorate and Charles II (r. 1660–1685) in 1661. Their political and religious manifesto appeared in print as, *A door of hope: or, A call and declaration for the gathering together of the first ripe fruits unto the standard of our Lord, King Jesus* ([London]: no printer, [1661]). See Richard L. Greaves, "Radicals, Rights, and Revolution: British Nonconformity and Roots of the American Experience," *Church History* 61, no. 2 (1992): 151–168; Bernard S. Capp, *The Fifth Monarchy Men: A Study in Seventeenth-Century English Millenarianism* (London: Faber and Faber, 1972); Louise Fargo Brown, *The Political Activities of the Baptists and Fifth Monarchy Men in England during the Interregnum* (Washington: American Historical Association, 1912).

upon the King's coronation unto all offenders, except murderers.[29] We were above four hundred prisoners kept all this time in Newgate because we refused to take the oaths of allegiance and supremacy.

After I was set at liberty out of prison, I went to Holland, and thence up into Germany, with my wife and two of my children, where we sojourned about two or three years. In my absence one Colonel Legge, a bedchamber man, and lieutenant of the ordinance, charged me in the Court of Exchequer for keeping a house and ground from the King, against whom I stood suit by my attorney.[30] But when Colonel Legge could not get my house from me by law, he and some others brought several red coat soldiers, and took it by force, thrust out those persons I had left in possession, and kept possession by soldiers, both of my house, garden and my goods, which had cost me above 700*l* with the purchase, bought of the Artillery Company of London, to whom I paid 300*l* and laid out 400*l* more in building upon the ground, which I had bought and paid for. I had at the same time 200*l* in Weavers Hall, which was given away to the King among many greater sums of other men's money. I spent above 150*l* more in Holland and Germany.

---

[29] Knollys is alluding to the coronation pardon of 1661. See, *A proclamation concerning His Majesties coronation pardon* (London: Printed by John Bill, Printer to the King's most Excellent Majesty, 1661); Matthew Jenkinson, *Culture and Politics at the Court of Charles II, 1660-1685* (Woodbridge: The Boydell Press, 2010) 69–70.

[30] The dignitary in question was William Legge (1607/8–1670). He was a royalist officer who fought for Charles I and remained loyal to his son, Charles II. Like many other royalist agents, Legge received numerous rewards for his allegiance. Under the Restoration he was reinstated to his former posts as master of the armories and groom of the bedchamber, and newly appointed as lieutenant-general of the ordnance. It appears that he claimed possession of Knollys' former house and school by virtue of his office as master of the armories. See Ian Roy, "Legge, William (1607/8–1670)," in *Oxford Dictionary of National Biography*, edited by H. C. G. Matthew and Brian Harrison (Oxford: Oxford University Press, 2004). Online ed., edited by Lawrence Goldman http://www.oxforddnb.com/view/article/16358 (accessed December 5, 2014); Geoffrey Smith, *Royalist Agents, Conspirators and Spies: Their Role in the British Civil Wars, 1640-1660* (Surrey and Burlington: Ashgate, 2011) 249. In December 1673, Knollys' made a petition to the King arguing his legitimate possession of the armory house in the Artillery Ground near Spitafields. See F. H. Blackburne Daniell, ed., *Calendar of State Papers, Domestic Series, November 1st, 1673, to February 28th, 1675* (London: Printed for His Majesty's Stationary Office, by Mackie and Co., 1904) 66–67. Knollys' predicament remained unresolved as late as 1679, when he was still petitioning the Crown for some kind of remedy. See William A. Shaw, ed., "Entry Book: November 1679, 11–20," *Calendar of Treasury Books, Vol. 6: 1679-1680* (London: His Majesty's Stationary Office, 1913) 257–265.

When I had spent all that, I was forced to sell all my goods there, to bring me to England again. In which return I met with two remarkable acts of providence towards my wife, two children, and me.[31] I had agreed with a skipper at Cullen [i.e. Cologne] in Germany to Rotterdam for a sum of money, and he was to pay all the tolls and licenses, which he did at two or three places, until we were come where we were strangers. Then he made me pay licenses at two places, and at a place called Rurote, upon the Rhine, he made me pay both toll and license, and kept me there two or three days at great charges. My wife being set and very sad in a harbor or victualling house, came in a gentleman, and observing her, asked me what the gentlewoman ailed. I told him she was my wife, and he understanding the Latin tongue, asked me what the matter was. I told him all my case, and what my condition was. "Well," said he, "if you be a son of Abraham, God will deliver you." So he went into his chamber, and sent for the skipper and toll masters, and caused him to produce our agreement, and understanding how he had wronged me—he being lord and chief over the toll masters there—he commanded them to take our goods from him, and to hire us another skipper to carry us and our goods to Rotterdam. He also made the skipper that had done me wrong to allow me so much as I had paid for licenses all the way thither. After we were come to Rotterdam and my wife, and son, and daughter were gone to England, God made two Catholics in Cullen instrumental to prevail with the Prince Dewitt[32] to send me by a bill of exchange 160 rix-dollar[33] for a house that I had built in his country and could not sell, which I received at Rotterdam.[34] And then came over to England myself, and came to my wife and children, whom I found at a friend's house in London.

Then I set upon teaching school again, and by God's blessing upon my honest labors, have provided things honest, necessary, and convenient for my family. To my eldest son, I had given 60*l* per annum during his life, which

---

[31] Original: "towards me, my wife, and two children."

[32] Knollys is probably referring to Johan de Witt (1625–1672) councilor pensionary of Holland (1653–1672). If so, then it is not clear why Knollys calls him "prince." Neither is it clear if the property was in Cologne or in an undisclosed location in the Netherlands.

[33] The rix-dollar was a small silver coin in use throughout the seventeenth century in the Netherlands and other parts of northern Europe.

[34] While still in Rotterdam, Knollys edited and published Katherine Sutton's *A Christian womans experiences of the glorious working of Gods free grace Published for the edification of others* (Rotterdam: printed by Henry Goddaeus, printer in the Newstreet, 1663).

he enjoyed above twenty-one years ere he died. To my next son, that lived to be married, I gave the full value of 250*l* in money, house, school, and household goods, and left him fifty scholars in his schoolhouse. To my only daughter then living, I gave upon her marriage above 300*l* in money, annuity, plate, linen, and household stuff, and left her husband fifty scholars in the said schoolhouse, in partnership with my said son. To my youngest son, that lived to be married, I gave more than 300*l*, besides it cost me above 60*l* in his apprenticeship, and 40*l* afterwards.

Thus my heavenly Father made up my former losses with his future blessings, even in outward substance, besides a good increase of grace, and experience, in the space of forty years, that I and my dear faithful wife lived together. We removed several times with our whole family; whereof once from Lincolnshire to London, and from London to New England. Once from England into Wales; twice from London into Lincolnshire, once from London to Holland, and from thence into Germany, and thence to Rotterdam, and thence to London again. In which removings, I gained great experiences of God's faithfulness, goodness, and truth in his great and precious promises. I have also gained some experience of my own heart's deceitfulness and the power of my own corruptions, and the reigning power of Christ, and his captivating and subduing my sins, making conquests of the devil, world and sin, and then giving me the victory, and causing me to triumph, and to bless his most holy name.

Three things made my latter sufferings very easy to be endured. First, the former straits and hardships, which I had undergone with patience. Second, the present lively acts and exercise of grace especially faith and hope under those latter and greater trials. Third, the light of God's countenance and the full assurance of his love and of eternal life. I would not want those experiences and teachings that my soul has enjoyed for all that ever I suffered.

My wilderness-mercies, sea-mercies, city-mercies, and prison-mercies afforded me very many and strong consolations. The spiritual sights of the glory of God, the divine sweetness of the spiritual and providential presence of my Lord Jesus Christ, and the joys and comforts of the holy and eternal Spirit, communicated to my soul, together with suitable and seasonable scriptures of truth, have so often, and so powerfully revived, refreshed, and strengthened my heart in the days of my pilgrimage, trials, and sufferings that the sense, yea, the life and sweetness thereof abides still upon my heart, and has engaged my soul to live by faith, to walk humbly and to desire and endeavor to excel in holiness to God's glory and the example of others. Though I confess many of the Lord's ministers, and some of the Lord's people have excelled and outshined me, with whom God has not been at so much cost nor pains, as he has been at with me. I am a very unprofitable servant, but yet, by grace, I am what I am. In the beginning of my ministry, I studied in the forenoon and visited my religious acquaintance in the afternoon, and some of my natural relations. I did preach constantly twice, often three times, and some Lord's Days four times; at Holton at seven in the morning, at Humberston at nine, at Scartho at eleven, at Humberston at three o'clock, all in the same day. I also preached every holiday once, at every burial, poor or rich. I have most commonly preached three or four times every week, if in any measure of health, for above forty years together, except, now and then, I got some other godly man to preach for me, but rarely. When I was in prison, I did preach usually every day, if well.

And God was pleased to confirm my call unto that great work. First, by the conversion of many sinners, who having declared the dealings of God with their souls, testified God did convince them, convert them, and establish many of them by my ministry, through the powerful and effectual operations of his Holy Spirit, and word preached by me unto them. Second, by some healing power of God put forth upon the sick and infirm bodies of several persons, who were suddenly restored to health, immediately in time of prayer with them, or by and through faith in Jesus Christ; especially in this city of London, and of the sickness called the plague, both in former years and in the year 1665. Not to me, but to God be given glory and praise, for in his name, through faith in his name, they were healed. Third, by enabling me, standing by me, and strengthening me by his Holy Spirit and sanctifying grace to preach the gospel in season and out of season, with all boldness, neither being ashamed, nor afraid to bear my testimony for Christ, his gospel, churches, ministry, worship and ordinances against the antichristian powers, ministers, worshippers, and traditions of the beast, the great mystical whore, and the false prophet. Nor have I been terrified by the adversary by virtue of the acts of Parliament touching private meetings and conventicles, commencing 10 May 1670.[35] I was taken at a meeting in

---

[35] In 1670, Parliament enacted a revision of the Conventicle Act of 1662. It outlawed the gathering of Nonconformists for worship. The Act was part of the Clarendon Code, alongside the Corporation Act (1661) the Act of Conformity (1662) and the Five-Mile Act (1665). For text see, David Charles Douglas, ed., *English Historical Documents, 1660-1714*, vol. 6 (London: Routledge, 1996) 375–386.

George Yard, and the then Lord Mayor committed me to the compter in Bishopsgate for preaching there, but having favor in the eyes of the keepers, I had liberty to preach to the prisoners there, twice every day of the week in the common hall, where most of the prisoners came and heard me and some of them blessed God that ever I came to that prison.[36] Soon after I was set at liberty, at the sessions in Old Bailey, God made me his prisoner by a sharp and painful distemper in my bowels, called the gripping of the guts, and he brought me near to the grave. But in time of my greatest extremity, god remembered mercy, forgave my iniquity, healed my disease and restored my life from death. No tongue can express my pains, yet God gave me much patience, wherein I possessed my soul. I had, first, a very clear discovery from the Lord of the causes why he so contended with me. One was the meritorious cause of some former visitations, and especially of this sore disease. Second, I saw the sin of my sinful nature, which was not so crucified, as that it was destroyed, but I found some motions of it of late stirring in my sinful heart. The sense of this was a very sore burden and trouble to my soul in this day of my calamity, for which I mourned in secret before the Lord, and lay at the throne of grace loathing myself, and begging, that God would kill that sin and destroy it, and all the rest of my sins. And I received this answer, his grace was sufficient for me [cf. 2 Corinthians 12:9], he had pardoned and he would subdue and destroy that and all other mine iniquities, according to his everlasting covenant of free grace.

Satan was sometimes very busy during this time of sickness, and tempted me sorely in the night season, sometimes suggesting to me that I was but a hypocrite, at other times that my evidences for heaven were not good, whom God helped me to resist steadfastly in the faith, and he fled away. Another cause why the Lord now contended with me was for the trial and exercise of my graces, which he had given me. It was the trial of my faith and the exercise of my patience, and that I might be to his praise and an example unto weak believers whose eyes were upon me, and were observing and hearkening how I did behave myself under all the great rebukes and chastisements of the Lord upon me. For they had heard, that God had taken one grandchild away by death, and visited another, who was

[36] *Oxford English Dictionary Online,* s.v. "compter," "the name of certain city prisons for debtors, etc., in London, Southwark, Exeter, etc.." The earliest recorded use of the term dates to 1428. See *Oxford English Dictionary Online* (Oxford: Oxford University Press, 2014) s.v. "compter, n.," http://www.oed.com/view/Entry/37923?redirectedFrom=Compter (accessed December 08, 2014).

above sixteen years old with the small pox and she was likely to die, and one son died and was buried during my sickness, and my eldest son was dead and buried in the country, whereof I was told before I was recovered. My other son's wife had sore labor, a dead-man-child, and she [was] likely to die, and my dear loving wife then began to be sorely afflicted with a pain and swelling in her face, of which she since died.

But God did give a proportionable measure of faith and patience to me his poor unworthy servant. Under all this his fatherly chastisements he did strengthen me with strength in my soul, and upheld me with the right hand of his righteousness; so that I fainted not nor was I weary, his rod and his staff did comfort me [cf. Psalm 23]. He brought out my will unto a free submission, subjection, and resignation to his own most wise and holy will. Yea, my Father's visitations did so preserve my soul that I did sing and rejoice under the sights and smiles of Christ, even whilst I was sighing and sorrowing for my transgressions.

Two learned, well practiced and judicious doctors of physic had daily visited me and consulted my cure several days together, and I was fully persuaded that they did what possibly they could to effect a cure. I also knew also that God did not succeed their honest and faithful endeavors with his blessing, although God had given a signal and singular testimony of his special blessing by each of them unto others of their patients, at least sixteen, at the same time. I resolved to take no more physic, but would apply to that holy ordinance of God appointed by Jesus Christ, the great physician of value (James 5:14–15). And I got Mr. Kiffin and Mr. Vavasor Powel,[37] who prayed over me and anointed me with oil in the name of the Lord and the Lord did hear the prayer and heal me. For there were very many godly ministers and gracious saints that prayed day and night for me—with submission to the will of God—that the Lord would spare my life and heal me, and make me more useful and serviceable to the Lord, to the church, and to the saints, whose prayers God heard. And as an answer of their prayers, I was perfectly healed, but remained weak long after. My dear wife remained weak and full of pain, and was very greatly afflicted with pain day

[37] Vavasor Powell (1617–1670) was a Welsh Baptist preacher with ties to the Fifth Monarchists. See Edward Bagshaw, *The life and death of Mr. Vavasor Powell, that faithful minister and confessor of Jesus Christ wherein his eminient conversion, laborious successful ministry, excellent conversation, confession of faith, worthy sayings, choice experiences, various sufferings, and other remarkable passages in his life and at his death are faithfully recorded for publick benefit: with some elogies and epitaphs by his friends* ([London]: no printer, [1671]).

and night, but the Lord gave her a great measure of faith and patience even to the end. She enjoyed the light of God's countenance, had full assurance of God's love, the pardon of her sins, and of eternal life. And having patiently endured six months sore pains, upon the thirtieth of the second month called April, 1671, being the Lord's Day, about four or five o'clock, slept in Jesus. I was doing my Master's work at that time in the congregation and toward the end of my sermon had a strong impulse upon my spirit, that my dear wife was departing, and in my prayer after sermon was drawn forth by faith to commend her to God that gave her to me, and blessed him for receiving her soul into Abraham's bosom, and placing her among the spirits of just men made perfect in the paradise of God.

Since the death of my dear wife it has pleased God to stretch forth his hand upon my only son then living, and to afflict him with a deep consumption, occasioned as I judge by grief for his dearly loving and beloved mother, for he drooped ever since she first was taken ill of that distemper of rheum, which fell from her head into her face, of which she died. And he has been worse and worse ever since she died.

Having had great expenses and a great charge of dear relations, and owing some considerable debts, I was necessitated to teach school again in my old age, that I might pay my debts, succor my dear relations, and not be too great a burden to the church of God. And this I have willingly and cheerfully undertaken, that if persecution do come upon me again—which I expect and prepare for—and I shall be haled to prison, or forced to fly, it may be my mercy and comfort—as at all other times of my many removals in the days of my pilgrimage and persecutions—that no person shall have any occasion to come to me and say, "Pay me what you owe me before you go." For I desire to owe no man anything but love and honestly to pay every man his own. And if death seize on my body, that I may leave enough of my own behind me to pay all my debts, and a little for the relief of God's poor, and some of my poorest natural relations. I had a summoning in June last to prepare myself for the grave by a sudden and sore fit of the wind-cholick[38]

[38] According to Morrissey, "wind-cholick" is "the gaseousness of a sour stomach." Henry Fielding, *Tom Thumb and The Tragedy of Tragedies*, ed., L. J. Morrissey (Berkeley and Los Angeles: University of California Press, 1970) 128. Thus John Maubray described it: "The wind-cholick traverses the belly, and gives an excruciating wandering pain in the viscera, or bowels." John Maubray, *The Female Physician, Containing all the Diseases Incident to that Sex, in Virgins, Wives, and Widows; Together with their Causes and Symptoms, their Degrees of Danger, and Respective Methods of Prevention and Cure* (London: Printed for James Holland, 1724) 85.

and vomiting. And on the 3rd of October last, 1671, I had another summons to be ready to depart this life by another sudden more violent tormenting fit of the wind-cholick and vomiting. And I am alarmed by these awakening visitations of the Lord to prepare and be ready that when my Lord and master comes or calls for me to come to him, I may be found so doing, that he may say, "Well done, thou good and faithful servant, enter thou also into the joys of thy master" [c.f. Matthew 25:21].

The next trial my heavenly Father saw needful for me to be exercised under was the sickness and death of my then only living son, my Isaac, my most loving and beloved son, who was translated the 15th day of November, 1671. Which great trial and loss God made gain to him, and easy to me by a manifest and powerful work of conversion, repentance and faith upon his soul in the time of his sickness, which administered much comfort to me, so that I sorrowed not for him as one without hope, who exercised very great patience under his very great pain, soreness and burning fever, whilst his flesh, marrow, and moisture consumed, and acted faith and hope very lively and constantly upon Christ in that word (John 6:37): "And him that cometh to me, I will in no wise cast off." Very often expressing his former bondage and slavery to sin and Satan, which he bewailed and acknowledged often God's free and rich grace in giving him Christ and pardon and salvation now at last, which he had neglected the offers and tenders of so often. Some combats he had, but after a manifestation of Christ to his soul, he died in faith and peace.

And albeit my natural affections caused me to weep often, and the sense of God's hand and rod upon me, caused me to mourn very much in secret, yet the Almighty by his rod and staff did so comfort me, that I walked through this valley also of the shadow of death without fear of evil and was assisted and enabled to perform the work of my ministry in the congregation without any omission or interruption [cf. Psalm 23]. And that very night my only son died, the Lord brought to my mind that Scripture (Micah 7:14): "Feed thy people with thy rod." Which was made a seasonable, suitable and powerful word by the teachings of the Holy Spirit unto my soul in my solitary condition; who thus administered food, yea and a feast also to my soul. For by this rod of God, I had served into my soul a dish of sour or bitter herbs, I mean sorrow for my sins. But I fed also on the Paschal Lamb, in whose blood I saw all my sins washed away. And the spirit of God witnessed with my spirit that I was the child of God and one of those children with whom God will keep covenant, and not take away his love from me, though he visited my transgressions with the rod and my iniquities with stripes (Psalm 89:28–34), which scripture was then brought again with power upon my heart.

The next dish of spiritual food under this rod, which God brought me, or sent me by his spirit in his word to feed upon, was full of love. Then that holy scripture came to me, not in word only but in power and in the spirit (Revelation 3:19–20), and in much assurance. Wherein he showed me his face and I saw my Father's face in that glass of the gospel (Hebrews 12:6–7), which the Holy Spirit held forth to me by this rod and shed abroad in my heart the love of the Father in his son Jesus Christ. After this the next day God gave me a dish of spiritual fruits by this rod to feed upon, served up in that Holy Scripture (Hebrews 12:11), "No affliction at the present is joyous, but grievous; but the fruit thereof shall be peace and righteousness to them that have been exercised thereby." And after God had thus fed me, feasted me several days and nights together with this his rod, he very graciously pronounced his blessing upon me by his rod, in these words: "Blessed is the man whom thou correctest and teachest out of thy law or word" [c.f. Psalm 94:12]. Unto which I was helped heartily to say, "Amen, it is good for me to be, and that I have been afflicted," etc. And after God had communed with me from his mercy seat, and had instructed me, I experienced such divine loves, shinings, and spiritual sweetness, as Jonathan did when he tasted a little honeydew on the end of the rod in his hand and was enlightened and refreshed [c.f. 1 Samuel 14:43]. So that I was enlivened, or revived, fed and feasted by the rod and word, even the bond of God's everlasting covenant of free grace, and love.

About four or five months after the death of my son, his wife married a gentleman of 300*l* per annum, and left me engaged to receive and pay all my sons debts. And to preserve his credit and his wife's, I borrowed 200*l* to help to pay his debts and suffered the loss thereof, which necessitated me still to keep school to pay my debts. And I having a granddaughter with me three years before, she being nineteen years old, did take the charge of my household affairs, and of my boarders, who managed all things with so much discretion, that my life was very comfortable and I had great content. In September 1672, my only daughter's husband went by her consent into the country, and left her.

[ANONYMOUS POSTSCRIPT][39]

Thus far was written with his own hand, and there we must be forced to break off, though abruptly. The remaining part of his life, written by himself, as this was, being—as Mr. Kiffin mentions in his Preface—unhappily lost. Which, because it is impossible to be supplied by any hand so particularly as his own, must be done in general by letting the Christian reader know that this holy man's life was all of a piece, and that he maintained his zeal, fidelity, and integrity in the latter part of it, as well as in the former, even to the end of it. He was not very long sick, not keeping his chamber above five weeks, nor his bed above ten days. All the time of his sickness he behaved himself with extraordinary patience, and resignation to the divine will, longing to be dissolved, and to be with Christ, not so much to be freed from pain and trouble, as from sinning. Which he expressed to one with him with a more than ordinary transport of joy.

[39] The document concludes with an anonymous postscript that makes a third person reference to Kiffin's preface. It explains the abrupt ending of Knollys' autobiography. It also provides a one-sentence introduction to the letter Knollys wrote on his deathbed to his London congregation: "A little before his death he wrote the following epistle, which he left as his last legacy to the church." Although the letter, also known as *Mr. Knollys' Last Legacy to the Church*, is included in the 1692 publication, the editors have decided to republish it separately in this volume.

MR. KNOLLYS' LAST LEGACY TO THE CHURCH, WRITTEN A LITTLE BEFORE HIS DEATH

(London, 1692)

INTRODUCTION

Knollys' last letter to his London congregation constitutes a truly remarkable summary statement of his pastoral theology and spirituality. He uses Galatians 4:18 as the biblical theme of the letter, encouraging the congregants to persist in his absence. In the letter he mentions by name his assistant pastor, Robert Steed, to whom—alongside the "ministering brethren" and other "helps in government"—he entrusts the congregation. He commends the leadership, namely the "ministering brethren" for their perseverance in times of persecution, especially during the year and four months of his imprisonment in London's New Prison.

The letter contains important doctrinal points that give a fuller picture of his theology and spirituality. For instance, he distinguishes between "administrations," among which he mentions "reading and expounding," on the one hand, and "ordinances," such as "prophesying and preaching," on the other. Equally important is his comment on the correct understanding of "zeal" as he attempts to provide a balanced definition of this moral disposition. "Zeal is," Knollys argues while referring to Galatians 4:18, "a fervent and constant affection of a gracious soul, in a good thing, managed with discretion." His reference to the "fund" is revealing as it affords us a rare glimpse at seventeenth-century Baptist institutional response to the Dominical imperative of charity (Matthew 25:31–46). Just as noteworthy is his concluding instruction to the church to "look out a minister of Jesus Christ." For Knollys the ideal candidate would be "qualified with such ministerial gifts and graces as may make him worthy" of the honor of serving as pastor. These are points that call for further reflection.

MR. KNOLLYS' LAST LEGACY TO THE CHURCH, WRITTEN A LITTLE BEFORE HIS DEATH[1]

(London, 1692)

To the Church whereof I am pastor, grace, love, and peace, by Jesus Christ our Lord and Savior, Amen. Holy brethren, partakers of the heavenly calling, I—not being able to preach any more unto you—do take liberty by writing to give you this as my last counsel, and I hope the whole church will seriously consider what I have written, as the last words of your very aged pastor, whose departure, as I hope, is at hand.

First of all, I do humbly beseech my reverend and beloved brother Steed,[2] for Christ's sake, that the fervent love to the church and the watchful

---

[1] Knollys' last letter to his London congregation; it appeared in print in 1692 as an appendix to Hanserd Knollys, *The life and death* (London, 1692) 44–52. Also known as, *Mr. Knollys' Last Legacy to the Church*, it was preceded by a postscript in which the anonymous author had this to say: "A little before his death, he wrote the following epistle, which he left as his last legacy to the church." Knollys, *The life and death*, 43. Knollys' *Last Legacy* was also included in the nineteenth-century edition of *The Life and Death* (London, 1812). Like *The Life and Death* it reflects the heavy hand of the nineteenth-century editor who incorporated biblical quotations—not just the citations—to the main body of the work. We are here restoring the 1692 text, while providing biblical quotations only when necessary. See Knollys, *The Life and Death* (London, 1812).

[2] Knollys was referring to Robert Steed, of Dartmouth. Steed was a Baptist since at least 1658, when he published an apology for the Baptists. See Robert Steed, *A plain discovery of the unrighteous judge and false accuser. Wherein is soberly, and in the fear of the Lord brought to light, and tendered to the examination of the upright in heart, the spirit of that pamphlet, intituled, The leper cleansed: published by Richard Ballamy of Tiverton* ([London]: Printed for Henry Mortlock, 1658). He was among the signatories who in 1689 endorsed the *Confession of Faith* first published in 1688. See *A confession of faith put forth by the elders and brethren of many congregations of Christians, (baptized upon profession of their faith) in London and the country: with an appendix concerning Baptism* (London: Printed for John Harris, 1688); Edward Bean Underhill, ed., *Confessions of Faith, and other Public Documents, Illustrative of the History of the Baptist Churches of England in the 17th Century* (London: Haddon Brothers and Co., 1854) 171. He became Knollys' assistant and succeeded him as pastor of the congregation, which was in 1691 meeting in Bagnio Court, Newgate Street in London. According to Walter Wilson, Steed's tenure ended in 1705, by which time the congregation was meeting in Currier's Hall, where it remained until 1799. See Walter Wilson, *The History and Antiquities of Dissenting Churches and Meeting Houses, in*

care over the particular members of it, expressed and published in his little epistle touching singing,[3] may be revived; and also that the brotherly love of the ministering brethren, and likewise of all my beloved brethren, who are helps in government, may be stirred up to help, to assist, to provoke the rest unto good works (Galatians 4:18).[4]

Now I do unfeignedly and without vain boasting commend many of you, my beloved brethren and sisters, for continuing in the apostles' doctrine and fellowship in breaking of bread and in prayer—but as for the rest, who forsake the assembling of themselves with the church on the Lord's day, I commend them not—especially not only in this time of liberty, but when it was a time of violent persecution, when I was shut up a year and four months—blessed be God for prison mercies—in New Prison. And having mentioned that time of persecution, can I pass it by without commending the constant assembling of our brethren and sisters all that time, every Lord's day to worship God? And may I not with great comfort commend the labor of love of our ministering brethren in the work and doctrine of the gospel without ceasing—as you well know—and among whom they still labor and faint not? And now some of our younger brethren begin to improve their gifts and talents for the glory of God and the edification of the church, whom I desire may be encouraged.

Another thing very commendable in this church is the charity, which they have added to their brotherly kindness (2 Peter 1:7). It was great brotherly kindness, which was manifested to the church, by those brethren who looked out our meetinghouse and prepared it for us as it now is. Unto

---

London, Westminster, and Southwark; Including the Lives of their Ministers, 4 vols. (London: no printer, 1808) 2:560–62; for more, see Robert Steed, "Letter from Robert Steed to Mr. Philip Cary, Exeter Jail," *The Congregational Magazine* 11, no. 37 (1828): 23–25.

[3] Robert Steed, *An epistle written to the members of a church in London, concerning singing, by one of their elders* (London: no printer, 1691) copy available at the Bodleian Library, University of Oxford, call number Pamph. 202 (21). Steed's *Epistle* was followed up by two other pamphlets that were written in response to it, see Thomas Whinnel, *A sober reply to Mr. Robert Steed's Epistle concerning singing* (London: no printer, 1691); also see, William Kiffin, *A serious answer to a late book stiled, A reply to Mr. Robert Steed's epistle concerning singing wherein the chief scriptures and arguments are examined, and the weakness thereof shewed: together with an answer to the several reflections, and false charges, against both churches and persons, recommended to the elders, ministers, and members of baptized churches* (London: no printer, 1692).

[4] Knollys employs the passage of Galatians 4:18, as rendered in the King James Version, as the keystone of his *Last Legacy*: "But it is good to be zealously affected always in a good thing, and not only when I am present with you."

this many of our brethren and sisters have added their charity in a free and very liberal collection and contribution, given into the trustees of the fund and I hope they will be ready to do the like again, when the like necessities call for it. Read, I pray you, the eighth and ninth chapters of the Second Epistle unto the Church of Corinth. All this and much more are the riches of grace, which God has freely given by our Lord Jesus Christ unto this church for his own glory.

Nevertheless, I must in love and faithfulness to your precious and gracious souls, holy and beloved, tell you of some things, not to shame you, for I myself am found guilty as well as you, and more than some of you, but to warn you, and to counsel you, as a father does [to] his children, and they are these. First, that several of us are fallen in some degree from our first love, cooled in our spiritual affections to Jesus Christ, and to the saints. Must not you and I confess that it is not with us now as it was in the day of our first espousals? God the Father, the Word, and the Holy Spirit remember it (Jeremiah 2:1–2). And we should remember from whence we are fallen, and should say, "I will go and return unto my first husband, for then was it better with me, than now" (Hosea 2:7; Revelation 2:4–5).

Now the first part of my counsel, which I desire to take and receive from Christ and to give unto you, my dearly beloved brethren and sisters, who are convinced and have confessed it before the Lord on several days of fasting and prayer. First, I do counsel you to repent (Revelation 2:5) and I must tell you, beloved, that our assembling once in four weeks, and spending four hours, from eleven to three, in praying and preaching, as we have often done, is not such a fast as will make our voice be heard on high (Isaiah 58:3–4). Several things are essentially necessary to evangelical repentance, that it may be acceptable unto God by Jesus Christ, namely, godly sorrow, which worked repentance, never to be repented of (2 Corinthians 7:9–10) [and] a broken contrite spirit; read these scriptures: Psalm 51:17; James 4:9–10; Isaiah 66:2–3; Isaiah 57:15; Zechariah 12:10–11. Alas, where are our tears of godly sorrow, our broken hearts, and our afflicted souls? Reformation after humiliation? "Repent and do thy first works" (Revelation 2:5). O holy brethren, let us do so, let you and I beg grace, that we may both mourn and turn from all our sins to the Lord with all our hearts. We have cause to repent of our formality and Laodicean[5] lukewarmness, especially for want of

[5] Pertaining to Laodicea, cf., Revelation 3:15–16.

zeal for the house of God (Psalm 69:9; Revelation 3:19; Colossians 4:12–13; John 2:17).

Secondly, I Counsel you to be zealous. Zeal is a fervent and constant affection of a gracious soul, in a good thing, managed with discretion (Galatians 4:18). If our zeal be not fixed upon a right object and good matter, it may be hot and great, but it cannot be good. Compare the zeal of Paul (Philippians 3:6) with the zeal of Epaphras (Colossians 4:12–13). To guide our zeal aright, two things especially ought to accompany it. First, the light of knowledge (Romans 10:1–3). Read the words again and again, and as often as you read this paper. Many professors of the law then were very zealous of establishing their own legal righteousness, and many professors of the gospel now are as zealous to establish their own legal righteousness, and not Christ's. "Oh!," say some, "if I could pray so, mourn so as others do, if I were so holy and so humble, etc., then I would believe." "Oh!," say others, "if I could get power over my corruptions, and strength against Satan's temptations, and victory over the allurements of this present evil world, then I would believe; but I have a heart full of vile affections, vain thoughts and doubts, that I cannot believe." Consider, are praying, mourning, humbling our souls, gospel duties? Even so is believing a gospel duty, which God commands (1 John 3:23); and he threatens to damn them that hear the gospel preached, and will not believe (Acts 13:41).

Secondly, the aim and end of our zeal must always be the glory of God, and guided, as I said, by discretions, wise as well as warm; greatest zeal, in greatest matters, and lesser zeal in lesser matters. Compare Galatians 5:11–13 with 1 Corinthians 11:13–16, 1 Corinthians 10:3 and Proverbs 19:11.

My counsel also is, and I humbly beseech our honored and beloved elder, and entreat our ministering brethren, who are helps in government, to join together to set in order these things. I mean no other things than those holy administrations which Christ, his apostles, and disciples practiced in the beginning. Search these scriptures, 1 Peter 2:21, Philippians 3:17, Luke 14:16–22, Acts 28:23–24, 28–31, 1 Corinthians 14:13–29, 1 Timothy 4:13, Colossians 4:16, 1 Thessalonians 5:27, and Revelation 1:3. Consider holy brethren that as reading and expounding are two different administrations, so are prophesying and preaching, yet both gospel ordinances (Romans 12:6–7).

Fourthly and lastly, my counsel to the church is that you will look out a minister of Jesus Christ, whom he has in some competent measure qualified with such ministerial gifts and graces as may make him worthy of so great honor as is due to a pastor and elder of the church of God; yea, of double honor (1 Timothy 5:17), both of maintenance and obedience (Hebrews 13:17).

And now my dearly beloved brethren and sisters, I commit you all to the word of his grace, which is able to build you up and to give you an inheritance among them which are sanctified. So I remain, while in this tabernacle,

Your Brother in the Lord
Hanserd Knollys.

PART III: THE HISTORIOGRAPHY OF HANSERD KNOLLYS:

CHANGING INTERPRETATIONS OF A SEVENTEENTH-CENTURY BAPTIST LEADER

THE HISTORIOGRAPHY OF HANSERD KNOLLYS

I. INTRODUCTION

The history of the interpretation of Hanserd Knollys suggests several reasons for the durability of his influence among Baptists. First, interpreters from the eighteenth century to the present have noted Knollys' sufferings for conscience' sake and found in him a champion for religious freedom.[1] Second, following his commitment to the Baptists in 1645, he articulated and defended Baptist principles until his death in 1691. He argued for believers' baptism and the congregational form of government as well as for religious toleration. Third, Knollys provided personal continuity of leadership for Particular Baptists during the first generation of their history. The combination of these factors established Knollys' reputation among Baptists of following generations.

In the nineteenth century New Hampshire historians also acknowledged Knollys' role in the history of their state, and nineteenth century Baptist scholars reiterated his role in the emergence of religious toleration. Analysis of studies published since the mid-twentieth century demonstrates a wide diversity in perspectives. While older themes have remained prominent in articulating Knollys' legacy, more recent studies have emphasized the nature of his Calvinism, his understanding of his Baptist identity, his millennial interpretations, and even his genealogy. This growing

---

[1] For discussion of the contrasrt between the terms "religious toleration" and "religious libert/religious freedom," see Part I: Hanserd Knollys' Life and Works, fn. 103.

variety of interpretations of Hanserd Knollys is due in some part to a recovery of new information about Knollys, but even more noticeably it reflects the plurality of interests of his interpreters.

II. THE AUTOBIOGRAPHY OF HANSERD KNOLLYS

Recovering the story of Hanserd Knollys begins with his own autobiography. Following the death of his wife and one of his children and his own serious illness in 1672, Knollys wrote an account describing key events of his life. His friend, William Kiffin, added notes on Knollys' final twenty years and in 1692 published the two parts together in *The life and death of that old disciple of Jesus Christ…Mr. Hanserd Knollys.*[2] This brief narrative is a sketch, but it nevertheless has provided the essential materials and even familiar phrases that have appeared in descriptions of Knollys' life ever since 1692. It is a unique source for reconstructing Knollys' biography since it is from his own hand, and it is the single most important source we possess for reconstructing Knollys' life and work. Some modern historians have described the autobiography as uncritical piety rather than analytical biography.[3] Knollys does focus heavily on his religious experiences and on providential assistance; also he omits references to some of his failures. Nevertheless, this book provides much important information about Knollys' life that is unavailable anywhere else. In this autobiography Knollys includes episodes from his early life, his education at Cambridge, and his lifelong work as a school teacher and minister. He mentions his sojourn to America and to the Continent, both prompted by persecution. He briefly discusses his dissenting religious quest and his conversion to new religious views. Finally, he highlights the persecutions he suffered under both Archbishop Laud and King Charles II. For the period of the 1670s and 1680s our knowledge of Knollys is noticeably diminished because Kiffin simply did not produce either the quantity or the quality of information about Knollys that appears in the autobiographical section. Knollys wrote to edify, but also to

---

[2] Hanserd Knollys, *The life and death* (London, 1692); Knollys, *The Life and Death* (London, 1812). Kiffin laments the lack of sources available for his part of the biography.

[3] John Craig is critical of *The life and death,* calling it a "work of spiritual edification [which] cannot be trusted as reliable history." See John Craig, review of *Erroneous and Schismatical Opinions: The Question of Orthodoxy Regarding the Theology of Hanserd Knollys (c. 1599-1691)* by Barry H. Howson, *Dutch Review of Church History/Nederlands Archief voor Kerkgeschiedenis* 83.2 (2003) 594–596, here 594.

justify his actions. The events recorded in the autobiography produce a remarkable portrait of an important early Baptist minister and leader. But the autobiography also provides an interpretation that frames Knollys' life in terms of persecution and suffering for the sake of religious conviction. Despite its limitations the historiography of Hanserd Knollys begins with *The life and death.*

The other contemporary primary source is Thomas Harrison's memorial funeral sermon for Knollys, preached at Pinner's Hall on October 4, 1691. It does not provide information pertaining to Knollys' career but rather provides an assessment of his character and qualities of life. As expected for this solemn occasion, the comment is brief and eulogistic in tone. Harrison judged that Knollys had "universal love to Christians.... [He] was not a man of narrow and private, but of a large and public spirit.... The difference of his fellow Christians' opinions from his did not alienate his affections from them.... [And Knollys demonstrated] courageous and cheerful suffering for his Master."[4]

III. EARLY BAPTIST HISTORIES: 1730–1850

Early Baptist historians gathered the sources available to them and uncritically compiled information about the denomination. The first published Baptist history was Thomas Crosby's *The History of English Baptists* (1738–1740). Crosby approached his task by collecting material about individual pastors and providing summaries of the work of these leaders. Crosby's description of Knollys includes his life, character, persecution, Baptist contribution, and bibliography. Crosby drew heavily on the autobiography to describe Knollys' life and features of his ministry. He noted that Knollys had been properly ordained by the bishop of Peterborough, and had preached to great effect at Great Saint Helen's in London. Moreover, he had gathered a congregation of Christians "baptized upon the profession of their faith" and was ordained as their pastor.[5] Second, Crosby gives much attention to Knollys' integrity and character. Detractors of Baptists said they were sectarian in spirit and Antinomian or Anabaptist

[4] Thomas Harrison, *A sermon on the decease of Mr. Hanserd Knollis, minister of the Gospel Preached at Pinners-Hall, Octob. 4. 1691* (London: Printed for H. Barnard, 1694) 57-58.

[5] Thomas Crosby, *The history of the English Baptists: From the Reformation to the Beginning of the Reign of King George I* (London: no printer, 1738) 1:155.

in belief. They were charged with factionalism and sedition.[6] Crosby's rebuttal emphasized Knollys' habits of regular prayer and reading of good books. He also emphasized Knollys' diligence in the performance of his duties as a minister, especially his frequent preaching, both before and after he became a Baptist.[7] Crosby reports that Knollys resigned his living for conscience' sake once it was clear that he did not believe what the Church of England taught.[8] As further evidence of Knollys' character he cites Harrison's funeral sermon which emphasized Knollys' irenic public spirit, humility, hard work, and courage.[9]

The third and major motif in Crosby's presentation of Knollys is that he was repeatedly imprisoned for his preaching, but was always exonerated by the authorities who found him innocent. In other words, Crosby depicted the Baptists as law-abiding Christians who were often wrongly imprisoned. Despite his innocence in the eyes of the law and his release from prison, Knollys repeatedly experienced difficulty and was forced to move to and from Lincolnshire, London, New England, Holland and Germany.[10] Crosby includes a letter by Knollys protesting the religious authorities who refused to support religious toleration.[11] He also quotes a graphic line directly from the autobiography when he records that Knollys' opponents "stoned him out of his pulpit."[12] Crosby records several aspects of Knollys' life and work, but his dominant interest is to show that Knollys and the Baptists were a people wrongly persecuted.

Fourth, Crosby does not neglect to point out Knollys' constructive leadership for early Baptists, citing his strong opposition to infant baptism and noting that he was responsible for the adult baptism of the nonconformist London pastor Henry Jessey, whom Crosby identifies as one of the most influential converts to the Baptists.[13] Finally, Crosby closes his account with a bibliography listing twelve of Knollys' Baptist writings.[14]

---

[6] Ibid., 1:227–228.
[7] Ibid., 1:335–337.
[8] Ibid., 1:335.
[9] Ibid., 1:340–342.
[10] Ibid., 1:339.
[11] Ibid., 1:230–231.
[12] Ibid., 1:228.
[13] Ibid., 1:336, 311.
[14] Ibid., 1:343.

Seventy years after Crosby, Joseph Ivimey began to publish *A History of English Baptists.*[15] Ivimey follows Crosby in many respects. Writing of the "pious and learned Hanserd Knollys," Ivimey retells the stories of Knollys' preaching, his arrests and his exoneration by the courts. [16] Ivimey summarizes Knollys' experience: "These instances show what difficulties the Baptist minister labored under at this period, and also what are the consequences of government's interfering with the church of Christ, and making laws for its direction."[17]In his interpretation of Knollys Ivimey strongly affirms the Baptist insistence on the separation of church and state.

Ivimey also documents Knollys' leadership among Baptists. He describes the making of the Confession of Faith by the seven London congregations, Knollys' role in the rebaptism of Jessey, and his opposition to "the intolerance of the Presbyterians."[18] He noted that "the sect [of Baptists was] everywhere spoken against;"[19] hence, like Crosby, Ivimey affirms the good character of Kiffin, Knollys, and Jessey among others. He describes the growth of the early Baptist movement, and cites additional sources, especially letters and documents carrying Knollys' signature. It is clear that in Ivimey's mind Knollys was a venerable leader who at advanced age once again acted on conscience and served months in jail rather than conform to religious practice he thought was wrong.[20] In their presentations of Knollys both of these early Baptist historians emphasize the Baptist heritage of acting according to the guidelines of conscience and opposing wrongful coercion by the state.

IV. KNOLLYS AND THE NEW HISTORICAL METHOD, 1850–1950

Modern critical historical scholarship developed in German universities duirng the nineteenth century, and the new method and discipline of history spread rapidly in academic circles. The study of Hanserd Knollys benefitted from this advance in a number of ways. In the mid-nineteenth century

[15] Joseph Ivimey, *A History of English Baptists* (London: Printed for the author, and sold by Burditt, Button, Hamilton, Baynes, 1811–1830).

[16] Ibid., 1:172.

[17] Ibid., 1:174.

[18] Ibid., 1:175, 180, 189.

[19] Ibid., 1:306.

[20] Ibid., 1:411

English Baptists honored Knollys by forming The Hanserd Knollys Society, a publication society created "for the reprinting of early Baptist writings and the publication of original records."[21] Baptists established the Society in London in 1846 and dissolved it, apparently in 1854, after issuing ten volumes of early Baptist writings.[22]

Because he was persecuted for expressing his dissenting ideas, Knollys sought opportunity for a fresh start in the new world. He arrived in Boston in July 1638. However, he was not welcome there, and he migrated with his family to Piscatagua plantation and settled in the town of Dover, New Hampshire. Knollys gave very little notice of his experiences in America, probably because he had little success and was constantly engaged in controversy. However, two centuries after publication of the autobiography, local anniversaries prompted historical publications which included recognition of Knollys' role in the history of Dover and its early church. In 1873 George B. Spalding, pastor of the Congregational Church of Dover, New Hampshire, published *A Discourse delivered in the First Church of Dover, May 18, 1873, on the Two Hundred and Fiftieth Anniversary of the Settlement of Dover, New Hampshire.*[23] In this anniversary history of the city of Dover, Spalding included references to histories of the region by John Winthrop and Daniel Neal, but gave particular attention to Knollys' autobiography, *The life and death*. Ten years later, the church published *The First Parish in Dover, New Hampshire: Two Hundred and Fiftieth Anniversary, Oct. 28, 1883*, celebrating the establishment of the church. This account notes that Hanserd Knollys "came here in 1638."[24] Both of these anniversary accounts focus especially on conditions in New Hampshire, on Knollys' role in founding the church, and on his unsuccessful struggle with his successor, Thomas Larkham. As founder of the Dover Congregational Church Knollys therefore has a permanent, if not necessarily distinguished, place in American religious history as both a church founder and a persecuted

---

[21] Sidney Lee, "Hanserd Knollys," in *Dictionary of National Biography* (New York: Macmillan and Co., 1892) 281.

[22] According to the listing in the Bodleian Library Catalogue, the Hanserd Knollys Society published ten volumes during the period 1846-1854. E.B. Underhill edited six of the volumes.

[23] George B. Spalding, *A Discourse delivered in the First Church of Dover, May 18, 1873, on the Two Hundred and Fiftieth Anniversary of the Settlement of Dover, New Hampshire* (Dover: Freewill Baptist Printing Establishment, 1873).

[24] *The First Parish in Dover, New Hampshire: Two Hundred and Fiftieth Anniversary, Oct. 28, 1883* (Dover: Printed for the Parish, 1884) 20.

dissenter. His role in the city's history is repeated in countless histories of New Hampshire. The American sojourn was a difficult time for Knollys. He did not believe that his efforts were successful, nor did he record any major change in his religious development. Nevertheless, the American experience remained a part of his outlook as one who had suffered for his convictions while he sought to establish a true church. Awareness of his American experiences—both positive and negative—helps create a fuller understanding of the man. Susan Hardman Moore places him in a larger context of ministers with similar experiences, noting that he was "one of twenty-five colonists who had held English parish livings before emigration" and returned to England in the 1640s or 1650s.[25]

In the second half of the nineteenth century scholarly encyclopedias and dictionaries proliferated, including British and American dictionaries of national biography. Both carried accounts of Hanserd Knollys. Sidney Lee's entry on Hanserd Knollys in the [American] *Dictionary of National Biography* in 1892 is succinct and balanced. He adds observations from Thomas Edwards' *Gangraena* (1646) that are critical of Knollys' theology and also notes that Knollys held "some offices of profit under Cromwell's government," evidence located in the Calendar of State Papers, Domestic, for 1653 and 1655.[26] These are references to Knollys' employment by the English government, first as examiner of the Customs and Excise and later as Clerk of the Check during Cromwell's rule. Alexander Gordon's "Hanserd Knollys" in the [British] *Dictionary of National Biography, 1885–1900,* provided a detailed survey of Knollys' life, an extensive list of his writings, and a useful list of sources.[27] Both of these late nineteenth-century entries identify additional sources and provide new information about Knollys' life. In the traditional model of dictionaries they provide very little interpretation.

The nineteenth century study of Knollys concluded in 1895 when James Culross, a biographer of William Carey and other Baptist leaders, produced a carefully researched major study entitled *Hanserd Knollys.*[28] Culross sought to highlight the struggle of dissenters in seventeenth-century

---

[25] See Susan Hardman Moore, *Pilgrims: New World Settlers and the Call of Home* (New Haven: Yale University Press, 2007) 202.

[26] Lee, "Hanserd Knollys," 281.

[27] Alexander Gordon, "Hanserd Knollys," *Dictionary of National Biography* (London: 1885–1900) 31:13.

[28] James Culross, *Hanserd Knollys* (London: Alexander and Shepherd, 1895).

England and above all to recount the sufferings of Knollys for conscience' sake. Culross called religious persecution "the error of the age."[29] Thus, in addition to recounting Knollys' personal narrative, throughout his study Culross adds significant material on the relationship of law to the practice of religion in English society during the seventeenth century. Culross discusses Puritans and Brownists (Independents) whose ideas attracted Knollys, the legislation of Elizabeth I and the Stuart rulers who denied religious toleration to dissenters, and the strenuous efforts of Archbishop Laud to make all of England conform to the Church of England. Persecution, in turn, was the reason for Knollys leaving England—first for the American colonies (1638) and later for Holland and Germany (1661). Culross gives much attention to the restrictive legislation passed by the Westminster Assembly of Divines and legal changes under the Commonwealth and Protectorate that temporarily favored religious toleration. During the reign of Charles II Baptists and others once again suffered under the restrictions of the Clarendon Code. Knollys was incarcerated in 1670, but soon released. At length, after James II fled from England, Parliament passed the Act of Toleration (1689), placing dissenters on new legal footing. Culross thus provided much of the essential seventeenth-century church-state context for understanding the significance of Knollys' life. He concluded that Knollys "was one of the men who helped pay the price of that civil and religious liberty that we enjoy today."[30] For Culross, Knollys is an illustrious example of a Baptist who suffered for his beliefs.

Historical scholarship in the nineteenth century thus honored Knollys by creating a Baptist publishing society bearing his name. In addition scholars also enhanced knowledge of Knollys by recovering his role in establishing the Congregational Church in Dover, New Hampshire, by recovering factual details of his life, and by assessing his experience of persecution by the state.

IV. KNOLLYS' MODERN INTERPRETERS, 1950–PRESENT

Interest in Knollys resumed in the second half of the twentieth century. In 1965 Southern Baptist historian Pope Duncan, published *Hanserd Knollys: a Seventeenth Century Baptist,* which is a concise fifty-five page

[29] Ibid., 61.
[30] Ibid., 109.

study.[31] Duncan gave particular attention to three issues: (1) Knollys' biography; (2) Knollys' Baptist Christian thought (including his views on redemption, the church, baptism, ministry, relations with other churches, and religious liberty); and (3) also Knollys' relationship with well-known mid-century English radical religious groups, including Seekers, Ranters, Familists, Diggers, Quakers, Levellers, and Fifth Monarchy Men.[32] All of these groups flourished during the more tolerant days of Cromwell, but all of them also came under attack by the established church. Knollys was familiar with concepts developed in these alternative Christian groups and showed sympathy for some of their ideas, notably those of the Fifth Monarchy Men, who taught the imminent end of the current age. Since they supported the rule of Christ in place of the English monarch and Knollys was sympathetic to some of their teaching, officials accused him of participating in an uprising led by Thomas Venner (January 6–9, 1661), whose aim was to overthrow the government of Charles II. As a result of this crisis Knollys left for Holland and Germany in 1661. Duncan pointed out that systematic examination of Knollys' theology had been neglected. He therefore devoted most of his study to analysis of Knollys' Baptist thought and it relations to contemporary Baptist interests in 1965. He wrote that Knollys repeated over and over the phrase "gathered church," and Duncan declared that "this is the heart of the Baptist view of the church."[33] He concluded, "Whenever and wherever men with integrity speak the words 'freedom,' 'competency,' or 'democracy' in the Christian context, they are speaking words which are the very genius of Baptists—whether seventeenth century or now."[34] Finally, Duncan also provides an admirable bibliography, including Knollys' writings, additional seventeenth-century English primary sources related to Knollys, and the key secondary sources published before 1965.

Barrington White, principal of Regents' College, Oxford (1972–1989), produced landmark studies of Separatist and early Baptist history. His *Hanserd Knollys and Radical Dissent in the 17th Century* appeared in 1977 as a publication in the Dr. Williams's Library lecture series.[35] White designed his

[31] Pope Duncan, *Hanserd Knollys: A Seventeenth Century Baptist* (Nashville: Broadman Press, 1965).

[32] See the essays in *Radical Religion in the English Revolution*, edited by J. F. McGregor and Barry Reay (Oxford: Oxford University Press, 1984).

[33] Duncan, *Hanserd Knollys,* 21.

[34] Ibid., 51.

[35] Barrington R. White, *Hanserd Knollys and Radical Dissent in the Seventeenth Century* (London: Dr. Williams's Trust, 1977).

succinct account of Knollys as a contribution to the broader history of seventeenth century dissent—the major focus of the Williams's Lectures. White provided a balanced summary of Knollys' life and thought. He included accounts of Knollys' engagements with other religious groups, and Knollys' theology, as well as analysis of early Baptist practices, including their relationships with the state. Significantly, in part to fulfill the purpose of the Williams's Lecture series, White concluded his essay with a list of several reasons that Knollys is important to the broader history of English religious dissent.[36]

The historiography of Knollys has intensified in recent years. In 1995 M. A. G. Haykin published *Kiffin, Knollys, and Keach: Rediscovering an English Baptist Heritage*, a study of the early Baptist leaders of the mid to late seventeenth century.[37] Haykin was chiefly interested in recovering the Calvinist heritage among early Baptists: he wrote that "The Calvinist Baptist heritage from the seventeenth century is a sorely neglected treasure."[38] His approach was to demonstrate Calvinist themes in the thought of Hanserd Knollys, Benjamin Keach, and William Kiffin—and to emphasize the Calvinist character of *The First London Confession of Faith* (1644, 1646) and *The Second London Confession of Faith* (1677, 1688). Haykin was also interested in discrediting the modern charismatic movement and argued that early Baptists rejected that expression of Christianity. He wrote: "Another area in which these Baptists can help their present-day descendants is with regard to the challenges posed by contemporary charismatic movements. [Early] Baptists had to contend with such groups. In their case, [the charismatic movement] was known to history as the Seekers and Quakers."[39] Haykin's study appears to be designed to find in Knollys precedent and support for present-day Baptists to embrace Calvinism and to reject modern charismatic movements.

Muriel James published *Religious Liberty on Trial* in 1997.[40] As her title indicates, she is keenly interested in religious persecution and the beginnings

---

[36] Ibid., 24.

[37] M. A. G. Haykin, *Kiffin, Knollys and Keach: Rediscovering our English Baptist Heritage* (Leeds, England: Reformation Today Trust, 1996).

[38] Ibid., 11. His chapter on Knollys is only eight pages long, thus sharply limiting his treatment of Knollys' thought.

[39] Ibid., 11.

[40] Muriel James, *Religious Liberty on Trial* (Franklin, Tennessee: Providence House Publishers, 1997). James' major field of inquiry and publication is psychology, with special emphasis on Transactional Analysis.

of religious toleration in seventeenth century England. Because of Knollys' suffering, she calls him a "hero."[41] Her study extends the long historiography which interprets Knollys primarily as an early persecuted Baptist. James' study was also prompted in part by her interest in tracing Knollys' geneology. Her research therefore provides information on Knollys' early life and especially on his family connections. She found evidence that Knollys' wife received a financial inheritance.[42] Her close study of the family history through wills and other sources also offers new evidence that suggests a revision of the date of Knollys' birth from 1598 to 1609.[43] Her later date is more plausible especially since it places the date of Knollys' matriculation into Cambridge University nearer his twentieth than his thirtieth birthday. Dennis Bustin credits James with being the first person to examine Knollys' early life with care.[44]

One of the most neglected aspects of Knollys' work has been his prolonged interest in and extensive publications on apocalyptic and millennial themes. Two publications appeared in 2000 that address this dimension of Knollys' theology. Kenneth Newport has a special interest in Biblical exegesis of apocalyptic texts and he included a study of Knollys in *Apocalypse and Millennium: Studies in Biblical Exegesis.*[45] In *Apocalypse How?* Mark Bell addressed the views of many mid-seventeenth-century Baptists regarding the return of Christ.[46] Knollys published more on this genre of theological literature than any other of his many interests. Millenarian views focus on the reign but more particularly on the time of the return of Christ. Some millenarians look to the distant future, but many, including Knollys, also apply their interpretation to their own days. They typically look for and find "signs" of Christ's near return in the persecutions they suffer at the

---

[41] Ibid., 44.

[42] Ibid., 59–60.

[43] See Dennis C. Bustin, "Appendix I: Hanserd Knollys' Date of Birth," in *Paradox and Perseverance: Hanserd Knollys, Particular Baptist in Seventeenth-Century England,* Studies in Baptist History and Thought, vol. 23 (Milton Keynes, England: Paternoster, 2006) 324–328. Bustin accepts the revised dating of Knollys' birth as does Leo Garrett, *Baptist Theology: A Four Century Study* (Macon: Mercer University Press, 2009) 62n60.

[44] Bustin, *Paradox and Perseverance,* 25.

[45] Kenneth G. C. Newport, *Apocalypse and Millennium: Studies in Biblical* Eisegesis (Cambridge: Cambridge University Press, 2000). See chapter 2, "Hanserd Knollys, Benjamin Keach and the Book of Revelation: a Study in Baptist Exegesis," 24–47.

[46] Mark R. Bell, *Apocalypse How?: Baptist Movements During the English Revolution* (Macon: Mercer University Press, 2000.

hands of their enemies, and often they attempt to predict the timing of the return of Christ. Bell notes that Knollys was sympathetic with the Fifth Monarchy Men, but that he did not share their willingness to use force. Bell's study is not a monograph devoted to Knollys; rather, he sets Knollys' apocalyptic thought in its early Baptist context. Bell concludes, "Knollys was…the most thorough and systematic millenarian thinker among the Particular Baptists. He is the only Baptist of his time to undertake an exposition of the entire book of Revelation."[47] The apocalyptic strain was pronounced in Knollys' thought and is now receiving scholarly attention.

Barry Howson's 2001 study examined the orthodoxy of Knollys' theology rather than developments in his life. He wrote, "This study is predicated on a proper understanding of the term 'orthodoxy' during the period of 1640–1660."[48] Like Haykin, Howson is interested in defending Knollys' Particular (Calvinist) Baptist identity. Howson defends Knollys against four opponents who charged him with positions deemed heretical: Antinomianism, Hyper-Calvinism, Anabaptism and Fifth Monarchism. Howson's method is to describe in separate chapters each of these positions in their seventeenth-century context and to examine the evidence to determine whether Knollys held some of their views.

Opponents in England and America charged Knollys with Antinomianism, the idea that since grace is all sufficient for salvation and works count for nothing, the moral expectations of the Christian life may be in danger of being ignored. The Antinomians responded that they wanted to give Christ all of the credit for salvation.[49] After examining Knollys' view of the role of grace in salvation, Howson concludes, "Knollys cannot properly be categorized as an Antinomian because he rejected most of their teachings."[50] Second, Howson answers another set of opponents who charged Knollys with hyper-Calvinism. Nineteenth century Baptist historian Joseph Ivimey had noted that hyper-Calvinist John Skepp, in the Preface to his book *Divine Energy* (1722), wrote that he was building on the foundation laid by Knollys. Ivimey, however, rejected this notion, as does Howson.[51] Howson notes that whereas ultra-Calvinists were reluctant or refused to offer general invitations of salvation to the unconverted, Knollys

---

[47] Ibid., 84.

[48] Howson, *Erroneous and Schismatic Opinions*, 24.

[49] Ibid., 104–105.

[50] Ibid., 132.

[51] Ibid., 7.

preached for conversions in his pastorate and during his itinerancy.[52] Howson accepts the designation High-Calvinist to describe Knollys, but he rejects the hyper-Calvinist label.

Critics of early Baptists often charged them with holding the most controversial views of Anabaptists, many of whom denied original sin and rejected the authority of magistrates. Howson notes that Baptists repeatedly distanced themselves from these positions, while accepting Anabaptist views of believer's baptism and the separation of church and state. According to the prefatory remarks for the 1644/1646 *Confession of seven London Baptist churches,* the latter signed by Knollys, the confession was written to show that Baptists were not Anabaptists.[53] Howson makes the case that Knollys was not an Anabaptist.

Fourth and finally, Howson takes up the Fifth Monarchy charge. Not only did Knollys write extensively about millennial themes, he showed sympathy with this movement and for this reason he encountered serious trouble with the authorities. This was, in fact, the probable reason for his leaving England a second time, this time for Holland and Germany. Duncan and others had addressed this issue, and Howson gives it extended treatment. Howson denies that Knollys was a Fifth Monarchist.[54] He does concede, however, that some elements of Fifth Monarchist ideas appear in Knollys' numerous millennial writings.[55]

Howson's coverage of these four alternatives to Baptist thought is a forceful reminder of the fluid nature of the theological identity of dissenters in the 1640s and 1650s. Knollys and other dissenters considered many views, borrowing, rejecting and modifying them as they shaped their own

---

[52] Much of Howson's extended discussion revolves around definitions and characteristics of High Calvinism and hyper-Calvinism (Howson, *Erroneous and Schismatical Opinions*, 138–193). The context for this discussion is the source or sources for the theology of John Gill and John Brinne, Baptist hyper-Calvinists of the eighteenth century (Howson, *Erroneous and Schismatical Opinions*, 132–133).

[53] The title of the document is "The Confession of Faith, of those Churches, which are commonly (though falsely) called Anabaptists." The Preface addresses some Anabaptist views that the Baptists rejected. See "London Confession, 1644" in William C. Lumpkin, ed., *Baptist Confessions of Faith* (Valley Forge: Judson Press, 1959) 153 and 155.

[54] Leo Garrett agrees that Howson has successfully defended Knollys from "erroneous and schismatical" opinions, but nonetheless judges that Knollys "was prone to eschatological vagaries." Garrett, *Baptist Theology*, 714.

[55] Howson, *Erroneous and Schismatical Opinions*, 307. It should be noted that most of Knollys' millennial writings were published well after the Venner Uprising of 1661.

theological positions. Howson concluded that Knollys' "theology changed very little."[56] Dennis Bustin, however, judges that while Howson has provided the fullest treatment of Knollys' theology, he failed to allow for changes in Knollys' thought and in the development of his theological ideas.[57]

Kenneth Newport has published the most recent concise scholarly summary of Knollys in his entry for the *Oxford Dictionary of National Biography*, with its characteristic format of succinct biography and thorough bibliography (published 2004; online 2010).[58] The author employs a critical assessment of sources to reconstruct the biography and bring together in one place much of the essential literature relating to Knollys.

Finally, in his exhaustive 2006 publication, *Paradox and Perseverance: Hanserd Knollys, Particular Baptist in Seventeenth-Century England,* Dennis C. Bustin has produced the most penetrating and useful account of Knollys. Bustin has done much to create better understanding of Hanserd Knollys. His research is thorough. He has consulted the primary sources and also has taken into account the scholarship that preceded his book. He begins his study with an historiographical overview of studies of radical religion and dissent, a review of Baptist histories and a summary of studies of Knollys. With careful attention to context Bustin provides relevant political, economic and social history of seventeenth-century England as well as major developments and debates in religion. For Knollys' biography Bustin follows *The life and death* narrative, but he also offers extensive additional information for each major phase of Knollys' life: his religious and educational background, his conversion to Baptist thought in the 1640s, his position *vis a vis* other radicals in the 1650s, and his struggles during the Restoration. Bustin gives special attention to understudied aspects of Knollys' thought—with full chapters devoted to both his apocalyptic views and his formidable legacy of articulating and defending key Baptist positions. To date, Bustin's study is the most comprehensive and most helpful interpretation of Knollys' life and legacy.

---

[56] Ibid., 308.

[57] Bustin, *Paradox and Perseverance,* 26.

[58] Kenneth G. C. Newport, "Knollys, Hanserd (1598–1691) " in *Oxford Dictionary of National Biography*, edited by H. C. G. Matthew and Brian Harrison (Oxford: Oxford University Press, 2004). Online ed., edited by Lawrence Goldman, January 2010. http://www.oxforddnb.com/view/article/15756 (accessed December 5, 2014).

The modern interpretation of Knollys emphasizes a variety of perspectives. It places him in the context of seventeenth-century history and English dissenting groups. It explores his methods of Biblical interpretation. It offers extended interpretation of his theological position. And finally, modern interpreters remind readers again of Knollys' suffering for his beliefs. In short, studies of the past two decades offer a fuller and much richer picture of Knollys.

CONCLUSION

The historiography of Knollys began with his own reflections on his life in *The life and death.* Early readers noted especially the emphasis that Knollys had placed on the sufferings he experienced for following Baptist teaching and practice. The earliest Baptist denominational historians, Crosby and Ivimey gave special attention to the ways that Knollys led the Baptists for a half century despite widespread opposition to the denomination. Mid-nineteenth century British Baptists honored the scholar-pastor by selecting his name for their newly formed Baptist publication series. On the occasion of the two hundred fiftieth anniversary of the city of Dover and its first Congregational church, local historians recognized Knollys' role in the early stages of the development of their city and church. Historical scholarship advanced rapidly in the late nineteenth century. The dictionaries of national biographies in England and in the United States both provided superb brief summaries of Knollys' life and work, and James Culross added a useful biography. In the past half century historians have studied many dimensions of Knollys' legacy, including his relationship to contemporary religious groups, his geneology, his understanding of key Baptist teachings, and his exegesis of scripture, especially its apocalyptic texts. Knollys' life and writings combined to influence his generation and to produce an important legacy. He continues to deserve careful study.

BIBLIOGRAPHY

A declaration of several of the churches of Christ, and godly people in and about the citie of London; concerning the kingly interest of Christ, and the present suffrings of his cause and saints in England. London: no printer, 1654.

A door of hope: or, A call and declaration for the gathering together of the first ripe fruits unto the standard of our Lord, King Jesus. [London]: no printer, [1661].

A proclamation concerning His Majesties coronation pardon. London: Printed by John Bill, Printer to the King's most Excellent Majesty, 1661.

Achinstein, Sharon. "Calamy, Edmund (1600–1666)." In *Oxford Dictionary of National Biography*. Edited by H. C. G. Matthew and Brian Harrison. Oxford: Oxford University Press, 2004. Online edition. Edited by Lawrence Goldman. Oxford: October 2007. http://www.oxforddnb.com/view/article/4355. Accessed November 21, 2014.

Alban, Kevin J. *The Teaching and Impact of the Doctrinale of Thomas Netter of Walden (c. 1374–1430).* Turnhout: Brepols, 2010.

Antoninus, de Florentia. *Summae sacra theologie, iuris pontificii, et caesarei, pars tertia.* Venice: Bernardum Iuntam et Socios, 1571.

Armstrong, Maurice W. "Religious Enthusiasm and Separatism in Colonial New England." *The Harvard Theological Review* 38, no. 2 (1945): 111–140.

Aquinas, Thomas. *Opera omnia, iussu impensaque Leonis XIII P. M.* Rome: Ex Typographia Polyglotta S. C. de Propaganda Fide, 1903.

———. *Commentaria in omnes epistolas divi Pauli Apostoli.* Paris: Dionysium Moreau, 1636.

———. *Commentary on Saint Paul's Epistle to the Ephesians.* Translated by Matthew L. Lamb. Albany: Magi Books, 1966.

Aventinus, Johannes. *Annalium Boiorum libri septem: accessit rerum et verborum memorabilium index copiosus.* Ingolstadt: Alexandrum et Samuelem Weissenhornios, 1554.

Ayer, Joseph Cullen. *A Source Book for Ancient Church History, from the Apostolic Age to the Close of the Conciliar Period.* New York: Charles Scribner's Sons, 1922.

Backus, Isaac. *A Discourse Showing the Nature and Necessity of an Internal Call to Preach the Everlasting Gospel.* Boston: Fowle: 1754.

———. *Isaac Backus on Church, State, and Calvinism: Pamphlets, 1754–1789.* Cambridge: The Belknap Press of Harvard University Press, 1968.

Bagshaw, Edward. *The life and death of Mr. Vavasor Powell, that faithful minister and confessor of Jesus Christ wherein his eminient conversion, laborious successful ministry, excellent conversation, confession of faith, worthy sayings, choice experiences, various sufferings, and other remarkable passages in his life and at his death are faithfully recorded for publick benefit: with some elogies and epitaphs by his friends.* [London], 1671.

Basil, Saint. *Libri quibus impii Eunomii apologeticus evertitur.* PG 29. Paris: J. P. Migne, 1857.

Bastwick, John. *Independency not God's ordinance: or A treatise concerning church-government, occasioned by the distractions of these times. Wherein is evidently proved, that the Presbyterian government dependent is God's ordinance, and not the Presbyterian government independent. To vvhich is annexed a postscript, discovering the uncharitable dealing of the independents towards their Christian brethren, and the fraud and jugglings of many of their pastors and ministers, to the misleading of the poor people, not only to their own detriment, but the hurt of church and state; with the danger of all novelties in religion.* London: John Macock, 1645.

Baxter, Richard. "A Confutation of the Strange Forgeries of Mr. H. Danvers, Against the Antiquity of Infant Baptism." In *More proofs of infants church-membership and consequently their right to baptism, or, A second defense of our infant rights and mercies in three parts.* London: Printed for N. Simmons and J. Robinson, 1675.

Bede. *Operum Venerabilis Bedae presbyteri tomus secundu, in quo subsequentes continentur eiusdem commentarii in Euangelium Marci Lib. IIII; in Euangelium Lucae Lib VI; in Acta Apostolorum Lib. I; Expositio nominum locorum in Actis contentorum, siue eiusdem, siue alterius au[to]ris; In Epistolas Catholicas; In Apocalypsim B. Ioannis Apostoli.* Paris: Josse Bade, 1521.

Bell, Mark R. *Apocalypse How? Baptist Movements During the English Revolution.* Macon: Mercer University Press, 2000.

Bell, Charles H. *John Wheelwright: His Writings, Including his Fast-day Sermon, 1637 and his Mercurius Americanus, 1645; With a Paper upon the Genuineness of the Indian Deed of 1629.* Boston: Prince Society, 1876.

———. *History of Exeter, New Hampshire.* Boston: Press of J. E. Farwell & Co., 1888.

Bellarmine, Robert. *De justificatione impii libre quinque.* Heidelberg: Johannis Lancelloti, 1615.

———. *De Papa Romano libri decem, scholasticè et theologicè collati cum disputationibus Roberti Bellarmini.* [Franeker], 1594.

———. *De translatione imperii romani a graecis ad francos, adversus Matthiam Flaccium Illyricum, libri tres.* Antwerp: Christophori Plantini, 1589.

———. *Liber primus: De beatitudine et canonizatione sanctorum. Quarta controversia generalis de ecclesia triumphante, tribus libris explicate.* In *De controversiis Christianae fidei adversus hujus temporis haereticos.* 4 vols. Venice: Joannem Malachinum, 1721.

———. *Liber secundus: De reliquis et imaginibus sanctorum. Quarta controversia generalis de ecclesia triumphante, tribus libris explicate.* In *De controversiis Christianae fidei adversus hujus temporis haereticos.* 4 vols. Venice: Joannem Malachinum, 1721.

———. *Opera omnia, Editio prima neapolitana iuxta Venetam anni 1721.* 6 vols. Naples: Josephum Giuliano, 1856–1862.

———. *Tertia controversia generalis, de ecclesia quae est in purgatorio. Duobus libris explicate.* In *Disputationes Roberti Bellarmini Politiani, S. R. E. cardinalis, de Controversiis Christianae fidei, adversus huius temporis Haereticos; quatuor tomis comprehensae.* Vol 3, col. 557–656. Paris: Tri-Adelphorum Bibliopolarum, 1608.

———. *Tertia controversia generalis, De summo pontifice, quinque libris explicate.* In *De controversiis Christianae fidei adversus hujus temporis haereticos.* 4 vols. Venice: Joannem Malachinum, 1721.

———. *Tertia controversia generalis, De sacramento eucharistiae, sex libris explicata, De controversiis Christianae fidei, Opera omnia,* 1857.

———. *Tractatus de potestate summi pontificis in rebus temporalibus, adversus Gulielmum Barclaium.* Cologne: Sumptibus Bernardi Gualtheri, 1610.

Bernard, Richard. *A key of knowledge for the opening of the secret mysteries of St Iohns mysticall Reuelation*. London: Felix Kyngston, 1617.

Bertrand, Dominique. "The Society of Jesus and the Church Fathers in the Sixteenth and Seventeenth Century." In *The Reception of the Church Fathers in the West: From the Carolingians to the Maurists*. 2 vols. Leiden and New York: Brill, 1996.

Beza, Theodore. *Iesu Christi Domini Nostri Novum Testamentum, sive novum foedus, cuius graeco contextui respondent interpretationes duae: vna, vetus: altera, Theodori Bezae*. Geneva: Sumptibus Haered. Eust. Vignon, 1598.

———. *Jesu Christi Domini Nostri Novum Testamentum, sive novum foedus, cujus graeco contextui respondent interpretationes duae: una, vetus; altera, Theodori Bezae*. Cantabrigiae: Rogeri Danielis, 1642.

Bietenholz, Peter G., and Thomas Brian Deutscher. *Contemporaries of Erasmus: A Biographical Register of the Renaissance and Reformation*. Vols. 1–3. Toronto: University of Toronto Press, 2003.

Blake, Thomas. *A moderate answer to these two questions, 1. Whether ther* [sic] *be sufficient ground in Scripture to warrant the conscience of a Christian to present his infants to the sacrament of baptism. 2. Whether it be not sinful for a Christian to receive the sacrament in a mixt assembly. Prepared for the resolution of a friend, and now presented to the public view of all, for the satisfaction of them who desire to walk in the ancient and long approved way of truth and holiness*. London: Abel Roper, 1645.

Bolton, Charles Knowles. *The Founders*. 3 vols. Boston: The Boston Athenaeum, 1919–1926.

Bouwsma, William J. *Venice and the Defense of Republican Liberty: Renaissance Values in the Age of the Counter Reformation*. Berkeley: University of California Press, 1968.

Bremer, Francis J. "Nye, Philip (1595–1672)." In *Puritans and Puritanism in Europe and America: A Comprehensive Encyclopedia*. Edited by Francis J. Bremer and Tom Webster, vol. 1, 184-86. Santa Barbara: ABC-CLIO, 2006.

———. "The Puritan Experiment in New England, 1630-1660." In *The Cambridge Companion to Puritanism*. Edited by John Coffey and Paul C. H. Lim, 127–142. Cambridge: Cambridge University Press, 2008.

Brook, Benjamin. *The Lives of the Puritans: A Biographical Account of those Divines who Distinguished Themselves in the Cause of Religious Liberty, from the Reformation under Queen Elizabeth, to the Act of Uniformity of 1662*. London: Printed for James Black, 1813.

Brown, Louise Fargo. *The Political Activities of the Baptists and Fifth Monarchy Men in England during the Interregnum*. Washington: American Historical Association, 1912.

Browne, Robert. *A booke which sheweth the life and manners of all true Christians and howe vnlike they are vnto Turkes and Papistes, and heathen folke. Also the pointes and partes of all diuinitie, that is of the reuealed will and worde of God are declared by their seuerall definitions and diuisions in order as followeth. Also there goeth a treatise before of reformation without tarying for anie, and of the wickednesse of those preachers, which will not refourme them selues and their charge, because they will tarie till the magistrate commanude and compell them*. Middelburgh: Richarde Painter, 1582.

Bucholz, Robert, and Newton Key. *Early Modern England, 1485–1714: A Narrative History*. 2nd ed. Oxford: Wiley-Blackwell, 2009.

Bühler, Curt F. "Observations on the 1562 Editions of Cardinal Reginald Pole's *De Concilio* and *Reformatio Angliae." Studies in Bibliography* 26 (1973): 232–234.

Burrage, Champlin. *The True Story of Robert Browne (1550?–1633), Father of Congregationalism.* Oxford: The University Press, 1906.

Bush, Sargent. "'Revising what we have done amisse': John Cotton and John Wheelwright, 1640." *The William and Mary Quarterly* 45, no. 4 (1988): 733–750.

Bustin, Dennis C. *Paradox and Perseverance: Hanserd Knollys, Particular Baptist in Seventeenth-Century England.* Studies in Baptist History and Thought. Vol. 23. Milton Keynes, England: Paternoster, 2006.

By the King. A proclamation commanding all persons being popish recusants, or so reputed, to depart from the cities of London and Westminster, and all other places within ten miles of the same. London: Printed by John Bill, Christopher Barker, Thomas Newcomb, and Henry Hills, 1678.

Bzowski, Abraham. *Annalium ecclesiasticorum post C.B. tomus XIII-XX, rerum in orbe christiano ab A.D. 1198 usque ad A.D. 1565 gestarum narrationem complectens.* Cologne: Boetzerus, 1616–1640.

Andrew, Archbishop of Caesarea. *In D. Ioannis Apostoli et Evangelistae Apocalypsin.* Ingolstadt: Sartorius, 1584.

Calamy, Edmund. *A Continuation of the Account of the Ministers, Lecturers, Masters and Fellows of Colleges, and Schoolmasters, who were Ejected and Silenced after the Restoration in 1660, by or before the Act of Uniformity.* London: Printed for R. Ford, 1727.

———. *The door of truth opened: or, A brief and true narrative of the occasion how Mr. Henry Burton came to shut himself out of the church-doors of Aldermanbury: published in answer to a paper, called, Truth shut out of doors: for the vindication of the minister and people of Aldermanbury, who are in this paper most wrongfully and unjustly charged; and also for the undeceiving of the underwriters, and of all those that are misinformed about this businesse. In the name, and with the consent of the whole church of Aldermanburie.* London: Printed for Christopher Meredith at the Crane in Pauls-Church-Yard, 1645.

Canons and Decrees of the Council of Trent. Translated by Theodore Alois Buckley. London: George Routledge and Co., 1851.

Capp, Bernard S. *The Fifth Monarchy Men: A Study in Seventeenth-Century English Millenarianism.* London: Faber and Faber, 1972.

Caron, Redmond. *Remonstrantia Hibernorum contra Lovanienses ultramontanasque censuras, de incommutabili regum imperio, subditorumque fidelitate, et obedientia indispensabili: ex S.S. Scripturis, patribus, theologis, etc. vindicate.* London, 1665.

Catechismus, Ex Decreto Concilii Tridentini: Ad Parochos, Pii Quinti Pont. Max. iussu editus. Rome: Manutius, 1566.

Chemnitz, Martin. *Examen Decretorum Concilii Tridentini. In Quo Ex Sacrae Scripturae norma, collatis etiam orthodoxis uerae & puriorus Antiquitatis testimonijs ostenditur, qualia sint illa Decreta, & quo artificio sint composite.* Frankfurt: Sigismundi Feyerabend, 1566–1573.

Chester, Joseph L. "Rev. John Wheelwright." *The New England Historical & Genealogical Register* 21, no. 4 (October 1867): 363–365.

Chrysostom, Saint John. *In Epistolam Secundam ad Thessalonicenses Commentarius, Homilia IV*. In *S.P.N. Joannis Chrysostomi, Opera Omnia Quae Exstant*. Edited by Jacques Paul Migne, *Patrologia Graeca* 62 (Paris: Migne, 1862).

———. *The Homilies of St. John Chrysostom, Archbishop of Constantinople, on the Epistles of S. Paul the Apostle to the Philippians, Colossians, and Thessalonians*. Edited and translated by Charles Marriott and E. B. Pusey. Oxford: James Parker and Co., 1879.

Clergy of the Church of England Database. http://www.theclergydatabase.org.uk/jsp/persons/CreatePersonFrames.jsp?PersonID=71066. Accessed December 8, 2014.

Clyde, William M'Callum. *The Struggle for the Freedom of the Press from Caxton to Cromwell*. New York: Burt Franklin, 1970.

Coffey, John, and Paul Chang-Ha Lim, eds. *The Cambridge Companion to Puritanism*. Cambridge: Cambridge University Press, 2008.

Collinson, Patrick. *The Elizabethan Puritan Movement*. Oxford: Clarendon Press, 1967.

______. *The Religion of Protestants: The Church in English Society, 1559–1625*. Oxford: Oxford University Press, 1982.

Concilium Tridentinum. In *Conciliorum oecumenicorum decreta*. Edited by Giuseppe Alberigo, et al., 657–799. Bologna: Instituto per la Scienze Religiose, 1973.

Condick, Frances. "Bastwick, John (1595?–1654)." In *Oxford Dictionary of National Biography*. Edited by H. C. G. Matthew and Brian Harrison. Oxford: Oxford University Press, 2004. Online edition. Edited by Lawrence Goldman, January 2008. http://www.oxforddnb.com/view/article/1659. Accessed December 5, 2014.

Conradus, Eubel. *Hierarchia catholica medii et recentionis aevi sive summorum Pontifucum*. 8 vols. Münster: Regensberger, 1923.

Coster, Franciscus. *Enchiridion controversiarum praecipuarum nostri temporis de religion*. Cologne: Arnoldi Mylij, 1596.

Coxe, Benjamin Hanserd Knollys, and William Kiffin. *A declaration concerning the publike dispute which should have been in the publike meeting-house of Alderman-Bury, the 3rd of this instant moneth of December; Concerning infants-baptisme. Together, with some of the arguments which should then have been propounded and urged by some of those that are falsly called Anabaptists, which should then have disputed*. London, 1645.

Craig, John. Review of *Erroneous and Schismatical Opinions: The Question of Orthodoxy Regarding the Theology of Hanserd Knollys (c. 1599-1691)* by Barry H. Howson. *Dutch Review of Church History/Nederlands Archief voor Kerkgeschiedenis* 83.2 (2003): 594–596.

Cranford, James. *Haereseo-machia: or, The mischiefe which heresies doe, and the means to prevent it. Delivered in a sermon in Pauls, before the Right Honourable, the Lord Maior, and the aldermen of the famous citie of London, February the first, M. DC. XLV. And now printed, for the satisfaction of the hearers, and others. / By James Cranford, pastour of Christopher Le Stocks, London*. London: Printed by James Young for Charles Green, 1646.

Crosby, Thomas. *The history of the English Baptists, from the Reformation to the Beginning of the Reign of King George I. [Vol. IV] Containing their History from the End of the Reign of King William III to the Reign of King George I, including some Part of His Reign*. London, 1740.

Crowdrey, H. E. J. *Pope Gregory VII, 1073–1085.* Oxford: Oxford University Press, 1998.

Como, David R. "Radical Puritanism, c. 1558-1660." In *The Cambridge Companion to Puritanism.* Edited by John Coffey and Paul C. H. Lim, 241-58. Cambridge: Cambridge University Press, 2008.

Courtney, William J. *Ockham and Ockhamism: Studies in the Dissemination and Impact of his Thought.* Leiden/Boston: Brill, 2008.

Culross, James. *Hanserd Knollys: "A Minister and Witness of Jesus Christ," 1598–1691.* London: Alexander and Shepherd, 1895.

de Cusa, D. Nicolai. *Utriusque juris doctoris, in omniqúe philosophia incomparabilis viri opera.* Basel: Sebastian Henricpetri, 1565.

Daniell, F. H. Blackburne, ed. *Calendar of State Papers, Domestic Series, November 1st, 1673, to February 28th, 1675.* London: Printed for His Majesty's Stationary Office, by Mackie and Co., 1904.

Danvers, Henry. *A treatise of baptism wherein that of believers and that of infants is examined by the Scriptures, with the history of both out of antiquity: making it appear that infants baptism was not practiced for near 300 years after Christ ... and that the famous Waldensian and old British churches and Christians witnessed against it: with the examination of the stories about Thomas Munzer, and John a Leyden: as also, the history of Christianity amongst the ancient Britains and Waldenses: and, a brief answer to Mr. Bunyan about communion with persons unbaptized.* London: Printed for Francis Smith, 1673.

———. *Innocency and truth vindicated, or, A sober reply to Mr. Wills'answer to a late treatise of baptisme wherein the authorities and antiquities for believers and against infants baptism are defended... with a brief answer to Mr. Blinmans essay.* London: Printed for Francis Smith, 1675.

Decimatertia centuria, Ecclesiasticae historiae... Basileae: Ex Officina Oporiniana, 1574.

Denzinger, Heinrich, and Peter Hünermann. *El magisterio de la Iglesia. Enchiridion symbolorum definitionum et declarationum de rebus fidei et morum.* 38th ed. Barcelona: Herder, 2000.

Dever, Mark S. *Richard Sibbes: Puritan and Calvinist in Late Elizabethan and Early Stuart England.* Macon: Mercer University Press, 2000.

Dionysius of Halicarnassus. *The Roman Antiquities.* 7 vols. Cambridge: Harvard University Press, 1984–1993.

"Dissenters' Schools, 1660-1820." *Transactions of the Baptist Historical Society* 4, no. 4 (1914): 220–227.

De Dominis, Marco Antonio. *De republica ecclesiastica libri X.* London: Ex officina Nortoniana apud Ioan. Billium, MDCXVII [1617].

Donagan, Barbara. "Nye, Philip (bap. 1595, d. 1672)." In *Oxford Dictionary of National Biography.* Oxford: Oxford University Press, 2004. Online edition. January 2008. http://www.oxforddnb.com/view/article/20417. Accessed December 5, 2014.

Doran, Susan, and Christopher Durston. *Princes, Pastors and People: The Church and Religion in England, 1500-1700.* 2nd ed. London: Routledge, 2003.

Douglas, David Charles, ed. *English Historical Documents, 1660–1714.* Vol. 6. London: Routledge, 1996.

Downame, George. *A treatise concerning Antichrist divided into two bookes, the former, proving that the Pope is Antichrist, the latter, maintaining the same assertion, against all the obiections of Robert Bellarmine, Iesuit and cardinall of the church of Rome.* London: Imprinted for Cuthbert Burbie, 1603.

———. *Papa Antichristus, siue Diatriba de Antichristo cuius duae partes: prior, kataskeue, quâ orthodoxa serenissimi Regis Iacobi, de Antichristo sententia demonstratur; posterior, anaskeue, quâ Leonardi Lessii sedecim demonstrationes, monitoriae Regis praefationi oppositae, refutantur. Auctore Reuerendo in Christo Patre, Georgio Dounamo Episcopo Derensi.* London: Ioan. Billium, 1620.

Duncan, Pope. *Hanserd Knollys: A Seventeenth Century Baptist.* Nashville: Broadman Press, 1965.

Dunning, Albert. *Congregationalists in America: A Popular History of their Origin, Belief, Politics, Growth and Work.* New York: J. A. Hill, 1894.

Eales, Jacqueline."White, John (1590–1645)." In *Oxford Dictionary of National Biography.* Oxford: Oxford University Press, 2004. Online edition. http://www.oxforddnb.com/view/article/29254. Accessed December 5, 2014.

Ebert, Frederic Adolphus. *A General Bibliographical Dictionary.* Oxford: The University Press, 1837.

Ecclesiastica Historia: Integram ecclesiae Christi ideam, quantum ad locum, propagationem, persecutionem, tranquillitatem, doctrinam, haereses, ceremonias… & statum imperii politicum attinet, secundum singulas centurias… ex… historicis, patribus, & aliis scriptoribus congesta; Per aliquot studiosos & pios uiros in urbe Magdeburgica. Basel: Oporinus, 1559–1574.

Edit 16. Censimento nazionale delle edizioni italiane del XVI secolo. Istituto Centrale perl il Catologo Unico delle Biblioteche Italiane e per le Informazioni Bibliografiche. http://edit16.iccu.sbn.it/scripts/iccu_ext.dll?fn=11&res=8559. Accessed December 5, 2014.

Edwards, Thomas. *The first and second part of Gangraena, or, A catalogue and discovery of many of the errors, heresies, blasphemies and pernicious practices of the sectaries of this time, vented and acted in England in these four last years also a particular narration of divers stories, remarkable passages, letters: an extract of many letters, all concerning the present sects: together with some observations upon and corollaries from all the fore-named premisses. Second part of Gangraena. Fresh and further discovery of the errors, heresies, blasphemies, and dangerous proceedings of the sectaries of this time.* London: T. R. and E. M. for Ralph Smith, 1646.

Ehler, Sidney Z., and John B. Morrall, ed. *Church and State Through the Centuries: A Collection of Historic Documents with Commentaries.* New York: Biblo and Tannen, 1967.

Erasmus of Rotterdam. *Collected Works of Erasmus: Notes to Poems.* Collected Works. Vol. 86. Toronto: University of Toronto Press, 1993.

Estius, Guilielmus. *Annotationes in praecipua ac difficiliora sacrae scripturae loca.* Douai: Typis viduae et heredum Petri Borremans, 1621.

———. *Annotationes aureae in praecipua ac difficiliora Sacrae Scripturae loca.* Cologne: Johann Crith von Witwe, 1622.

Evans, B. "Incidents in the Life of Hanserd Knollys." *The Baptist Magazine* (February 1866): 92–100.

Featley, Daniel. *Katabaptistai kataptüstoi, The dippers dipt, or, The anabaptists duck'd and plung'd over head and eares, at a disputation in Southwark: together with a large and full discourse of their 1. Original. 2. Severall sorts. 3. Peculiar errours. 4. High attempts against the state. 5. Capitall punishments, with an application to these times*. London: Printed for Nicholas Bourne and Richard Royston, 1645.

Fielding, Henry, and L. J. Morrissey, eds. *Tom Thumb and The Tragedy of Tragedies*. Berkeley and Los Angeles: University of California Press, 1970.

Fincham, Kenneth. "Dove, Thomas (1555–1630)." In *Oxford Dictionary of National Biography*. Oxford University Press, 2004. Online edition. January 2008. http://www.oxforddnb.com/view/article/7952. Accessed December 5, 2014.

The First Parish in Dover, New Hampshire: Two Hundred and Fiftieth Anniversary, Oct. 28, 1883. Dover: printed for the Parish, 1884.

Firth, C. H., and Robert S. Rait, eds. *Acts and Ordinances of the Interregnum, 1642–1660*. Vol. 1. London: His Majesty's Stationary Office, 1911.

François, Wim. "Augustine and the Golden Age of Biblical Scholarship in Louvain (1550–1650)." In *Shaping the Bible in the Reformation: Books, Scholars and their Readers in the Sixteenth Century*. Edited by Bruce Gordon and Matthew McLean, 235–290. Leiden: Brill, 2012.

Garrett, Leo. *Baptist Theology: A Four Century Study*. Macon: Mercer University Press, 2009.

Gee, Henry, and William Hardy. *Documents Illustrative of English Church History*. London: Macmillan and Co., 1896.

Génébrard, Benedictine Gilbert. *Chronographiae libri quatuor*. Paris: M. Sonnium, 1580.

Giovio, Paolo. *Pauli Iouii nouocomensis episcopi Nucerini, De vita Leonis Decimi Pont. Max. libri quatuor.: his ordine temporum accesserunt Adriani Sexti Pont. Max. et Pompeii Columnae Cardinalis vitae*. Florence: Laurenti Torrentini, Florence, 1599.

Goadby, Joseph Jackson. *Bye-Paths in Baptist History*. London: Elliott Stock, 1871.

Godwin, Thomas. *Romanae historiae anthologia: an English exposition of the Romane antiquities, wherein many Romane and English offices are parallel'd, and divers obscure phrases explained*. Oxford: Printed by Iohn Lichfield, and Iames Short, for Henry Cripps, 1620.

Gordon, Alexander "Hanserd Knollys." In *Dictionary of National Biography, 1885–1900*. Vol. 31. London: 1885–1900.

Greaves, Richard L. *Deliver Us from Evil: The Radical Underground in Britain, 1660–1663*. New York: Oxford University Press, 1986.

———. *Enemies Under His Feet: Radicals and Nonconformists in Britain, 1664–1677*. Stanford: Stanford University Press, 1990.

———. "Radicals, Rights, and Revolution: British Nonconformity and Roots of the American Experience." *Church History* 61, no. 2 (1992): 151–168.

———. *Saints and Rebels: Seven Nonconformists in Stuart England*. Macon: Mercer University Press, 1985.

———. *Secrets of the Kingdom: British Radicals from the Popish Plot to the Revolution of 1678-1689*. Stanford: Stanford University Press, 1992.

Green, I. M. "The Persecution of 'Scandalous' and 'Malignant' Parish Clergy during the English Civil War." *The English Historical Review* 94 (1979): 507–531.

Hackman, Alfred. *Catalogus librorum impressorum Bibliothecae Bodleianae*. Vol. 3. Oxford: University Press, 1843.

Hall, David D., ed. *The Antinomian Controversy, 1636–1638: A Documentary History*. 2nd ed. Durham: Duke University Press, 1990.

Hammond, Henry. *A paraphrase, and annotations upon all the books of the New Testament briefly explaining all the difficult places thereof.* London: Printed by J. Flesher for Richard Royston, 1653.

———. *A Paraphrase and Annotations upon all the Books of the New Testament, Briefly Explaining all the Difficult Places Thereof.* Vol 3. Oxford: The University Press, 1845.

Harrison, Thomas. "Sermon." In *Erroneous and Schismatical Opinions: The Question of Orthodoxy Regarding the Theology of Hanserd Knollys (c. 1599–1691),* Studies in the History of Christian Thought, no. 98. Edited by Barry H. Howson, 57–58. Leiden: Brill, 2001.

Haykin, M. A. G. *Kiffin, Knollys and Keach: Rediscovering our English Baptist Heritage.* Leeds, England: Reformation Today Trust, 1996.

Heinsius, Daniel. *Aristarchus sacer, sive ad Nonni in Iohannem metaphrasin exercitationes.* Lugduni Batavorum: ex officina Bonaventurae et Abrahami Elzevier, 1627.

———. *Paraphrasis sancti Evangelii secundum Joannem.* PG 43. Paris: J. P. Migne, 1864.

Hildebrand, Stephen M. "A Reconsideration of the Development of Basil's Trinitarian Theology: The Dating of Ep. 9 and 'Contra Eunomium'." *Vigiliae Christianae* 58, no. 4 (2004): 393–406.

Hill, Christopher. *The World Turned Upside Down: Radical Ideas During the English Revolution.* New York: Penguin, 1975.

Hill, Joseph, and Cornelis Schrevel. *Lexicon manuale, Graeco-Latinum & Latino-Graecum primò conncinatum, térque editum à Cornelio Schrevelio: vocabulorum octo quasi millibus locupletatum, plurimisque praeterea in locis auctum & adornatum, prout ex praefatione constat / studio atque operâ Josephi Hill; ad calcem adjecta sunt sententiae Graeco-Latinae, quibus omnia Gr. L. primitiva comprehenduntur; item tractatus duo, alter De resolutione verborum, De articulis alter; uterque perutilis & adhuc desideratus.* London: John Field, 1663.

"House of Commons Journal Volume 5: 9 March 1647." *Journal of the House of Commons: volume 5: 1646-1648.* British History Online. http://www.british-history.ac.uk/report.aspx?compid=25040. Accessed December 5, 2014.

"House of Lords Journal Volume 13: 1 November 1678." *Journal of the House of Lords, volume 13: 1675–1681 (1767–1830).* British History Online. http://www.british-history.ac.uk/report.aspx?compid=11591. Accessed May 28, 2014.

How, Samuel. *The sufficiencie of the spirits teaching, without humane-learning: or A treatise, tending to proue humane-learning to be no help to the spirituall understanding of the Word of God. Written (if it may be) for the silencing of such false and scandalous reports, as have been rumored about concerning this matter; and also for the affording of true information to all such as desire to know the truth.* Amsterdam: Cloppenburg Press, 1640.

Howell, T. B., ed. "Proceedings in the Star-Chamber against Dr. John Bastwick, Mr. Henry Burton, and William Prynn, esq. for several libels." In *A Complete Collection of State Trials and Proceedings for High Treason and other Crimes and Misdemeanors from the Earliest Period to the Year 1783, in 21 Volumes.* 21 vols. London: T. C. Hansard for Longman, Hurst, Rees, Orme, and Brown, 1816.

Howson, Barry H. *Erroneous and Schismatical Opinions: The Question of Orthodoxy Regarding the Theology of Hanserd Knollys (ca. 1599–1691)*. Studies in the History of Christian Thought, no. 98. Leiden: Brill, 2001.

Hudson, Anne "Netter, Thomas (*c.*1370–1430)." In *Oxford Dictionary of National Biography*. Oxford: Oxford University Press, 2004. Online ed. Edited by Lawrence Goldman, 2008. http://www.oxforddnb.com/view/article/19907. Accessed December 5, 2014.

Hughes, Ann. *Gangraena and the Struggle for the English Revolution*. Oxford: Oxford University Press, 2004.

Ivimey, Joseph. *A History of English Baptists*. 4 vols. London: Burditt, Button, Hamilton, Baynes, 1811–1830.

James, Muriel. *Religious Liberty on Trial*. Franklin: Providence House Publishers, 1997.

Jenkinson, Matthew. *Culture and Politics at the Court of Charles II, 1660–1685*. Woodbridge: The Boydell Press, 2010.

Jerome, Saint. *Adversus Jovinianum libri duo*. PL 23. Paris: J. P. Migne, 1883.

———. *D. Hieronymi Opera Omnia*. 9 vols. Paris: C. Guillard, 1533–1546.

Jewel, John. *A defense of the Apologie of the Churche of Englande Conteininge an answeare to a certaine booke lately set foorthe by M. Hardinge, and entituled, A confutation of etc. Whereunto there is also newely added an answeare vnto an other like booke, written by the saide M. Hardinge, entituled, A detection of sundrie fowle errours etc. Printed at Louaine, Anno. 1568. and inserted into the foremer answeare, as occasion, and place required, as by special notes added to the margine it maie appeare*. London: Henry Wykes, 1571.

———. *The Works of John Jewel*. Edited by Richard William Jelf. 8 vols. Oxford: Oxford University Press, 1848.

Jones, Henry. *A sermon of antichrist preached at Christ-Church, Dublin, Novemb. 12. 1676*. London: for Nathaniel Ponder, 1679.

"Jottings by John Lewis of Margate, 1742." *Transactions of the Baptist Historical Society*, 4.4 (1914): 206.

Kenyon, J. P. *The Popish Plot*. London: Heinemann, 1972.

Kiffin, William. *A serious answer to a late book stiled, A reply to Mr. Robert Steed's epistle concerning singing wherein the chief scriptures and arguments are examined, and the weakness thereof shewed: together with an answer to the several reflections, and false charges, against both churches and persons, recommended to the elders, ministers, and members of baptized churches*. London: no printer, 1692.

———. "Epistle to the Reader." In *The life and death of that old disciple of Jesus Christ and eminent minister of the Gospel Mr. Hanserd Knollys who dyed in the ninety third year of his age written with his own hand to the year 1672; and continued in general in an epistle by Mr. William Kiffin*. London: Printed for John Harris, 1692.

Klaiber, A. J. "The Gospel Minister's Maintenance Vindicated." *Baptist Quarterly* 2, no. 5 (1925): 224–231.

Knollys, Hanserd. *A declaration concerning the publike dispute which should have been in the publike meeting-house of Alderman-Bury, the 3rd of this instant moneth of December; Concerning infants-baptisme. Together, with some of the arguments which should then have been propounded and urged by some of those that are falsly called Anabaptists, which should then have disputed. By Benjamin Coxe, Hanserd Knollys, and William Kiffen, etc.* London, 1645.

———. *A Moderate Answer Unto Dr. Bastwicks* [sic.] *Book, Called, Independency not God's Ordinance. Wherein, is declared the manner how some churches in this city were gathered, and upon what tearmes their Members were admitted; That so both the Dr. and the Reader may judge, how near some Beleevers who walk together in the Fellowship of the Gospell, do come in their practice to these Apostolicall rules which are propounded by the Dr. as God's method in gathering Churches and admitting Members.* London: Printed by Iane Coe, 1645.

———. *An answer to a brief discourse concerning singing in the publick worship of God in the Gospel-church, by I. M. [Isaac Marlow] 1690.* London: printed for the author H. K. [Hanserd Knollys], 1691.

———. *An exposition of the 11th Chapter of Revelation wherein all those things therein revealed, which must shortly come to pass, are explained.* London: no printer, 1679.

———. *An exposition of the first chapter of the Song of Solomon. Wherein the text is analysed, the allegories are explained, and the hidden mysteries are unveiled, according to the proportion of faith. With spiritual meditations upon every verse.* London: W. Godbid, 1656.

———. *An exposition of the whole book of the Revelation wherein the visions and prophecies of Christ are opened and expounded: shewing the great conquests of our lord Jesus Christ for his church over all his and her adversaries pagan, arian, and papal.* London: William Marshall, 1689.

———. *An impartial account of divers remarkable proceedings the last sessions of Parliament relating to the horrid Popish Plot, etc. Viz. The manner of choosing their speaker. The speeches of divers worthy members, relating to that. The vote of the House at large in defence of the King, and the Protestant religion. The articles of impeachment against the five Lords in the Tower. The articles of impeachment against Thomas Earl of Danby, and his letter. The Earl of Danby's pardon in Latin and English, and his plea. The reasons and narrative of the proceedings betwixt the two Houses of Parliament, concerning the Lords in the Tower, etc. The proceedings of the House of Lords, concerning the Lords in the Tower, and the names of those Lords that entered their protest. A copy of the bill relating to the Duke of York. The Earl of Shaftsburies speech in the House of Lords. Mr. Powel's speech concerning the Earl of Danby. Mr. Palme's report about the temporary laws.* London, 1679.

———. *Apocalyptical mysteries, touching the two witnesses, the seven vials, and the two kingdoms, to wit, of Christ, and of Antichrist, expounded. Wherein is contained some things necessary for the saints in this present generation to know.* London, 1667.

———. *Christ exalted; a lost sinner sought and saved by Christ; God's people are a holy people. Being a sum of diverse sermons preached in Suffolk.* London: Iane Coe, 1646.

———. *Christ exalted: in a sermon begun to be preached at Debenham in Suffolk, upon the 14. day of Febr. last, upon Coloss. 3. 11. By Hanserd Knollys. Who was stoned out of the pulpit (as he was preaching) by a company of rude fellowes, and poor women of that town; who were sent for, called together, and set on by a malignant high-constable, who lives in the same town. Also, another sermon, preached at Stradbrooke in Suffolk, the 13. day of Febr. last, concerning sanctification; upon Ephes. 1. 4.* London, 1645.

———. "Courteous Reader." In *A Christian woman's experiences of the glorious working of God's free grace*, by Katherine Sutton. Rotterdam: Henry Goddaeus, 1663.

———. "Hanserd Knollys to Robert Simon, February 19, 1640." *Suffolk Deeds*, vol. 1. Boston: Rockwell and Churchill, City Printers, 1880, 18-20.

———. *Mystical Babylon availed wherein is proved, I. That Rome-papal is mystical-Babylon, II. That the Pope of Rome is the beast, III. That the Church of Rome is the great whore, IV. That the Roman-priests are the false prophet: also A call to the people of God to come out of Babylon.* London: no printer, 1679.

———. *The life and death of that old disciple of Jesus Christ and eminent minister of the Gospel Mr. Hanserd Knollys who dyed in the ninety third year of his age written with his own hand to the year 1672; and continued in general in an epistle by Mr. William Kiffin.* London: Printed for John Harris, 1692.

———. *The Life and Death of that Old Disciple of Jesus Christ, and Eminent Minister of the Gospel, Mr. Hanserd Knollys, who died in the Ninety-third Year of his Age. Written with His Own Hand to the Year 1672, and Continued in General, in an Epistle by Mr. William Kiffin. To Which is Added his Last Legacy to the Church.* London: E. Huntington, 1812.

———. *The parable of the Kingdom of heaven expounded, or, An exposition of the first thirteen verses of the twenty fifth chapter of Matthew.* London: no printer, 1674.

———. *The rudiments of the Hebrew grammar in English. Published for the benefit of some friends, who being ignorant of the Latine, are desirous to understand the Bible in the originall tongue.* London: Moses Bell, 1648.

———. *The shining of a flaming-fire in Zion. Or, A clear answer unto 13. exceptions, against the grounds of new baptism; (so called) in Mr. Saltmarsh his book; intituled, The smoke in the temple, p. 15, &c. Which exceptions, were tendered by him to all believers, to shew them, how little they have attained; and that there is a more glorious fulnesse to be revealed. Also, a postscript; wherein (to the like end) some queries are propounded unto believers.* London: Iane Coe, 1646.

———. *The world that now is; and the world that is to come: or The first and second coming of Jesus Christ Wherein several prophecies not yet fulfilled are expounded.* London: Thomas Snowden, 1681.

———. "To the Churches of God in London and elsewhere in all places with the Bishops and Deacons." In *Mysteries unvailed wherein the doctrine of redemption by Jesus Christ, flowing from the glorious grace and everlasting love of God, the very fountain of life and salvation unto lost sinners, is handled: the most usuall Scriptures explained and reasons answered, which are urged for the universality of the death of Christ for all persons : vvherein the unsoundness of this opinion, together with divers other conclusions as depending upon it, are discovered and the truth unveiled.* Robert Garner. London, 1646.

———. "To the Courteous Reader." In *Instructions for children: or, The child's & youth's delight, teaching an easie way to spell & read true English. Containing the father's godly advice; directing parents in a right and spiritual manner to educate their children. With a Christian catechism, wherein all the chief principles of true Christianity are clearly opened. Together with many other things both pleasant and useful for the education of children.* Benjamin Keach. London: Printed for Thomas Knowles at the corner of Tower-Street, and John How without Bishopsgate, 1683.

———. "To the Honourable Committee of Examinations." In *Christ exalted: a lost sinner sought, and saved by Christ: Gods people are an holy people. Being the summe of divers sermons preached in Suffolk; by Hanserd Knollys. Who for this doctrine had the meeting-house doores shut against him, and was stoned out of the pulpit (as he was preaching) by a rude multitude; who were gathered together, and set on by a malignant high-constable. Which hath been proved by divers witnesses of good reputation, before the Honourable Committee of Examination at London*. London: Printed by Iane Coe, 1646.

Knollys, Hanserd, et al. *The Baptists answer to Mr. Obed. Wills, his appeal against Mr. H. Danvers*. London: no printer, 1675.

Kreitzer, Larry J. "The Anabaptist Petitions of 1660 and 1661: William Kiffin and the Particular Baptists." *Exploring Baptist Origins*. Edited by Anthony R. Cross and Nicholas J. Ward, 81–99. Oxford: Regents Park College, 2010.

De Krey, Gary Stuart. *London and the Restoration, 1659–1683*. Cambridge: Cambridge University Press, 2005.

Lamont, William. "Blake, Thomas (1596/7–1657)." In *Oxford Dictionary of National Biography*. Edited by H. C. G. Matthew and Brian Harrison. Oxford: Oxford University Press, 2004. Online edition. Edited by Lawrence Goldman. January 2008. http://www.oxforddnb.com/view/article/2583. Accessed November 21, 2014.

Langley, A. S. "17th Century Baptist Disputations." *Transactions of the Baptist Historical Society* 6 (1918–1919): 216–243.

Lapide, Cornelio Cornelli. *Commentaria in Apocalypsin S. Ioannis Apostoli*. In *Commentaria in Sacram Scripturam*. Edited by Sisto Riario Sforza. Vol. 10. Naples: I. Nagar, 1859.

Laurence, Anne. *Parliamentary Army Chaplains, 1642–1651*. In Royal Historical Society Studies in History, vol. 59. Woodbridge: The Boydell Press, 1990.

Lee, Sidney. "Hanserd Knollys." In *Dictionary of National Biography*. New York: Macmillan and Co., 1892.

Leo X, Pope. *Sa. Lateranen concilium novissimum, sub Julio et Leone X celebratum*. Rome: I. Mazochius, 1521.

"Levellers." *The Oxford Dictionary of the Christian Church*. Edited by Cross, F. L., and E. A. Livingstone, 3rd rev. ed. Oxford: Oxford University Press, 2005. http://www.oxfordreference.com. Accessed December 5, 2014.

Lindley, Keith. "Adams, Sir Thomas, first baronet (*bap.* 1586, *d.* 1668)." In *Oxford Dictionary of National Biography*. Edited by H. C. G. Matthew and Brian Harrison. Oxford: Oxford University Press, 2004. Online edition. Edited by Lawrence Goldman, January 2008. http://www.oxforddnb.com/view/article/132. Accessed November 21, 2014.

Livy. *Ab urbe condita*. Edited by Christina Shuttleworth Kraus. Cambridge: Cambridge University Press, 1994.

Lumpkin, William C., ed. *Baptist Confessions of Faith*. Valley Forge: Judson Press, 1959.

Lynch, Kathleen. *Protestant Autobiography in the Seventeenth-century Anglophone World*. Oxford and New York: Oxford University Press, 2012.

MacPherson, John, ed. *The Westminster Confession of Faith, with Introduction and Notes*. Edinburgh: T&T Clark, 1881.

Mancini, Celso. *De iuribus principatum libri novem*. Rome: Gulielmi Facciotti, 1596.

Mansi, Giovanni Domenico, ed. *Sacrorum conciliorum nova et amplissima collectio.* 35 vols. Florence: Antonii Zatta Veneti, 1759-1798.

Marlorat, Agustin. *A catholike exposition vpon the Reuelation of Sainct Iohn. Collected by M. Augustine Marlorate out of diuers notable writers, whose names ye shal find in the page following.* London: H. Binneman, 1574.

Marlow, Isaac. *A brief discourse concerning singing in the public worship of God in the Gospel-church.* London: no printer, 1690.

Marshall, Peter. "Charles I's Reformation 1625-42." In *Reformation England, 1480-1642.* Edited by Peter Marshall. 2nd ed. London: Bloomsbury Academic Press, 2012.

Marshall, Stephen. *A sermon of the baptizing of infants preached in the Abbey-Church at Westminster, at the morning lecture, appointed by the Honorable House of Commons.* London: Richard Cotes for Stephen Bowtell, 1644.

Mason, Alistair. "Arminianism." In *The Oxford Companion to Christian Thought.* Edited by Adrian Hastings, Alistair Mason, and Hugh Pyper, 41. Oxford: Oxford University Press, 2000.

———. "Reformed Theology." In *The Oxford Companion to Christian Thought.* Edited by Adrian Hastings, Alistair Mason, and Hugh Pyper, 603-04. Oxford: Oxford University Press, 2000.

Maubray, John. *The Female Physician, Containing all the Diseases Incident to that Sex, in Virgins, Wives, and Widows; Together with their Causes and Symptoms, their Degrees of Danger, and Respective Methods of Prevention and Cure.* London: Printed for James Holland, 1724.

Mantuanus, Baptista Spagnuoli. *Baptistae Mantuani Carmelitae theologi Adolescentia, seu, Bucolica, breuibus Iodoci Badij commentarijs illustrata: his accesserunt Ioannis Murmeillij in singulas eclogas argumenta, cum annotatiunculis eiusdem in loca aliquot obscuriora: accessit, & index, non ille vetus, & indigestus, sed nouus omnino, ac locupletior multo, opera Barthol. Laurentis.* London: Ioannes Kyngstonus, 1569.

McBeth, H. Leon. *The Baptist Heritage.* Nashville: Broadman Press, 1987.

McGinn, Bernard. "Wrestling with the Millenium: Early Modern Catholic Exegesis of Apocalypse 20." In *Imagining the End: Visions of Apocalypse from the Ancient Middle East to Modern America.* Edited by Abbas Amanat and Magnus Bernhardsson, 148–167. London: I. B. Tauris, 2002.

McGregor, J. F., and Barry Reay, eds. *Radical Religion in the English Revolution.* Oxford: Oxford University Press, 1984.

Menache, Sophia. *Clement* V. Cambridge: Cambridge University Press, 2003.

Mendle, Michael. "Grub Street and Parliament at the Beginning of the English Revolution." In *Media and Revolution.* Edited by Jeremy D. Popkin, 31–47. Lexington: University Press of Kentucky, 1995.

Mezeray, François Eudes. *Abrégé chronologique, ou Extrait de l'histoire de France... divisé en trois tomes.* Paris: T. Jolly, 1568.

Miller, Perry. *The New England Mind: The Seventeenth Century.* Cambridge: Harvard University Press, 1983.

———. "'Preparation for Salvation' in Seventeenth-Century New England." *Journal of the History of Ideas* 4, no. 3 (1943): 253–286.

Moore, Susan Hardman. *Pilgrims: New World Settlers and the Call of Home.* New Haven: Yale University Press, 2007.

Moore, Norman. "Windet, James (d. 1664)." In Oxford Dictionary of National Biography. Revised by Michael Bevan. Edited by H. C. G. Matthew and Brian Harrison. Oxford: OUP, 2004, Online edition. Edited by Lawrence Goldman. http://www.oxforddnb.com/view/article/29718. Accessed May 27, 2014.

Mosconio, Isidoro. *De maiestate militantis ecclesiae. Libri duo. Quibus ecclesiae maiestatem ex religione Christiana prodire demonstrator. Atque de ipsius religionis statu.* Venice: Florauantem Pratum, 1602.

Neal, Daniel. *The History of New England Containing an Impartial Account of the Civil and Ecclesiastical Affairs of the Country to the Year of Our Lord, 1700.* 2 vols. London: printed for J. Clark, R. Ford, and R. Cruttenden, 1720.

Netter, Thomas. *Tomus primus doctrinalis fidei ecclesiae catholicae contra Witclevistas et Hussitas: eorum[que] sectatores.* Paris: Josse Badius, 1532.

Newport, Kenneth. "Knollys, Hanserd (1598–1691), Particular Baptist minister and author." In *Oxford Dictionary of National Biography.* Oxford: Oxford University Press, 2004–2010. Online edition. January 2010. http://www.oxforddnb.com/view/article/15756. Accessed December 5, 2014.

———. *Apocalypse and Millennium: Studies in Biblical Eisegesis.* Cambridge: Cambridge University Press, 2000.

Nicolaus, de Bibera. *Occulti Erfordensis, Carmen satiricum. Eine quelle de XIII jahrhunderts.* Edited by Theobald Fischer. Halle: Buchh. des Waisenhauses, 1870.

Nuttall, Geoffrey F. "Abingdon Revisited, 1656-1675." *Baptist Quarterly* 36 (April 1995): 96-103.

Osorio, Juan. *Concionum.* Antwerp: Joannem Keerbergium, 1594–1597.

Ovid. *Tristium libri v.* Edited by S. G. Owen. Oxford: Oxford University Press, 1889.

Owen, John. *An exposition of the two first chapters of the Epistle of Paul the Apostle unto the Hebrews.* London: Robert White, 1668.

———. *Exercitations on the Epistle to the Hebrews also concerning the Messiah wherein the promises concerning him to be a spiritual redeemer of mankind are explained and vindicated, his coming and accomplishment of his work according to the promises is proved and confirmed, the person, or who he is, is declared, the whole oeconomy of the mosaical law, rites, worship, and sacrifice is explained: and in all the doctrine of the person, office, and work of the Messiah is opened, the nature and demerit of the first sin is unfolded, the opinions and traditions of the antient and modern Jews are examined, their objections against the Lord Christ and the Gospel are answered, the time of the coming of the Messiah is stated, and the great fundamental truths of the Gospel vindicated : with an exposition and discourses on the two first chapters of the said epistle to the Hebrews.* 4 vols. London: Robert White, 1668.

Panopolitanus, Nonnus. *Conversio Evangelii secundum Ioannem, Graecis versibus conscripta.* Cologne: Apud Maternum Cholinum, 1570.

———. *Translatio vel Paraphrasis S. Evangelii secundum Ioannem... cum versione Latina.* Basel: Ex officina Chalcographica Petri Perna, 1571.

———. *Paraphrasis sancti Evangelii secundum Joannem.* PG 43. Paris: J. P. Migne, 1864.

———. *In Evangelium S. Ioannis Paraphrasis Graeca.* Hagenau, 1528.

Paiva de Andrade, Diogo. *Orthodoxarvm Explicationvm Libri Decem: In quibus omnia ferè de religione capita, quae his temporibus ab haereticis in controuersiam vocantur, apertè & dilucidè explicantur: Praesertim contra Martini Kemnicij petulantem audaciam, qui*

Coloniensem Censuram, quam à uiris Societatis Iesu compositam esse ait, unà cum eiusdem Sanctiß. Societatis uitae ratione, temerè calumniandam suscepit; Cum neceßariis indicibus, rerum verborum, et explicatae scripturae sacrae. Cologne: Cholinus, 1564.

Petrarch. *Liber sine nomine.* Edited by Ugo Dotti. Roma: Editori Laterza, 1974.

Pererius, Benedictus. *Commentarius in Danielem Libri XVI.* Antwerp, 1594.

Piepho, Lee. "Mantuan's Eclogues in the English Reformation." *Sixteenth Century Journal* 25, no. 3 (1994): 623–632.

Pio V. *Regnans in excelsis*, in *Bullarum diplomatum et privilegiorum sanctorum romanorum pontificum, taurinensis edition.* Edited by Francisco Gaude, et al. Vol. 7. Turin: Seb. Franco and Henrico Dalmazzo, 1862.

Possevin, Antonius. *Bibliotheca selecta, qua agitur de ratione studiorum in Historia, in Disciplinis in Salute omnium procuranda.* Rome: Typogr. Apostolica Vaticana, 1593.

Prance, Miles. *A true narrative and discovery of several very remarkable passages relating to the horrid popish plot as they fell within the knowledge of Mr. Miles Prance.* Dublin, reprinted, 1679.

Prideaux, John. *Viginti-duae lectiones de totidem religionis captibvs, praecipve hoc tempore controversis, prout publicè habebantur Oxoniae in vesperiis quibus accesserunt Tredecim orationes inavgvrales de totidem theologiae apicibus scitu non indignis, prout in promotione doctorum in comitiis habebantur: subnectuntur Sex conciones pro more habitae ad artium baccalaurios in die cinerum.* Oxford: Hen. Cripps, Hen. Curteyn, & Thom. Robinson, 1648.

Prideaux, Mathias. *An easy and compendious introduction for reading all sorts of histories: contrived, in a more facile way then heretofore hath been published.* Oxford: Leonard Lichfield, 1648.

Propertius, Sextus. *Elegies.* Edited and translated by G. P. Goold. Cambridge: Harvard University Press, 1990.

Pole, Reginald. *De Concilio liber.* Rome: Paulum Manutium Aldi F., 1562.

———. *Libri duo d. Reginaldi Poli laudatissimi Cardinalis, quos pietate, gravitate, doctrina, ac eloquentia summa refertos, et ante hac in Germania nunquam excusos moriens reliquit. Primus liber de Concilio agit...* Dillingen: Sebaldus Mayer, 1562.

———. *Reginaldi Poli Card. amplissimi liber, De Concilio...* Venice: Jordani Zileti, 1562.

Questier, Michael. "Conformity, Catholicism and the Law." In *Conformity and Orthodoxy in the English Church, c. 1560-1660.* Edited by Peter Lake and Michael Questier, 237–261. Woodbridge: The Boydell Press, 2000.

Quint, Alonzo H. "The Memorial Address." In *The First Parish in Dover, New Hampshire: Two Hundred and Fiftieth Anniversary.* Dover: Printed for the Parish, 1884.

Quintrell, Brian. "Williams, John (1582–1650)." In *Oxford Dictionary of National Biography.* Oxford University Press, 2004. Online edition, January 2008. http://www.oxforddnb.com/view/article/29515. Accessed December 5, 2014.

Rademaker, C. S. M. *Life and Work of Gerardus Joannes Vossius (1577–1649).* Assen: Van Gorcum, 1981.

Renihan, James M. "Henry Danvers' *A Treatise of Baptism*: A Study in Seventeenth-Century Baptist Historiography." *BRT/RBT* 7, no. 1–2 (Spring/Fall 1997): 27–47.

de Ribera, Francisco. *In sacram b. Iohannis apostoli & euangelistae apocalypsim commentarij ...; his adiuncti sunt quinq[ue] libri de templo & de ijs quae ad templum pertine[n]t ad multorum locorun tam apocalypsis quam reliquorum librorum intelligentiam cum primis vtiles*. Salamanca: Pedro Lasso, 1591.

———. *Commentarius in sacram beati Ioannis Apocalypsim*. Salamanca, 1591.

Roberts, Stephen K. "The House of Commons, 1640-1660." In *A Short History of Parliament*. Edited by Clyve Jones, 110-25. Woodbridge: Boydell Press, 2009.

Roy, Ian. "Legge, William (1607/8–1670)." In *Oxford Dictionary of National Biography*. Oxford: Oxford University Press, 2004. http://www.oxforddnb.com/view/article/16358. Accessed December 5, 2014.

Russell, John. *A brief narrative of some considerable passages concerning the first gathering and further progress of a church of Christ, in gospel order, in Boston, in New England, commonly (though falsly) called by the name of Anabaptists; for clearing their innocency from the scandalous things laid to their charge*. Boston: Printed by J. D., 1680.

de Sá, Manuel, S.J. *Aphorismi confessariorum, ex variis doctorum sententiis collecti*. Cologne: Petri Amorfortii, 1599.

Saltmarsh, John. *The smoke in the temple. Wherein is a designe for peace and reconciliation of believers of the several opinions of these times about ordinances, to a forbearance of each other in love, and meeknesse, and humility. With the opening of each opinion, and upon what Scriptures each is grounded. With the several exceptions which may be made against each opinion from the Scriptures. With one argument for liberty of conscience, from the national covenant. With another argument to prove the Gospel, or New Testament of Jesus Chirst the very Word of God; tendred to all the beleevers, to show them how little we have attained, and that there is a more glorious fulnesse to be revealed. With a discovery of the antichristian way of peace, etc. for opinions. With a full answer to Master Ley, one of the assembly of divines, against my late new Quere. With some spiritual principles drawn forth of the controversie*. London: Ruth Raworth, 1646.

Sander, Nicholas. *De visibilii monarchia ecclesiae: libri octo*. Louvain: Fouler, 1571.

Sandys, George. *Sacrae heptades, or Seaven problems concerning Antichrist 1. of his place. 2. Of his state. 3. Of his names. 4. Of his rising. 5. Of his raigne. 6. Of his words and actions. 7. Of his times. Necessarie to be read and knowne of all men, who professe Christ Iesus, and hope to be saved by no other name*. Amsterdam: Successors of Giles Thorp, 1625.

Sharp, Andrew. "Lilburne, John (1615?–1657)." In *Oxford Dictionary of National Biography*. Edited by H. C. G. Matthew and Brian Harrison. Oxford: Oxford University Press, 2004. Online edition. Edited by Lawrence Goldman, October 2006. http://www.oxforddnb.com/view/article/16654. Accessed August 13, 2014.

Shaw, William A., ed. "Entry Book: November 1679, 11–20." *Calendar of Treasury Books, Vol. 6: 1679-1680*. London: His Majesty's Stationary Office, 1913.

———. "Introduction." In *Minutes of the Committee for the Relief of Plundered Ministers, and of the Trustees for the Maintenance of Ministers; Relating to Lancashire and Cheshire, 1643-1660, Part I, 1643-1654*, xvi–xvii. London and Redhill: Wyman and Sons, LTD, 1893.

Sion College, Founded by Thomas White, D. D. London: P. White and Son, 1854.

Skerpan-Wheeler, Elizabeth ed. *Life Writings, The Early Modern Englishwoman: Printed Writings, 1641–1700*, Series 2, Part 1. Aldershot: Ashgate, 2000.

Smith, Geoffrey. *Royalist Agents, Conspirators and Spies: Their Role in the British Civil Wars, 1640-1660*. Surrey and Burlington: Ashgate, 2011.

Spalding, George B. *A Discourse delivered in the First Church of Dover, May 18, 1873, on the Two Hundred and Fiftieth Anniversary of the Settlement of Dover, New Hampshire.* Dover: Freewill Baptist Printing Establishment, 1873.

Steed, Robert. *A confession of faith put forth by the elders and brethren of many congregations of Christians, (baptized upon profession of their faith) in London and the country: with an appendix concerning Baptism.* London: Printed for John Harris, 1688.

———. *A plain discovery of the unrighteous judge and false accuser. Wherein is soberly, and in the fear of the Lord brought to light, and tendered to the examination of the upright in heart, the spirit of that pamphlet, intituled, The leper cleansed: published by Richard Ballamy of Tiverton.* London: Printed for Henry Mortlock, 1658.

———. *An epistle written to the members of a church in London, concerning singing, by one of their elders.* London, 1691.

———. "Letter from Robert Steed to Mr. Philip Cary, Exeter Jail." *The Congregational Magazine* 11, no. 37. 1828.

Stoughton, John. *History of Religion in England from the Opening of the Long Parliament to 1850: Church of the Commonwealth.* 4th ed. London: Hodder and Stoughton, 1901.

Strada, Famiano S.J. *De bello Belgico decas prima [- secunda].* 2 vols. Rome: Francisci Corbelletti, 1632–1647.

Strauss, Gerald. *Historian in an Age of Crisis: The Life and Work of Johannes Aventinus, 1477–1534.* Cambridge: Harvard University Press, 1963.

Suárez, Francisco. *Defensio fidei catholicae, et apostolicae adversus Anglicanae sectae errores, cum responsione ad apologiam pro iuramento fidelitatis, & praefationem monitoriam serenissimi Iacobi Angliae regis.* Coimbra: Didacum Gomez de Loureyro, 1613.

———. *Selections from Three Works of Francisco Suárez, S.J.: De legibus, ac deo legislatore, 1612; Defensio fidei catholicae, et apostolicae adversus anglicanae sectae errores, 1613; De triplici virtute theologica, fide, spe, et charitate, 1621.* Oxford: Calrendon Press, 1944.

Sutton, John. "Leigh, Edward (1603–1671)." In *Oxford Dictionary of National Biography.* Oxford: Oxford University Press, 2004. Online ed., January 2008. http://www.oxforddnb.com/view/article/16378. Accessed December 5, 2014.

Sutton, Katherine. *A Christian womans experiences of the glorious working of Gods free grace Published for the edification of others.* Edited by Hanserd Knollys. Rotterdam: printed by Henry Goddaeus, 1663.

Teglatije, Stefan. *Oratio.* In *Tomus Quartus Conciliorum omnium, tum generalium, tum provincialium atque particularium.* Cologne: Gervinum Calenium et Haeredes Iohannis Quentelij, 1567.

The Confession of faith of those churches which are commonly (though falsy) called Anabaptists presented to the view of all that feare God, to examines by the touchstone of the Word of truth, as likewise for the taking off those aspersions which are frequently bot in pulpit and print, (although unjustly) cast upon them. London: Matthew Simmons, 1644.

The New Testament of Iesus Christ faithfully translated into English, out of the authentical Latin, diligently conferred with the Greek, & other editions in diuers languages: with arguments of books and chapters: annotations, and other helps, for the better vnderstanding of the text, and specially for the discouerie of corruptions in diuers late translations: and for clearing controuersies in religion of these days. Douai: John Cousturier, 1633.

de Thou, Jacques-Auguste. *Jacobi Aug. Thuani Historiarum sui temporis*. 5 vols. Paris: Ambrosium & Hieronymum Drouart, 1604–1608.

Tolmie, Murray. *The Triumph of the Saints: The Separate Churches of London, 1616–1649*. Cambridge: Cambridge University Press, 1977.

Tombes, John. *An examen of the sermon of Mr. Stephen Marshal about infant baptisme in a letter sent to him*. London: R. W. for George Whitington, 1645.

———. *Antipaedobaptism*. 3 vols. London: 1652, 1654, 1657.

Trapp, Damasus. "Angelus de Dobelin, Doctor Parisiensis, and His Lectura." *Augustinianum* 3 (1963): 389–413.

Underhill, Edward Bean, ed. *Confessions of Faith, and other Public Documents, Illustrative of the History of the Baptist Churches of England in the 17th Century*. London: Haddon Brothers and Co., 1854.

de Valencia, Gregorio S. J. *Commentariorum theologicorum tomi quatuor. In quibus omnes materiae quae continetur in Summa Divi Thomae explicantur*. 4 vols. Ingolstadt: David Sartorius, 1591–1597.

Van De Wiel, Constant. *History of Canon Law*. Louvain: Peeters Press and Eerdmans, 1991.

Vázquez, Gabriel. *De cultu adorationis libri tres*. Alcalá de Henares: Juan Gracian, 1594.

Venn, J., and J. A. Venn, eds. *Alumni Cantabrigiensis*. 4 vols. Cambridge: Cambridge University Press, 1922-27.

Vernon, E. C. "Cranford, James (1602/3–1657)." In *Oxford Dictionary of National Biography*. Edited by H. C. G. Matthew and Brian Harrison. Oxford: Oxford University Press, 2004. Online edition. Edited by Lawrence Goldman, January 2008. http://www.oxforddnb.com/view/article/6610. Accessed November 21, 2014.

Viegas, Blasius. *Commentarii Exegetici in Apocalypsim Ioannis Apostoli*. Evora: E. de Lyra, 1601.

———. *Commentarii exegetici in Apocalypsim Ioannis Apostoli*. Paris: Dionysium Binet, 1606.

Viguerius, Joannes. *Institutiones ad christinianam theologiam, sacrarum literarum, universaliumque conciliorum authoritate, necnon doctorum ecclesiasticorum eruditione confirmatae, ... His annecti curavimus eiusd. Viguerij commentaria antea nunquam excussa, in D. Pauli epistolam ad Romanos*. Antwerp: Viduae et Haeredum Ioannis Stelsii, 1572.

Virgil. *Georgics*. Edited by Richard F. Thomas. 2 vols. Cambridge: Cambridge University Press, 1988.

Vossius, Gerardus Joannes. "Disputatio theologica prima de baptism." In *Theses theologicae et historicae de variis doctrinae Christianae capitibus; quas, aliquot abhinc annis, disputandas proposuit in Academia Leidensi*. Oxford: Excudebat Guilielmus Turner, impensis Guilielmi Webb, 1628.

Wall, William. *The History of Infant-Baptism*. Edited by Henry Cotton. 4 vols. Oxford: The University Press, 1835.

Watts, Michael. *The Dissenters*. 2 vols. Oxford: Clarendon Press, 1978, 1995.

Webster, Tom. "Marshall, Stephen (1594/5?–1655)." In *Oxford Dictionary of National Biography*. Edited by H. C. G. Matthew and Brian Harrison. Oxford: Oxford University Press, 2004. Online edition. Edited by Lawrence Goldman, October

2009. http://www.oxforddnb.com/view/article/18148. Accessed November 21, 2014.

Westminster Directory. A Directory for the publicke vvorship of God throughout the three kingdoms of Scotland, England, and Ireland with an act of the Generall Assembly of the Kirk of Scotland for establishing and observing this present directory : together with an act of the Parliament of the kingdom of Scotland approving and establishing the same : an act of the committee of estates concerning the printing thereof : and an act of the commission of the Generall Assembly for the printing and for the present practice of it throughout the said kingdom of Scotland. Edinburgh: Printed by Evan Tyler, 1645.

Westminster Shorter Catechism. The A. B. C. with the catechisme that is to say, an instruction to be taught and learned of every childe before he be brought to be confirmed by the bishop. London: Printed for the Company of Stationers, 1605.

Westminster Shorter Catechism. The grounds and principles of religion, contained in a shorter catechism (according to the advice of the Assembly of Divines, sitting at Westminster) to be used througout the kingdom of England and dominion of Wales. 1646.

Whinnel, Thomas. *A sober reply to Mr. Robert Steed's Epistle concerning singing.* London, 1691.

White, Barrington R. *Hanserd Knollys and Radical Dissent in the Seventeenth Century.* London: Dr. Williams's Trust, 1977.

———. *The English Separatist Tradition from the Marian Martyrs to the Pilgrim Fathers.* London: Oxford University Press, 1971.

White, John. *The first century of scandalous, malignant priests made and admitted into benefices by the prelates, in whose hands the ordination of ministers and government of the church hath been, or a narration of the causes for which the Parliament hath ordered the sequestration of the benefices of severall ministers complained of before them, for vitiousness of life, errors in doctrine, contrary to the articles of our religion, and for practising and pressing superstitious innovations against law, and for malignancy against the Parliament.* London: Printed by George Miller, 1643.

———. *The way to the true church wherein the principall motiues perswading according to Romanisme and questions touching the nature and authoritie of the church and scriptures, are familiarly disputed, and driuen to their issues, where, this day they sticke betweene the Papists and vs: contriued into an answer to a popish discourse concerning the rule of faith and the marks of the church. And published to admonish such as decline to papistrie of the weake and vncertaine grounds, whereupon they haue ventured their soules. Directed to all that seeke for resolution: and especially to his louing countrimen of Lancashire.* London: [R. Field], 1608.

Whitley, W. T. "A Retrospect: The Contribution of Nonconformity to Education to the Victorian Era." *Transactions of the Baptist Historical Society* 4, no. 4 (1914): 1–16.

———. "Debate on Infant Baptism, 1643." *Transactions of the Baptist Historical Society* 1 (1908–1909): 237–45.

———. "London Churches in 1682." *The Baptist Quarterly* 1 (1922–1923): 82–87.

William of Malmesbury. *De gestis pontificum Anglorum libri quinque.* In *Rerum Anglicarum scriptores post Bedam praecipui, ex vetustissimis codicibus manuscriptis nunc primum in lucem editi. Willielmi monachi Malmesburiensis de gestis regum Anglorum lib. V. Eiusdem Historiæ nouellæ lib. II. Eiusdem de gestis pontificum Angl. lib. IIII. Henrici Archidiaconi Huntindoniensis Historiarum lib. VIII. Rogeri Houedeni Annalium pars *prior & posterior. Chronicorum Ethelwerdi lib. IIII. Ingulphi abbatis Croylandensis historiarum lib. I. Adiecta ad finem chronologia.* London: G. Bishop, R. Nuberie, & R. Barker, 1596.

Wills, Obed. *An Appeal to the Baptists against Henry D'Anvers, Esq.* London: Printed for Jonathan Robinson at the Golden-Lion in St. Paul's Church-yard, 1675.

———. *Censura censurae, or, A just censure of the unjust sentence of the Baptists upon an appeal made against Mr. Henry D'Anvers by Obed Wills.* London: Printed for Jonath Robinson, 1676.

———. *Infant-baptism asserted & vindicated by Scripture and antiquity in answer to a treatise of baptism lately published by Mr. Henry Danvers: together with a full detection of his misrepresentations of divers councils and authors both ancient and modern: with a just censur of his essay to palliate the horrid actings of the anabaptists in Germany: as also a perswasive to unity among all Christians, though of different judgments about baptism.* London: Printed by Jonathan Robinson, 1674.

——. *Vindiciae vindiciarum, or, A vindication of a late treatise, entituled, Infant-baptism asserted and vindicated by Scripture and antiquity in answer to Mr. Hen. D'Anvers his reply: to which is annexed, the Right Reverend Dr. Barlow (now Bishop-elect of Lincoln) his apologetical-letter: also An appeal to the Baptists (so called) against Mr. Danvers, for his strange forgeries, and misrepresentations of divers councils and authors, both antient and modern / by Obed Wills.* London: Printed for Jonathan Robinson, 1675.

Wilson, Walter. *The History and Antiquities of Dissenting Churches and Meeting Houses, in London, Westminster, and Southwark; Including the Lives of their Ministers.* 4 vols. London, 1808.

Winship, Michael P. "Wheelwright, John (1592?–1679)." In *Oxford Dictionary of National Biography.* Edited by H. C. G. Matthew and Brian Harrison (Oxford: Oxford University Press, 2004). Online ed., edited by Lawrence Goldman. http://www.oxforddnb.com/view/article/66155 (accessed December 5, 2014).

Winthrop, John. *Winthrop's Journal: History of New England 1630-1649.* Edited by James K. Hosmer. 2 vols. New York: Charles Scribners, 1908.

Wright, Stephen. *The Early English Baptists, 1603–1649.* Woodbridge: The Boydell Press, 2006.

Wycliffe, John. *Tractatus de ecclesia. Now First Edited from the Manuscripts with Critical and Historical Notes.* Edited by Johann Loserth. London: Published for the Wycliffe Society by Trübner & Co., 1886.

Zeger, Tacitus Nicolaus. *Scholion in omnes Novi Testamenti libros quo loci difficiles aut etiam ambigui juxta originalem Scripturae phrasim... sunt explicati... pars prima [Scholion in locos difficileis... epistolarum apostolicarum... pars secunda, scholia in locos difficileis... libri Apocalypseos... pars tertia.* Cologne: Haeredes Arnoldi Birckmanni, 1553.

INDEX

SUBJECT INDEX

SCRIPTURE INDEX